PRESENT-DAY THINKERS
AND THE
NEW SCHOLASTICISM

AN INTERNATIONAL SYMPOSIUM

EDITED AND AUGMENTED
BY
JOHN S. ZYBURA, Ph.D.

SECOND, REVISED EDITION

WITH AN INTRODUCTION BY
THE VERY REV. JOHN CAVANAUGH, C.S.C., D.D.
President Emeritus of Notre Dame University

B. HERDER BOOK CO.,
15 & 17 SOUTH BROADWAY, ST. LOUIS, MO.,
AND
33 QUEEN SQUARE, LONDON, W. C.
1927

INTRODUCTION

That the prefatory word to this valuable study
was not written by one of the foremost exponents of
Scholastic philosophy in his generation is the reader's
—and the world's—misfortune. The illness that
closed the holy, beneficent, and inspiring career of
the late Cardinal Mercier began to arouse painful
apprehension among his friends just about the time
when he would probably have been at work on the
Introduction to Dr. Zybura's newest contribution to
the literature of philosophy in English.

That the Great Belgian Cardinal would have been
the ideal interpreter and sponsor of the book will be
admitted by all. His mastery of both Scholasticism
and the variant modern philosophies, his lofty
position in the academic world, the longitude of his
seeing and the latitude of his judging, his catholic
hospitality of mind, his keen and sympathetic insight
into other mentalities, his genius for composing sit-
uations, made him one of the outstanding leaders in
a movement of thought that seems to promise much
for the advancement of philosophy and science.

It is the spirit of this enlightened and fervent
lover of truth, therefore, that one should like to see
pervading and dominating the inquiry instigated here.
Certainly if one may judge from the spirit mani-

iii

fested in the contributions of both Scholastics and moderns—assembled by Dr. Zybura with so much painstaking and such brilliant success—a very comfortable *rapprochement,* if not a complete one, is easily within the horizon of hope. At the present time unquestionably the Scholastics are a thousand times more familiar with the so-called modern philosophies, than the moderns are with Scholasticism. Surely Neo-Scholastic thinkers will rejoice when all serious teachers of philosophy have made such headway as to show interest, understanding, and respect for the best medieval thought and for the efforts to make it serviceable for the problems of to-day. Scholastic philosophers seemingly will be the chief gainers by the change; in reality the men who will profit most will be the earnest and brilliant searchers after truth in our day to whose minds Scholasticism has hitherto been so largely a closed book.

It is a pleasant duty to pay tribute to the scholarship, industry, and deep devotion to philosophy which Dr. Zybura has brought to the completion of this work, despite the handicap of a long and painful illness. I am convinced that great good will come of his work; I believe he has started a movement that is destined to be far-reaching in its beneficial effects on the course of philosophic thought in English speaking countries. For what better way could be found to bring about a closer acquaintance and more sympathetic understanding—so much to be desired —between modern Scholastics and modern non-

Scholastics, than the publication of this symposium, made up of original and authoritative statements from leading representatives of both schools of thought, and on the very subject of a better understanding itself? It is because this volume has found a new and wonderful thing to do and has done it so specially well, that I believe it will prove of vital interest to philosophers of all schools and to educated readers in general.

Another service of a lesser kind but still a most important one the labors of Dr. Zybura have already rendered. His questionnaire, addressed to a long list of professors of philosophy, differing in training, tradition and mental complexion, was sent out on January 3rd, 1925, and during the days following. The questions proposed seemed to be just the stimulus needed to impel certain Scholastic philosophers in the United States to rise to the duties and responsibilities of the hour. I have no authoritative information on the subject, but I find that many Catholic teachers and chiefly some of those who attended the birth of the American Catholic Philosophical Association, are of the opinion that Dr. Zybura's initiative gave the first impulse which led to the formation, a year later, of that most necessary and promising organization with its valuable by-product, *The New Scholasticism: A Quarterly Review of Philosophy.* This view is also supported by other facts which need not be mentioned here. It is then an act of simple equity, in which I am sure the readers of this book and teachers of philosophy will cheerfully join, to make due acknowledgment of the services of the author, who had already done much to promote the study of Scholasticism by his recent translation of Dr. Olgiati's *L'Anima di S. Tommaso* under the title "The Key to the Study of St. Thomas" (Herder, 1925).

JOHN CAVANAUGH, C.S.C., D.D.

PREFACE

THOSE who have read history deeply and by the clear light of truth, are now appraising at its proper value the Renaissance myth about the inferiority or utter worthlessness of all medieval thought and culture. "The conception of the Middle Ages as a period of dark ignorance, crude taste, and blind fanaticism has few supporters left. . . . It is more and more apparent that in letters and institutions, philosophy and art, the Middle Ages present a chapter in the development of civilization which the student of human progress can ill afford to neglect." [1] The rashly attempted breach of the law of continuity at the dawn of the modern era and the consequent lack of wise control produced "a speed so great as to be against our own good; for it has been too rapid to enable that genuine assimilation which alone can make for safe development. We have passed through in decades what should have required centuries, if character is to keep pace with intellectual and cultural exploitation. The rapid loss of the sense of transcendental values, with its correlated taking on of positivism, has been an in-

[1] *Speculum:* A Journal of Mediaeval Studies (January, 1926), editor's preface, p. 3. Cfr. Ralph Adams Cram, *Mediaevalism and Modern Life,* address delivered at the first annual meeting of the Mediaeval Academy of America (*The Commonweal,* Vol. IV, No. 1, p. 9).

evitable consequence of this propulsion forward. Similarly the situation at the beginning twentieth century, and the Great War, were inevitable consequences of the same fact. We need to slow down if we are to save ourselves. An important means to this end is turning back upon the stages passed through, to pick up what we have foolishly thrown aside in our eager rush forward. From this point of view, the study of thought in the Middle Ages is exceedingly important. Indeed, I know of no single direction of cultural effort which can prove so fruitful as can this. I am hopeful that this insight may prevail, and with conviction. When it does there should be much recasting of values as regards what is commonly called 'modern' thought in the light of what went before." [2]

In our era of reappraisals and readjustments it is being increasingly realized that in order to secure the structure of civilization, we must plan to build on the bed-rock of perennial principles, of absolute and transcendental values: reliance on the shifting sands of scientism and sentimentalism, of relativism and romanticism has led but to disaster. It is this insight which inspires the present noteworthy trend of many of the best-trained minds to that type of philosophical thinking whose very soul is absoluteness, objectivity, wholesome common sense, the reign of intelligence. Deeply rooted in the imperishable achievements of that beautifully balanced Hellenic mind whose character is so indelibly

[2] From Professor Longwell's statement in Part I, Chap. I, *infra*.

stamped on other phases of our culture and
civilization, nurtured and developed by the best
intellects of the early and medieval Christian era,
Scholastic thought is of the very warp and woof
of the Western mind, and therefore of great significance for the successful solution of present
problems. "Modern thought cannot ignore its own
middle age; to do so is to ignore itself. It is not
enough to say that the thirteenth century is close
to us. The thirteenth century is in us, and we cannot get rid of it by denying it any more than a
man can deliberately detach himself from his past
by merely forgetting that he has a past." [3]

The *New Scholasticism* has a claim to the serious
attention of present-day thinkers by a threefold
title: it is heir at once to the best thought of the
ancient and of the medieval past; it aims to make
this double treasure functional for the present; by
a fruitful union of the best in past and present it
seeks to prepare the birth of a new and a richer
synthesis in the future: it is loyal to the spirit and
best traditions of the *Philosophia perennis*. In the
great cultural centers of the European continent
there is a growing sympathy and co-operation with
its programme and ideals, and its representatives
are there increasingly making contact with other
currents of contemporary thought.

Unfortunately, as much cannot be said for some
English-speaking countries, and especially for our

[3] Étienne Gilson, *La Philosophie au Moyen Age* (Paris, 1922),
II, p. 155.

own. Here, the movement toward a *rapproche-ment* has hardly been started. The non-Scholastic and Neo-Scholastic currents unconcernedly continue along parallel lines, and no appreciable effort has yet been made to bend them to the point of a better mutual understanding and co-operation on the problems which are of vital interest to both. "There is a most regrettable lack of contact and intercourse between Catholic and non-Catholic philosophers in this country,—a condition which contrasts very unfavorably with the conditions existing on the continent of Europe." [4] This is all the more deplorable at the present time when "it seems to be a prime desideratum that Scholastics and non-Scholastics should come to some genuine understanding of one another. For the time seems ripe for such an understanding." [5]

Prompted by a like conviction, I invited prominent representatives of both sides—the non-Scholastic and the Neo-Scholastic—to a frank and friendly exchange of ideas on the subject in the present symposium, in the hope that this mutual declaration of positions and the liquidation of misunderstandings would lead to a better acquaintance and be the first move towards eventual co-operation.

In the first place, a questionnaire was submitted [6] to sixty-five professors of philosophy in the lead-

---

[4] Professor Perry, in Part I, Chap. I, *infra.*

[5] Professor Blake, *ibid.*

[6] This questionnaire was sent out during the first days of January,

ing non-Catholic universities of the United States, Great Britain, and Canada. An expression of opinion was requested on the following points: present attitude of non-Scholastic thinkers towards Scholastic and Neo-Scholastic philosophy; reasons for the unfriendliness or indifference towards it,— whether they are to be found in the content, or method, or other aspects of that philosophy; the contributions which it can make towards the solution of contemporary problems; present prospects for a *rapprochement* between it and other currents of present-day thought; the means to be used for bringing about a better understanding and closer co-operation in the domain of philosophy. Thirty-three professors returned answers for publication; the others who replied admitted that insufficient knowledge of Scholasticism disqualified them for expressing an opinion on the points submitted. To preserve the personal touch, the answers received for publication are given in their original form; they are then summarized and grouped as commendations, counsels, criticism; this constitutes Part I of the present volume.

For the presentation of the Neo-Scholastic side, in Part II, eminent Neo-Scholastics of various countries were requested to contribute original articles on the nature, aim, methods of the New

1925, and was followed by requests for Neo-Scholastic contributions. In May of the same year the first steps were taken towards the formation of the American Catholic Philosophical Association. See *Proceedings* of the First Annual Meeting of The American Catholic Philosophical Association, p. 3.

Scholasticism; on its attitude towards modern and contemporary thought; on the progress of the movement in the several countries since the issuance of the encyclical *Æterni Patris* (1879). I have made a faithful rendition of the contributions originally written in French, German, and Italian. All these scholars wrote their articles quite independently of one another. The contributions are here given in their entirety, despite the fact that they overlap on certain points. For while agreeing on fundamentals, they display a freedom in aspects and a diversity in emphasis which furnish a concrete proof that Scholasticism, far from being the rigid and monotonous system many believe it to be, gives ample play to a reasonable variety in essential unity.

In Part III, I have devoted three chapters to a question of vital moment to the New Scholasticism. As several of our non-Scholastic contributors attest,[7] many still regard the following charge as fatal to the Neo-Scholastic programme: Scholasticism was permanently superseded by the new science and philosophy of the transition period because found to be incompatible with them; how, then, can Neo-Scholastics hope to synthesize it with that science and philosophy as they are to-day, after centuries of wonderful progress? On the basis of the best authorities, I have endeavored to establish the true view of the fortunes of Scholastic

[7] See, for example, the statements of Professors Perry, Hocking, and Hudson, in Part I, Chap. I, *infra*.

philosophy during the Humanism-Renaissance period. This view then furnishes the groundwork
for a presentation of the status and standpoint of
the New Scholasticism, for a statement of the law
and fact of continuity, and for some further considerations on the ideals and methods of the Neo-
Scholastic movement.

I wish to repeat here my very cordial thanks to
all who have contributed to the present symposium.
Their gracious response and open-minded attitude
are most gratifying tokens of a readiness for
further co-operation toward a better understanding,
and are sure to be deeply appreciated by all who
have the fruitful progress of human thought and
culture at heart.

J. S. ZYBURA

Colorado Springs, Colo.

CONTENTS

CONTENTS

CONTENTS

PAGE

PART I

OPINIONS OF NON-SCHOLASTIC PHILOSOPHERS ON SCHOLASTICISM

CHAPTER I

Professor Ralph Barton Perry, of Harvard University

I SHALL try to answer your questions in order: As to the attitude of non-Scholastic philosophers to Scholasticism, I think they regard Thomism as a part of the *history* of philosophy, and as such esteem it as they do any great historic system such as that of Plato or Descartes. The present drift towards realism ought to bring about a revival of interest in this system, but I do not think it has had much effect as yet.—Non-Catholic philosophy both in the eighteenth and in the nineteenth centuries was, of course, largely a reaction against Thomism, and most contemporary philosophers were reared in either the eighteenth or the nineteenth century tradition. So the common attitude to Thomism is the historical retrospective attitude, as to a system that has had its day.

As to the content of Scholasticism: the lack of sympathetic interest is not due to anything in the doctrines themselves. Professor Royce, for example, was greatly influenced by Scholastic doctrine in his conception of individuality (cfr. his "Conception of God"). Personally, I find many points of agreement, such as Realism, and the Thomist doctrine of the irreducibility of the person to social and political unities. I have found much in common with Père Kremer (cfr. his *Le Néo-Réalisme Américain*), and with Professor De Wulf, whom we are proud to have as a member of our department here.

As to the Scholastic method: the main objections are made on the ground of method and they are reducible to two: it is believed, in the first place, that the Scholastic philosophy is essentially an apologetic system, that is, devised to lend support to doctrines accepted on other grounds, such as those of authority or faith. There exists the feeling that Neo-Thomists and Neo-Scholastics are not really thinking for themselves but merely re-editing a system which they accept on non-philosophical grounds. Now the spirit of modern secular philosophy is radically critical. It does not tolerate the closing of any questions, but reconsiders all beliefs, not with a view to their rejection, necessarily, but with a view to accepting whatever conclusions reason and experience may appear to justify. It is generally believed that the outcome of Scholastic philosophizing is determined in advance, and that the processes of reasoning are therefore somewhat of an empty show. Furthermore, no non-Scholastic philosophers that I know of believe that the Scholastic proofs are real proofs—or believe that the deductive method can be carried through in metaphysics.

The temper of the present age is empirical, experimental, hypothetical, as opposed to the rationalistic sense of certitude prevailing down through the seventeenth century.—In the second place, it is felt that Scholastic philosophy is stationary and unprogressive. We find that philosophy has outgrown the great Scholastics and moved forward—not rejecting them, but assimilating them and adding more. There is a general feeling that contemporary adherents of the Scholastic system are living in the past, and that we have, therefore, nothing to learn from them. It is believed that St. Thomas, for example, has become an authority in the sense in which free-thinking and autonomous intellect can acknowledge no authority. Moreover, American Catholic philosophers do not appear to keep abreast of changing philosophical interests. They do not focus on the same points as ourselves, and so there is a lack of contact. This brings me to the next question.

As to a better understanding between Scholastics and ourselves. On this point I have very positive convictions. There is, I think, a most regrettable lack of contact and intercourse between Catholic and non-Catholic philosophers in this country—a condition which contrasts very unfavorably with the relations existing on the continent of Europe. Why is it, for example, that the Catholic teachers of philosophy in this country do not attend meetings of the American Philosophical Association and contribute articles to the philosophical periodicals, such as the *Journal of Philosophy?* Their participation would be warmly welcomed, and I do not see why we should not speak out our differences and come to understand one another better. It is not merely a question of philosophy in the stricter sense but of all our common social, economic, and cultural interests. In France, for example, conditions are quite different; there Catholics and non-Catholics, although they disagree sharply, seem to belong to one intellectual world. Catholics rank high among the influential thinkers of the day and are in constant contact and discussion with their non-Catholic colleagues.

*Professor William Ernest Hocking, of
Harvard University*

When I was a student of philosophy, the Scholastic period was usually treated rather briefly in the historical course, because it was felt that the importance of the great Schoolmen for the thought of to-day lay in their premises, which were held largely in common and could therefore be discussed together, rather than in their careful and voluminous deductions from those premises. The systems were so carefully articulated that the principles could be stated with some precision and generality; and if these were held to be superseded in any respect, it was held unnecessary to go into the details.

Now the sense was strong at that time, and is still strong, that the starting-points of Scholasticism were to some extent superseded in the period of the Renaissance. It seemed necessary that the results of Scholasticism should be as it were lost and rediscovered, since the presence of the principle of authority as offering a source of finished truth which reason might support, and to some extent reinterpret, but not deviate from in substance, was felt to fix conclusions too much in advance. The development of methods of inductive science, as modes of climbing to principles from which, in turn, deductions were to be made, was regarded as an essential part of the treasury of philosophy, and as necessary to the zest of philosophical discovery. In sum, the great defect of Scholasticism was felt to be its independence of experience, which was held to have some essential contribution to the content of metaphysical belief.

Since that time, there has come about a distinct change of attitude toward Scholasticism. There is a widespread re-awakening of interest in its content as well as in its method. The whole mediaeval period is studied with greater care and appreciation. At Harvard Professor Maurice De Wulf, of the University of Louvain, perhaps the greatest authority on the history of Scholasticism, has been giving courses of lectures, especially on St. Thomas. In the notable work of Professor W. H. Sheldon of Yale, called "The Strife of Systems," there is an extensive and highly appreciative chapter devoted to St. Thomas. The change of temper is due in part to a new realization of the essential wealth of thought of the Middle Ages, and in part to a disappointment with the results of the scientific method in philosophy. Where philosophies of everlasting flux prevail, there cannot but be impatience with an intellectual world in which well ordered systems, to remain eternally valid, are striven for; but thinkers for the most part realize that permanence of truth and the growth of truth are not incompatible, any more than the identity of an individual is incompatible with his growth. When this truth is well understood, many of the difficulties between modernism and traditionalism, both in philosophy and in doctrine, will disappear.

It will always be true that the philosophical mind will prefer to start, as Descartes tried to do, without presuppositions, and be carried to its conclusions by the necessities of dialectical advance. Plato and Hegel will be the great types of metaphysical method (the overdrawn schematism of Hegel being discarded). But with this there will be recognized the necessity of making a place for *data,* features of the world which resist at least our human efforts at rationalization, and which must be accepted as matters of experience. Intuition has for its aim the widening of the scope of perception to include data beyond the region of sense; and with the admission of intuition, there appears a type of authority which comes from the existence of varying degrees of intuitive capacity. The insight of the mystic may become, under certain circumstances, a valid source of metaphysical evidence. The method of St. Thomas, again, would not resist statement in terms of a free Platonic dialectic; and the content of Scholasticism remains, of course, one of the permanent types of philosophical doctrine. We shall never overcome the disposition of reason to produce varieties of doctrine, nor should we wish to do so. But we can continue to make clear where the issues lie, to study the limits of pure reason, and to overcome the misunderstandings due to prejudice.

The movement known as "New Realism" is of

large importance in this country and in England.
It marks a reaction against the subjectivistic trait
of much idealism, a disposition to take the world
anew at its face value and to seek the solution of
philosophical problems on other lines than the
comparatively simple and unprofitable line of taking everything up into the mind and calling the
thing done. In this respect, it is an undoubted
advance; it requires of idealism a more concrete
statement of the place of mind in the universe,
and of the significance of its concept of the Absolute.
It is a retrogression in another respect, finding itself boggled in the epistemological problems of the
eighteenth century without noteworthy improvement on the older statements. This suggests that
the epistemological work of William James and
Santayana has been more effective on its critical
than on its constructive side. Apart from the
school of John Dewey, there are fewer pragmatists
among teachers of philosophy than there were a
generation ago, though there are doubtless more
persons in the community who think in pragmatic
terms. Neo-realism arises as an alternative criticism of idealism, *i. e.,* an alternative to pragmatism;
and as neo-realism, due in this country largely to
the influence of Santayana, grows, pragmatism
declines. Bergson supplies a third alternative,
more significant than that of neo-realism; for although Bergson is pragmatical with respect to
science, he is an intuitionist in respect to the living
basis of the world. And through the essential in-

stability of the intuitionist standpoint, the path of
the next years leads to an internal rationalization
of the content of intuition; that is, to a reaffirma-
tion of metaphysical idealism on new grounds.
When this route has been followed in the general
philosophical consciousness, Hegel and Royce will
be revalued, as at this moment in Italy the Hegelian
point of view is being ably restated and developed.

Professor Wilmon H. Sheldon, of Yale University

The present attitude of non-Scholastic philosophers varies in different parts of our country. Here at Yale I gave a seminar on the *Summa Theologica,* using the Dominican Fathers' translation. In the future I may alternate between the *Summa* and Leibniz. The seminar was taken chiefly by divinity students and went very well. In my graduate-student days, Charles S. Peirce used to urge us to study Scholasticism. I find graduate students uniformly eager to learn about Scholasticism. I think the attitude of many of our Western colleges is not so favorable, influenced as their thinkers are by pragmatism; but it is possible that I am mistaken in this.

This pragmatic temper is perhaps the greatest influence working against the study of Scholastic philosophy—and indeed against any metaphysics. I think there must first be an interest in metaphysics —and I doubt if there is much of such interest at more than a few universities. Another reason is the belief that Scholasticism works wholly by authority—that the thinker is committed beforehand to certain conclusions. This objection affects the works of all Protestant-trained philosophers. Thus it is in a sense the method rather than the content that causes much of the trouble. Again, our psychology is largely materialistic and eschews all connection with religious interests.

I do not see any signs of an *early* "rapprochement" between the two camps of Scholasticism and modern philosophy; but surely no good thing comes easily, and it is always worth while to work for that end. As I said above, the democratic Protestant and *most of all* the pragmatist *hates* the idea of authority: it is a red rag to a bull from his point of view. That is the strategic point, I think. And herein I have, so far as I can, answered the other question: the stone of stumbling and rock of offence to the Protestant is the feeling that the Scholastic cannot inquire freely and empirically. Of course, I do not agree with this view, except in so far as I think any inquiry is bound to give a result agreeing with common sense and with what is vouchsafed from divine sources. Hence one should insist on the common sense and the practical character of Scholasticism.

There is a part of your question to which it ought to be possible to give a pretty direct answer; but I am afraid I do not have the knowledge that would justify me in pretending to speak with authority. Whether Scholasticism has points of contact with non-Catholic philosophies that will make fruitful coöperation possible is a question of fact, which supposes however an accurate understanding as to just what Scholasticism is; and it has been so many years now since I have paid any attention to this field that I hesitate to pronounce judgment. In a general way I should say that the answer will depend on the type of philosophy one is inclined to. Most of the current schools, including those that for the last century have been most popular, are so far away from Scholasticism both in aims and methods as to have no apparent common ground. On the other hand, certain of the forms of recent Realism would probably, on a number of points, find themselves taking sides with Scholasticism against some of its historical rivals. This is especially the case with the more general aspects of logical theory. But how much influence these newer tendencies will have is still problematical; and even in their case I hesitate, as I say, to pronounce on the degree of sympathy that is logically possible, in the absence of an adequate acquaintance with the Scholastics.

What I have to add to this is a purely personal opinion which can be taken for what it is worth. After all, the chance of intellectual coöperation depends even more on psychological considerations than it does on logical ones. And if I were asked what the psychological probabilities are of Scholastic and non-Scholastic thinkers getting together in the near future, I should have to say that they seem to me on the whole rather small. I don't mean to imply that the fault is all on one side. But since you ask for criticisms, I may be permitted to call attention to one obstacle in particular for which the Catholic philosopher is more directly responsible. I assume that what is wanted is discussion, a mutual give and take, such as has for a long time now been almost lacking between Catholic and non-Catholic philosophers. Now discussion does not require any considerable identity of belief; on the contrary, it seems to flourish more vigorously as differences widen. But it does normally presuppose a certain psychological attitude. It assumes principles to be really open to argument in terms of reason alone, and differences of opinion to be really arbitrable. And as soon as a disputant comes to feel that this is not the case, and that he is up against a settled test of orthodoxy which his arguments assail in vain, his zeal for controversy is sure to wane. It is undeniable that this is what non-Catholics feel about Scholasticism; and as long as Scholastics assume, or cause others to suppose they assume, that they are defending a system rather than engaged in an open-minded search for truth, especially when this system is suspected of having other foundations than purely rational ones, I think they will have to be content to go their own way and leave others to go theirs. Not that I really suppose Scholastics to be much more stubborn in holding to their opinions than other philosophers. But in the case of these last the reason is at least a personal one, and ideally the hope always remains of convincing them; whereas if their belief also has been institutionalized and connected with an authoritative religion, the hope departs, and with it goes also the chance of real intellectual coöperation. Discussion will then mean only proselytizing, which is not discussion at all.

Professor Charles M. Bakewell, of Yale University

I am very much interested indeed in your undertaking. The great period of Scholastic philosophy is not given, in non-Catholic schools, the consideration it deserves. This is not due to a hostile attitude, but rather to the fact that there are no texts available that are intelligible to the normal youth. If you will pardon my saying so, I think that the modern defenders of Scholastic philosophy have been over-timid. They have clung to the words and phrases of the Scholastic writers instead of translating their ideas into the language of everyday life as it is lived to-day—instead of translating them, to use Professor James' phrase, "into their cash value in terms of actual experience." The result is that the college student does not get beyond the words and phrases—they do not bite in.

The Scholastic philosophers' knowledge of the physical world was slight indeed as compared with that of modern scientists, but their knowledge of the inner life,—of the soul, its nature, its aspirations, its needs, was profound. Here they were in close touch with experience. The philosophy they built on this foundation is correspondingly important. In these days, when in so many quarters the current seems to be setting in the direction of outright materialism, it is particularly important that the voice of the Scholastic philosophers should be heard,—but it is not heard unless it is understood.

Speaking about the prospect of a "better understanding," another point occurs to me. Why do not the modern defenders of Scholastic philosophy meet and cross swords with their colleagues in the meetings of our philosophical associations? They keep themselves apart, and give the impression of an unwillingness to grapple with problems with the freedom of an open mind seeking truth, as if they assumed that the book of reason was closed and that they held the keys, and could speak with authority, and from a different plane than that occupied by all other philosophers.

I. As to the present attitude of non-Scholastic thinkers to Scholastic philosophy:

One must distinguish between those who are engaged in teaching philosophy and those who are actively doing research work. Again, in the latter group, a distinction should be made between those who are interested in systematic philosophy and those who are interested in historical research. I will take up each of these in turn.

(a) Present-day teachers in philosophy are essentially thorough-going rationalists by temperament; they are, so to speak, in sympathy with Liberalism as against Fundamentalism. They feel themselves to be emancipated as regards the traditional theology, or Church doctrine of any kind. This does not indicate the absence of religious interest; on the contrary, I believe the average of such interest, and conviction, is very high among teachers of philosophy. But it does indicate a spirit of rationalism so thorough-going, in intention, as to determine all interests and attitudes.

Now the philosopher of average acquaintance with thought in the Middle Ages—and that is a very limited acquaintance—regards Scholasticism as a philosophy bound up with the Roman Catholic

Church, and therefore under constraint and hindering the free movement of reason as such. He takes the same view of Scholasticism in its more recent form (Neo-Scholasticism). Hence this philosophy fails to engage his interest sufficiently to lead him to a closer study of it; and he is unwilling to give the time required for a proper understanding of it.

Again, being conscious that we are in an age of specialization, he gives himself to the mastery of some special field. Hence, even when he is interested, he is precluded by the limits of time from mastering the scholastic philosophy.

Finally, the present-day teacher of philosophy has strong faith in the evolving character of knowledge; and, generally speaking, the last is for him the best. Consequently the Greek philosophy of the 5th and 4th centuries B. C. and the "modern" philosophy of the 18th and 19th centuries constitute the objects of his major attention. Frequently he knows even his Plato and his Aristotle but poorly, and he is primarily interested only in the late 19th century and the contemporary philosophy.

These facts—taken out of my own observation and experience, to be sure—indicate to me rather an attitude of indifference than of hostility to the philosophy in question; and it tends to pass away from indifference toward respectful appreciation whenever the individual has opportunity of increasing his knowledge.

(b) Those who have worked in systematic philosophy have been dominated by a thorough-going rationalism and faith in the evolving character of thought. Hence they have usually regarded all mediaeval philosophy as outworn and kept alive only by the imprimatur of the Roman Catholic Church. Thus some form of Idealism or Realism or Naturalism or Pragmatism has engaged their major attention and effort. This does not mean that they have been unmindful of the value lying in the scholastic synthesis or in the scattered contributions and suggestions out of the mediaeval philosophy. The contrary is the case wherever they have the knowledge. But the lack of interest or time has withheld them from a closer study which might enrich their own systematic formulations. In this group there is occasionally distinct hostility, based upon conviction as regards the truth; but such hostility is essentially similar to that of the Realist as against the Idealist, for example, though it may be intensified by the spirit of liberalism in protest against institutionalism of any kind.

(c) The group of historians is comparatively small. Under the pressure of specialization they tend to limit themselves either to ancient or to modern philosophy, and indeed even more restrictedly. Some few are interested in the mediaeval philosophy. Now and then a man seeks to cover the whole range of philosophy in its historical development; but when he does so he finds it exceedingly difficult to master all—and especially the mediaeval field, which until recently has been more or less a closed record. Generally speaking, this group is not hostile to Scholasticism; on the contrary, it is warmly appreciative. Increase in knowledge of this field tends always, I believe, to increase both sympathy and appreciation.

II. As to the specific inquiry regarding "method or content":

The non-Catholic philosopher is not accustomed to the dialectic of Scholasticism, but is trained in science and critical analysis. The result is that he has little taste for the rigor of logic, and his real faith lies the way of empiricism. Moreover, the development of methodology since Kant gives him good ground for refusing to rely simply on the logic of Aristotle in the search for truth; and he does not know of the concessions, in this regard, made by the Neo-Scholastics.

The result is that he is lacking both in the training and confidence necessary for a proper understanding of Scholasticism. It is not likely, I think, that this defect in training will be remedied within the scheme of Protestant education; but then acquaintance with the procedure of Neo-Scholasticism may do much to effect a cure.

As for the content. Thomism is usually regarded, within the circles I speak of, as an antiquated system of thought. It is to them simply one of the possible syntheses; but their engagement with the succession of syntheses, in the history of thought, tends to check confidence in any synthesis as final. Hence they regard Thomism as not meriting the implicit confidence accorded to it by Catholic thinkers. Remedy of this condition will come, I believe, with a better knowledge on their part of the Thomistic synthesis and the whole round of mediaeval thought,—that is, when they see this synthesis in its integrity as they see other syntheses with which they are acquainted.

III. The Scholastic philosophy has undoubtedly, as I view the matter, much to contribute in the solution of problems in metaphysics and epistemology and religion. It is in the last named field especially where present-day thinkers may gain most by a study of mediaeval thought. For in that age they labored with a conviction and zeal regarding transcendental values which has never been matched; and their acquisitions have yet to be seen at their full value. Moreover, the world's present need of a restored belief in such values would make this contribution especially significant (cf. *infra*).

IV. As to the prospects of a *rapprochement:* The prospects are excellent, but not in the sense of accepting Thomism as a body of philosophic doctrine. The *rapprochement* will be rather of the kind that comes whenever a better understanding is had between minds of diverse thinking. This better understanding has been withheld thus far by the backward state of our knowledge of philosophy in the Middle Ages; but that condition is rapidly passing. The Ancient and the Modern periods have now been so worked over that attention is more readily given to the intervening *"terra incognita.*" Moreover, it is being seen more and more that this field deserves closer attention not only for itself but as a connecting link between ancient and modern. It has long been my own conviction that the so-called philosophy of the Middle Ages is in reality the early or beginning modern philosophy; and that neither the one nor the other is intelligible when viewed in the customary manner—namely, as a distinct period in and for itself. When both History and the History of Philosophy are seen and taught as "ancient" set over against "modern," each with its "mediaeval" period, we may expect that fruitful comprehension of human events and thought which we ought to have.

I see various encouraging signs of this insight spreading; and though these signs are scattered and partial, I believe they betoken the coming of a view that will make the study of the philosophy of the Middle Ages as necessary a part of our education in that field as is now the study of ancient philosophy and modern philosophy. With that will come of course the interest in mediaeval philosophy which all serious seekers for truth have at heart, as they scan the pages of man's thought-history eager for aid from whatever source.

I may add, as a matter of conviction and deep interest, a certain idea I have concerning the whole movement of thought in what I choose to call the "modern" world,—that is, from about the 4th century A. D. This thought is essentially the expression of a stock, the Teutonic; this stock is one possessed of tremendous energies, and of potentialities for either good or bad, in a degree heretofore unknown in history. In consequence of this energy they have moved ahead at very high speed; a speed so great as to be against their own good, for it has been too rapid to enable that genuine assimilation which alone can make for safe development. We have passed through in decades what should have required centuries, if character is to keep pace with intellectual and cultural exploitation. The rapid loss of the sense of transcendental values, with its correlated taking on of positivism, has been an inevitable consequence of this propulsion forward. Similarly the situation at the beginning of the 20th c. and the Great War, were inevitable consequences of the same fact. We need to slow down, if we are to save ourselves. An important means to this end is returning back upon the stages passed through, to pick up what we have foolishly thrown aside in our eager rush forward. From this point of view, the study of thought in the Middle Ages is exceedingly important. Indeed, I know of no single direction of cultural effort which can prove so fruitful as can this. I am hopeful that this insight may prevail, and with conviction. When it does there should be much recasting of values as regards what is commonly called "modern" thought in the light of what went before.

V. As to the means to be used for bringing about a better understanding and closer co-operation:

In Protestant circles one cannot count on much being done to this end, saving by the few directly interested. They will continue to do what usually has been done by those who penetrate into the mediaeval mind—that is, spread the gospel of new-found truth. This number has been growing of late years, as an aftermath of the knowledge made available by increased research in the history of mediaeval thought. Addition to these numbers will continue to depend on increased availability of such knowledge—an availability which, for the present, must continue to be chiefly the task of Catholic scholars.

The Catholics can, I am sure, do most by con-tinuing to promote historical research in this field and by making their results more readily accessible. I would suggest, for example, two especially fruit-ful directions in this connection. First, an in-creasingly liberal attitude on the part of the Vatican authorities in making manuscripts easy of access for impartial and critical research. Second, making translations (especially into English) both of the original sources and of the secondary sources—that is, of the leaders of thought in the Middle Ages and of the various subsequent outstanding discus-sions or treatments of the leaders and the move-ment in mediaeval thought.

Professor A. A. Bowman, of Princeton University [1]

Scholastic philosophy is not my field, but as one who is professionally in touch with the contemporary world of philosophy I wish to say that in my opinion you are quite wrong in your supposition that present-day thought is hostile to Scholasticism. On the contrary, I find the best thought of the day very sympathetic to the keen thinking of the Schoolmen. As evidence of this let me mention the fact that Mr. C. D. Broad of Trinity College, Cambridge (England), has somewhere remarked (I have lost the reference but I think it must have been in one of the philosophical journals) that no serious thinker of the present day would treat Scholasticism with anything but respect. Mr. Broad in my opinion is the keenest mind among the younger generation of English thinkers, and, as his training and viewpoint are ultra-modern and scientific, such a statement as coming from him is particularly significant.

I might also mention the work of Mr. Reginald

[1] This letter and those of Professor Alexander of Nebraska University and of Professor Hudson of the University of Missouri, were originally written to Mr. C. J. Steiner, S. J., of St. Louis University, and are here used with his and the authors' kind permission.

Harris, Fellow of All Souls, Oxford, on Duns
Scotus as evidence of the serious interest young
England has in the Scholastic philosophy. It is
true that many disparaging remarks on the subject
are to be met with in uninformed writers, but you
may take it from me that the best-trained minds
are turning in a noteworthy way to the great systems of the Middle Ages.

Professor John Dewey, of Columbia University

In reply to your very interesting letter I will make the following statements:

It is difficult to make any sweeping generalization regarding the attitude of non-Scholastic philosophers toward Scholasticism at the present time. The neglect of Scholasticism is in part due to psychological and pedagogical reasons rather than to logical ones. There are, of course, certain fashions, to use a harsh term, in thought as well as in other matters, and the neglect of the Scholastic system is in some measure due to the fact that the thinkers and writers outside of the Catholic Church do not have at present a lively interest in the problems and issues with which Scholasticism is primarily concerned. It is my impression, however, that there is now a growing interest, connected partly with the revival of realistic theories of knowledge, and partly with increased study of Aristotle and consequent interest in the relation of mediaeval thinkers to the Aristotelian system.

The chief causes for indifference rather than positive unfriendliness are these: (1) The fact that non-Scholastic thinkers have mostly been brought up in the Protestant tradition and have,—more or less unconsciously,—identified Scholasticism with the theological dogmas which they do not accept. The teachers themselves were educated under these influences. The courses in the history of philosophy given in institutions under Protestant auspices emphasize the Greek thought and modern movement since Bacon, rather than Scholastic philosophy, and consequently the habit of neglect tends to perpetuate itself. (2) A more objective cause of this attitude of mind is, I think, the decay of acute interest, if not actual belief, in the content of Christian revelation. (3) The Scholastic method seems too rationalistic and not sufficiently empirical to appeal to one school of contemporary thought, while those who are rationalistically inclined seem to prefer at present to follow the model set by recent mathematics. (4) The development of natural science since the formulation of the main tenets of Scholasticism, and the fact that it does not seem possible to find harmony between the points of view developed in this science and the positions of Scholastic philosophy, is another reason. The new problems, moreover, which the development of modern science (in its methods and results) introduced, are more widely and intensely appreciated than the problems with which Scholasticism is concerned. (5) The rise of many new social and political problems upon which Scholasticism does not appear to throw any light, because it had been developed in a period before these presented themselves.

As to bringing about a better understanding, the

only suggestion that occurs to me in connection with this point is the desirability of a presentation of the main points of Scholasticism apart from a definite reference to the theological doctrines of the Church, and a more sympathetic interest in at least problems of modern empirical and rationalistic philosophers than has been displayed by some of those writing from the Scholastic point of view. What I mean is, a tendency which I have occasionally observed in some of these writers to assume that the truth is so finally and clearly stated in Scholasticism that most modern European philosophy is a kind of wilful and perverse aberration. Now while there is a growing dissatisfaction with many of the results of eighteenth and nineteenth century philosophy, there are probably no non-Scholastic thinkers who do not believe that they represent a sincere attempt to deal with genuine problems.

Professor Edgar S. Brightman, of Boston University

Answering your questions categorically, I should reply: (1) That there is more interest in Neo-Scholasticism at present than there was a quarter of a century ago; but that in America interest in Scholasticism of the Middle Ages is at a low ebb largely because the historical study of philosophy has declined of late.

(2) As to present-day reasons for the unfriendliness or indifference of non-Scholastic philosophers to Scholasticism, this is the hardest to answer of your questions. There is no doubt that the *odium theologicum* enters in; fashion dictates a good deal, and one is so busy studying the things that are being "talked about" that one neglects much that is more significant. Another factor is the Scholastic terminology, which is forbidding, and which often defines problems in a fashion that has little relation to the contemporary approach.

(3) I should say that the prospects for a *rapprochement* of any and all schools ought always to be good, in the sense of furnishing a welcome hearing to the presentation of every well-considered point of view. There are several things that might aid it. If Scholastic philosophers were to write more frequently for the philosophical journals, were

to attend the meetings of the Association (both Eastern and Western Divisions), and were to write books that interpreted the relation between Scholastic and modern thought, the situation would improve, I believe. The sort of book that I have in mind is indicated by Schulte, *Die Gottesbeweise in der neueren deutschen philosophischen Literatur,* Kremer, *Le Néo-Réalisme Américain,* or Maher's *Psychology,* or Ryan's new *Introduction to Philosophy* (although I have not had time to examine the last named very carefully as yet).

For myself, I think that one of the chief reasons for my not paying more attention to Neo-Scholasticism, apart from the poor excuse of pressure of other matters, is the fact that I find both dualism and also the "soul" so hard to understand. In my forthcoming book on *Introduction to Philosophy* (Henry Holt & Co., N. Y., 1925) I have a chapter on consciousness in which I criticize the concept of soul; but I am sure you will feel, and feel justly, that I have not adequately considered the Scholastic presentation of the subject.

Professor *Walter Goodnow Everett, of*
Brown University

The attitude towards Scholasticism on the part of philosophical students and teachers, outside of your own schools, is due, I think, to several causes. In the first place, most of our philosophers would insist that Scholastic philosophy represents only a phase of the historic development of thought, not a final or definitive system. I should hold—and many others would, with differing degrees of emphasis, be found in substantial agreement on this point—that philosophy is a progressive unfolding of human thought in the process of civilization, and that complete finality never is or can be reached. Conceptions of the universe and of man's place within it are necessarily modified by the fresh winnings of knowledge. The elements of truth in an historical system, in Platonism or Aristotelianism, for example, do not reappear unchanged; they stand in new relations and possess a different significance. This progressive view of philosophy does not mean that no secure truth is won and no problems settled, but rather that one's world-view cannot be rounded off to the exclusion of new discoveries and fresh insights.

Personally, I should also hold as a corollary of what has been expressed that, for a genuinely moral

34

and spiritual interpretation of life, man is not dependent upon the finality of his metaphysics. Such dependence would indeed be calamitous. Rather are the values which give the most enduring nobility and worth to his existence—and also the most enduring satisfaction—discoverable within human experience. This is an open book whose pages are a thousand times more legible than are the complexities and mysteries of the universe concerning which the best and most truth-loving minds have reached such different hypotheses.

I note that you inquire whether the reasons for an attitude of possible friendliness or unfriendliness to Scholasticism are to be found in the content, or method, or other aspects of that philosophy. I am inclined to think that the primary defect lies in certain unchallenged presuppositions which affect both the content and method of Scholastic philosophy. These presuppositions concerned both its view of the physical world, its philosophy of nature, and its philosophy of history. The results of science, now almost universally accepted, have changed the entire outlook upon these problems. Scarcely less significant, within the limits of its own field, has been the work of literary criticism. One gladly recognizes that the great thinkers of the Scholastic period were as earnest in their search for truth as the thinkers of any age have been, but they all wrought under the limitations of their time and of the historical-cultural life of which they were a part.

On one point I should like to say a further word. In a general course in the history of philosophy I give a larger place to mediaeval philosophy than do many teachers. I find it not wanting in interest to students. Three phases of the period have proved of distinct value in such an historical survey, viz.: (1) the course of thought on the relations of faith and reason; (2) the development of Christian mysticism; and (3) the time-honored problem of realism and nominalism. The treatment of these features of mediaeval philosophy has seemed essential to an appreciation of the continuity of thought. The linkage both with classical Greek and Alexandrian philosophy makes it clear to the student how unbroken was the course of philosophical speculation.

Permit me to add that I warmly appreciate the admirable spirit of your inquiry, and that I shall be happy to see the results when they are made public.

Professor Edgar A. Singer, Jr., of the University of Pennsylvania

In the department of philosophy of this University as many courses are given in the mediaeval period, as in the classic; and have been, as far back as the number of students would warrant it. They are in charge, as are the classic courses, of a full professor who has made this period his special study. The courses in mediaeval philosophy are indeed less followed than those in ancient and modern. But is not this true of mediaeval history in general? However, I venture to guess that the insistence now being put upon the continuity of history is rapidly restoring a balance which the beginnings of modern criticism upset. I may add that our plans for next year (1926) include the opening of a course in Neo-Scholasticism.

Professor Joseph A. Leighton, of the Ohio State University

The method of St. Thomas Aquinas does not appeal to me because it seems to me too predominantly *authoritarian* and *deductive* and that, in the consideration of the various articles, the analysis is over-elaborated. His clinching arguments appear to me frequently to consist in citations (and explanations of the citations) from the Scriptures, Aristotle, and the Church Fathers. Unless one admits the absolute and final authority of these sources, as interpreted by Thomas, one naturally is not convinced by his arguments.

Professor H. B. Alexander, of the University of Nebraska

It is difficult to give a simple or direct reply to your inquiry relative to Scholastic philosophy. My impression is that the antipathy you mention is actual and proceeds from both motives—aim and method of Scholasticism. In addition I should say that ignorance of the Scholastic writers is a large prejudicial factor, for I believe few instructors in philosophy have more than a cursory acquaintance with Scholastic thought.

In regard to the first issue, the matter of harmonization of reason and dogma, undoubtedly much of the modern attitude is an inheritance from the scientific and religious controversies of the past three centuries; but I believe something is due also to the fact that many of our contemporary teachers of philosophy are agnostic or even anti-Christian. At any rate, the prevailing idea that "truth" is known only when it is "scientific," narrows the possibility of sympathy with a mode of thought which has an avowed subordination to faith. Here also the prejudice in the matter of method enters. Modern science feels itself free to investigate any possible subject without prejudice as to conclusions. A method which involves deduction from accepted truths is distasteful to the scientific temper. I am

inclined to think, however, that the existence of the
censorship and Index forms the greatest obstacle
of all: it is difficult to take as genuine a philosophy
which is expressed under such formal restrictions.

In the preceding I have given what I regard as
the chief sources of the general attitude.   Coming
to particulars, I believe that you will find a reasonable sympathy with Scholastic thought in many instances, and I am inclined to classify the University
of Nebraska as one of them.   My colleague, Professor Hinman, has repeatedly used the translated
works of Dr. De Wulf and those of Dr. Coffey in
his undergraduate courses in metaphysics.   My
own subject is the history of philosophy, and I
give about equal weight to Scholastic and to
Modern Philosophy (something quite unusual in
non-Catholic schools).   I may say that I had the
advantage of some schooling on the subject under
Father Shanahan, S.J., and I have also from time
to time used Dante (*Divina Commedia*) as subject
matter for an introduction to the thought of the
Middle Ages.

As to my personal attitude, I believe that you
can best get it from my recently published *Nature
and Human Nature,* in the two essays, "The Goodness and Beauty of Truth," and "Apologia pro
Fide,"—the latter my presidential address before
the American Philosophical Association a few years
since.   Certainly I have a deep respect for Scholastic philosophy.   I feel that at present it over-

emphasizes St. Thomas Aquinas, and that it might make a stronger appeal to our generation if it were more boldly to espouse the cause of faith and make less pretensions in the field of pure reason.

Professor E. L. Hinman, of the University of Nebraska

My own belief is that a measurable *rapprochement* between Scholastic and non-Scholastic philosophy may reasonably be expected, so much at least as to engender a more appreciative mutual understanding. But there are some reasons for aloofness that may not soon be done away.

Teachers of philosophy in America must commend their subject to an educated audience greatly under the influence of the achievements of science. If the philosophers were then to accept the principle of authority in its Scholastic form they would at once put themselves out of court. This consideration has some merited weight; but it has also gained an enormous unmerited weight by reason of the ignorance which exists among the scientists, among the general educated public, and among many of the philosophers themselves, concerning the finer meaning of Scholastic philosophy. The attitude of the scientists is easily understood. Here, as Dr. De Wulf points out, Scholasticism is simply paying the penalty for the mistakes of policy of its leaders of the past. In Protestant lands other influences also have reinforced this argument, while there has been little effective spokesmanship on the other side. Explicit avowal of conformity to an external authority would therefore cost a man his audience.

A further cause of alienation, as I see it, is the different method used in the two camps of treating philosophical discussion. The non-Scholastics study thoroughly any and all of the great philosophers, any and all of the vexed cultural questions, and try to distil the truth for to-day from such a discussion. The Scholastics concentrate chiefly upon one system, Thomism, and do not engage closely with the literature of modern philosophy. Criticisms of modern classics that have issued from the Scholastic camp have often read as if the writers were of course arguing to a foregone conclusion, and also had never understood the modern philosophical classics in such wise as to see eye to eye with the modern non-Scholastic student. More recently a few Catholic scholars have shown the power to get beyond this; but on the whole, the two parties have not yet come to speak the same intellectual language or do battle on the same terrain. For this I hold the Scholastics chiefly responsible, although I also believe that non-Scholastic university instruction is suffering from the failure to concentrate enough. "What should Scholastic philosophers do to bring about a better understanding between themselves and non-Scholastic thinkers of to-day?" I think that if they could produce a discussion of modern philosophical classics that was appreciative of the problems there raised, but able effectively to show how on the merits of the issues the Scholastic interpretation was the better grounded, that would be something. While we have something of this, much more will be needful, if the parties are even to meet on the same intellectual terrain.

I think I see signs of something like a *rapprochement*. The narrowly scientific or mechanical view of the world has been riddled with effective criticism. The "low categories philosophies" of a few years ago are discredited, and with them the narrow type of intellectualism which raises the banner of the physical sciences alone. Even a psychologist may now believe in a soul. Indeed, there are many phases of the strongly held philosophy of to-day that might engage closely with much of the Scholastic teaching. But I do not share the apparent conviction of some Catholic writers that the New Realism is to foster a better understanding. The New Realism is in danger of becoming another "low categories philosophy." The pronunciamento of the "Six Realists" has proved incapable of development, but it contemplated a radical mechanism. Critical Realism also simply consecrates the categories of physics, and issues in what one of its representatives calls Neo-Materialism. Nor is the English Neo-Realism of Bertrand Russell and Samuel Alexander more satisfactory. I wonder if the Scholastic writers who seem to welcome that kind of thing are properly discerning.

My own supposition is that there is more of promise in the remodeling of the Kantian and post-

Kantian idealism, in such wise as to bring it into closest relation with the philosophy of Aristotle. The writings of Professor A. S. Pringle-Pattison, for instance, contain much that would seem to me very suggestive along that line. But this is much nearer to the orthodox development of modern philosophy than is the kind of thing that is now trying to get itself stated as the so-called New Realism.

Professor George H. Mead, of the University of Chicago

I must confess that I am not sufficiently familiar with Scholastic philosophy or with present-day Neo-Scholasticism to be able to judge in how far there is in them a basis for sympathy with other types of philosophic speculation. This in a manner implies that it has not seemed to me necessary that I should give to the study of mediaeval Scholasticism and its continuance in modern times, the attention which I have given to the philosophies of the ancient world, and those that have arisen since the Renaissance, and in this admission I think that I reflect the attitude of my colleagues in this and other universities, with the exception of a few who lay more stress on learning than I.

My defense is that the movement of thought has seemed to me to have left Scholasticism at one side, nor to have returned to it for renewed light or inspiration. It is true the basis both of modern rationalism and empiricism are to be found in Scholastic thought, and in particular I have been realizing recently that an adequate account of the very complex and ambiguous conception of consciousness, giving an entirely new orientation to the thought of the modern world, must begin with St. Augustine and proceed down the doctrines of both Nominalists and Realists, and that Abélard is one of the most refreshing modern figures.

The fundamental difference of attitude which I have recognized between Scholastic thought and that of other schools, lies in the acceptance of authority as an immediate ground for determining the judgment on the part of Scholastic thought,— at least as I have understood it in its history. I think all disagreements and unfriendliness that may exist come back to this: the principle of authority appears to us to have rendered static and immobile the Scholastic mind, when once the *Summa* of Aquinas had been definitely erected. There exists within it no place for unshackled scientific question, investigation, and imagination. *Scientia* has in the modern spirit become science, and every philosophy since the days of Galileo has willingly or unwillingly acknowledged the necessity of finding within itself a place not only for the results but also method of scientific investigation. The inhibitions of reverence may well attend the results of research. They stifle the eager search for the exception, and the experimental proof of the hypothesis.

Professor Jay William Hudson, of the University of Missouri

The typical attitude towards Scholasticism is not so much one of adverse criticism as indifference. Most academic philosophers regard Scholasticism as a dead issue, of historical interest only, representing a stage in the history of philosophy—an important stage—that has served its purpose. They are likely to feel that one who still adheres to a Scholastic system does not adequately recognize the later advances in philosophical thinking.

You ask whether it is the content, spirit, or method that gives most offense. The spirit, I should say, if by spirit you include the aim and motive of Scholastic philosophy, as they are understood. For the average philosopher thinks of Scholasticism as the handmaid of theology—the dogmatic theology of the Church—whose aim is either to substantiate that theology in rational terms, or, at least, to present a philosophy that is perfectly compatible with that theology. This means that the Scholastic philosopher does not trust his reason alone, but that he is committed beforehand to certain dogmatic premises, so that his philosophy becomes a sort of special pleading, and not a fair and impartial judgment of the issues at stake. With such a spirit motivating a philos-

48

ophy, its method and content seem to be vitiated.

Please observe that the above is my opinion of the attitude of the average academic philosopher outside the Church. My own views on the matter are much too complicated to express here. In the last resort, of course, a system like that of St. Thomas Aquinas has to be considered and evaluated on its own merits, and not in terms of preconceptions regarding his aim or religious affiliations. In doing this, I am certain one finds in him one of the great systems of all time. But I wonder how many really understand the great master?

Professor James B. Pratt, of Williams College

I wish to express my very real sympathy with your undertaking, and my earnest hope that your efforts will be successful.—My acquaintance with the Scholastic philosophy is neither so wide nor so deep as I could wish, but I have profound respect for it, and especially for St. Thomas, whom I rank very high among the world's systematizers.

The principal reasons for a certain unfriendliness toward the Scholastic philosophy on the part of many non-Scholastic thinkers are, perhaps, the following: (1) The slight use it makes of the results of natural science, and its seeming unwillingness to recognize the importance of scientific facts. (2) Its reliance upon authority and its consequent dogmatism. (3) Its retention of methods and terms as important which the non-Scholastic thinker finds difficult to use without seeming to give up his case. (4) The seeming limitation of its interest to the ancient problems.

I should add that personally I feel very friendly toward Scholasticism for the following reasons: (1) It presents a view of the universe and of man that gives much needed play to individual religion and cultivation of the individual soul. It stands for a point of view somewhat similar to that of the great Indian philosophy, in this respect. *The soul has a chance in Scholasticism.* (2) I like its crisp and exact logic.

I think the feeling of most non-Scholastic philosophers of my acquaintance toward Scholasticism is neither friendly nor unfriendly, but rather one of complete neglect and indifference, and too often one of very great ignorance.

As to the question of a better mutual understanding and co-operation between Scholastic and non-Scholastic thinkers, my answer is largely implied in what I have already said. If Scholastic thinkers would throw off authority and their seeming dogmatism, and would deal with our modern problems in more modern fashion, there might result a helpful exchange of views between them and the non-Scholastics. If they would mix with us more—in our meetings and in our journals—this also would help. We get the feeling that Scholastic thinkers are living and want to live in a little sacred world of their own.

The effort that you are making is a fine and long step in the right direction, and I feel like thanking you personally for having undertaken it.

Professor William K. Wright, of Dartmouth College

In reply to your inquiry, I can only speak for what I suppose to be the typical attitude of professors of philosophy in secular colleges and universities, such as for the most part constitute the membership of the American Philosophical Association. And as I have not often heard the questions discussed, about which you inquire, it is likely that what I say may be simply my own personal attitude, though I suppose it to be representative.

The attitude toward Scholasticism and Neo-Scholasticism is not so much one of friendliness or hostility as of comparative ignorance. We know what the standard histories of philosophy say about medieval philosophy. Most of us have probably read the short treatises of St. Anselm in translation (*Proslogium,* etc.), and we have read here and there in translations of the *Summa* of St. Thomas. We have read a few semi-popular books like those of De Wulf, Turner, *et al.,* and an occasional article in journals like the *Revue Néo-Scholastique.* We have read Newman's books, or some of them. And that is about all.

The chief reasons why we do not devote more time to Scholasticism and Neo-Scholasticism are probably lack of time and the belief that we have more to learn from systems of more recent origin, that have been influenced more by the development of the modern natural and social sciences. It is not that we feel any particular hostility to Scholasticism or Neo-Scholasticism. The former, we know, performed great services in the Middle Ages; and the latter, we are sure, has much to contribute to-day. But teaching occupies most of our time, our hours for independent study are limited, and our Latin is rusty.

Personally, though a liberal Protestant, I have much respect for Scholasticism and Neo-Scholasticism, and I believe that the latter is a valuable constructive movement in contemporary thought. In saying this, however, I do not wish to be misunderstood. There can, for me, be no doctrines that must be accepted *"de fide"*; all must be suggested to reason and experience, and nothing can be retained that cannot be reconciled with the general drift of the modern inductive sciences,— not only with what has been *established* by them, but with what they render fairly *probable*. Philosophy to-day, is no longer *"ancilla theologiae,"* but has become *"ancilla scientiarum."* However, I believe that very much of what has been considered vital in the Christian faith—Catholic as well as Protestant—can be reconciled with science. The work of Sir Bertram Windle is instructive in this respect.

To bring about a better understanding between themselves and non-Scholastic thinkers of to-day,

Scholastic philosophers might write more books and articles dealing with the non-theological aspects of Scholasticism, in comparison with the other philosophical schools of to-day. Our "neo-realists" and "critical realists," for instance, would be glad to know more about the attitude of Scholastic realism on the problems in which they are interested. The critical realists just now are much concerned with the doctrine of essences, which they have borrowed from Scholasticism, without, I suspect, understanding very much about it. An account of recent developments in Catholic political and social philosophy and ethics (beginning perhaps with the Encyclical of Leo XIII regarding labor, and coming down to the present time, recounting both the official pronouncements of prelates, and the writings of professors) would be of great interest to us. We are laymen, and our interests are not primarily theological.

The tables of contents in recent years of our principal philosophical journals in this country and England, and the chapter headings of recent "Introductions to Philosophy" will give an idea of the kinds of questions with which we are most concerned. Light on what either St. Thomas or more recent Scholastics have to say on these matters would be of interest. There is a chapter on the method of St. Thomas entitled the "Practical Synthesis" by Professor W. H. Sheldon in his *Strife of Systems and Productive Duality,* which is the most serious attempt of which I know in recent years by a Protestant to make use of Scholasticism, and to compare it with recent developments in non-Scholastic philosophy.—I hope that the publishers will send us a circular of your book. We endeavor to place all more important Catholic books on philosophy in our library, but Catholic publishers sometimes neglect to send us circulars.

Professor Ralph M. Blake, of the University of Washington (Seattle)

I am very glad to answer the questions which you put, to the best of my ability, as follows:

(1) "The present attitude of non-Scholastic thinkers to Scholasticism and Neo-Scholasticism as a *philosophy*." The attitude of different men in this respect would naturally be very different, and it is therefore rather difficult to generalize. I should estimate the matter somewhat as follows. By the majority of non-Scholastics the Scholastic writers are pretty much ignored, although there is a growing interest in mediaeval Scholasticism from the purely historical point of view. Others have made some more or less superficial acquaintance with the Scholastic views as presented by their modern defenders, and have felt themselves repelled by what seems to them the dryly abstract and logical form in which they have found them presented. Relatively few have studied the Scholastic views with care and attempted a sympathetic understanding, and still fewer are conscious of any positive sympathy or agreement with such views.

(2) "The sources and present-day reasons for the unfriendliness or indifference of some towards it. Are these reasons to be found in the content,

or method, or other aspects of that philosophy?"
The state of the Scholastic Philosophy as described
by Pope Leo XIII in the encyclical *Aeterni Patris*
is one of the historical sources of such unfriendliness or indifference. Admittedly it had fallen
into a corrupt and decayed condition. It was pursued in a half-hearted manner; it presented itself
largely in inadequate "outlines" and "compendia,"
and in a dryly dogmatic form; it took little or no
account of contemporary non-Scholastic thought.
The life had pretty much gone out of it. There
has been since that time, of course, much change for
the better in all these respects; but it is not unnatural that those educated in different traditions
have not, for the most part, been fully aware of
these changes. And this is partly due to the aloofness of the Scholastics themselves. Scholastic philosophy is cultivated almost exclusively by Catholics, and among them it is only the clergy who are
engaged upon it in any positive and creative way.
Scholastic treatises are produced for ecclesiastics
by ecclesiastics; published by Catholic publishing
houses, advertised and reviewed, for the most part,
by Catholic journals. Scholastic writers seldom
contribute to philosophical journals published under
non-Catholic auspices; they seldom join or attend
philosophical associations of a prevailingly non-
Catholic and non-Scholastic character; in a word,
they do not make themselves heard or felt in the
world of philosophical discussion with which non-
Scholastics are familiar. Nor do they encourage

non-Scholastics to take any active part in their own enterprises. Hence they are little known or understood by their non-Scholastic contemporaries. It tends to be felt that the Scholastic philosophy is not and cannot be anything but the rather humble "handmaid of theology," and that it properly belongs to the strictly ecclesiastical realm, to which, for the most part, it seems willingly to confine itself.

Another reason for the neglect of Neo-Scholastic works, at least in English-speaking countries, is to be found in the fact that the Neo-Scholastic works of serious importance and genuine ability in the English language can still practically be counted on the fingers. Furthermore, even these are chiefly outlines, text-books, and compendia; and even when they make more serious pretensions they rarely seem to be fully abreast of modern non-Scholastic discussions of the topics dealt with. There is a tendency to present the Scholastic views with insufficient depth and clearness; to give inadequate attention to a thorough explanation of the grounds upon which these views rest; to neglect to relate the Scholastic views to other contemporary views of the same problem, and to give careful and impartial consideration to such objections as really weigh in the minds of their present-day critics. One constantly feels that Neo-Scholastic writers are so sure of the correctness of their own views that they do not feel the necessity either of working them out in careful detail, or of considering them in the light of a thorough study of non-Scholastic writers.

(3) "Is that philosophy capable of making any valuable contributions towards the solution of present problems in the various departments of thought and life?" In my opinion the Scholastic philosophy is in a position to make very valuable contributions to the solution of philosophical problems of the present day. In fact, that Scholastics and non-Scholastics should come to some genuine understanding of one another seems to me to be a prime desideratum, particularly at the present time. For the time seems to be ripe for such an understanding. There are already strong currents in contemporary non-Scholastic thought which are very closely allied to the Scholastic on many fundamental points, and much might be accomplished by the union of these divided forces. I refer especially to the very marked tendency to realistic views, both in metaphysics and in theory of knowledge, in the discussions of present-day non-Scholastics. Scholastics might easily exert a profound influence upon the course and the outcome of these discussions.

(4) "What are the prospects for an early *rapprochement* between that philosophy and the other currents of modern philosophic thought?" I have already indicated my view that there already exists a sound basis for such a drawing together of Scholastic and non-Scholastic currents. In fact I believe that a whole section of non-Scholastic thought

is definitely and strongly moving in the direction of some sort of Scholastic view, although those who are doing most to further this movement, and indeed Scholastics themselves seem to be largely unconscious of this fact. Fundamentally Scholastic views of substance, cause, universals, truth, knowledge, error, etc., seem to be coming more and more strongly into prominence.

(5) "What should be done to bring about a better understanding and a closer co-operation in the domain of philosophy?" In order to further better understanding and co-operation the following seem to me to be important:

(a) Scholastics must abandon the "aloofness" of which I have spoken.

(b) They must become thoroughly and intimately familiar with contemporary non-Scholastic thought in all its phases, but especially with the ideas of contemporary realists. To this end they must have, more particularly, a thorough understanding of the newer developments in logic (especially on its symbolic and mathematical side); of the basic conceptions of contemporary theory in the realms of physics, psychology (in the former especially the theory of relativity and the new ideas of time, space, motion, etc., involved; in the latter especially the Freudian and the "behaviouristic" development), and biology.

(c) They must definitely and sympathetically *enter into* these speculations, not with preconceived notions as to the issue, not with the primary inten-

tion of refuting them or of criticising their errors
(though this will naturally be involved), and in
general not with the attitude of defending a system
once for all pretty much given and fixed. On the
contrary they must be ready and willing to profit
by whatever they can find of value in these ideas,
even if this involve considerable modification in
the details of their metaphysical or epistemological
theories. I am confident that they will find their
fundamental ideas largely borne out and sustained,
and will be helped to elaborate and develop these
ideas into a richer and more fruitful philosophical
synthesis than either they or their non-Scholastic
contemporaries have yet attained.

(d) Non-Scholastics must be brought to understand and to enter sympathetically into the deeper
thought of Scholastics. This can best be accomplished by the multiplication of thoroughly informed and solidly worked out Scholastic treatises
on themes of contemporary interest and importance.
I do not think that Scholastics will find their non-
Scholastic contemporaries unready or unwilling to
enter freely into discussion, or to give a full and
fair consideration to the Scholastic positions when
these are adequately and fully expounded by men
thoroughly familiar with the whole range of contemporary thought.

CHAPTER II

OPINIONS OF NON-SCHOLASTIC THINKERS IN GREAT
BRITAIN AND CANADA

Professor Clement C. Webb, of Oxford University

I MUST first point out that, while I am very far
from being an "authority" on Scholastic philosophy,
I have some acquaintance with some of its mediaeval representatives; but of Neo-Scholasticism I
have only a very slight knowledge, and cannot speak
of it from anything that can be called first hand
study.

(1) *The present attitude of non-Scholastic thinkers to Scholasticism and Neo-Scholasticism.*—I
should be inclined to say that there was now, far
more than in my younger days, a general agreement among competent scholars that the Schoolmen, especially the best known of them, St. Thomas,
were really important thinkers, from the study of
whom much can be learned as to the problems which
have in all ages engaged the attention of philosophers and apart from the study of whom the
history of thought cannot be rightly understood.
The notion which was prevalent 100 to 150 years
ago and later, that their speculations were a solemn
trifling or even that their submission to certain dog-

mas as revealed was such as to deprive their work of all claim to freedom and originality, is now rarely held by the instructed. While a certain reaction towards *realism*, which has been marked in the philosophy of the last quarter of a century in England, Germany, and America has helped in drawing attention to a group of thinkers who all shared the general standpoint of Aristotelian realism, away from which the current of thought from Descartes onwards took its course so strongly. On the other hand the extreme idealism of Croce and Gentile has (partly under the influence of a patriotic predilection for Italian philosophy) gladly sought points of attachment in such illustrious Italian thinkers as St. Thomas and St. Bonaventure.

But I think that very many who would thus be more than willing to learn of the mediaeval masters would be less disposed to seek for enlightenment from the *Neo-Scholastics:* they might be quite ready to discuss problems with them as with other fellow-students, but they would suspect that they were really taking up a position inconsistent with the full recognition of the complete freedom of thought to follow the argument whithersoever it leads, by adhering to positions which the main stream of historical development has passed by and trying to force modern knowledge into a particular *cadre*, which had been found acceptable chiefly because it was reconcilable with dogmas which the Neo-Scholastics concern themselves to be bound to accept as of divine authority.

(2) The above remarks go some way towards answering your question as to *the sources and present-day reasons for the unfriendliness or indifference of some towards Scholasticism*. There is I think now a much more open-minded attitude prevalent than in the past towards the *content* of Scholastic philosohy. But its *method* is unfamiliar to those not trained in Catholic schools, and they do not move easily in it. This applies to non-Scholastics of all schools; but in the case of "absolute idealists" the strong *realistic* bias and the hostility to *immanentism* which characterizes Scholastic thought seem to them radically opposed to certain tendencies of their own thinking which are in their judgment essential to philosophical advance. It has been expressed by one of them in the epigrammatic definition of Scholasticism as "the philosophy which denies the divinity of the human spirit." Some who take up this position (*e. g.,* Gentile) would be disposed to find in some of the great Schoolmen—especially in St. Bonaventure—a tendency in the direction which they regard as the fruitful one, though still hampered by the realistic tradition of the Greeks, which they would regard as really hostile to the essentially Christian thought of the taking of the manhood into God; and would see in the persistent adherence of the Neo-Scholastics to the realism of the mediaeval Schoolmen (I am using "realism" not in its mediaeval sense as opposed to "nominalism," but in its modern sense as opposed to idealism) a re-rivetting

on the Christian spirit of pagan chains from which it had succeeded in the idealistic speculation of Kant's successors in shaking itself free.

(3) As to *the capacity of Scholastic philosophy for contributing to the solution of present problems* I certainly think that it has such a capacity. In the first place its thoroughness of method is of great value. The reaction from the pedantry into which the later mediaeval schools no doubt fell certainly encouraged a looseness in argument from which even very great thinkers in the subsequent period—*e. g.,* Locke—were not exempt. And even those of us who are not prepared to go *back* to the Aristotelian realism, as though Descartes, Kant, and Hegel had all been on the wrong track, may yet feel,—probably most of those who were, as we of my generation in Oxford were, nurtured on Plato and Aristotle, do feel,—that the idealism which thirty to forty years ago was dominant in our schools had not thoroughly learned the lesson of that realism before deserting it.

(4) I think my previous remarks will answer so far as I can the question about *the present prospects of a "rapprochement."* They grow greater with *the growth of that historical sympathy* in which the seventeenth and eighteenth centuries were in comparison with our time so lacking, and with the *decrease of sectarian animosity* which makes men less unwilling to coöperate in the pursuit of truth with men of other religious confessions.

(5) I hope that I shall not offend in saying that

what *Scholastic thinkers* should do to bring about a *better understanding and closer coöperation* is to do what can be done to remove the impression that they are maintaining Scholasticism as a philosophy less from independent conviction of its superiority than in obedience to ecclesiastical authority. On the other hand *non-Scholastics* should consider that what is most important objectively in the pursuit of truth is the validity of the reasonings employed and not the motives which incline individuals to attend to particular lines of argument; and also that irrelevant motives are not necessarily absent where they are less readily suggested than in the case of the Scholastics who all, I suppose, belong to one Church and that a Church acknowledging an infallible authority exercised by its visible head.

You asked me for a frank expression of my opinion and I have therefore not hesitated to give it. I shall look forward with interest to your book.

Professor A. E. Taylor, of Edinburgh University

Scholastic philosophy is little known in general to most of our students in philosophy, partly because what time they have to spare is so much taken up with the study of Plato and Aristotle (at least in this country) and one or two of the big men like Kant. After all, life is short and only to know one great philosopher as Plato or Kant thoroughly takes a man all his time. Also, I am afraid the mere fact that the great Scholastics wrote in Latin and used a highly elaborated technical terminology which is remote from the terminology shaped in later times by the influence of all sorts of points of view in the sciences unknown before the great advances made in the seventeenth century, inevitably stands in the way. It is hard to understand Aristotle himself unless one is a thorough Greek scholar and has learned the habit of putting questions to one's self in Greek, so to say. And to understand the great Scholastics I think one needs not only to be at home in their Latin, but to turn a great deal of their language into the Greek of Aristotle or Plotinus. And I should add that the mere difficulty of being adequately provided with texts of their works is also a serious one. How hard it is, for example, even to have copies of Duns Scotus or

Ockham at hand. I know very little about Ockham for this reason. His works are simply not accessible to me, as I am too busy to go where I could get at them.

Also the method, or what is felt to be part of the method, of the Schoolmen is against them. There is the feeling that to a very large extent they are spending their time in making subtle formal distinctions to which nothing empirically real corresponds. One must recollect the deep impression made in all subsequent philosophical thought by Kant's doctrine of the limits imposed on speculation by the necessity that, to be productive of truth, it must be employed on a material supplied by "experience." It is hard to convince students that the Schoolmen are not trying to spin truth out of their own interior, like the spider with whom Francis Bacon compared them. Of course the popular conception of them as indifferent to empirical fact is an exaggeration and a bad one. But there is a side to them which gives some justification for it, and it is hard to eradicate. I should say that on the whole philosophers of the present, even when they reject empiricism as a philosophy, are thorough believers in the necessity of the empirical method. Even in mathematics this is a marked characteristic—I should say a good one—for the present day, and there is a largely unjustifiable notion abroad that the Schoolmen in general were viciously *a priori* in method. For example, you know how much the great men like St. Bonaventure and St.

Thomas have to say about such a thing as the way in which angels know. A modern student feels, I think, that all this is unprofitable, because, first, he would say that the existence of angels has to be established before we discuss their intellectual operation, and a mere appeal to authority no longer suffices to establish the point, and secondly, even if we are satisfied that angels exist, it is useless for us to discuss the way their intelligence works, since we have no data to go on.

To the question "whether Scholasticism is capable of making any valuable contributions towards the solution of present problems" I should say yes, remarking particularly that it seems to me that the Scholastic metaphysics is specially valuable as a corrective to the Kantian substitution of a theory of knowledge for a theory of being (a theory of the *objects* of our knowledge), that their works abound in excellent psychological analyses, and that the thorough objectivity of their ethical doctrine gives it the highest importance. And I should add in particular that they are the most valuable corrective of the sentimental idolatry of the "state," which I think the great defect of too much of our contemporary ethics. They do full justice to human individuality, as Kant did, without, like Kant, virtually reducing all that distinguishes one man from another to the level of the merely "phenomenal."

"What should Scholastic and non-Scholastic thinkers do to bring about a better understanding and closer coöperation in the domain of philos-

ophy?" I think Scholastics could do two things:
they could attempt to translate the doctrines of
their masters into a terminology which will make
them appeal more readily to minds brought up in
the tradition of modern philosophy. And what is
more important, they could attempt more than they
do a thoroughly sympathetic study of the modern
philosophers. You never really "refute" anyone
until you have learned by critical and historical study
to see how he came to put his questions in the way
he did and to give the answer he did to them.
And something more is needed. You need to go
on to see *how far* a man's theory will really take
you, and how much truth can be got out of it, and
just where and why it breaks down. It is useless
to set out to "refute" anyone without thoroughly
understanding him first. As a writer in the Louvain *Revue de Philosophie* said the other day, it is
futile to ask us to believe that all the most eminent
philosophers from Descartes on have merely been
talking puerile nonsense. One must start by readiness to believe that men like Descartes, Leibniz,
Kant, Schopenhauer really meant something not
wholly absurd and that it is worth while to make
the strenuous attempt to discover what they meant.
Men who write of all thinkers since 1600 in the
tone of Jacques Maritain,[1] for example, are acting
as absurdly as Beattie, who set out to "confute"
Hume's criticism of causality and personal identity

[1] Maritain explains his misunderstood position in *Réflexions sur
l'Intelligence,* p. 291; also cfr. Dr. Noël's article in Part II.   (Z.)

by vociferating that he was not going to be convinced, no matter what Hume's arguments might be, and insinuating that Hume's object must be to propagate atheism and rob mankind of the "consolations of religion." Too much Neo-Scholastic writing tends to be mere denunciation, and denunciation never "refutes" anyone. In enucleating philosophic truth by criticism *il faut de la patience, et encore de la patience, et encore de la patience,* to parody Danton's famous phrase about *l'audace.*

The "modern" has to learn that there really is no such thing as a breach of continuity in the history of philosophy. There was no arrest of philosophic thought between A. D. 600 and A. D. 1600 which will allow him to jump from the Greeks to Descartes, and he will never understand Descartes himself without some knowledge of the thought of the thirteenth century,[2] so much of which remains embodied in the *Meditations.* And the Neo-Thomist needs to remember that mankind have not simply been playing the fool since 1274. Entire understanding can only come as the result of the conviction that each party has *something* worth saying to say and that slap-dash criticism made from either side without any real attempt to understand what the other means is mere useless wrangling which breeds nothing but bad temper and self-complacency. After all there is only the *philosophia perennis* and that is not so much a body

[2] Cfr. Part III, Chap. III, on Continuity and Descartes' debt to Scholasticism. (Z.)

of formulae as an attitude of the living mind. What we want to do is not to repeat what St. Thomas said or what Kant said, but to say, if we can, what they would say to-day if they could look out at the world of our positive knowledge with the same single-minded devotion to truth which they both possessed, and without the personal limitations which the most objective of thinkers derives from the conditions of his age and place, his own individual bias, the specific peculiarities of his own education and the like. For example, we don't want simply to repeat what St. Thomas said about Plato and Platonism; we want to say what he might, with his clear head and love of truth, have said if like we he had the whole of Plato's works before him and had the knowledge we have of the character of Plato's teaching in the Academy.[3] We don't want to repeat what Kant said, on the basis of very imperfect knowledge, about the "old" philosophy, but to say what he might have said after a really adequate and sympathetic attempt to understand it. I don't say that if we act thus, differences in philosophy will all disappear; I don't know that it is desirable that they should, since no one mind of man can take in all truth adequately. But we shall at least find ourselves converging towards the same point and shall discover that a great deal of our most heated recrimination was based on mere misunderstanding of one another's language.

[3] Cfr. Prof. Taylor's recently published work on *Platonism and its Influence,* Boston, 1924. (Z.)

Professor H. Wildon Carr, of the University of London

I find no difficulty in replying to your questions in one comprehensive answer: I am conscious of no unfriendliness or indifference towards Scholasticism, old or new. Philosophy is to me the living search for truth, and in this search it does not seem to me there is any privilege. No age can hand over its philosophy to another age as truth discovered. Every age has to think out its own problems for itself.

Professor George Santayana [4]

Since my retirement from teaching I am less able than ever to feel the pulse of academic opinion; but the question you raise is interesting to me, and I will add some observations on it.

There are various reasons why the disdain in which Scholasticism has long been held should have much abated in recent years.

1. The dryness of Scholasticism, the absence from it of eloquence, passion, and personal humors, has come to seem a merit to those who would welcome an accurate, sober philosophy, and are tired of romanticism, of views which being brand new will to-morrow be obsolete, and of popular appeals to fancy or prejudice.

2. The fixity and clearness of the Scholastic vocabulary are also a relief from the Babel of figurative terms and perverse categories confusing modern philosophy and making the despair of any one who wishes to think cogently and not be misunderstood.

3. Science, which many supposed had superseded all speculative philosophy, has itself now become obscure and dubious in its foundations, so that its authority is much impaired, except as a language

[4] Professor Santayana was for many years professor of philosophy at Harvard; he now resides in London. (Z.)

convenient in the practical routine or investigations of scientific men.

4. In technical philosophy, especially in England and America, there is a lively movement towards realism, both in the epistemological and in the logical sense of this term; so that the gibes about Scholastic trifling and quibbling have ceased, or have become a sign of ignorance. Such questions as how many spirits might dance on the point of a needle are seen to be pertinent and inevitable in any clear theory of the relations of mind and body.

5. The natural history of Aristotle, just because it records the facts of animal life without any assumptions about its mechanism, finds much favor among some biologists; and although I do not know that his psychology has shared in this renewed esteem, I think that it deserves to do so, since it connects mind with body in the only natural or morally intelligible way.

6. In its association with Christian faith Scholasticism is also more welcome than it was: many have abandoned the attempt to minimize, modernize, or explain away the historical and religious dogmas of Christianity; in Scholasticism these persons hear for the first time the sound of an honest note; and they are, in more than one Church, the young, the spiritual, and the growing party.

7. Nevertheless Scholastic philosophy, except in its application to theology, can hardly appeal to the modern man, because its subject-matter is remote from his interests, and the problems it studies

are not those that puzzle him or seem to him vital. His point of view is historical, political, adventurous; he wishes to know how things have come about and in what direction they are tending. Scholasticism, on the contrary, is analytical of things and their static properties; it is a sort of geography of the logical and moral world, rather than a programme for evolution or revolution. I think therefore that a long time and many a disappointment will have to intervene before a modern public can be content with any Scholastic statement of the eternal order of things.

Professor J. H. Muirhead, of the University of Birmingham

I think that the comparative neglect of Scholasticism at the present time among philosophers is largely owing to the extraordinary expansion of the study of philosophy itself both in psychology and metaphysics, which is so marked a characteristic of our time. It is like the absorption of so much of the ordinary man's attention with the newspapers and the recentest novels or monographs in science, biography and history which leaves no time for classical literature. There is certainly no antipathy to it in itself. There is no unfriendliness, but simply preoccupation. On the other hand there are a select few, of whom Professor A. E. Taylor is one, who in reaction from this preoccupation and a certain secularizing in the life of our time are seeking spiritual sustenance from these sources and under whose influence there may be a revival of interest.

Nevertheless there is in the method of modern philosophy and of much of mediaeval a pretty fundamental antithesis which is apt to repel students who are deeply imbued with either from each other. To characterize this distinction would take me too long, but it might partly be indicated by the contrast between such words as speculative or

critical and dogmatic, deductive and inductive; or
by such phrases as *"intelligo ut credam"* and *"credo
ut intelligam."* Perhaps a freer attitude in mediaeval scholars would assist the *"rapprochement"*
you speak of. I am sure it would be met on the
part of others with a less bigoted and self-satisfied
one.

Professor S. Alexander, of the University of Manchester

To my profound regret, I have only a superficial
and second-hand knowledge both of Scholastic and
Neo-Scholastic philosophy. Whenever I do come
into direct contact with them I feel the real loss
which such ignorance entails. I should say that
the attitude of non-Scholastic thinkers is not so
much hostility or indifference, as due, like my own,
to want of knowledge. I may mention that when
the Dominicans celebrated last year (1924) the
sixth centenary of the canonization of St. Thomas
and held in Manchester a course of lectures on his
philosophy, the University lent a lecture room for
the purpose, and two non-Roman Catholics, Professor T. F. Tout of Manchester and Professor
A. E. Taylor of St. Andrews (now of Edinburgh),
gave two of the lectures, which have been published.[5]

So far as I can see, the only way to bring about
a better understanding is for Scholastics and non-
Scholastics to meet in philosophical societies and
the like, and become better acquainted, as our philosophical society here welcomed the other day a
paper from one of the Jesuit Fathers of Stony-

[5] Published under the title *St. Thomas Aquinas*, Basil Blackwell,
Oxford, and B. Herder Book Co., St. Louis, 1925. (Z.)

hurst.   There is one real difficulty to coöperation in the suspicion felt on the non-Scholastic side that the Scholastics are limited in their freedom, but that too may be due to ignorance.

Professor John Laird, of the University of Aberdeen

(1) Scholasticism, I suppose, would include Bonaventure and Duns Scotus as well as Aquinas. It is unreasonable, therefore, to expect a single attitude of "non-Scholastic thinkers" to "Scholasticism." And again, "non-Scholastic thinkers" differ very much on nearly all points, and therefore, presumably on this one. I do not see, for example, how Dewey, Inge, Bertrand Russell, and Croce could be expected to have the same or a similar attitude towards anything. Consequently, I think the most that could be said on this head would be that the importance of the great schoolmen and the instruction to be obtained from their works is now very generally recognized, and in a degree much greater than formerly. As to Neo-Scholasticism there is obviously room for difference of opinion concerning the relation of philosophy to authority set forth in the encyclical *Aeterni Patris*. What would be generally agreed, however, would be that M. Gilson's work or the studies from Louvain (perhaps, even, from Stonyhurst or Maynooth) are of the greatest service to all historians of philosophy and to modern thinkers.

(2) This disposes, I think, of the alleged "un-

friendliness or indifference." I do not see any greater "unfriendliness or indifference" here than towards, say, Malebranche or Fichte. Philosophers cannot be expected to have expert acquaintance with *all* other philosophers—even in the European tradition. And different philosophers must continue to have different preferences and affinities.

(3) A philosophy incapable of making "valuable contributions" is no philosophy. The general admission, therefore, that the great schoolmen were independent thinkers of incontestable merit and assiduity, is a sufficient answer to the question. The possible *sufficiency*, as distinguished from the *importance* of Scholastic philosophy for the modern world, is another question. Personally, I should be sorry to think, say, of Leibniz, Plato or Hegel as legislators for all times in the commonwealth of philosophy. And I should have the same regrets so to regard Ockham or Suarez.

(4) In so far as *"rapprochement"* means good will, or mutual sympathy and understanding, this exists at present in great measure; but improvement in these respects is to be hoped for, as in all other cases of speculative eminence or, for that matter, sincere thinking. If the implication of the question, however, is that it is desirable for all philosophers to settle their differences and present an agreed programme, I do not believe that this *can* be, *should* be, or *is likely to* be. And I should hope to find no such agreement among the Scholastics themselves. There is little in ultimate

speculation, I think, which is demonstrative; and
for the rest a profound difference of opinion in
speculative matters is a healthy symptom.—
"Scholastic" and "non-Scholastic" thinkers should
cultivate good will, and at the same time dispute
with the utmost vigor and pertinacity.

Professor J. W. Scott, of University College, Cardiff, Wales

(1) It seems to me that in the more advanced quarters of English philosophy to-day the respect for Scholasticism as a philosophy is growing.

(2) Any unfriendliness or indifference that may exist should be set down, I think, to the content rather than to the method of Scholasticism.

(3) It seems to me that Scholasticism may be capable in a high degree, of furnishing a way of striking a consistent attitude on rather a large number of different issues which arise in present-day thought. But finding a consistent attitude on many questions may be a very different matter from attaining in regard to any of them a solution which cuts the ice, when the question is taken in the concrete setting which modern life gives to it.

(4) Between the realistic vanguard of contemporary philosophic thought on the one hand, and the *method* of Scholasticism on the other, there may be, I think, enough sympathy to suggest the possibility of some *"rapprochement"*; but not, I imagine, between any of the other contemporary currents and Scholasticism. Moreover, even in the case of the realistic vanguard, the lack of sympathy with the content of Scholasticism may be serious

enough to be a factor hindering a *"rapprochement."*

(5) As to the way of bringing about a better understanding and closer coöperation, I can only say that it seems to me that Scholastic thinkers have not yet revealed to nearly all the modern philosophers who would be interested, nearly all the points of contact with modern thought which Scholasticism has to show.

(1) I imagine that non-Scholastic thinkers are in the main somewhat indifferent although not positively unfriendly towards Scholasticism.

(2) The reasons for this attitude are: prejudice or preconception that mediaeval philosophy contains little that is new or valuable; belief that all its conclusions are anticipated in Greek philosophy and the writings of the early Christian Fathers; conviction that subservience to theology is fatal to the spirit of philosophic enquiry, which must be free and untrammelled in order to be fruitful.

(3) I believe that Scholastic philosophy is capable of making valuable contributions towards the solution of present problems, although I cannot lay claim to any thorough or sufficient knowledge of it. —I have seen no signs of an early *rapprochement* between Scholasticism and the other currents of contemporary philosophic thought.

(4) Perhaps if academic representatives of Scholasticism should attend philosophical association meetings, present papers, and enter freely into discussions there, it would help to bring about a better understanding and closer co-operation. But they should not confine themselves to simple reitera-

tion of cut and dried definitions and principles and conclusions, no matter if they are accepted by high ecclesiastical authority, for such a policy will be met by impatience.

Professor G. S. Brett, of the University of Toronto, Canada

The general question of the relation between Scholastic and non-Scholastic types of philosophy seems to me complex rather than difficult. I will state a few opinions on different points to illustrate my meaning.

(1) Wherever the association between philosophy and religion still continues to seem most important, a very irrelevant antagonism is created between a supposed "philosophy of Protestantism" and either Scholastic or other types. It is worth noticing that this antagonism is distributed for similar reasons over both Scholasticism and Pantheism.

(2) The most recent tendency being to affiliate philosophy with scientific method, there has again arisen a complicated relationship. Some emphasize the repression of free enquiry as the mark of mediaeval authority and consequently dislike all the Scholastic tradition, but historical research is tending to make this attitude unreasonable. Others have followed on from scientific method to Realism, and a Realism which is Platonic or mathematical will have no quarrel with Scholasticism, or at least only the antagonism originally felt against Nominalists!

(3) There can be little doubt that the essence of the matter lies in the question whether philosophy is or is not the "handmaid of theology." Undoubtedly many feel to-day that Scholasticism implies a censorship of thought and has no place for complete freedom of expression. In so far as this is true, there can be no hope of any effective coöperation between Scholastic and non-Scholastic writers. But two facts tend to mitigate this trouble. One is the fact that it is possible even for Protestants to "protest too much." The excess of loose theorizing and the futile type of philosophy manufactured to suit people who think it worth while to cry "Peace, Peace" when there is no peace, —in short the spiritual anarchy which is now rampant will tell heavily in favor of a "Philosophy of Authority" and by consequence create a friendly attitude toward the pattern of Scholasticism. What other craving really sustains all the recent praise of guilds, the study of all forms of mediaeval civilization, the eager desire to reconstruct a life which was at least believed to have an intelligible structure and an intelligent Ruler?

The other fact is the ambiguous position of psychology. Nobody pretends to dig up the modern theories in the barren fields of Scholasticism, yet some of the best modern work has come out with the official "imprimatur." Here again the excesses of the unrestrained have told against them. Behaviorism and Freudianism have not been wisely handled, so that the Roman Church can wait its opportunity and find plenty of sympathy for an official rebuke in due season. In its own field psychology can progress "without a soul," but by so doing it will limit its outlook and sooner or later the problems of universals, of "mind as pure act," and other aspects of "rational psychology" will discover for themselves a new status and redress the balance.

Speaking for myself only and wishing to be understood as having no natural or acquired connection with the Roman Catholic tradition, I should say that modern philosophy tended to free itself from the religious and political considerations which have obscured the good features of the Scholastic tradition. I should consider that a proper understanding of Plato and Aristotle would show that the merits and defects of Scholasticism are to be measured by the degree to which political, social, and literary conditions caused misunderstanding of these sources; that the process of restoring a true philosophical attitude has been continuous from 430 A. D. to the present time; that consequently the fundamental task of making philosophy adequate to a growing experience, involving the satisfaction of demands arising from Greek, Hebrew, Christian and secular (scientific) sources, will in time be viewed as a common problem to which each period has made its specific contribution. My answer to your questions will therefore be that philosophy must not degenerate into propaganda, but take as its basis the appeal to reason, and on this basis with due regard to historical development we can respect without subservience the great principles of dignity, order, and clarity which were the merits of the scholastic mind and the essence of its enduring achievements.

Professor Sir Bertram Windle, F.R.S., of St. Michael's College, University of Toronto, Canada [6]

In English-speaking countries—omitting the United States, of which I cannot speak—there has been a very remarkable change of opinion as to the value of Scholastic philosophy. Not so many years ago people, who knew little or nothing about it, either laughed at it or considered it waste of time to think about it. How little it was understood may be seen from a letter of Huxley's boast that he had mastered in one summer afternoon the whole argument of Suarez respecting evolution. He, who did not know the first word of the technology of that subject, would have been very scornful of anybody who, being equally ignorant of biology, attempted in several afternoons to tear the heart out of one of his scientific papers.

One of the things which has led to this change of opinion was the publication of the Stonyhurst Series and more especially the volume on Psychology by my late very dear friend Fr. M. Maher, S.J. When he obtained his D.Lit. in London University

[6] The statements of the two eminent scholars, Sir Bertram Windle and Dr. F. Aveling, are placed here because they are mainly an expression of the non-Scholastic attitude as known to these scholars.

for this book, it was placed on the optional list I think in both Oxford and London.   Since that time, chairs of the subject have been started in more than one university.   My friend and colleague M. De Wulf, who is a professor here as well as in Louvain and comes to St. Michael's at intervals to give a course, is also a professor at Harvard.   Here in Toronto there is a good deal of activity, for our Society is the only philosophical one at the University and is attended by professors of other kinds of philosophy.   At our meetings I see that they are interested in our philosophy and at any rate realize that it is a complete scheme—*totus, teres atque rotundus*.   Of course all of them have studied Plato and Aristotle and thus they have the foundations of Scholasticism and of Augustinian thought in them and are always interested to see how we develop them.   But the real gain—and that we have made—is that the outside world should see that Scholasticism is a thing to be reckoned with.

Professor F. A. Aveling, King's College, University of London

The present attitude of non-Scholastic philosophers to Scholasticism, as far as I know it, is not unfriendly. Scholasticism is conceived of as it is—Aristotelianism with modifications. But the modifications are considered to be so closely bound up with the system of Catholic dogma that they are, on that score, suspected. Non-Scholastics, as a general rule, are not familiar with Scholastic writings in the original.

The sources of the comparative indifference are to be traced, I think, to decadent Scholasticism, formalism, and the general revolt dating back to the Renaissance. Further, scientific advances have not fitted in well to the old philosophical system. Neo-Scholasticism has made the attempt at synthesis. But it is felt that no system can claim to be final, or even entirely valid at any time so long as further discovery may modify or invalidate it. I should imagine that, in the main, the content of Scholasticism is the reason of the indifference.

Personally I believe that synthesis of all the philosophical currents is unlikely. There appear to be—and always to have been—different attitudes taken with regard to philosophical problems. And much, in the way of their solution, depends upon the subjective attitude from which philosophy is approached. More stress appears to be put now-a-days upon the instinctive and emotional interpretation of life, for example: and it seems that the intellectual abstractions of Scholasticism are suspected. In psychology, to take an instance in point, the doctrine of the sub-conscious and the unconscious have profoundly altered the general outlook.

Finally, the remedy is to employ a method of philosophic doubt, and attempt a synthesis without prejudice in favor of any system. I am writing, of course, of both sides. But that, it appears to me, would be a difficult task, in view of the—I almost wrote innate—system each of us possesses ready made when he begins to reflect.

Professor Leslie J. Walker, S.J., of Campion Hall, Oxford [7]

Since Galileo knocked out Ptolemy, there has been, in my opinion, no successful attempt to show that the fundamental principles of Aristotle's philosophy lead to the same conclusions as are reached in modern science on the basis of more numerous and less coherent hypotheses. Our philosophy of Nature, which should be a science of Nature, seems to the modern mind to have about as much to do with nature as have the speculations of Kant or Hegel. Yet, Aristotle's theory of material energy is the same as that used in modern physics, or more precisely, in thermodynamics. The world of physics is deserting Galileo and Newton and is going back to Aristotle without knowing it. I might add, perhaps, that we also seem often to be ignorant of this very important tendency. . . . I hope to have the Cosmology ready soon, and shall there try to substantiate what I claim for the Aristotelian Physics.

[7] This extract from Fr. Walker's letter to Mr. C. J. Steiner, S.J. (St. Louis University), is here inserted with the kind permission of both.

Professor R. F. Alfred Hoernlé, of the University of Witwatersrand, Johannesburg, South Africa

I have never had an opportunity of studying Scholasticism thoroughly from within and at first-hand, or of having it expounded by a teacher who believed in it. . . . What little I know, mostly at second-hand, of Scholastic philosophy, and especially of the teaching of St. Thomas Aquinas, has always filled me with respect for its thoroughness and intellectual power. But, in general, I am a victim of the tragic fact that European civilization runs in two separate channels—a Roman Catholic one, and another which cannot even be characterized, in general, as "Protestant," and the various components of which have little more in common than that, in varying degrees and on widely different grounds, they reject the first principles of the Roman Catholic world-view. If your efforts can do anything to bring about a better understanding, I wish them success most heartily.

CHAPTER III

COMMENDATION, COUNSEL, CRITICISM

The material presented in the two preceding chapters is sufficiently ample and varied to furnish a valuable cross-section of opinion, and to give us an adequate insight into the attitude of contemporary non-Scholastic thinkers in the English-speaking world towards Scholasticism. It seems best—despite the repetition entailed—to group and review these highly interesting contributions to our symposium under three main heads: (1) Opinions favorable to Scholasticism, whether on general grounds, or for specific reasons, or because of its points of contact with present-day non-Scholastic thought; (2) helpful hints to Neo-Scholastics, suggesting ways to a better mutual understanding and closer coöperation in the domain of philosophy; (3) criticisms of Scholasticism old and new.

§ I. *Commendation*

1. In their *general commendations* our non-Scholastic friends are well nigh unanimous in bearing witness to the distinct and striking change of attitude towards Scholasticism that has come about

in recent times, as well in academic circles as among the general cultured public. Neglect and unfriendliness are giving way to a wide-spread re-awakening of interest alike in the content and the method of Scholastic philosophy. Disdain and ridicule are yielding to a profound esteem and sincere sympathy for the medieval masters of thought and their modern disciples. Ignorance and misunderstandings are being gradually dissipated by closer study and clearer comprehension of their doctrines. "No serious thinker of to-day would treat Scholasticism with anything but respect, and disparaging remarks on the subject are made only by the uninformed."

"There is now a general agreement among competent scholars" and "in the more advanced quarters of English philosophy" that the Schoolmen were really great and important thinkers, profound and independent thinkers of incontestable merit and assiduity,—as earnest in their search for truth as the thinkers of any age have been. The notion prevalent some generations ago and later, that their speculations were a solemn trifling or even that their submission to certain dogmas as revealed was such as to deprive their work of all claim to freedom and originality is now rarely held by the instructed. "It is now very generally recognized" that from the study of their works much can be learned as to the problems which have in all ages engaged the attention of philosophers. The best thought of the day is very sympathetic to their keen thinking, and the best-trained minds are turning in a noteworthy way to the systems of the Middle Ages.

It is beginning to be realized that Scholasticism is a complete system,—a compact, well-knit, well rounded out whole. A profound esteem is felt for the great principles of dignity, order, and clarity which were the merits of the Scholastic mind and the essence of its enduring achievement. St. Thomas is ranked very high among the world's great systematizers. The Neo-Scholastic movement, too, and some of the works it has produced, are acknowledged to be of great service to modern thinkers; Neo-Scholastics are recognized as being capable in a high degree of furnishing a way of striking a consistent attitude on rather a large number of different issues in contemporary thought, and of making valuable contributions to the solution of philosophical problems of to-day.

Finally, several professors testify to the fact that medieval philosophy is now being studied with greater care and appreciation by their students; that more time is being devoted to it in the general courses of the history of philosophy; that chairs of Scholastic and Neo-Scholastic philosophy have been, or are about to be, established in some of the leading universities in English-speaking countries.

2. The *specific reasons* assigned by the several contributors for this growing interest in Scholasticism, for this remarkable change of temper and opinion as to its value, are deserving of careful consideration.

The insistence now being put upon the *continuity of history and of thought* is rapidly restoring a balance which the beginnings of modern criticism had upset. It is now seen that the study of Scholasticism is essential to an appreciation of this continuity: apart from this study the history of thought cannot be rightly understood, while with it the student clearly sees how unbroken was the course of philosophical speculation.

The *content* of Scholasticism is seen to be one of the permanent types of philosophic doctrine. Its *common sense and practical character* are being appreciated. There is a new realization of the essential wealth of the thought of the Middle Ages on the one hand, and on the other disappointment with the results of the scientific method in philosophy. Science, which many supposed had superseded all speculative philosophy, has itself now become obscure and dubious in its foundations, so that its authority is much impaired, except as a language convenient in the practical routine or investigations of scientific men.

The *thoroughness of the Scholastic method* is seen to be of great value, as an effective remedy against the looseness in argumentation and theorizing from which even very great thinkers of the modern period (*e. g.,* Locke) were not exempt. The absence from it of eloquence, passion, and personal humor has come to seem a merit to those who would welcome an accurate, sober philosophy, and are tired of romanticism, of views which being brand new to-day will be obsolete to-morrow, and of popular appeals to fancy and prejudice.

There is admiration for the *crispness and exactness of Scholastic logic* and for the *fixity and clearness* of Scholastic *terminology*. They are valued as a relief from the Babel of figurative terms and perverse categories confusing modern philosophy and making the despair of anyone who wishes to think cogently and not be misunderstood. What is more, the gibes about Scholastic subtleties have ceased, or have become a sign of ignorance.

Scholastic *metaphysics* is found specially valuable as a corrective to the Kantian substitution of the theory of knowledge for the theory of being, *because that metaphysics is a theory of the objects of knowledge*. It is said to have greatly influenced the speculation of Josiah Royce.[1]—Scholastic *psychology* deserves renewed esteem since it connects mind and body in the only natural or morally intelligible way. The Scholastics had a profound knowledge of the inner life,—of the soul, its nature, its aspirations, its needs. Their works abound in excellent psychological analyses. Here they were in close touch with experience, and the philosophy they built on this foundation is correspondingly important. In these days, when outright materialism seems about to prevail in so many quarters, it is considered particularly imperative that the voice of the Scholastics be heard.—The *natural history* of

---

[1] Cfr. Francesco Olgiati, *Un Pensatore Americano, Josiah Royce,* Milan, 1917.

Aristotle, just because it records the facts of animal life without any assumptions about its mechanism, finds much favor among some biologists.

It is furthermore recognized that the *thorough objectivity of the ethical doctrines* of Scholasticism gives it the highest importance. The Thomist doctrine of the irreducibility of the person to social and political unities is admired. These doctrines are found to be a most valuable corrective of the sentimental idolatry of the "State," which is looked upon as the great defect of too much of our contemporary ethics. Scholastic teaching on these matters does full justice to human individuality, as Kant did, without, like Kant, virtually reducing all that distinguishes one man from another to the level of the merely phenomenal.

It is admitted that Scholasticism presents a view of the universe and of man that gives much needed play to individual *religion* and the cultivation of the individual *soul*. "The soul has a chance in Scholasticism." In its association with *Christian faith,* Scholastic philosophy is also more welcome than it was: many have abandoned the attempt to minimize, to modernize, or explain away the historical and religious dogmas of Christianity; in Scholasticism these persons hear for the first time the sound of an honest note,—and they are, in more than one Church, the young, the spiritual, and the growing party. In reaction from a certain secularizing tendency of our time there are those who are seeking spiritual sustenance from medieval thought. The excess of loose theorizing and the spiritual anarchy which is now rampant will tell heavily in favor of Scholasticism. The craving that really sustains the recent praise and study of all the aspects of medieval civilization is the eager desire to reconstruct a life which was at least believed to have an intelligible structure and an intelligent Ruler.

3. For all these reasons, and for those following, the feeling is gaining ground that Scholastics and non-Scholastics should come to some *rapprochement,* to some genuine understanding of one another. What is more, this union of intellectual forces is looked upon as a prime desideratum, particularly at present, when the time seems ripe for such an appreciative mutual understanding. Attention is called to the fact that there are already *many points of contact,* and that many strong currents in contemporary non-Scholastic thought are very closely allied to Scholasticism on many basic points: fundamentally Scholastic views of substance, cause, universals, truth, knowledge, error, etc., seem to be coming more and more strongly into prominence.[2] One whole section of contemporaneous thought, known for its marked tendency to realistic views (Realism, New [3] and Critical),[4] is regarded as definitely and

[2] In their statements the Neo-Scholastics give further details on this subject.

[3] Cfr. R. Kremer, *Le Néo-Réalisme Americain,* Louvain and Paris, 1920.

[4] Cfr. *Essays in Critical Realism,* London, 1920.

strongly moving in the direction of some sort of Scholastic conception. Such conditions of present-day thought inspire the belief that much might be accomplished by a closer drawing together and co-operation of these divided forces, and that Neo-Scholastics might exert a profound influence on the outcome of these discussions. Furthermore, it is admitted that even those who are not prepared to go *back* to the Aristotelian realism, yet feel that the idealism which thirty to forty years ago was dominant, had not thoroughly learned the lesson of that realism before deserting it.

Nor is this all. Some think that the fundamental principles of Aristotle's philosophy lead to the same conclusions as are reached in modern science on the basis of more numerous and less coherent hypotheses. Aristotle's theory of material energy is found to be the same as that used in modern physics, or more precisely, in thermodynamics. The world of physics is said to be deserting Galileo and Newton and to be going back to Aristotle without knowing it. The narrowly scientific or mechanistic view of the universe has been riddled with effective criticism: the narrow type of intellectualism which raised the banner of physical science alone is discredited. The ambiguous position of modern psychology is favorable to Scholasticism; the excesses of the unrestrained have told against them, and it is now seen that Behaviorism and Freudianism have not been wisely handled. "Even a psychologist may now believe in a soul." The psychology which tries to do "without a soul" will limit its outlook, and sooner or later the problems of universals, of "mind as pure act" (Giovanni Gentile), and other aspects of *rational psychology* will discover for themselves a new status and redress the balance. On the other hand, it is conceded, some of the best modern work along these lines has come from Neo-Scholastics.

The *present prospects of a rapprochement* are seen to grow still brighter with the growth of that historical sympathy in which the seventeenth and eighteenth centuries were in comparison with our times so lacking, and with the decrease of sectarian animosity, thus making men less unwilling to coöperate in the pursuit of truth with those of other religious confessions.—It is true that one or two express their misgivings as to the probability or even the possibility of closer coöperation; their reasons for this attitude are contained in the objections raised against Scholasticism.

§ II. *Counsel*

What means should Neo-Scholastics adopt in order to make all the sterling and timely qualities of their doctrines better known and justly appreciated? What should they do to remove the obstacles barring the way to a better understanding and coöperation in the domain of philosophy?

The suggestions offered by the several contributors are here brought together.[5]

The emphasis that marks non-Scholastic testimony as to the recent revival of interest in Scholasticism, likewise characterizes their charge of *aloofness* against the Scholastics of English-speaking countries,—of aloofness, that is, from the representatives and interests of non-Scholastic contemporary thought. That this indictment is in a large measure justified will hardly be gainsaid by anyone familiar with present academic and broadly cultural conditions. Whether the responsibility for these conditions lies entirely on one side is another question. In England, it is true, a start in the right direction was made at Manchester during the recent commemorations of the sixth centenary of the canonization of St. Thomas,[6] and by the Summer School of Catholic Studies at Cambridge.[7] But on the whole, and especially in this country, "there still exists a most regrettable lack of contact and intercourse between Catholic and non-Catholic philosophers,—a condition which contrasts very unfavor-

[5] The Neo-Scholastics likewise offer valuable suggestions in the chapters that follow.

[6] The papers then read were published, as noted above.

[7] *St. Thomas Aquinas.* Papers from the Summer School of Catholic Studies, held in Cambridge, August 4–9, 1924; B. Herder Book Co., St. Louis, 1925.—Sir Bertram Windle informs me that non-Scholastic professors attend, and take an active part in, the meetings of the Philosophical Society of St. Michael's College, University of Toronto, Canada.

ably with the relations existing on the continent
of Europe." "We get the feeling," writes another
American non-Scholastic, "that Scholastic thinkers
are living and want to live in a little sacred world
of their own." "Why," ask others, "do they not
attend meetings of the American Philosophical
Association and contribute articles to our philosophical journals?"

Why, indeed? "Their participation would be
warmly welcomed and to-day, especially, it is
important that the voice of Scholastic philosophers
should be heard." But "they keep themselves
apart and give the impression of an unwillingness
to grapple with problems."—Surely, no one would
venture to ascribe this "unwillingness" to a consciousness of incompetence. In the 216 Catholic
colleges, seminaries, and universities of the United
States [8] there are many professors of philosophy
well equipped to enter into a fruitful exchange of
ideas, "to cross swords with their non-Scholastic
colleagues" in their meetings and journals alike.
However, there will be little cause for surprise if
what is now courteously styled "the impression of
an unwillingness" gradually develops into a more
harmful impression, unless a decided change of
front takes place in the near future. In this connection, the present writer makes bold to call attention to another, and at least equally pertinent aspect
of the situation. Is not the time ripe for the

[8] The Catholic Press Directory, 1925 Edition (J. H. Meier,
Chicago).

founding of a Philosophical Association of our own,[9] with a philosophical periodical of our own, after the example of the Neo-Scholastics of Belgium, France, Germany, Italy, and Spain? Undoubtedly we have the requisite mental and material forces to launch and to develop what appears to be a most opportune and necessary enterprise. But until this is done—*and may it be soon!*—why not take advantage of the gracious invitation to expound the Scholastic position in non-Scholastic journals of philosophy? It would redound to the benefit of all concerned.

As it is, there has been little effective spokesmanship for Scholastic philosophy; its representatives do not make themselves heard or felt in the world of non-Scholastic philosophical discussion. *"Nor do they encourage those of the other side to take part in their own undertakings."* Hence the fault is partly theirs if they are little known or understood by those of their contemporaries who were educated in different traditions. Scholastic philosophy is cultivated almost exclusively by Catholics, and among them it is only the clergy who are engaged upon it in any positive and creative way. Scholastic treatises are produced for ecclesiastics by ecclesiastics, published by Catholic publishing houses, advertised and reviewed for the most part by Catholic journals.[10] Thus it tends

[9] This was written five months (in July, 1925) before the writer received news (in December) that the preparations for launching such an Association had been begun in May.

[10] For this our Catholic publishers are often blamed. They do

to be felt that this philosophy properly belongs to the strictly ecclesiastical realm, to which, for the most part, it seems willing to confine itself.—

This spirit of aloofness seems to indicate that some Neo-Scholastics have forgotten the heavy penalty paid for a like isolation in the past. Accordingly, the most effective remedy for this deplorable tendency seems to be the vivid realization of the factors that brought about the decadence of Scholasticism some centuries ago.[11] For, as we shall see, one of the chief causes of the discredit and comparative oblivion into which Scholastic philosophy lapsed during the period of the Renaissance and after, was precisely such cloistered aloofness and indifference to fresh currents of thought and to new scientific interests. *Vestigia terrent,*—or should do so. What had been a robust and flourishing system, full of promise for the future, was condemned to centuries of solitude, precarious vegetation, and senile decay in schools and monasteries, through the shortsightedness of mere mechanical repeaters, wrong-headed partisans, blind

not advertise enough. They do not send review copies of their publications to non-Catholic journals. They do not—as one contributor complains—send circulars of their books to non-Catholic educational institutions. The publishers' answer to this objection is that the potential sale of Catholic philosophy books among non-Catholics is too small to justify the outlay of circularizing non-Catholic institutions and review copies sent to non-Catholic periodicals are, as a rule, either ignored or condemned without regard to their merits.

[11] Cfr. Part III, Chapter II.

pedants, closeted logic-choppers, Quixotic champions
of defunct physical theories.

Such timid or self-complacent parochialism is
not only sure to lead to complete estrangement and
stagnation, but it is diametrically opposed to the
very nature and spirit of Scholasticism as it existed
in the period of its finest flowering. What it
achieved then, it can accomplish to-day. Essentially this philosophy is so vital and vigorous, so
broad and deep, so perennial and universal, as to be
fully capable of creatively and synthetically assimilating everything that is new *and* true, if only
it be brought into proper contact with it.[12]   Moreover, the attitude of aloofness belies the very ideal
of the New Scholasticism: *Nova et vetera; vetera
novis augere.* Evidently, the realization of this
progressive programme emphatically demands that
Neo-Scholastics make known the perennial content
and true spirit of the *old* in a way to be understood
by the modern world; that they themselves earnestly
strive after a full and sympathetic knowledge of
whatever is available in the *new,*—and all this with
a view to realizing a harmonious and fertile union
of both: and over both must brood the creative
spirit.

Some *specific suggestions* are offered by our non-
Scholastic contributors. In the first place, Neo-
Scholastics should attempt to *translate the doctrines
of their masters* into a terminology which will

[12] Cfr. Part III, Chapter III.

make them appeal more readily to minds brought up in the tradition of modern philosophy. They should present those doctrines in the language of everyday life as it is lived to-day, instead of timidly clinging to words and phrases that have no meaning for the modern student. The lack of such intelligible texts is one of the reasons why Scholasticism does not receive the consideration it deserves. In their books, articles, and discussions modern Scholastics should not confine themselves to a simple reiteration of cut and dried definitions and conclusions, with an appeal to authority, for such a policy will be met with impatience.

In the exposition of their doctrines Scholastic thinkers should do what can be done to remove the impression that they are maintaining Scholasticism as a philosophy less from independent conviction of its superiority than in obedience to ecclesiastical authority. The main points of their philosophy should be presented apart from any definite reference to theological doctrines of the Church. What is wanted is discussion, a mutual give and take. Scholastics should show that they are engaged in an open-minded search for truth, that they are not propagandists defending a system which is suspected of having other than purely rational foundations.

Scholastic thinkers, our friends say, have not yet revealed to nearly all the modern philosophers who would be interested, nearly all *the points of contact with modern thought* which Scholasticism has to show. Neo-Realists and Critical Realists would be glad to know more about the attitude of Scholastic realism on the problems in which they are interested.[13] The doctrine of essences should be made clear to the Critical Realists. An account of recent developments in Catholic political and social philosophy and ethics would be of great interest to non-Scholastic professors and to the general educated public.

The *attitude of Neo-Scholastics towards modern and contemporary philosophy should be more reasonable and more sympathetic.* Some of them show a tendency to assume that the truth is so finally and clearly stated in Scholasticism that most modern European philosophy is a kind of wilful and perverse aberration. It is futile to ask the non-Scholastics to believe that all the eminent philosophers from Descartes on have merely been talking puerile nonsense. Neo-Thomists need to remember that mankind has not simply been playing the fool since 1274. Criticisms of modern philosophical classics that have been issued from the Scholastic camp have often read as if the writers were of course arguing to a foregone conclusion, and also had never understood the modern philosophical classics in such wise as to see eye to eye with the modern non-Scholastic student.[14] Too

[13] Cfr. R. Kremer, *op. cit.;* also, Sister Mary Verda, *New Realism in the Light of Scholasticism,* Macmillan, 1926.

[14] The articles of Professors Olgiati and Noël, and of Dr. Jansen in the chapters that follow, tell a different story.

much of Neo-Scholastic writing tends to be mere denunciation, and denunciation never refutes anyone. What Professor Taylor says about the right method of "refuting" deserves careful consideration. Scholastics should produce discussions of modern philosophical classics that will be appreciative of the problems there raised, and *effectively show how on the merits of the issues the Scholastic interpretation is the better grounded.*

Neo-Scholastics must become thoroughly familiar with contemporary non-Scholastic thought in all its phases, empirical and rationalistic, but especially with the ideas of contemporary realists. To this end they must have, more particularly, a thorough understanding of the newer developments in logic, of the basic conceptions of present-day theory in the realms of physics (especially the theory of relativity and the new ideas of time, space, motion, etc.), psychology (especially the Freudian and Behavioristic developments), and biology. They should *enter into* these speculations definitely and sympathetically, not with preconceived notions as to the issue, nor with the attitude of defending a system once for all pretty much given and fixed. Rather, they must be ready and willing to profit by whatever they can find of value in these ideas, even if this involve considerable modification in some details of their own system. They should multiply thoroughly informed and solidly worked out Scholastic treatises on themes of contemporary interest and importance. They should endeavor to interpret the relation between Scholastic and present-day thought, remembering the while that there are probably no non-Scholastic thinkers who do not believe themselves to represent a sincere attempt to deal with genuine problems.

It is further asserted that American Neo-Scholastics do not appear to keep abreast of changing philosophical interests, and do not focus on the same points as non-Scholastics. The two parties have not yet come to speak the same language or do battle on the same terrain. But is it only, or chiefly, the Neo-Scholastics who are responsible for this state of affairs? American non-Scholastics themselves confess that until recently most of them failed to show a sympathetic interest in Scholasticism, and to obtain a first-hand knowledge of it. They admit that even to-day "non-Scholastic university instruction is suffering from the failure to concentrate enough" on the subjects in question. Now the endeavor to reach an understanding should be *mutual;* hence it would seem that the lack of it may be more or less equally apportioned to both sides.

Neo-Scholastics are sure to welcome these frank suggestions, and to profit by them. In their contributions they in turn point out the means which they believe should be adopted by non-Scholastics with a view to a better understanding. If both sides display the genuine philosophic temper, if both are actuated solely by a sincere love for truth, if both strive earnestly to put aside whatever could bedim the cold, white light, or distort the vision, of truth, then the hope will be well founded that eventually a more united front in thought and action will be presented against the grave dangers that continue to threaten our common culture and civilization.

§ III. *Criticism*

The objections raised against Scholasticism old and new likewise indicate the reasons for the indifference or unfriendliness towards it; indeed, in the opinion of one or two, they also point out the insurmountable obstacles that bar the way to a *rapprochement*. With varying emphasis they are directed against the content, the method, and less important aspects of Scholastic philosophy. Some are of the psychological and pedagogical rather than of the logical order.

Scholastic philosophy was dealt a deathblow by the new thought and science of the Renaissance period. It was "weighed and found wanting," and superseded by modern philosophy: the subsequent movement of thought has left Scholasticism at one side, nor has it returned to it for renewed light and inspiration. Accordingly, "the typical attitude towards it is the historical retrospective one, as to a system that has had its day." "Most academic philosophers regard Scholasticism as a dead issue, of historical interest only."—This is the most sweeping as it is the most serious of all the charges, in that it denies the very possibility of a Scholastic revival, and hence the very *raison d'être* of the New Scholasticism. For that reason it will be considered at some length in Part III.[15]

Second in importance is the allegation that Scholastic philosophy was and is to-day *subservient to the dogmatic authority of the Church;* but true philosophy must be fully autonomous; reason alone must be its source and guide; therefore, Scholasticism cannot be a true philosophy. The settled conviction or grave suspicion as to the truth of the indictment expressed by the major premise is,—to use the words of Professor Sheldon,—"the stone of stumbling and rock of offence ('a red rag to a bull') to all Protestant-trained philosophers," and of course, and most of all, to outright rationalists. The objection receives various formulations, but the one idea of dependence on ecclesiastical authority underlies and motivates them all: Scholastic philosophy is identified with theological dogmas; its outcome is determined in advance by the principle of authority; it is admittedly "the handmaid of theology"; it is essentially an apologetic system; Scholastics are not thinking for themselves, but merely re-editing a system accepted on non-philosophic grounds; they are not free to follow the argument whithersoever it leads, but are guided by theological prepossessions; hence discussion with them is

[15] The other objections are considered in the several chapters of Part II.

futile and their processes of reasoning are felt to be an empty show.

In this connection may be stated another reason given for the indifference or unfriendliness to Scholasticism; it is in striking agreement with what Professor Maritain says on the same point in his contribution.[16] "A more objective cause of this attitude of mind is the decay of acute interest, if not of actual belief, in the content of Christian revelation" (Prof. Dewey). "I believe something of the antipathy to Scholasticism is due also to the fact that many of our contemporary teachers of philosophy are agnostic or even anti-Christian" (Prof. H. B. Alexander). Of course, Scholasticism is not accountable for this.

Then come several aspects of the criticism made *from the viewpoint of the sciences*. The Scholastic thinkers wrought under the scientific and cultural limitations of their time, and their speculations were affected by their imperfect or mistaken views of the physical world and of the philosophy of nature. As the main tenets of their system were formulated before the development of natural science, it does not seem possible to harmonize the points of view established by scientific advances with the position of Scholastic philosophy. For this reason the scholars of to-day believe that they have more to learn from the systems of more recent origin, inasmuch as these systems were directly influenced by the development of modern natural and social sciences.

[16] In Part II.

This much as to the *content* of Scholasticism. But its deductive *method*, too, is distasteful to the modern scientific temper. Philosophy to-day is no longer *ancilla theologiae*, but has become *ancilla scientiarum*. Modern science feels itself free to investigate any possible subject without prejudice to conclusions. The Scholastics of to-day make slight use of the results of natural science and seem unwilling to recognize the importance of scientific facts.

The subject-matter of Scholastic philosophy has little appeal to the modern man because the problems it studies are so remote from his interests, from the aims, methods, "fashions" of present-day thought, from the things "talked about," as to have no apparent common ground with most of the current and popular schools of philosophy. On the other hand, many new social and political problems have arisen upon which Scholasticism does not appear to throw any light because it had been developed in a period before these problems presented themselves.

Scholastics seem to claim that theirs is *a final or definitive system*, while most non-Scholastics would insist that it is but a phase of the historical development of thought. Philosophy, they say, is a progressive unfolding in the process of civilization, and complete finality never is or can be reached. No age can hand over its philosophy to another age as a truth discovered; every age has to think out its own problems for itself. And especially where philosophies of perpetual flux prevail, there cannot but be impatience with an intellectual world in which well-ordered systems, to remain eternally valid, are striven for.—There can be no mutual understanding in the sense that philosophers settle their differences and present an agreed programme; this they are not likely to do, nor should they, nor can they do it, because of the insuperable disposition of reason to produce varieties of doctrine. It would be regrettable if any of even the greatest thinkers, ancient or modern, Scholastic or non-Scholastic, should become legislators for all times in the commonwealth of philosophy.—As to the Neo-Scholastic attempt to synthesize the old philosophy with modern scientific advances, some think that no final or even entirely valid system can be reached at any time, so long as further discoveries may modify or invalidate it.

Because Scholasticism is disposed to regard itself as a "finished system," it also tends to be *backward and unprogressive.* Scholastics are living in the past, and it is believed that we have, therefore, nothing to learn from them. Then there is the prejudice or preconception that medieval philosophy contains little that is valuable because all its conclusions are anticipated in Greek philosophy and the writings of the early Christian Fathers.

Closely linked with the two preceding is the exception taken to the alleged *unphilosophical adherence of Scholastics to one system.* There is said to be an *over-emphasis of St. Thomas,* who, it is charged, has become an authority in a sense in which a free-thinking and autonomous intellect can acknowledge no authority. Hence, also, the difference of the method used in the two camps of treating philosophical discussion. The non-Scholastics study thoroughly any and all of the great philosophers, any and all of the vexed cultural questions, and try to distil the truth for to-day from such discussion. The Scholastics, on the contrary, concentrate chiefly upon one system,—Thomism; nor do they engage closely with the literature of modern philosophy.

The *Scholastic method seems too rationalistic, aprioristic, deductive,* to an age whose temper is empirical, experimental, hypothetical. Its great defect is thought to be *its independence of experience.* It appears as if Scholastics were trying "to spin truth out of their own interior." There is the feeling that to a large extent they are spending their time in making subtle formal distinctions to which nothing empirically real corresponds. Their proofs are not real proofs, and their intellectual abstractions are suspected. The modern man's point of view is historical, political, adventurous; he wishes to know how things have come about and in what direction they are tending. Scholasticism, on the contrary, is analytical of things and their static properties.

The alleged *independence of experience* is one of the sources of the *objection to Scholastic metaphysics.* Speculation, to be productive of truth, must be employed on a material supplied by experience, which has some essential contributions to make to the content of metaphysics. Most non-Scholastic philosophers believe that the deductive method cannot be carried through in metaphysics. Again, it is said that the pragmatic temper, so much in evidence to-day in English-speaking countries, is perhaps the greatest influence working against the study of Scholasticism, because that temper is opposed to *all* metaphysics. Only a few American universities seem interested in metaphysics. From an opposite standpoint, idealists dislike *the strong realistic bias of Scholastic thought,* and its characteristic hostility to immanentism. All Scholastics share the general standpoint of Aristotelian realism, away from which the current of thought from Descartes onwards took its course so strongly.—Finally, more stress appears to be put now-a-days upon the instinctive and emotional interpretation of life. In psychology the doctrines of the subconscious and the unconscious have profoundly altered the general outlook.—The connection of this and the foregoing objection with *theories of knowledge* is evident.

The *Scholastic method of exposition* tends to repel the modern student because it is unfamiliar to him. It is dryly abstract and logical in form. It often defines problems in a fashion that has little relation to the contemporary approach, and rarely seems to be fully abreast of modern non-Scholastic discussions of the problems dealt with. The Scho-

lastics present their own views with insufficient
depth and clearness; they give inadequate attention
to a thorough explanation of the grounds upon
which these views rest, and to the objections which
really weigh in the minds of their present-day critics.

Another factor that is said to be adverse to the
study of Scholastic philosophy is its forbidding *terminology*. Its highly elaborate technical nature is
remote from the terminology shaped in later times
by the influence of all sorts of viewpoints in the
sciences unknown before the great advances made
in the seventeenth century. Besides, the great
Scholastics wrote in Latin; but, as one of the American professors confesses, "our Latin is rusty."
And Neo-Scholastic works of serious importance
and genuine ability in the English language can still
practically be counted on the fingers; even these
works are chiefly outlines, text-books, and compendia.

Finally, it is frankly admitted that much of the
indifference, unfriendliness to, and prejudice against,
Scholasticism is owing to *"comparative, or very
great ignorance" of that philosophy*—especially as
to its finer meanings—among students, scientists, the
general educated public, and among many of the non-
Scholastic philosophers themselves.

*The most satisfying and conclusive answer to
these charges* will be a presentation of the authentic
position and achievements of the New Scholasticism
by some of its leading representatives of to-day.

Their words *and works* are the best refutation.
An open-minded and careful perusal of the chapters
that follow will make clear that the really important objections raised against Scholasticism have
their source in serious misunderstandings of Scholasticism, old and new.   Once the mists of misconception and prejudice are dissipated and Scholasticism is seen in its true light, earnest thinkers will
find it worthy of a more intensive and extensive
study.   Having gained a clearer and deeper insight into its doctrines, they will proceed to institute a dispassionate and thorough comparison of
the foundations on which the cardinal points of
these doctrines rest with the grounds of their own
philosophical conceptions, and like true philosophers they will be loyal to the truth wherever
found.   As Professor Blake says, "non-Scholastics
must enter sympathetically into the deeper thought
of Scholastics. . . . They must give a full and fair
consideration to the Scholastic positions when these
are adequately and fully expounded by men thoroughly familiar with the whole range of contemporary thought."

On the other hand, the spirit that should animate
the efforts of Neo-Scholastics to bring about a better understanding and coöperation has been recently
outlined by an eminent Neo-Scholastic.[17]   "The
essential requisite of a 'Catholic philosophy' is to
go through the world not hurling condemnations

[17] Erich Przywara, S.J., in *Stimmen der Zeit,* Vol. 108, p. 317
(Freiburg i. Br., January, 1925).

and execrations, but 'seeking what was lost.' The only determining factor in its attitude towards *all* individual philosophies must be the untiring quest for the kernel of truth they contain, the quest, that is, for the σπέρμα τοῦ λόγου, for the seed of the *Logos*. The 'anathema' of Catholic philosophy is essentially never directed against the *contents* of truth, but against the idolizing of *portions* of truth. Accordingly, its method (if it would be genuinely Catholic) does not consist in drawing the greatest possible number of limits or in casting the deepest possible trenches, but in looking *everywhere*—even beneath the deepest rubbish and rubble—for the sheen of the all-pervading *Logos*."

If a living and fruitful contact of Scholastic and non-Scholastic thought is to be achieved, if the two currents are not to continue along parallel lines, nay, to diverge more widely and become more deeply estranged, then *both sides* must put in practice the precious counsel contained in Professor Taylor's statement and beginning with these words: "Entire understanding can only come as the result of the conviction that each party has something worth saying to say, and that slap-dash criticism made from either side without any real attempt to understand what the other means is mere useless wrangling which breeds nothing but bad temper and self-complacency."

PART II

THE NEO-SCHOLASTIC MOVEMENT
EXPLAINED BY ITS REPRESENTATIVES

CHAPTER I

NATURE AND PROBLEMS OF THE NEW SCHOLASTICISM IN THE LIGHT OF HISTORY

By Msgr. Dr. Martin Grabmann, of the University of Munich

THE New Scholasticism means the renewal, the revival of the Scholasticism of the Middle Ages, the transference of the philosophical content and method of the medieval world of thought into our modern intellectual life. When a plant is to be transplanted from one place to another, it must be disengaged from its former soil and conditions of life, take root in the new soil, and thrive under the new vital conditions. The gardener who undertakes this transplanting must be familiar at once with the soil in which the plant has hitherto prospered and with the nature of the new ground with which it is now to be vitally united. The case is similar when there is question of transplanting intellectual contents and forms of life which in bygone centuries could attain a thriving development under determinate historical conditions and connections, into the totally different soil of present-day intellectual life. Here two things are equally indispensable: a knowledge of the relations and circumstances under which this world of thought of former ages came into being and flourished, and an understanding for the intellectual situation of to-day. For mental assimilation likewise has its laws, according to which the intellectual contents and values of the past develop and operate in new conditions and vital relationships. Even though one holds fast to eternally valid truths and fundamental convictions in philosophy, none the less one cannot put aside the subjective psychological determinations nor the historical conditions in which these perennially sound truths at a given time find their expression and elaboration. In this matter we must needs seek and find the middle course between a one-sided psychologism and an exaggerated objectivism. The Scholastic dictum that "everything is received after the manner of the recipient,"—*quidquid recipitur, secundum modum recipientis recipitur,*—holds true not only of individuals but also of entire epochs: their mental make-up influences the forms and functions of philosophic thought.

We can rightly apply these general reflections to a fundamental consideration of the nature of the New Scholasticism. If this movement is to be a renewal of the philosophy of medieval Scholastics, —particularly of that of their prince, St. Thomas Aquinas,—and a renewal that is fruitful and effective for the problems of our day, then, on the one hand, we must enter into the mental life of the Middle Ages and familiarize ourselves with the genesis, rise, and decline of Scholasticism as well as with the causes at work during these several periods; on the other, we must keep our mind alert and open for the movements and needs of the present.

I

A deep and thorough historical study of the course of development of medieval Scholasticism and of the laws of this development, enables us to discriminate between those aspects of Scholastic thought that were dependent on the conditions of the period, and those parts of it that contain perennially valid truths and convictions; it likewise qualifies us to fix the limits between what was the common property, the synthesis of Scholastic thought, and the manifold differences of schools and tendencies. We must also realize that the natural science substratum of medieval thinking was limited by the time-conditions and presented a world-picture which modern science has almost entirely set aside. Indeed, the basic researches of P. Duhem confront us with the fact that the Nominalist school of Ockham,—which from the viewpoint of content does not enter into the New Scholasticism,—is most intimately connected with the amazing anticipation of the scientific world-picture of a Copernicus and a Galileo. The question arises whether and to what extent we can establish the dependence of medieval philosophy on the natural science of that period. It is especially of great moment to know whether metaphysics, the core of

Scholasticism old and new, is to share the shifting fortunes of the development of the natural sciences.

Scholastic philosophy is largely determined by the transmission of intellectual material, by the influx of new sources, by the joint action of tradition and independent penetration of traditional treasures of thought. It is precisely in this continuity of life and inheritance, in this organic and progressive unfoldment of previous fundamental doctrines of philosophy, that it manifests and proves itself as the *philosophia perennis*. Clemens Baeumker, in whom the historical investigation of Scholasticism has only too prematurely lost its great master, traced the historical line of this perennial philosophy in the following manner:[1] "That profound system of metaphysics, such as it was grounded by Plato and Aristotle, as it was fashioned in the Christian spirit by Patristic thought, as it was rounded off by Scholasticism, especially in the imperishable lucid form and logical elaboration given it in the light of first principles by St. Thomas Aquinas, as it was in its essential traits accepted by Leibniz as the *philosophia perennis:* surely, this system can and must be continued and further developed, enriched, thoroughly secured and poised in its foundations—especially in its theory of knowledge,—maintained in progressive relation with the advances of empirical science; but it cannot without detriment be aban-

---

[1] Cl. Baeumker, *Philosophische Welt- und Lebensanschauung* in *Deutschland und der Katholizismus,* Freiburg i. Br., 1918, I, p. 69.

doned as to its groundwork and leading propositions. This is particularly true of the proofs for the existence of God."

Medieval Scholasticism is based above all on the ancient philosophy of Plato, Aristotle, the Neo-Platonists, and Augustine. The Berlin philosopher A. Trendelenburg, who had for pupils such eminent Neo-Scholastics as G. von Hertling and O. Willmann, wrote as follows:[2] "We must abandon the prejudice of the Germans that a newly formulated principle has yet to be discovered for the philosophy of the future. The principle is found: it lies in the organic world-view which was grounded in Plato and Aristotle and propagated itself from them." J. Maritain, one of the leading Neo-Scholastics, has expressed the same truth in the sentence that "he [Aristotle] has laid the foundations of true philosophy for all time."[3] The historical researches of recent years have thoroughly cleared up the ways by which the writings of Aristotle came into Scholasticism, as well as the forms taken by the translation, utilization, and evaluation of the Stagirite; they have likewise thrown abundant light on the rôle of Platonism, Neo-Platonism, and Augustinianism in Scholasticism. These historical results of research must be turned to account for the understanding of the content of the Christian Aristotelianism of Albert the Great and particu-

[2] A. Trendelenburg, *Logische Untersuchungen*, Berlin, 1870, I, IX.

[3] J. Maritain, *Éléments de Philosophie*, Paris, 1920, I, p. 50.

larly of St. Thomas Aquinas. The true nature of this Christian Aristotelianism is now becoming clearer, since the interpretation of Aristotle given by the Parisian Faculty of Arts,[4] uninfluenced as it was by any theological interest, is becoming ever better known through the examination of manuscripts. In a Munich library I have discovered *Quaestiones* pertaining to a considerable portion of the Aristotelian writings of Siger of Brabant, the noted head of Latin Averroism at the University of Paris. I shall edit these questions; the motives and methods of the Thomistic interpretation and utilization of Aristotle will then become more distinctly known. The representative of the New Scholasticism, he, too, whose orientation is not primarily historical, but systematic and speculative, will do well to imitate the great medieval Scholastics in their familiarity with the writings of the Stagirite. Also in later Scholasticism, after Thomistic philosophy had long since become the common property of Catholic scholarship, the immediate and intensive pre-occupation with the works of Aristotle was by no means discontinued. I call attention only to the commentaries on Aristotle of Paul Soncinas, Dominic of Flanders, Toletus, Fonseca, Sylvester Maurus, the *Complutenses* and *Coimbricenses,* etc.

For the understanding of the writings of Aristotle we have ready to our hand, from the philological viewpoint, quite different helps than the

[4] The Faculty of Philosophy at the University of Paris.

medieval philosophers could command; their knowledge of Greek was insufficient for conducting independent Aristotelian researches in the original sources. When one realizes all the labor devoted in the Middle Ages to the translations of Aristotle directly from the Greek and to the revision of previous translations, especially when one sees the care and exactness with which St. Thomas sought to construct his Aristotelian investigations on the best possible text-foundation, then one will be only too glad to profit by modern means and methods for the study of Aristotle. Above all, it will be necessary to become thoroughly familiar with Aristotle in the original Greek, and also to put under contribution the Greek commentaries on Aristotle which are now available in a larger measure than they were in the Middle Ages, thanks to the magnificent edition put out by the Berlin Academy. So, too, all that German, English, and French researches on the Stagirite have achieved during the last century, especially from the philological point of view, will have a valuable quickening effect on Neo-Scholastic philosophy. The Aristotle of the Middle Ages was in the main an impersonal Aristotle; his writings were analyzed and appraised in detachment from the personality of the author. To-day it is notably the Greek scholar of Berlin, W. Jaeger, who traces the inner development of the Stagirite and the genesis of his literary activity. These are highly significant researches, not to be heedlessly overlooked by the New Scholastic.

It is very gratifying that at the centers of Neo-Scholastic, Thomistic philosophy,—I would call special attention to the *Institut Supérieur de Philosophie* of Louvain University, and to the *Collegium Angelicum* in Rome,—courses are being given on the philosophy of Aristotle. The Louvain *Institut* has brought out valuable publications on the study of Aristotle by Mansion, Defourny, and Colle. Among the manuals of Thomistic philosophy, it is especially the excellent *Elementa Philosophiae Aristotelico-Thomisticae,* of P. J. Gredt, O.S.B., which make even the beginner acquainted with the Greek text of Aristotle. The more intensive occupation with Aristotle as well as the contact with modern Aristotelian research has the further advantage of bringing Neo-Scholastic philosophy to move on a common terrain with present-day thinkers and scholars who are alive to the greatness and depth of the Aristotelian world of thought, but cannot as yet find their way to Scholasticism. It is a most welcome sign of this *rapprochement* between Thomism and the modern investigation of ancient philosophy that such an eminent scholar in Greek philosophy as Professor A. E. Taylor (of Edinburgh University) took an active part in the celebration in honor of St. Thomas at the University of Manchester.

Side by side with Aristotelian philosophy, Augustinianism exerted a most important influence on the formation of medieval Scholasticism. One of the most valuable results of the researches in medieval philosophy is the precise elaboration, along historical lines, of the two great fundamental tendencies of thirteenth-century speculation, Aristotelianism and Augustinianism. Here Cardinal Ehrle has won the highest merit because his treatises on Augustinianism and Aristotelianism in the second half of the thirteenth century, published forty years ago, pointed the way to subsequent researches; in a new investigation which appeared in the *Xenia Thomistica* he disclosed fresh material for this purpose.[5] We are likewise much indebted to the Franciscans of Quaracchi, because through splendid editions and specialized researches they give us a deep insight into the world of thought of Franciscan Augustinianism. The works of the great theologians of the Franciscan Order, in whom the Augustinian tradition of the Victorine school of a Hugh and a Richard of St. Victor continues to live, —Alexander of Hales, St. Bonaventure, Matteo d'Acquasparta, Walther von Brügge, Roger Marston, etc.—are especially adapted to give an effective presentation of the Augustinian outlook on the world, the beauty and sublimity of which grips the whole man, more especially his heart and will. Whoever has attentively read the splendid work of E. Gilson on the philosophy of St. Bonaventure will

[5] Fr. Cardinale Ehrle, S.J., *L'Agostinismo e l'Aristotelismo nella Scolastica del Secolo XIII, Xenia Thomistica*, Rome, 1925, pp. 517-588.

receive the impression that the clear and warm light of truth and love has streamed into his soul. We stand in need of a thorough knowledge of Franciscan Scholasticism, based on sources; for such a knowledge is necessary for an understanding of medieval mysticism. The operation of the mysticism of the Seraphic Doctor, of which P. Ephrem Longpré has drawn a strikingly beautiful picture, was immeasurably wide and deep during the whole of the later Middle Ages down to the time of Thomas à Kempis. While the philosophy of Bonaventure, so rich in content, is mainly embedded in theological connections, the writings of his pupil Matteo d'Acquasparta, for the most part still unpublished, contain an abundance of purely philosophical *Quaestiones*.

The opposition between Augustinianism and Aristotelianism in the thirteenth century does not mean that in the thought-world of St. Thomas the Augustinian element had been dislodged by Aristotle. He who is at all familiar with the *Summa Theologiae* knows how strong was the Augustinian influence in the theology, dogmatic and moral, of the Angelic Doctor. The source analysis of Thomistic ethics allows us to see the sure and judicious manner in which Aquinas combined Aristotelian forms with Augustinian content. In Thomistic metaphysics, too, which is decidedly more than a mere copy and reproduction of the metaphysics of Aristotle, the Augustinian element is distinctly in evidence. Baeumker's characterization of Thomistic meta-

physics is very pertinent:[6]   "Through compactness
in the whole and nicety in the execution of details
the metaphysical system of St. Thomas receives a
formulation that is classical for its time and its kind.
The dominant temper in this world of thought is
Aristotelian. But at the same time this current
carries not only many Augustinian and several Neo-
Platonic elements along with it, but over and above
that, in the ultimate questions of world-view, it
receives its decisive direction from the Augustinian
tradition. The Aristotelian setting of Thomistic
philosophy as against the Augustinianism of the
Franciscan school comes to light above all in the
domain of the theory of knowledge, psychology, and
the philosophy of nature. I cannot enter into details here. In these fields of thought Aquinas departed from the Augustinian tradition only after
mature deliberation. His refusal to accept the
Augustinian theory of illumination, for example,
had for its deeper reason the efforts of the Angelic
Doctor to stress and secure the natural power of
human thought, to ground and guard the independence of philosophy in its own domain, and to fix
a sharp and clear line of demarcation between faith
and knowledge, between the natural and the supernatural. His preference for Aristotelian psychology over the Augustinian grows out of the need of
giving the doctrine of the soul an empirical foundation and of taking the facts of consciousness into

[6] Cl. Baeumker, *Die christliche Philosophie des Mittelalters,* in
Kultur der Gegenwart (Leipzig, 1923), I, 5, p. 46.

account. However, also in the theory of knowledge and in psychology the Augustinian element is by no means totally obliterated. If we compare the Thomistic doctrine with the purely Aristotelian-Averroistic conception of Siger of Brabant, we shall easily perceive the Augustinian note also in those parts of the philosophy of Aquinas where the Aristotelian bent predominates. In the further elaboration of the Thomistic system during the following period of Scholasticism, the Augustinian element was perhaps not felt nor developed equally with the Aristotelian. In Germany at present Max Scheler and the Catholic adherents of *Phenomenology* are bringing into prominence, as against Scholastic Thomism, an Augustinianism that has a gripping appeal for the modern man. But in reality there is no such opposition between Augustine and Thomas, let alone the fact that the philosophers just mentioned lack the historical direction and are concerned more with shibboleths than with texts. The historical significance of Augustine, especially in medieval thought, imposes on the representative of the New Scholasticism the necessity of allowing himself to be gripped by the force of Augustinian thought in fashioning the structure of the philosophic system. Augustinian spiritualism guards us against an exaggerated dialectic, against a form of philosophical exposition that smacks too much of the schoolroom and has little appeal to modern taste; it imparts to philosophic thinking the charm of psychological immediacy and sharpens the mental

vision for the viewing of great and wide relationships. M. Baudin has very emphatically pointed
out the necessity of combining Thomism and Augustinianism in philosophic thought.[7]

The history of medieval philosophy is instructive for the orientation of the New Scholasticism
also because it introduces us to the conflicts about
individual problems, and shows us how controversy
clarified points in question, brought out shortcomings and difficulties, and indicated new solutions.
The knowledge of this polemic literature allows us
to see the style and method by which Scholasticism
handled individual problems. I can here adduce
only some outstanding instances. Among the most
momentous results of the historical investigation of
thirteenth century Scholasticism is the discovery of
the sources of Latin Averroism at the University
of Paris and the presentation of the scientific life-
work of Siger of Brabant, particularly as it is given
us in the great work of Mandonnet. Through the
recently discovered *Quaestiones* of Siger on Aristotle we are enabled to know the details of this
philosophic tendency. So, too, investigation increasingly unveils the reaction of Scholasticism,
which took its position on the terrain of faith,
against this Averroism that was shaking the basic
convictions of Christianity. Hitherto we had a
near acquaintance only with the polemic treatise *De
Unitate Intellectus,* which St. Thomas composed in
1270 against the monopsychism defended in Siger's

[7] M. Baudin, *Revue des Sciences Religieuses,* 1923, pp. 518-519.

commentary on *De Anima*. In the light of manuscript research the critical position taken by the Franciscan school to the doctrines of Siger is now becoming increasingly clearer. This polemic literature has a present value in the sense that it treats of discussions of philosophic doctrines which under another name are again making their appearance today, and are directed against the fundamentals of the Christian and theistic world-view.

A further instance of instructive philosophical polemics and criticism, to use a collective designation chosen by Cardinal Ehrle, is the conflict about the doctrine of St. Thomas during the first fifty years following his death. Cardinal Ehrle has the great merit of having established, on literary and historic grounds, this controversial literature, which was heretofore hidden in manuscripts. In my opinion the editing of this literature in its most important forms would be valuable not only for the historical knowledge of Scholasticism, but also for the understanding and critical appraisal of the debated points of Thomistic doctrine. The Franciscans of Quaracchi are preparing an edition of the *Correctorium* of William de la Mare, in which the Franciscan reaction against Thomistic Aristotelianism found its first comprehensive presentation. Of the numerous writings of the Dominicans against the attacks of this English Franciscan,—an enthusiastic follower of St. Bonaventure,—only a single one has thus far been published under the name of Aegidius of Rome. It is gratifying to know that

P. Glorieux is arranging the publication of the defensive treatise of the Dominican John Quidort of Paris. Nothing has as yet been published of the controversial literature which grew out of the discussion of the oldest pupils of St. Thomas with Henry of Ghent, James of Viterbo, Robert Cowton. An extensive volume on Durandus, prepared by J. Koch on the basis of manuscripts and appearing in the *Beiträge zur Geschichte der Philosophie des Mittelalters*, will furnish information on the attack made by the Dominican Durandus against the great member of the same Order, Thomas Aquinas, and on the polemic repulse of this attack by the Dominicans. Hitherto the polemic writings of John Duns Scotus, which issued from the opposition between the Thomistic and the Scotistic schools, were predominantly utilized for the systematic exposition of Thomistic philosophy. To be sure, these expositions were not always based on the requisite familiarity with the texts. To elucidate the actual relations between the *Doctor Subtilis* and the *Doctor Communis* it will be necessary to institute a more penetrating investigation of the defensive writings which were given out by the Dominicans to safeguard Thomistic doctrine. This whole controversial literature, on one and the other side alike, is by no means mere pamphleteering; its character and setting is strictly scientific and objective. It was the aspiration and striving for the knowledge of the truth in difficult questions that gave the impulse to these polemical discussions. The circumstance that one of these controversial writings was composed with more temperament than another does not affect the scientific nature of the conflict, which, on the whole, always retained its objective character. Unquestionably this polemic literature can give some precious hints for clearing up difficult points of Thomistic doctrine and those that have received different interpretations.

A third group of Scholastic polemic literature is represented by the discussions between the *Via Antiqua* and the *Via Moderna* in the fourteenth and fifteenth centuries. This is the conflict between the old Scholasticism,—one portion of which held fast to St. Thomas, the other to Scotus,—and the Nominalism that attached itself to the person of William of Ockham; it is one of the most interesting but as yet for the most part unknown domains of the history of philosophy. Denifle's monumental *Chartularium Universitatis Parisiensis* has garnered valuable authentic and new material for the preceding as well as for this period of Scholasticism. In his book on *Petrus von Candia*,[8] Cardinal Ehrle has presented totally new results of research on this strife of "the two ways." Regarding the conceptual and historical connections of Nominalism we are indebted to C. Michalski for a series of investigations which draw entirely new lines through the philosophic movements of the later Middle Ages, while A. Birkenmajer has given us valuable literary and historical information on John of Mirecourt,

[8] Münster, 1925.

one of the leading champions of Ockhamistic Nominalism. From the standpoint of a theory of knowledge marked by a subjectivistic bent, Nominalism directed its criticism against the metaphysics of thirteenth-century Scholasticism. Thus William of Ockham tried his critical acumen on Scotus' proofs for the existence of God. The Nominalism of the later Middle Ages is an era of criticism and skepticism, which dragged the validity of the concept of substance and of the principle of causality into the region of doubt, and so anticipated in many respects the philosophical tendencies of the modern epoch. It is not without reason that Nicholas of Autrecourt has been styled the David Hume of the Middle Ages. In matter of fact, the old Scholasticism of the Thomistic and Scotistic schools undertook no definitive reckoning with philosophic Nominalism, which had become well nigh exclusively dominant in the German universities. The medieval period has given us no scientific discussion and appraisal of William of Ockham, one of the most influential thinkers of the Middle Ages. From the theological standpoint the innovations of the *Venerabilis Inceptor* were countered, as we learn from a professional opinion discovered by Msgr. A. Pelzer. In the *Defensiones Theologiae D. Thomae Aquinatis* of John Capreolus, the *Princeps Thomistarum,* Ockham is overshadowed by Scotus, Petrus Aureoli and other older opponents of Thomistic doctrine, and theological problems stand in the forefront of the discussion. It is a very welcome fact that his-

torical research is now turning with greater brisk-
ness to the history of Nominalism and is beginning
to draw a faithful picture of this powerful intellectual movement from the laborious study of manuscripts difficult to decipher.   For the problems of
the New Scholasticism these investigations are by
no means worthless.   The philosophy of Nominalism contains much philosophic acumen and propounds difficulties which still agitate philosophic
thought.

This conflict with Nominalism, ending as it did
in a victory for the old Scholasticism during the
great Scholastic restoration of the sixteenth and
seventeenth centuries, is a striking historical proof
for the perennial value of the classic Scholasticism
of the thirteenth century, above all, of the Scholasticism of St. Thomas.   In alliance with Christian
Humanism, Thomistic Scholasticism was revived in
Spain in the sixteenth century by the school of the
great Dominican Francis of Vittoria, and enjoyed
a long period of flowering.   It is again the merit
of Cardinal Ehrle,—in whose path Spanish Dominicans like Getino Beltrán de Heredia and others
followed,—to have pointed out, on the basis of
rich new material, the great significance of the Dominican school of Salamanca.   Not only did this
Spanish Scholasticism brilliantly solve the theological tasks imposed by the Council of Trent, but it
also continued to work vigorously in the purely
philosophical domain.   And these Spanish Scholastics can also serve as a model in regard to literary

form.   The Latinity of our present-day text-books
of philosophy could gain much by following their
example.   These men were not satisfied with a
mere reproduction of the thoughts of medieval
Scholasticism; they strove to develop it, more particularly that of St. Thomas, in reference to the
newly arising tasks and problems.   But little research has as yet been devoted to discover how the
relations between modern philosophy and this Scholasticism of the Baroque period shaped themselves.
Recently the German theologian Eschweiler has indicated at least the essential points of this question
in a book on Hermes and Scheeben.[9]   The New
Scholasticism may not heedlessly overlook this
epoch, which has achieved excellent expositions of
the whole of Thomistic philosophy, besides successfully treating of individual questions.   On the other
hand, it will not do to rest satisfied with viewing
medieval Scholasticism, above all that of St.
Thomas, through the admittedly very fine ground
lenses of sixteenth and seventeenth century commentators.   Valuable as these helps are, they are none
the less too remote from the Middle Ages to replace
or render superfluous the study of Scholasticism in
its sources, as well as in the writings of the earliest
followers of St. Thomas.   A weighty witness to
the great intellectual power contained in the Scholasticism of the post-Tridentine period are the dogmatic treatises of Scheeben, whose highly gifted

[9] K. Eschweiler, *Die zwei Wege der neuen Theologie: Georg
Hermes—Matth. Joseph Scheeben*, Augsburg, 1926.

speculation was modeled on the folios of this time. One thing especially the New Scholasticism of to-day,—philosophical and theological alike,—can learn from this period, that is, the harmonious combination and mutual penetration of speculatively energetic thinking and of familiarity with positive historical sources.

Such are some of the considerations on the historical orientation and grounding of the New Scholasticism. The Catholic philosophy of our day can draw very precious lessons from its great past, and it is precisely through the historical contemplation of itself that it can acquire a certain broadness of vision. It is therefore necessary also for those representatives of the New Scholasticism who treat it systematically, to utilize the results of historical research and to base the structure of their intellectual labors on the broadest possible foundation of the study of Scholastic sources. To give only one example: how very differently will a philosopher see his way and secure a calm, objective judgment in the much debated question about the real distinction between essence and existence in created things, if he knows the whole history of this problem in detail, if he sees this disputed question spread out before him in faithful historical reality from its first appearance in thirteenth-century Scholasticism onward, with all the varied attempts and grounds of solution. Particularly, historical investigation will teach us to distinguish the lasting and valid content of truth in Scholasticism from what is dependent on the transient conditions of a given period. Herein, too, are to be found valuable motives and momenta for the transference of Scholastic, Thomistic philosophy to the philosophic problems of the present.

II

In attributing to the New Scholasticism, rightly understood, a living development, sound progress, broadness and open-mindedness for the philosophic problems of the present, we are unquestionably thinking and acting in harmony with the mind of St. Thomas. Historical research is bringing out with increasing clearness the fact that for his time St. Thomas was a very modern and progressive philosopher and theologian. For this we have the testimony of his pupil and oldest biographer, William of Tocco, who writes of St. Thomas: *"Erat enim novos in sua lectione movens articulos, novum modum et clarum determinandi inveniens et novas reducens in determinationibus rationes, ut nemo qui ipsum audisset nova docere et novis rationibus dubia definire, dubitaret quod eum Deus novi hominis radiis illustrasset, qui statim tam certi coepisset esse judicii ut non dubitaret novas opiniones docere et scribere, quas Deus dignatus esset noviter inspirare."* [10] Thomas Aquinas was convinced of the human mind's power for truth, and in a number of

[10] Cfr. A. Masnovo, *La Novità di S. Tommaso d'Aquino,* in Volume Commemorativo del Sesto Centenario della Canonizzazione, Milano, 1923, pp. 41–50.

passages, especially in his commentaries on Aristotle, he has expressed some very noteworthy thoughts on the development and progress of science. In his criticism of theories which he could not accept he was at pains to separate truth from error. For no error is wholly such, but variously distorted truth. It is the mark of a mind at once broad and noble to recognize what is true in an opponent's views and to make it one's own. St. Thomas was an independent thinker: he conscientiously weighed and availed himself of the achievements of earlier and contemporary philosophers and theologians, but he penetrated and fashioned all this traditional material with the power of his mighty genius. The source analysis of the writings of St. Thomas is without doubt important and valuable; but we must not regard the Thomistic world of thought as a mere summary, as a mere architectonic conjunction of alien materials skilfully combined. And though P. Duhem deserves high credit for his researches on the natural science of Scholasticism, nevertheless his assertion that one cannot speak of a really independent Thomistic philosophy because St. Thomas only brought together the results of previous thinking, has been justly rejected. The independence of St. Thomas shows itself not only in regard to the traditional Augustinian tendency, which felt the Thomistic doctrine to be something new, but also in regard to his teacher, Albert the Great. One needs but to compare the *Summa* of Ulric of Strasbourg, the most loyal follower of Albert, with the *Summa Theologiae* of Aquinas in order to notice at once that Thomas did not stop at the views of his teacher, but constructed and rounded off his Christian Aristotelianism by further independent effort. That the attitude of St. Thomas was modern for his time is also manifested by the position he took towards the Faculty of Arts and Latin Averroism at the Paris University. It is true that in his treatise *De Unitate Intellectus,* written against Siger of Brabant, he rejected and refuted the pernicious errors of the Averroists. In a number of paintings art has justly glorified the triumph of St. Thomas over Averroism. But these errors by no means prevented him from recognizing the true views of the Aristotelianism of the Faculty of Arts. The *Quaestiones* of Siger of Brabant on Aristotle, which I have discovered, prove that on a number of questions St. Thomas was in agreement with the philosophy of the Faculty. The fact that by the decree of condemnation issued by Bishop Stephen Tempier, of Paris, in 1277, wherein 219 propositions of the Averroists were rejected, also a number of propositions of St. Thomas were unjustly included,—this fact likewise points to this relation of Aquinas to the Faculty of Arts. This relation explains why, after the all too premature death of the Saint, it was precisely the Paris Faculty of Arts,—not the theological Faculty, to which he had belonged,—that sent such an affecting letter of condolence to the general chapter of the Dominican Order.

An achievement of St. Thomas which is highly significant from the viewpoint of the history of philosophy is that he established philosophy as an independent science. Heretofore Scholasticism, especially that of the Franciscan school,—the admirable booklet of St. Bonaventure, *De Reductione Artium ad Theologiam* is an example thereof,— but also that of the Dominicans, as is evident from the legislation of the Order, had conceived and evaluated philosophy exclusively, or at least predominantly, as a science auxiliary to theology, the science of faith. St. Thomas, on the basis of his fundamental regulation of the relation between faith and science, undertook to establish a clear-cut distinction between philosophy and theology, appointing to each its own domain as well as its own principles and methods.[11] And even in the domain common to both—as in that of natural metaphysical theology and dogmatic theology—there is no commingling or confusing of the two fields of knowledge because the view-point from which both disciplines regard their common object is different. In his fine work on *The Philosophy of St. Thomas Aquinas*, E. Gilson has very aptly characterized this Thomistic standpoint:[12] "With a full consciousness of all the consequences of such an attitude, St. Thomas accepts simultaneously both his faith and his reason, each with all the demands proper to it. His thought,

[11] On this question see M. Grabmann, *Die Kulturphilosophie des hl. Thomas*, Augsburg, 1925, pp. 111–147.
[12] pp. 31, 32, Cambridge and St. Louis, 1924.

therefore, does not aim at achieving as economically as possible a superficial harmony wherein the doctrines most easily reconcilable with the traditional teaching of theology may find room, but he insists that reason should develop its own content in full liberty and should set out its demands in their utmost stringency; the value of his philosophy lies not in the fact that it is Christian, but in the fact that it is true. . . . In this lies the whole secret of Thomism, in this immense effort of intellectual honesty to reconstruct philosophy on a plan which exhibits the *de facto* accord with theology as the necessary consequence of the demands of reason itself, and not as the accidental result of a mere wish for conciliation." Hence St. Thomas is a resolute champion of the independence, the autonomy of philosophy and the profane sciences in their own domain. This standpoint is especially evident in his *Responsio ad Magistrum Ioannem de Vercellis de Articulis XLII*, a professional opinion rendered to the General of his Order, John of Vercelli, concerning forty-two propositions taken from Peter of Tarantasia's commentary on the *Sentences*. At the very outset St. Thomas points out that for the most part these articles do not belong to theology, but are of a purely philosophical nature. It is very harmful (*multum nocet*), he says, to assert or deny propositions which do not pertain to the sphere of faith and theology as if they were the concern of the latter. Here St. Thomas takes a firm stand against the undue interference of theology in the purely philosophical domain, as well as against the attempt to treat philosophical theses after the manner of truths of the faith. In one passage of this opinion, where there is question of an interpretation of an Aristotelian text, St. Thomas remarks: *"Nec video quomodo pertineat ad doctrinam fidei, qualiter Philosophi verba exponantur."*

I have dwelt at some length on this attitude of St. Thomas towards the progress and independence of philosophy because herein lie valuable hints as to the possibility, nay the necessity, of such a development and rounding out of the New Scholasticism as will meet the needs of the present. Like an echo of the Thomistic conception are the words penned by the recently departed Cardinal Mercier, the greatest representative of systematic Neo-Scholasticism in our day, in his writings on the programme for establishing the *Institut Supérieur de Philosophie* which he founded at the University of Louvain by order of Leo XIII: [13] "The science of to-day is above all a science of the most exact individual research. . . . Let us train, in greater numbers, men who will devote themselves to science *for itself,* without any aim that is professional or directly apologetic, men who will work *at first hand* in fashioning the materials for the edifice of science. . . . An immense field is open to scientific investigation. The boundaries of the old philos-

---

[13] D. Mercier, *Rapport sur les Études Supérieures de Philosophie, Présenté au Congrès de Malines,* Louvain, 1891, p. 17.—Cfr. D. Mercier, *Psychologie,* Introd.

ophy have become too narrow: they must be extended. Man has multiplied his power of vision; he enters the world of the infinitely small and fixes his scrutinizing gaze upon regions where our most powerful telescopes discern no limits. Physics and chemistry progress with giant strides in the study of the properties of matter and of the combination of its elements. Geology and cosmogony reconstruct the history of the formation and origins of our planet. Biology and the natural sciences study the minute structure of living organisms, their distribution in space and succession in time; and embryogeny explores their origin. The archeological, philological, and social sciences remount to the past ages of our history and civilization. What an inexhaustible mine is here to exploit, what regions to explore and materials to analyze and interpret! Finally, what pioneers we must engage in the work if we are to gain a share in all those treasures!" The Cardinal then proceeds to show how the achievements of these particular sciences, how these acquisitions of observation and analysis call for a comprehensive synthesis, and how precisely the Aristotelian-Scholastic philosophy is the expansive framework in which the results of research in the modern sciences should be gathered up in such a synthesis. And this development of Scholastic philosophy should be carried out in union with St. Thomas, "that striking incarnation of the spirit of observation united with the spirit of synthesis, that genius who ever deemed it a duty to fertilize philosophy by science and at the same time to elevate science to the heights of philosophy." Cardinal Mercier is right when he sees precisely in the modern development of the particular sciences the reason for the necessity of a corresponding evolvement of Scholastic philosophy. In his opusculum *In Boethium de Trinitate* (which deserves to be more studied than it is), in which he has most fully developed his teaching on science and method, St. Thomas has deeply grasped and presented the intrinsic connection between philosophy and the other profane sciences; and it is quite in keeping with the tendency of his thought to hold that the advance of the special sciences exerts an influence also on the development and rounding out of philosophic thought, without detriment to the eternally valid principles and basic convictions of the *Philosophia Perennis*. There are solid grounds for asserting that the principles of Aristotelian-Scholastic philosophy can be regarded as the presuppositions of the particular sciences with greater reason than can those of modern idealistic and positivistic philosophy, which either explains away the specific significance of the individual sciences, or conversely, allows itself to be absorbed by them. Ch. Sentroul, a prominent representative of the Louvain school, has clearly shown that this combination of a duly developed Scholastic philosophy with the particular sciences can be fruitful, because it is precisely this philosophy which lends certainty, expansion, and unity to our thought. This philosophy

overcomes scepticism, which undermines the certitude of human thought and thereby dampens the
ardor for truth of the particular sciences. This
philosophy overcomes Idealism (in epistemology),
which would impart unity to our thought, but bars
access to the world of reality. Finally, this philosophy overcomes Positivism, which remains fixed to
a multiplicity of individual cognitions and external
observations, and is incapable of embracing them in
one comprehensive synthesis. In the organization
of the *Institut de Philosophie* Cardinal Mercier ac-
tualized on a large scale his conception of the importance of the profane sciences for the further development of philosophy by establishing a large
number of chairs for those natural sciences which
stand in immediate contact with philosophy.

I cannot here enter upon the fields of endeavor
in which Thomistic philosophy has partly to reach
an understanding with modern thought, and partly
stands in a give-and-take relation to it. For I
should have to enlarge on the movement towards
Critical Realism, on the awakening sense for metaphysical problems, on Neo-Vitalism, on the waning
of materialism in psychology, on experimental psychology, on the modern philosophy of values, and
on so many other movements and currents in the
philosophic thought of to-day, which point to a contact with Scholastic philosophy. I should have to
speak of the works of Catholic philosophers like
Mercier, Noël, Geyser, Maritain, Maréchal, and
others in the domain of logic and epistemology; I

should have to treat of the works of deep meta-physicians like Garrigou-Lagrange, Descocq, Balthasar, and others; I should have to give an account of the researches of Neo-Scholastics like Gemelli, Fröbes, Barbado, Nys, Gutberlet, Peillaube, etc., in psychology and philosophy of nature; with special pleasure I could describe the rich work done in the field of ethics, jurisprudence, and social philosophy by Catholic philosophers like Deploige, Lottin, Mausbach, Schilling, Cathrein, Gillet, to mention only a few; finally, I could call attention to the achievements of the New Scholasticism in pedagogy, —I need only mention the name of O. Willmann,— in the philosophy of religion, in esthetics by men like Menendez y Pelayo and M. De Wulf. For the advancement of Neo-Scholastic philosophy and for its contact with present-day problems it is important that a scientific division of labor be made. A clear distinction should be drawn between philosophy as propaedeutic to theology (the philosophic formation of future theologians and priests), and philosophy for philosophy's sake, that is to say, specialized philosophic research which is to make of Thomistic philosophy an influential factor in modern intellectual life also outside Catholic circles. For the needs of a thorough instruction in philosophy for theological students a single scholar may be able to compose a satisfactory manual of Thomistic philosophy, —we already have a goodly number; but a division of labor will be imperative for specialized research in philosophy that is to yield new results. There is one kind of research, the history of literature and ideas, which will be rendered fruitful especially by the study of manuscripts. Then there must be specialists for the problems of logic and epistemology; keenly penetrating metaphysicians are indispensable; a rich field of labor beckons philosophers of nature and psychologists who have been well grounded in the natural sciences; the religious and mystical movement of to-day is favorable soil for investigations in the psychology of religion; in a very special manner the imperishable truth-value of the Thomistic philosophy in ethics, jurisprudence, political and social philosophy will always stand the test. This division of labor is carried out in the institutes of philosophy, especially in the *Institut Supérieur de Philosophie* of Louvain. So, too, in collective works in which the various parts of philosophy are elaborated by different specialists, this division of labor has yielded good results. The *Philosophia Lacensis* of the German Jesuits made a praiseworthy beginning. An especially instructive instance of this division of labor is the great *Cours de Philosophie* which the *Institut Supérieur* of Louvain is publishing. German Catholic philosophers have likewise united in such a common undertaking, that of the *Philosophische Handbibliothek*, of which ten substantial volumes have appeared.

This division of labor in no way disturbs the unity of thinking within Neo-Scholastic philosophy. The common love for truth,—a reflection of the eternal divine Truth,—the loyal love for the Church, the closeness to the *Doctor Communis,* the far-sighted and large-hearted St. Thomas Aquinas, whom Francis Silvestris of Ferrara styled the *"homo omnium horarum,"*—such is the common bond that unites Catholic philosophers. I close with the beautiful words of J. Maritain:[14] "Apostle of the intelligence, teacher of truth, restorer of the intellectual order, St. Thomas did not write for the thirteenth century, he wrote for all time."

[14] J. Maritain, *Saint Thomas, Apôtre des Temps Modernes, Xenia Thomistica,* I, 76.

CHAPTER II

By Paul Gény, S.J., Professor of Philosophy at the Gregorian University, Rome

To form an accurate idea of Scholastic philosophy and appraise its value impartially is not an easy matter. Two mistakes are possible: the exaggeration of its difference from modern philosophy, or the undue attenuation of the same. To my mind, the best way to avoid both excesses is to adopt a historical point of view, not by immersing oneself in the current that carries human thought along and determines its development, but by dominating the aggregate of the changes which have taken place in the manner of conceiving philosophy.

When Greek speculation was born, the great systems of the Ionians, old and new, of the Eleatics, and the Pythagoreans, all had one and the same ambitious end in view: to wrest her secret from nature and to embody this secret in a formula. I say advisedly, the *secret,* not the *secrets* of nature; for in matter of fact, the Greeks did not ·set about to scrutinize the phenomena one by one so as to lay bare their laws and gradually rise to the highest generalizations. Not at all. By a sort of intui-

161

tion they understood that detailed researches could well be put off to a later period, and that the most universal laws of being could be readily discovered with the sole aid of the most obvious facts and the first principle of reason.

Here is not the place to show that the grandiose syntheses of the sixth and fifth centuries B. C., though undoubtedly tainted with gross errors, contain precious gems of truth; nor can I stop to make clear, what would be so much to my purpose, how across the errors these systems gradually form, and give an ever greater precision to, the important doctrine of act and potency, in order to explain the universal *becoming* of the things of experience. Plato is almost fully familiar with this doctrine. Aristotle applies to it his clear and orderly mind and formulates its various laws: in the being that becomes he shows us the potency that receives and the act that is received; the former he calls the *material cause,* the latter the *formal cause* of the being that is produced. To our question: Whence comes the act which perfects the potency? he answers that the act is educed from the potentiality of the subject; but as this answer does not satisfy, he points to the *efficient cause,* itself an act, which exerts its influence on the potency so as to actualize it, and it can exert this influence because it loves a good, also an act, that moves it after the manner of a *final cause.* This is the cause of causes, the ultimate reason of becoming, and, for the rest, not necessarily distinct from the efficient cause, so that at the apex of the universe there can be and there must be a pure Act, at once the first Mover and the first End, simple, infinite, immutable, eternal, the Thought that thinks itself and in thinking itself finds an unlimited happiness. Thus the Physics of Aristotle serves as the basis for a sublime Metaphysics, which expands into a well nigh perfect Ethics.

It is a marvelous synthesis, which the founders of schools during the following centuries did not know how to preserve; nevertheless it continues to live, more or less pure, in the Academy and the Lyceum. The Lyceum does not deteriorate much, it is true, but neither does it mount very high: its activity is absorbed in commenting on the works of the Master. In the Academy are first developed the germs of scepticism contained in the separation made by Plato between the sensible and the intelligible world; subsequently, from contact with Oriental religions and above all with Christianity, a new period of splendor sets in: Plotinus gives a new form to the theory of ideas; furthermore, though unable to guard adequately against the error of pantheism in explaining the origin of beings and their return to the first principle, he none the less preserves many precious platonic and peripatetic elements. This heritage is passed on to the Christian West, first directly by Augustine and Boëthius, and then in a roundabout way through the Syrians and Arabians: and so Scholastic philosophy is being constituted.

This philosophy, as we know,—and shall know still better when so many unpublished treasures now reposing in libraries will have been given to the public,—develops with a multiplicity of currents which give proof of its vigorous vitality. Great schools are formed: that of St. Thomas, the most faithful to the peripatetic spirit; that of Scotus, which takes up again certain theses of the preceding epoch; that of Ockham, which is a prelude to modern Empiricism. There are minor schools, such as those of St. Bonaventure and Aegidius. Original thinkers like Henry of Ghent and Durandus also make their appearance. However, all these currents have in common a stock of peripatetic doctrines that constitutes their unity and assures the continuity of human thought.

On the other hand, it is difficult to speak of continuity at the close of the fifteenth century. Scholasticism still lives, it is true, but has fallen into discredit through the obstinate attachment of its followers to physical doctrines once for all overthrown by modern science, and is confined to schools, especially those conducted by religious Orders. And there we now no longer find any creative activity; this activity takes hold of the minds of individual thinkers who, having placed themselves outside the traditional influences, now attempt new ways of thought: Bacon, Descartes, Hobbes, Locke, Geulinckx, Malebranche, Spinoza, Leibniz, Berkeley, Hume, found new systems which have some sort of common parentage, or at least may be grouped according to similar tendencies, but are far removed from the philosophy of Plato and Aristotle. They are no longer based on ancient physics which, side by side with monstrous errors, had a central part based on obvious, indisputable facts, particularly on the fact of change, explained, as we have seen, by the doctrine of the four causes, or of potency and act. Instead, the mechanistic tendency now holds 'sway and seeks to explain change,—even substantial change,—by the local motion of particles in themselves unchangeable; the root of this tendency is the predominance of imagination which prefers to stop short at the concrete, and refuses to resolve it into matter and form.

As a result, one system overthrows the other, but none takes a permanent, overmastering hold of men's minds. There is no longer a correspondence between the sensible and the intelligible, and thereupon, among the sensists and the intellectualists alike, the idealistic tendency begins to develop, destined soon to invade the entire world of modern philosophic thought, and with more or less rigor to lord it over the various factions that compose it.

Intoxicated by its achievement of emancipation and autonomy, modern philosophy preserved a certain ardor of life down to our own times. Kant had aroused vast expectations, and in matter of fact, one entire century lived on his thought. It is found even in Pragmatism and Positivism. But now the fever seems to have abated; Kantianism no longer satisfies. On the other hand, the simple study of facts with their reduction to more or less exact laws cannot be said to constitute philosophical investigation. A "philosophy of values" has received considerable attention, but how are values to be determined without standards derived from ontology? In short, philosophers are scanning the horizon, and the cultured public, loath to renounce thinking, is anxiously asking: "Watchman, what of the night?" As yet, nothing new is in sight.

There exists a philosophy as old as man himself, or at least as old as the man of classic culture. We have seen that it was in course of preparation even before Socrates, that it had its season of flowering in Plato and Aristotle, that it remained in a state of more or less vital preservation during the following centuries. Later it was impregnated with a strong religious sense by Plotinus. Purified and rounded out, it became resplendent during the Middle Ages, above all in St. Thomas Aquinas. It did not die after his time, no, not even after the partly deserved neglect into which it fell after the Renaissance era; on the contrary, in the sixteenth and seventeenth centuries it enjoyed a new period of splendor, and it was then that it set about gradually to strip itself of those errors of a special physics which had done it so much harm. But being too feeble,—perhaps because the diversity of schools made it difficult to realize that the best hopes of life lay in the pure peripateticism of St. Thomas,—it offered no resistance to the slow penetration of modern philosophy, particularly of Cartesianism. And so, towards the end of the eighteenth century it had lost well nigh all of its vital sap, and in most of its followers there remained only a dry foliage of notions and distinctions. After the French Revolution, when altars and thrones were being raised again, Christian philosophy was likewise reconstructed, but no one thought of looking for its principles to Scholasticism. Various ways are tried, such as Traditionalism and Ontologism, but all prove unsuccessful. Then thinkers begin to turn to Scholastic philosophy. Some, for fear of becoming isolated, seek to temper it with Cartesianism, but along these lines they fail to give it compactness and coherence; besides, the sun of Cartesianism itself begins to set. Others return to pure Christian peripateticism and place themselves bravely within the traditional current: these receive repeated encouragement from the Church. Naples, Rome, Louvain, Fribourg, Paris, Milan, have seats of higher learning where Scholastic philosophy flourishes. A more intimate contact with the great masters, to the end of profoundly penetrating their thought, makes felt the need for becoming better acquainted with the environment in which they lived, with the books they studied, with the various currents of thought that had been formed among them. This gives rise to historical works, critical studies, the publication of unedited texts: the editions of Quaracchi and Louvain, the collections made under the direction of

Cardinal Ehrle and Denifle, of Baeumker and Grabmann, of Prof. Gilson, furnish a rich material to be made fruitful. Scholastic philosophy is being eagerly studied not only by its followers but by others, in ever growing number.

This movement will surely continue on its forward course. But will Scholasticism ever recover its scepter in the realm of intelligence? Such a question is difficult to answer. To-day no one dares to maintain any longer that the Middle Ages were a pause in the history of thought; but only a few are as yet ready to acknowledge that Greek and medieval philosophy possesses an *absolute* and *perennial* value. Modern mentality shrinks from any static conception of philosophic truth; to believe that a system conceived over two thousand years ago should still be able to satisfy the intelligence of to-day and to offer solid bases for a construction answering the needs of our times,— looks like an absurdity to most. But is it really an absurdity? In so many other branches of culture the Greeks are still our masters; could they not be such also in philosophy? Is it necessary for every philosopher, not only to rethink philosophy, but likewise to reconstruct it differently from his predecessors? Is it reasonable to liken philosophy to a work of art, which has a strictly personal value, is indelibly stamped with the name of its author, and may never again be repeated, but only imitated? Is it perhaps not true that the human mind is identically constituted in all men?

Do not the same laws, the same principles, the same demonstrations hold good for all?

Here, it seems to me, we touch the outstanding difficulty made against the efforts of the Scholastics to have their philosophy accepted. This difficulty is further re-enforced by the conviction, very widespread among philosophers to-day, that we cannot know things as they are in themselves, but only the phenomena which,—mayhap under the influence of an external reality,—our mind produces within itself. Knowledge, it is averred, is immanent, that is to say, it is entirely achieved within the thinking subject, and for this reason cannot lay hold of an external reality; at most, the mind can infer the existence of such a reality, conjecture its main outlines, but nothing more. The great philosophical problem, then, is the critical problem. Now Scholasticism either passes this problem by, or solves it hastily by an appeal to evidence, and without further ado intrepidly penetrates into the domain of absolute being and constructs an ontological physics and metaphysics: how is it possible to grant it this pretension?

I shall state my opinion frankly: I believe that the Scholastics have not yet answered this difficulty with sufficient force. Not that there exists or should exist for them any real doubt as to the certainty of their position; but its legitimacy should be established more effectively. Above all, it should be made clear that the setting of the critical problem in modern philosophy is artificial, even un-

natural, because, since the time of Descartes, it has
issued from a false interpretation of the immanence
of thought. There are some valuable works on
the subject, such as those of Cardinal Mercier and
Prof. Maritain; but something more remains to be
done if we are to dissipate the equivocation that
has lasted for three centuries.

To tell the truth, philosophers of the English-
speaking world seem best equipped to take this
step: the very excesses of Idealism have produced
a violent reaction in England, and still more in the
United States, due, no doubt, to the practical and
realistic sense of the race. Dr. Kremer's study,
Le Néo-Réalisme Américain, has shown the hopes
that may be harbored in this regard.

No doubt other objections are holding modern
minds aloof from Scholastic philosophy. But they
are better known, more superficial, and, if I mistake not, more easily refuted. It is sufficient, for
example, to have become familiar with the Neo-
Scholastic atmosphere, say, of Louvain, Fribourg,
Paris, Milan, *and* Rome, in order to be convinced
that thought is there developed with true freedom.
Faith,—which is a faith equipped with motives of
credibility studied according to all the rules of
criticism, and by that token reasonable, a *ratio-
nabile obsequium,*—guards against certain errors,
suggests certain solutions, but by no means hinders
their discussion, nor the search for arguments from
experience and pure reason, nor the attentive examination of every objection brought against them.

For the rest, this aid given by faith pertains only to the principal questions, to those that concern the moral life; for the remainder, that is, for a vast domain, the widest freedom prevails. Neo-Scholastics make abundant use of this freedom, as is evinced by the innumerable controversies which exist and will continute to exist between them, in proof of the sincerity and seriousness of their investigations. Be it well noted that at the present hour,—as for well nigh a century,—it is the Church that strenuously defends the worth of human reason (in this she remains true to her tradition), and vigorously protests against the pretensions of a tyrannical voluntarism and of a desperate pragmatism: the will, the Church teaches, can and should apply the intellect to the consideration of its object; it can and should lead from the known credibility and "credentity" (duty to believe) of Revelation to faith in the same; but it should not and cannot command an assent without due justification. *"Credo quia absurdum"* is a downright absurdity; *"Credo ut intelligam"* has need of an explanation; and it is readily seen why some reproach Scholasticism, and especially Thomism, with a certain "rationalism."

In a neighboring domain, and for an analogous reason, some accuse Scholastic Peripateticism (and here, too, the other schools single out Thomism) of being too close to Empiricism, of giving too much weight to experience, of binding spirit too closely to matter, soul to body. Much, yes; too much, no.

Aristotle was greatly devoted to experience; far from establishing an abyss between spirit and matter, he associates them most intimately in man: for him the spiritual soul is the principle that constitutes primal matter,—itself a pure indetermination,—in the grade of a body, confers upon it the mechanical, physical, and chemical properties as well as the vital energies; he looks upon sensation as a product not of the soul alone, but of the composite of body and soul. Hence the problem of the union of body and soul, the problem of the "communication of substances," as it was called at one time, that is, of the relations between the physical and the moral,—a problem that has led to the "desperate" solution called psychophysiological parallelism,—is solved with the greatest facility in Thomistic Peripateticism. Shall we say that the solution remains incomplete because the dualism, spirit-matter, is not reduced to unity? But why mutilate the datum of experience by absorbing spirit in matter or matter in spirit, as is done by materialistic or spiritualistic monism? Besides, the dualism cannot be said to be irreducible: matter, too, is an actualization of thought; Peripateticism, as has been picturesquely said, makes of the material universe "a thought that does not think itself, suspended from a Thought that thinks itself."

But can the cosmological doctrines of the Stagirite be reconciled with modern physics? We have already noted the distinction between the general cosmological doctrines,—such as the hylomorphic composition of bodies, the nature and function of quantity, the relation of qualities to substance,— and such special doctrines as that of the four elements, the incorruptibility of the stars, the natural place of the elements. The latter are the result of a rudimentary experience, have been shown to be erroneous, and are no longer held. The former, however, have endured because they are based on obvious experience which is not exposed to error. At one time Mechanism believed to have overcome it together with Peripateticism, and to be in a position to impose on us the abandonment of Aristotle for Democritus. But in its ulterior development science itself solved the difficulty; Poincaré, Duhem, Mach, Ostwald, have taught us to distinguish between facts and the hypotheses invoked to explain them, to bind them together in theories, and to deduce laws from them. The facts, and they alone, command assent; the hypotheses are subject to philosophic criticism. This criticism has been recently instituted in regard to the atomic and electronic theories, and it has been shown that the Scholastic philosopher can very well look to them for a description of the external aspect of phenomena, but remains free to interpret it by his own principles: it seems that true molecules exist, distinct, even distant, at least in bodies in an amorphous state; that in the molecules there are some parts having the aspect and the properties of atoms; that in these latter, still smaller parts have the aspect and the properties of electrons; but whether these corpuscles are true, distinct individuals, or parts of a continuous, qualitatively heterogeneous whole, the science of physics does not and cannot say.

I believe I have touched upon the principal objections which are being made against Scholasticism to-day. The others are really of little account. Some, for example, find fault with Scholastic terminology. I admit that it differs considerably from that of modern philosophy. However, anyone who takes the trouble to study it admires its precision, while in the other he discovers much that is vague and unstable; then why make a change? Truth is a thing so precious that one who seeks it sincerely should be ready to learn another language if necessary. The Scholastics respected the terminology of Aristotle, and they made translations that might seem barbarous even to men of the Middle Ages; for example, *potentia* to signify the receptive principle, or *quod quid erat esse* to designate essence. Many Neo-Scholastics still use Latin as the medium of expression, and the Church approves of it; not that Latin is a more philosophical idiom than the modern languages; rather, it is less so because it is too synthetic; besides, the usual vocabulary of a dead language is always less rich. But this retention of Latin has the immense advantage of facilitating the reading of the old Scholastics, and of furnishing an instrument for international communication much more suitable than any of the artificial languages, Volapük, Esperanto, or Ido.   Moreover, Scholastics are able to express themselves in the modern languages: these are used at Louvain, Paris, Milan; nor is there lack of clearness in the works of Cardinal Mercier, Sertillanges, Rousselot, Maréchal, Maritain, Gemelli.   And when they so wish, they can find equivalent substitutes for the most technical expressions: thus, under the pen of Cardinal Mercier, *"species impressa"* has become the *déterminant cognitionnel*.   But in ordinary practice, it is perhaps more to the purpose to retain the traditional phrases and explain their meaning.   And then, do we not see modern authors introducing a terminology that seems most suitable to them?   Is not that of Kant all his own?   Does not Driesch speak of *entelechy* and *equipotential systems?*

I heartily agree with those who would have the Scholastics become more clear, adopt a more sympathetic mode of expression, and a more flowing and colorful style.   In my opinion, the manner in which the books on Neo-Scholastic philosophy are written is often defective.   Apart from the texts for the use of schools, which because of their strictly limited scope address themselves to a very restricted public, the philosophical works which represent Neo-Scholastic production do not give in their *ensemble* a very flattering impression.   Beside some really excellent ones (we have cited some illustrious names above, and the list is not complete), many present a pallid appeorence.   And it is not only the exposition that needs to be reformed, but likewise the method. Decadent Scholasticism exaggerated the rôle of deduction, preferred the arguments *a priori,* consulted experience but little, and overlooked synthetic work. Aristotle, instead, always showed how the highest problems of metaphysics arise from ordinary experience, crystallized in common speech. This beneficial contact with concrete reality, which gives security before mounting to abstract regions, this genetic method which makes clear the real value of problems, is what constitutes the true peripatetic tradition; this it is that has made the fortune of the system, assured its sway over minds for so many centuries, and determined in its favor the choice of the great thinkers of the thirteenth century,—a choice made not in compliance with a command of the Church, but against the prohibitions formulated by her in the first period.

I recall having heard Prof. Brochard in the Sorbonne conclude a series of lectures on the Ethics of Aristotle with these enthusiastic words: "In the Stagirite we have not *an* ethics, but *the* ethics." I believe that anyone who will have the courage to study the Christian Peripateticism of St. Thomas dispassionately and deeply will say: "In it we have not *a* philosophy, but *the* philosophy."

CHAPTER III

THE SPIRIT OF THE NEW SCHOLASTICISM

By Professor Dr. B. W. Switalski [1]

THE question as to the attitude of contemporary non-Catholic philosophers to Neo-Scholasticism cannot be satisfactorily answered without some preliminary considerations. In the first place, within the Neo-Scholastic movement itself there exist various tendencies which, while at one on fundamental doctrines, sharply differ on many other points. It is therefore necessary,—and sufficient for our present purpose,—to set forth those essential qualities which are common to every Neo-Scholastic tendency truly worthy of this title. Neo-Scholasticism as such is characterized by a standpoint and an orientation which is decidedly objective: it is firmly convinced that the human

[1] Dr. Switalski is professor of philosophy and pedagogy at the State Academy of Braunsberg (East Prussia), an institute for advanced philosophical and theological studies. In 1923 he was honored with the doctorate in theology by the University of Bonn; in 1924 he declined a call to the University of Freiburg. In 1922 the German episcopate, headed by Cardinal Schulte, commissioned him to found the *Albertus Magnus Academy,* to which he refers at the end of this chapter, and with which he is connected. His noteworthy work, *Probleme der Erkenntnis,* was published in 1923 (Aschendorff, Münster).

mind is capable of grasping the order of reality. For this reason it presses into its service the philosophy that was given a distinctly objective direction and character by its foremost masters, especially by St. Thomas Aquinas, from whom it received a model elaboration. Under the inspiration and guidance of this philosophy Neo-Scholastics aim to anchor all present knowledge and values in theocentric Idealism,—grounded by those same masters on unshakable foundations,—and from this point of departure to fashion them into a harmonious and lucid whole.

To preclude all misunderstanding, it should be noted that by theocentric Idealism is meant that conception of the universe which holds that all the reality of being, order, and activity is ultimately grounded in one, self-subsisting, personal God, who is also the last end to which all reality is ordained. To this world-view is opposed every kind of anthropocentric Idealism, which seeks to shape, or at least estimates, everything *with man alone as the starting-point, and refers everything to man,* to his "salvation," that is, to his well-being. It goes without saying that every truly Catholic philosophy must of necessity be theocentric; its followers see the foundation of their viewpoint in the need of explaining the world of experience, which, in the light of self-evident principles, leads them up to a personal God, the author, ordainer, and end of all reality.

Neo-Scholasticism, thus understood, has several

advantages over modern philosophy: the stability of its standpoint, the clearness, depth, and expanse which characterize its statement of problems, the confidence it has in the possibility of their solution, and the sublimity of its mission, which serves to keep alert the energetic effort to comprehend and turn to account the divinely established and all-controlling order of being and of duty.

On the whole, the philosophy of the nineteenth century maintained an adverse attitude to Neo-Scholastic endeavors. This was partly due to ignorance of the intellectual treasures of Scholasticism, which for a long time was harbored and cultivated in small circles, to "the exclusion of the general public"; however, the main reason of this aloofness is to be found in the subjectivistic, or naturalistic, but at all events immanentistic (anti-ontological) orientation and fundamental attitude of modern philosophizing in general. More especially, it was the transcendental Idealism of Kant and his successors, representative of a sublimated subjectivism consistently "thought out to the end," that could find no way of approach to an unbiassed appraisal of Scholasticism. Its direct and indirect influence seeped far into Catholic circles in a manner to arouse grave misgivings. The urgent summons of the Popes since Leo XIII to a return and close adherence to St. Thomas was primarily prompted by the hardihood of modern attempts of philosophic construction, apparent also in certain Catholic thinkers. The threatening danger was descried from the high watch-tower of the Church's teaching office even before it could be fully realized by the thinkers who were in the thick of the intellectual conflict.

For a long time the papal warnings were misunderstood in Catholic and non-Catholic quarters alike. They were thought to impose the obligation of slavish adherence to the letter. Quite naturally modern philosophers declined on principle a programme that was wrongly interpreted as imputing to thinkers a readiness to renounce philosophical independence. On the other hand, there were among Catholics over-anxious souls,—perhaps poorly endowed with the philosophic spirit,—who would have nothing else than a word-for-word restoration of Thomism, and this against the express and authoritative interpretation of the ecclesiastical decisions.

A new appraisal of Scholasticism and the philosophic movement that goes back to it was prepared during the last third of the nineteenth century by the historico-critical works of Denifle, Ehrle, Baeumker, Mandonnet, De Wulf, Grabmann, and others; by modern scientific methods they disclosed the treasures of medieval philosophy, and at the same time showed their connection with the history of the times and ideas. Non-Catholic thinkers, too, now directed their efforts to the cultivation of this hitherto disparaged field of thought.

In addition to this, after the close of the nineteenth century, Catholic philosophers reached the

conviction that a fruitful explanation and understanding between Scholasticism and modern philosophy was possible only when the results of the
latter were not only known, but also pondered
from within and in all their parts by minds as dispassionate and incorruptible as was that of St.
Thomas.   The work of Cardinal Mercier and his
Louvain school can serve as a model in this respect.
For these reasons Neo-Scholastic philosophy can
point to many noteworthy achievements in the field
of the history of philosophy and in systematization,
which go far beyond the confines of a school and
command the attention of scholars with outspokenly
modern tendencies.

The first years of the twentieth century saw a
significant *volte-face* in the valuation and treatment
of philosophical questions, and thereby made the
modern thinker more responsive to the Scholastic
way of putting and clarifying problems: Husserl's
rediscovery of absolute foundations,—above all in
the logical domain,—the investigation of Meinong's
school on his "object theory" ("Gegenstands-
theorie"), Külpe's calling attention to the existence
of imageless spiritual acts in the life of the soul,
the newly aroused sense for metaphysics which,
having been strengthened by the prodigious riddles
of the world-crisis, will never again allow itself to
be silenced by formalistic subtleties,—these are the
main reasons of the change that has recently taken
place.   Positivism, "Historism," in fact, every
kind of Relativism has been found wanting.   Men

are seeking ultimate, fixed foundations and standards for thought and action. From the subject,
which is beginning to despair of its self-glorification,
they are again turning to the object, firm in itself
and capable of lending steadiness to the subject; the
phenomenological method, introduced by Husserl
and arbitrarily remodeled by Scheler, even promises to give final insights into the essential relations
of reality.

The points of contact of these tendencies with
Scholastic methods are quite obvious. For all
that, it would be a mistake to take for granted
that they have already bridged the gulf between
Scholasticism and modern thought. To be sure,
the appreciation of Scholasticism is on the increase
also in non-Catholic circles; men are beginning to
realize that only a return to unbiassed, objectively
determined ways of viewing things can save modern
man from utter disintegration. But they do not
find the courage to take the final step because of
a lack of confidence either in their own powers or
in the soundness of Scholastic tenets. Hence while
the efforts of Neo-Scholastic thinkers to achieve a
strictly objective synthesis of "the old and the
new" are received with respect, they meet with
considerable reserve. An understanding between
the two camps has not as yet been reached. Only
individual investigators, and mostly along individual lines, are returning to the Scholastic conception.
Especially noteworthy in this connection is the fact

that the concept of entelechy is again being recognized as valid in the biological domain.

From the present situation, as here outlined, there arises for the representatives of Neo-Scholasticism a very responsible and difficult, but also a very fruitful and meritorious task: after the treasures of Scholasticism have been made accessible in a manner that is scientifically unobjectionable, they are to be deeply and energetically pondered; their meaning and whatever in their content has a perennial significance must be determined by a calm realization of the situation and with the aid of those instruments of criticism which have been given such a fine edge in the modern treatment of problems. Only then will it become possible to confront, compare, and balance those treasures with the conclusions of modern philosophy, thoroughly investigated in the same manner; for only in this way can the two conceptions be reduced to quantities which are comparable with each other. By conscientiously occupying himself with the mental heritage of Scholasticism, the mature and unprejudiced thinker will also gain this benefit: he will learn to survey and to appraise the ever changing creations of present-day philosophy, not with the eyes of the time-spirit, whose children we all are, but in the light of the essentially purer atmosphere of a world-conception which by its very principles is withdrawn from change and firmly established in itself. And so Neo-

Scholasticism, with its truly philosophic foundation
and equipment, promises not only to supply fixed
fundamentals, but, what is of equal importance, to
sharpen and clarify men's vision for whatever has
genuine worth and universal validity.

Penetrated by the conviction that Neo-Scholasticism, as we have described it, should be promoted
with all possible energy, the German episcopate,
under the leadership of the Archbishop of
Cologne, His Eminence Cardinal Karl Joseph
Schulte, and with the express approbation and
furtherance of the Apostolic See, founded at
Cologne in 1922 a *Catholic Institute for Philosophy,*
called the *Albertus Magnus Academy* (after the
teacher of St. Thomas, Blessed Albert the Great,
who taught in Cologne for a time). Its aim is
gradually to become a center for the exposition and
interchange of philosophic ideas, with a view to
a better understanding between Neo-Scholastics
and modern philosophers. This work, while animated by the Catholic spirit, will be guided by
strictly philosophic criteria. The beginnings are
promising, but the task is extremely difficult.
Everyone who is convinced of its importance,—and
what earnest man of culture is not?—should contribute, intellectually and materially, towards the
success of this Institute.

CHAPTER IV

THE CONTEMPORARY ATTITUDE TOWARDS
SCHOLASTICISM

By Professor Jacques Maritain, of the Institut Catholique, Paris

In the following pages I wish to summarize the actual attitude of non-Scholastic thinkers towards Scholastic philosophy, the main reasons for this attitude, and the prospects for a *rapprochement* between that philosophy and the other currents of present-day thought.

I

On the whole, modern philosophers have never been friendly, or even just, to Scholastic philosophy. The philosophy that is natural to the human mind had of necessity to engender enmity in those who refuse to take into account the natural conditions of human thought. For some generations, nay for centuries, they have been attacking and aspersing the origins, structure, and tendencies of that philosophy, whilst remaining wholly ignorant of, or misconstruing, its spirit and the very principles on which it is founded. Such an attitude may well cause amazement; but anyone can readily convince himself of its actuality by a glance at any of the usual manuals of the history of philosophy.

However, this state of affairs could not last. There were hearts and minds that rebelled against the void in which they were being forced to languish and to die. A movement marked by an eager interest in all true philosophic realism began to take form. Scholastic philosophy was found to answer this rightful longing for truth. The movement thus initiated,—too complex to be analyzed here, —was by no means barren, since it issued in bringing Thomism to the attention of sincere investigators.

Its influence began to spread and eventually made itself more or less felt in various quarters. It can be truly said that to-day there are no longer any French philosophers wholly ignorant of Scholastic philosophy. For many years the ablest representatives of Thomism endeavored to rehabilitate intelligence by drawing attention to the emptiness of current doctrines (Bergsonism and Pragmatism) in respect of the *real,* which alone is of moment for the intellect.[1] Their efforts were successful in arousing in the souls of men that profound yearning,—so characteristic of the most significant aspirations of to-day,—for a *return to the real and the absolute by way of the intellect and the primacy*

---

[1] Dr. Maritain has recently published a penetrating work on this subject: *Réflexions sur l'Intelligence et sur sa Vie Propre,* Paris, 1924. (Z.)

of the spirit. Since then, the existence of a Scholastic thought as a living, original, and prolific
form of human thought has been recognized,—and
that no longer of the human thought of only one
period, one ethnic temperament, one place or
country, but of human thought purely and simply,
in so far as it is human.

Among non-Scholastic philosophers there are
some who possess enough independence of mind to
avow the admiration they entertain,—even despite
their prejudices,—for the order, coherence, perfect
unity, and plasticity of the Scholastic method. At
the Sorbonne a historian of philosophy, Professor
E. Gilson, author of several notable works on the
philosophy of St. Thomas, has made an effective
contribution towards bringing about a recognition
of the absurd injustice that weighed heavily on a
long period of investigations and of thought directed to the quest of truth. "From the strictly
historical point of view," he says in part, "it is unlikely that one can regard several centuries of
philosophic speculation as simply non-existent."

After so many efforts and labors there has ensued
in France a general acknowledgment of the importance of Thomism for the solution of certain
questions that are in the foreground of public preoccupation. And so it has come about that quite
a number of problems are beginning to be treated
in function of the Scholastic position, and particularly in the light of the principles laid down by
Thomistic philosophy. Then, too, whether one's

position be favorable or unfavorable to Scholastic philosophy, one sees himself constrained to give serious consideration to the solutions which it adduces, as well as to the attitude of mind which it recommends. Some go so far as to see in it a sheet-anchor for modern intelligence. A thinker like Gonzague Truc, for example, who is an essayist rather than a philosopher, an agnostic and even an atheist, confesses that he cannot actually see any salvation for the intellect except in a *return* to Scholastic discipline and method. Another writer, M. Thibaudet, literary critic of the *Nouvelle Revue Française,* admits in his *Réflexions sur la Littérature* the undeniable existence of a Thomist critique penetrating into the domain of literature, as well as a renovated classicism represented by MM. Ghéon and Massis. Others, like M. Rougier, set the whole philosophical and logical problem in function of the Scholastic doctrine, only to declare themselves against the latter and to range themselves among its adversaries; for the rest, I must confess that side by side with a certain material erudition they betray a regrettable ignorance of the elements that are essential and vital for the discussion.

The most recent generations of intellectuals have shaken off the dominance of the mistaken teachers of the nineteenth century and,—even when they have not been led to an outright adherence to Catholicism, and with the firm tranquillity bestowed by faith walked in the footsteps of the greatest philosophers of the Church behind St. Thomas

Aquinas, the apostle of modern times,—have at
least given vigorous tokens of a springtime of metaphysics, of a spirit distinctly opposed to Materialism and Positivism. And even when these minds,
in the impetuosity born of their emancipation and
amid the illusions by which they sustain their *élan,*
take a violent stand against metaphysics and tend
toward a new "revolutionary" mysticism, it is still
the Scholastic reaction which from afar and indirectly has made possible their opposition to the influence of official science. This movement, which
is as yet indeterminate and undisciplined, finds
expression in the review *Philosophies;* its partici-
pants group themselves around Pierre Morhange
and with him frankly declare themselves to be "mys-
tics pure and simple"; as yet, however, this mysticism is rather vague.

The need of escape from egocentric subjectivism
toward reality is to-day so genuine and so profound
that even philosophers from whom one would least
expect it give serious indications of a *rapprochement* to Scholastic doctrines and method.

II

We now come to consider the reasons of the
unfriendliness towards Scholasticism, and to inquire
whether these reasons are to be found in its doctrinal content, or in its methods, or in other aspects
of this philosophy.

In a general way, it is easy to understand the opposition of "modern" philosophers to everything that implies any kind of submission of the mind to the external world in the formation of ideas. On the side of method, science in the modern sense is adverse to anything that brings to light the imma- nent [2] and genuine activity of the mind in the con- quest of truth. In this wise it condemns itself to empiricism, to idealistic and empirical agnosticism; and so modern philosophy, too, must needs antago- nize the traditional, realistic-conceptual philosophy.

Since Descartes, and through the influence of Kant, man pretends to have emancipated his knowl- edge from the absolute standards imposed on it by the object; hence that *indocility* in regard to being, that *attempt to arrogate for man the absolute aseity, the self-subsistence proper to God alone,* which characterizes the subjective idealism of the moderns. Nothing flies more in the face of the spirit of Thomism which, in harmony with common sense, demands that in knowledge the mind be pro- portioned to things.

It is then in the ineradicable idealistic prepos- session, in the propensity to treat philosophy as a "subjective poem," that we must look for the doc- trinal and sentimental disposition which is the cause of the aversion and hostility that "modern" philos- ophers show toward Thomism.

It should be sought also, and above all, in the at- titude of mind that is purely empirical and experi-

---

[2] *Immanent* is here used as opposed to *transitive*, not as opposed to *transcendent*. (Z.)

mental,—only too often confused with "scientific" method and, in matter of fact, incidentally countenanced by the marvelous success of the experimental sciences,—which repudiates all metaphysics, and *a fortiori* the metaphysics of Thomism. Contemporary empiricists would fain be, so they aver, more modest than the metaphysicians. But in reality they hardly succeed in proving themselves other than pusillanimous. These dispositions of mind found expression recently in an article by M. Ramon Fernandez, in which he says: "Whence comes it that we esteem the mental escapement of even the smallest discovery in 'the detail of phenomena' far more than the well-oiled gears of a system that supposes the full understanding of a universe which we do not know except in part?" This betrays ignorance of the formal object of the intellect and, it would seem, of its very functioning, precisely in so far as it is intellect, in the knowledge of this object. "When," continues the same author, "shall we find sufficiently powerful reasons for breaking with our intellectual habit of giving ourselves over to a science of Being of which we are not quite sure that it is not a mere science of words?"

The numerous and close relations which exist between Scholastic philosophy and faith,—the latter, as is known, finds in the former the purely rational principles and the motives of credibility which are, humanly speaking, its support,—raise the aversion of many "modern" thinkers for this philosophy to its highest pitch. The hatred of Christianity, —the anti-theological prejudice,—fosters and exasperates their hatred of Scholastic philosophy, in which they disdainfully insist on seeing nothing more than what they style "a theological philosophy."

Another cause is the absurd dogma, so prevalent in our day, that progress is continuous and necessary; everything modern is regarded as good simply because it is modern; the *future,* naturally, will be still better. The past was undoubtedly good when it was modern; having been outstripped, it is to be for evermore discarded.

Added to this is a certain "historicism," very much in fashion, which would have us believe that all moments of human thought,—though destined to be surpassed without end by other moments,— are in themselves venerable: this, of course, excludes all distinction between the true and the false in historical judgments, and is tantamount to an utter abdication on the part of philosophy.

III

We may well ask: What are the prospects for a *rapprochement* between Scholastic philosophy and the other currents of contemporary thought?

The prospects certainly exist, but as yet their realization appears well in the distance. So much is certain: the great ideologies of the nineteenth cen-

tury seem to have had their day, or are dying
away peacefully because of well-nigh unanimous indifference. Kantian idealism and the system of
Positivism are now represented, here or abroad,
but by a few superannuated professors, who are
wearing themselves out in the *milieu* of intellectual
confusion which they engendered. As a legitimate
reaction against the raging intellectual epidemic and
against what has been termed "the poison of the
intellect," there prevails everywhere, in minds and
hearts alike, a general yearning,—the yearning for
the *real*. Even more than in the philosopher, it
is dominant in the man on the street, in those pre-
occupied with moral and political problems, in those
in quest of beauty, the artists and the poets, in the
curious, in the lovers of life,—more in all these
than in the professional philosophers, whose preoccupation too commonly consists in upholding by
their logomachies the ideology received in the
schools.

It is unquestionably true that this deep longing
for realism too often seeks satisfaction through any
means whatsoever, and at times rests content with
the most mischievous pseudo-philosophical pallia-
tives. Be that as it may, it remains true that in
every quarter and in almost every country, the light
is dawning and the imperious need of truth and
absoluteness is asserting itself. It is *reality* that is
wanted, that is to say, truth reached *through the
channels of the intellect and the primacy of the*

spirit. And this accounts for the eager and sympathetic movement of metaphysical curiosity which we are witnessing.

These spiritual phenomena have been noted by the Russian philosopher Berdiaeff, who maintains that we are entering upon an entirely new historical era,—another Middle Age. According to him, this period will be marked by the predominance of spiritual discussions, by the return to metaphysics, by the religious setting given to the most important problems. All the grand ideas that guided the three last centuries, particularly the dogma of progress, have by now become obsolete.

This new disposition of mind and heart in favor of realism, intellectualism, and spiritualism, Scholastic philosophy alone is equipped to satisfy, foster, and develop, and eventually to make it bring forth most abundant fruit. Consciously or unconsciously, in principle if not yet in fact, there exist remarkable possibilities for Scholasticism.

Here and there one already sees the tendencies and prospects of a *rapprochement* with Scholastic philosophy taking shape. Here and there a great step forward has been taken. Thus the American Neo-Realists, with Perry and Santayana, are renewing contact with Aristotelian realism by their critique of Kantian Criticism; the philosophies of the concept, like that of Husserl in Germany, are harking back to the logic of Aristotle; the philosophic deepening of biological problems is eliciting a return to the animism of Aristotle, as is seen, for

example, in the works of Driesch in Germany and
in those of Dr. Remy Colin in France.   Attention
should also be called to the anti-transformist position of the famous French anatomist Vialleton.   The
American biologist W. R. Thompson, director of
the laboratory of entomology at the islands of Hy-
ères, makes a clear and intelligent avowal of the
doctrine of St. Thomas Aquinas.

CHAPTER V

THE PREJUDICES AGAINST THE NEW SCHOLASTI-
CISM: THEIR CAUSES AND REMEDIES

*By Dr. R. Kremer, C.SS.R., Fellow of the Institut
Supérieur, Louvain University; Professor at
the Redemptorists' House of Studies,
Tillet, Belgium*

IN the following pages I shall try to answer the
proposed questions according to the knowledge and
general impression derived from the reading of
books and periodicals, from attending lectures, and
from personal intercourse with Scholastic and non-
Scholastic philosophers. It would be rash to attempt a definitive pronouncement on so vast a subject; but it is hoped that one who is sincerely interested in philosophy and has had the opportunity
of observing present-day currents of philosophic
thought, may give some useful hints in one or the
other direction, without intending his suggestions
and appraisals to be final, or in any way offensive
to those who may hold a different opinion.

I

It is impossible to sum up in a single phrase the
present attitude of modern philosophers to Scho-

lasticism. Many do not even take it into consideration, or have only a very vague idea of its nature.
However, a certain disdainful way of judging it,—
quite common some time ago,—seems to be going
out of fashion. The legend of the dark, ignorant
Middle Ages is no longer admitted by serious students, and as a consequence it is no longer possible
to despise medieval philosophy. On the contrary,
recent researches have shown, as Prof. Gilson, one
of the foremost historians and students of medieval
philosophy, testifies, that this period was as fertile
in minds possessed of great acumen and even genius as any other in history. M. Gilson has gathered a large and sympathetic audience around his
chair at the Sorbonne, and young men of ability attend his lectures. The work of other scholars
such as De Wulf, Baeumker, Grabmann, etc., has
long since been recognized, and medieval philosophy
is being more justly appreciated.

As a result, Neo-Scholasticism, too, has won the
esteem of all who realize that we can profit by
the wisdom of those medieval philosophers whom
the Neo-Scholastics have chosen as their guides.
Moreover, this movement has proved that it possesses real vitality and is an important current of
thought in contemporary philosophy. Scholastic
works and periodicals are no longer scorned, but
their scientific value is recognized; as an instance I
may mention the friendly notices by Prof. A. E.
Taylor in *Mind*. The lectures of Prof. De Wulf at
Harvard, the chairs of Scholastic philosophy at the

universities of Amsterdam, Utrecht, London, and Oxford, show that there is a real interest in these doctrines. The celebration of the centenary of St. Thomas Aquinas, not only in Catholic universities and centers of learning, but also in secular universities and meetings, as in Munich, Manchester, and chiefly Naples, has called attention to the historical importance of the Angelic Doctor and to the adaptability of his doctrines to present needs. The programme set forth by Father Agostino Gemelli, Rector of the Catholic University of Milan, in his address at the Congress of Naples, met with a sympathetic reception; on the whole it embodies the aims and methods of Neo-Scholastics everywhere. And the appreciative way in which Prof. Liebert, President of the Kantgesellschaft, compared St. Thomas with the great German Criticist, shows that the permanent merits of Aquinas, and consequently the possibility of the success of Neo-Scholasticism, are being widely recognized.

Thus there seems to exist a real interest and curiosity as to what Scholastic philosophy is and what it has to offer to the present generation. But at the same time there still remains a lingering feeling of surprise, as some one put it, that students who show a real knowledge of contemporary thought should go back to an ancient, obsolete way of thinking. There are keen thinkers to-day who suspect that Neo-Scholasticism is rather an archæological fancy, than a really living philosophy; their respect for it is mingled with considerable scepticism as to its actual value and aims. I think this scepticism and distrust are not justified in fact, and I now proceed to examine their chief causes and remedies.

II

(1) It must be a difficult task for a non-Scholastic philosopher to get information on the subject which interests us. In the first place, he may say that the books dealing with Scholasticism are not easily found and, moreover, not intended to furnish information to those of his mental attitude. As I shall state later what I consider to be the duty of Scholastics in this matter, I shall here indicate what the non-Scholastic ought to do. He will get little or no reliable information from his usual sources. And if he opens a book by an old or new Scholastic, he is likely to be startled by new words, new ways of thinking and of stating and solving problems. His first temptation will be to look upon all this as quite obsolete and unworthy of serious consideration. But should he not rather regard it as deserving of at least as much attention and sympathy as is shown to many ancient and modern authors who are otherwise but little known? Most contemporary Scholastics take great pains to understand and appreciate, say, Kant, Bergson, or James; should not the other side be equally just and painstaking in regard to Scholasticism? This effort will perhaps be greater and certainly more necessary because of the current prejudices to be over-

come. For a genuine understanding of Scholasticism it is not enough to quote a text-book here and there, or even to read a manual like that of Father Rickaby, as William James did for his work, *Some Problems of Philosophy*. A careful perusal of current Scholastic literature,—such as is to be found in periodicals like the *Revue des Sciences Philosophiques et Théologiques,* or the *Revue Néo-Scholastique de Philosophie,*—is indispensable. Books like the *Cours de Philosophie* of Louvain, the *Stonyhurst Series,* and the more specialized researches of Sertillanges, Rousselot, and others, should be attentively studied.

(2) But another difficulty faces students who are alive to the richness and variety of medieval Scholastic philosophy. Which of the several tendencies does Neo-Scholasticism follow? Does it adhere to the Intellectualism of St. Thomas, or to the Intuitionism of the Augustinian school, or to the Voluntarism of Duns Scotus, or to the Experimentalism of Roger Bacon? It should state its position clearly on this point. Some allege that it holds too exclusively to Thomistic Intellectualism and unduly neglects the freer tendencies of St. Bonaventure and others.

I think no one should find fault with the Neo-Scholastic movement for showing a greater variety than is commonly believed. Such divergences as existed formerly are a token of vitality and freedom of speculation. As to the present, it is undeniable that St. Thomas is the chief inspiration of the movement. The main reason is that historical development of the doctrines and arguments has shown him to have realized more fully and profoundly than others the capital points of Scholastic teaching. As time went on, the splendor of his genius became ever more apparent. His doctrines and spirit are more comprehensive than is generally admitted by those who do not know him from personal study. His Intellectualism, for instance, as the late lamented Pierre Rousselot has conclusively shown in his brilliant work, *L'Intellectualisme de Saint Thomas,* is by no means that narrow and bigoted idolatry of human concepts which is generally attached to this term. On the contrary, it is capable of assimilating all the really vital elements of Intuitionism and Voluntarism without losing any of its originality. Therefore, I for one, and many others, convinced Thomists as we are, should rejoice if the effort were made to revive the spirit and systems of the other great Schoolmen; the more quickening such a restoration would be, the more useful it would become to Thomism itself. Besides, some would be likely to find more immediate satisfaction for their intellectual needs in the other systems of Scholasticism.

(3) This confidence in the future proves that Scholasticism, far from being a system that is dead, has aims, methods, and problems as modern as those of any other philosophy. It aims to make a full analysis of the essential features of reality, life, and the sciences; by means of thorough ob-

servation and deduction it seeks to form a systematic view of God, nature, man, society, science, and art,—a view that is not a mere subjective fancy, but affords a deeper insight into reality. Its method is nothing else but the application of the natural powers of the mind to that task. It is no more exclusively deductive than other great philosophies. I am afraid some of those who demand "a closer contact with reality," a less abstractive method, are not very clear in their own mind as to the difference between philosophy and empirical science; logically they should condemn Kant or Hegel more severely than St. Thomas on the score of the deductive, rationalistic nature of their method.

Scholasticism in its most flourishing period kept close contact with observation and science as they existed at that time. Neo-Scholastics admit that the subsequent neglect of this contact was one of the chief causes of the decay of Scholastic philosophy in the sixteenth and seventeenth centuries,— and Professor De Wulf has strongly emphasized this point. Therefore, true to the peripatetic spirit, Neo-Scholastics consider it imperative to be familiar with the actual state of the natural and of other sciences; at Louvain, for instance, the academic training in philosophy comprises lectures in these various branches and even practical work in the laboratories, such as that of psychology. But philosophy is not to be confused with science, nor has it simply to accept and develop the conclusions of the latter. Its task is rather to reflect on the methods of science and to criticize them from its own point of view; furthermore, to consider the findings and theories of science so as to discover the image of the world and mind which they imply. Such being the case, it becomes clear how a medieval philosophy can still be true and useful to-day, despite the fact that the scientific doctrines with which it was for a time associated have been superseded; for the essential, metaphysical principles do not depend on experimental enquiry, but are gained by the simple, natural activity of the mind on commonsense facts and elementary perception. However, I readily grant that in the exposition of their doctrines Neo-Scholastics could at times describe more fully the facts which serve as starting-points of reflection, be they strictly scientific or merely those of every-day observation. But is this not a question of literary description rather than of philosophy proper? Nevertheless, as we shall indicate later, it remains true that the analytical side of Scholastic doctrine should be more fully developed than before.

(4) At first blush it may seem that Scholasticism lacks actuality as to the problems it discusses. What does the doctrine of the real distinction between essence and existence, between the soul and its faculties,—what does the operation of the *intellectus agens,* or the controversy between Thomists and Molinists, mean to the modern mind? I admit that certain obsolete, fanciful problems and useless

subtleties current in the period of Scholastic decadence still linger in some books; such are especially certain atomizing ways of conceiving the relation of substance and accidents, matter and form, and so on. But most of the problems that to some may seem devoid of actuality flow from fundamental theses which Scholasticism first proves or seeks to prove; it is simply preposterous to judge them apart from the questions and principles out of which they issue. Such, for example, are the discussions on the attributes of God and on the soul and its faculties. Moreover, the chief questions in philosophy are, on the whole, always the same; actuality exists only with respect to the form they assume at different times. An attentive and sympathetic observer will soon recognize those persistent problems in Scholasticism: they all center around God, man, nature, knowledge. Recent Scholastics have repeatedly discussed the problem of knowledge even in its latest forms. There remains still more to be done for the philosophy of science. But then Neo-Scholasticism does not pretend to have finished its task. Moreover, one sometimes gets the impression that the doctrines themselves, rather than the problems, create aversion to Scholasticism. Theism, the substantiality of the soul, and other points of Scholastic doctrine are often pronounced to be quite outworn and no longer worthy of discussion. But what else is this but sheer prejudice? Scholasticism should at least be given a fair trial.

(5) It is sometimes urged that Scholastics hold

themselves aloof from non-Scholastic currents of contemporary thought. If by this is meant that they do not admit certain theses which are common to modern philosophers, but combat them vigorously, the statement is true. But does not every philosopher define and defend his own ideas by endeavoring to refute those of his fellow-philosophers with which he cannot agree? However, it must be granted that some Scholastics fail to give due attention to modern systems; at times they distort them or use rather strong language in qualifying them. But are they themselves not often misunderstood? Have their opinions not been frequently subjected to harsh treatment? This, of course, is but a feeble excuse. On the whole, however, present-day Scholastics, and certainly those who are looked upon as leaders in their own camp, study modern philosophy with eager sympathy, even when they dissent from it. The collection of the school of Louvain contains several books on modern philosophy which have been praised for their thoroughness. In Germany Geyser and Przywara have recently examined such contemporary movements as the "Phenomenology" of Husserl and Scheler; I could give a whole bibliography in this connection, but for the present it is sufficient to refer the reader to the above mentioned periodicals and their exhaustive reviews of such works..

(6) I think the main reason which leads modern philosophers to regard Scholasticism with distrust

may be summed up in the celebrated dictum: *Philosophia ancilla theologiae*. Modern philosophy is obsessed with the fear of becoming a slave; it rejects all authority. In its eyes Scholasticism cannot be a true philosophy because its conclusions are dogmatically predetermined by the Church. I waive here the discussion of the original sense of the celebrated and much abused phrase.[1] I simply wish to state some facts which define the actual position of Scholasticism with regard to authority. First of all, it must be emphasized that Scholastic philosophy is quite distinct from theology. Theology, as understood by the Scholastics, presupposes faith, relies on divine authority, and draws its conclusions from dogmatic premises by means of reasoning; it also investigates the life of dogma in the Church. Philosophy, according to the Scholastic conception, is not derived from authority or faith, but is the achievement of reason. It does not accept blindly a system handed down to it, but examines it critically. Human authority is no true argument, but only an invitation to consider a meaning seriously. As to divine authority, whether of Scripture or of Tradition (to speak in the language of Catholic theology, as the matter requires us to do), philosophy has not to consider it directly, nor does it draw its conclusions from it: neither are its conclusions determined beforehand by the Church. Being a rational in-

[1] A clear exposition of it is given in Chap. VI by Olgiati-Zybura, of *The Key to the Study of St. Thomas*, St. Louis, 1925. (Z.)

vestigation, it is in itself truly autonomous. But this does not mean that it can contradict Revelation or the teaching of the Church, nor that it can explain away all mysteries. Philosophy is possible even though it cannot demonstrate all truth; it is enough that every demonstrated proposition is true. Besides those demonstrable truths, there may be a large number of truths which can be known only on divine authority (which authority must of course be shown to apply to that particular case;—this is the task of theology). For a believer in dogmatic religion,—be he a Catholic or an orthodox Protestant,—even if he is not a Scholastic, faith and philosophy cannot contradict each other, because they are both undeniably true. Precisely for the same reason every independent thinker must hold that philosophy cannot contradict a well established fact; if it does, it is a sign that the seemingly assured conclusion does not follow from the premises, supposedly true and proved, from which it is claimed to be derived; and a closer scrutiny will expose the logical flaw. The same procedure would be applied by the Scholastic to a so-called philosophic proposition which would happen to contradict dogmatic truth. But in that case, too, he would be seeking true rational evidence.

The fact that Scholastic philosophy has been adopted by the Catholic Church has not altered the intrinsic nature of that philosophy. The Church needs a philosophy to explain and prove those religious truths which are demonstrable by pure reason,

and to furnish theology with the rational principles which this science uses. To fulfill its office,
the philosophy used by the Church must be a true
philosophy, that is to say, it must be a rational,
not a dogmatic and authoritative system. The
same proposition can be held by the philosopher
and the theologian, but each will prove it by his
own method without confusing their arguments.
Even if the same man is both a philosopher and a
theologian, he may and must reasonably confront
his knowledge of one and the other origin, but he
will not take the one for the other.

It will be urged that the cases are not parallel
inasmuch as faith is not an objective, accurately
ascertainable fact, but a subjective state of mind.
This, however, is no refutation of the Scholastic
theory of faith and reason; it is merely the assertion of the rationalistic, as opposed to the rational,
view. Moreover, the present question is not as to
which view is true, but whether Scholasticism con-
fuses faith and reason, and makes philosophy
directly dependent on authority; and this must be
emphatically denied. On the contrary, strange as
it may seem, this conception of dogmatic faith and
of reason shows a greater confidence in reason because it trusts the human mind as being capable
of attaining certitude in a large domain and of correcting its errors; besides, it gives a restful security
and serenity in scientific research which the out-
sider cannot rightly appreciate.

The question can also be solved in another way.

Let the non-Scholastic philosophers test the starting-points and conclusions of the Scholastic system and see whether or not they are derived from reason, as they claim to be. This can be done without any general discussion of programmes. But the test must not be simply some modern system or some received "principles"; it must be a thorough and independent investigation of the question, taking account of the genuine sense of Scholastic doctrines, as has been said above (II, 1).

III

I do not believe that a complete and formal *rapprochement* between Scholastic philosophy and modern currents of thought will be realized in the near future. But all the tokens of sympathy mentioned above (I) tend to bring about a better mutual understanding and a diminution of useless discussions. Once the controversy has been brought to bear on the central points, it can become fruitful, and many hitherto unsuspected affinities can be detected. On the other hand, philosophical progress does not consist in the renunciation of one's standpoint or in compromises; but the frank exchange of ideas can be made to bear fruit.

Scholasticism will find some kindred tendencies in contemporary thought, such as the objectivistic analysis of Husserl and his school, the realistic doctrines of Külpe and of the English and American Realists (New or Critical) ; more generally, in the revival of interest in metaphysics which is in evidence especially in Germany.

Scholasticism itself will impress the other philosophers of to-day mostly by its systematic, definite character, and by the full and well-balanced answers it gives to all vital questions. Prof. W. H. Sheldon has aptly expressed the feeling of awe inspired by Thomism as the most massive and lasting system known to history (cfr. "The Vice of Modern Philosophy," *Journal of Philosophy, XII,* 1915, pp. 5 and 15).

IV

Scholastic philosophers themselves can do much to help the Neo-Scholastic movement by striving to make the latter better known. There are such practical means as writing,—not only for Scholastic periodicals, but also for others where their contributions would be welcomed,—and presenting their views at general congresses and other meetings. Here especially, but also in less occasional works, much depends on the manner of proposing their ideas and making them intelligible to those not familiar with Scholastic thought.

(1) They should put their arguments in a way that analyzes the starting-points more carefully and makes them more readily recognizable. The logical and psychological origin of notions should be explained more in detail than is usually done in cur-

rent books. The meaning of words should be explained, especially where widespread confusion exists. The value of the arguments should be critically examined. This would also lead to a true internal progress of Scholastic doctrine.

(2) There is a certain way of quoting St. Thomas and other Scholastic writers that may turn out to be a hindrance rather than a help to non-Scholastic readers; for it may give them the false impression that these writers are alleged as "authorities" and substituted in place of proofs. Not that well-selected texts may not be truly illuminating; but too frequently quotations, especially in matters where the text really adds nothing to the simple statement of fact or idea, are misleading. On the whole, a book may be more effective without containing any "texts," provided its whole development is inspired and pervaded by a genuine knowledge of Scholastic doctrine and by true philosophic insight.

(3) In order to adapt themselves to the present-day mentality, Scholastics should treat of questions which have a peculiar attraction for the modern mind, such as the theory of knowledge, the philosophy of science, evolution, etc. Useful work has been done on the first subject by Cardinal Mercier, Prof. Noël, Dr. Coffey, Dr. Vance, Prof. Geyser, and others; but these questions need a fuller treatment and readaptation. Natural theology should be treated with more attention to the problems of religious psychology. On a closer examination of

recent philosophical literature, other problems will readily suggest themselves, such as the philosophy of history, of the "Geisteswissenschaften."

(4) Such an examination will yield a knowledge not only of the problems of to-day, but also of the best way of treating them in order to impress contemporary readers. It is indispensable for those who write for the non-Scholastic public to have an accurate knowledge of the dominating tendencies. It is not always necessary to discuss these systematically or even to allude to them explicitly; but when this is done, special care must be taken not to misrepresent these tendencies. The discussion of modern systems must consist chiefly in testing their internal consistency and the validity of their foundations, rather than in a simple juxtaposition to Scholastic theses; of course, this latter method can be usefully employed to make Scholastic ideas known; and in a short critical notice it may be the only possible way of rapidly stating the principal points of agreement and disagreement.

(5) But adaptation is not a blurring of differences and much less a shallow dissertation on commonplaces. Neo-Scholasticism must first of all be true to itself. Like all philosophy it must plunge into the depths of the analysis of reality. An acute mind, even though lacking a finished style, does more for the progress of a doctrine than a brilliant essayist. Success is more surely achieved by painstaking work than by hasty compromises.

Such are the views of Neo-Scholastics, so far as

I know them, bearing on the proposed questions. Their hopes and their programme may seem ambitious. But why should they not be realized in course of time and with the collaboration of students from different places and with different formations of mind? Here, too, one can apply the phrase of St. Thomas: *"Fiat aliqualiter per plura, quod non potest fieri per unum."*

CHAPTER VI

THE NEO-SCHOLASTIC MOVEMENT IN FRENCH-SPEAKING COUNTRIES

By Professor L. Noël, of the University of Louvain

UNQUESTIONABLY, the starting-point of the Neo-Scholastic movement is to be found in the efforts and works of Cardinal Mercier, and in his teaching at the University of Louvain.

Well nigh half a century ago, immediately upon ascending the papal throne, Leo XIII urged the Catholic world to return to the philosophy of St. Thomas. This philosophy was no longer known. The higher institutes ignored it. The seminaries taught doctrines labeled as Thomistic in connection with theology. These were taken from manuals or from dry and meager formulas, abridging not so much the thought of the master as that of his recent disciples. The Pope's intention was to go farther back to authentic sources. But he did not wish the Thomistic doctrine to be merely disinterred and left in the passive state of an archæological curiosity; his aim was to have it become the ground-work of a thought that was actual and living. He hoped that it would enlighten the modern mind and cure social anarchy by becoming a remedy for the anarchy of ideas.

centuries-old home of national education, endowed with all the rights of a State institution, and sovereignly teaching all branches,—literary, scientific, professional,—to the intellectual *élite* of a country situated at the center of modern civilization. What an advantage for the study of religious problems which could be pursued in the light of researches directly made in all scientific domains by members of the same institution! On the other hand, what a benefit for the scientific researches themselves to be conducted in the atmosphere of a large-hearted and lofty Catholicism that quickens an institution of such proportions. The Belgian nuncio had seen all these opportunities for furthering the mutual penetration of scientific life and Christian thought, and when he was ready to actualize his dream of a Thomistic revival, his thoughts quite naturally turned to the University of Louvain.

In July, 1882, at the request of the Pope, the executive council of the University of Louvain established a chair of Thomistic philosophy and entrusted it to Canon Mercier. Immediately after his appointment Canon Mercier left for Rome, where Leo XIII wished to become personally acquainted with the man to whom the realization of his projects was to be committed. No ordinary interview this, between the great Pope of modern times and the young professor who one day was to become the illustrious primate of Belgium. Leo XIII was a severe master; his requirements were as high as his genius and as his consciousness of the greatness and prestige of the Church. This time, however, he had to be satisfied; these two men understood each other. Like Leo XIII, the young professor had a generous faith in humanity, in reason, in science. He loved his age. And like Leo XIII, he wished to draw science and the age closer to the Truth. Instead of clinging to a literal and narrow interpretation of the Pope's intentions, he caught their spirit and set about to realize them with a breadth of view which in the end was more faithful in proportion as it was more personal and less servile.

First of all, since Leo XIII wished that Thomism make contact with modern thought and science, Canon Mercier began to make a thorough investigation of this science and thought. In the course of his teaching at Malines he had mastered the doctrines of St. Thomas, he had appraised the solid good sense of these doctrines, at once so serene and so positive, scaling the loftiest heights of things divine without losing touch with sensible realities or for a moment letting go the rigorous chain of logical reasoning. He had likewise examined the works of the teachers who dominated European thought about this time: the positivists and the English and French psychologists. Everything in their works was traced to experience, and forthwith a *rapprochement* between these tendencies and the Aristotelian aspect of Thomism presented itself. In order to reach contemporary minds, it was of great importance to point out to them how the highest speculations of Scholastic doctrine were linked with the data of facts. But it would not be enough to appeal to every-day observation. For the nineteenth century the reality of things disclosed itself in its truest aspect in the retort of the chemist, under the scalpel of the anatomist, under the microscope of the biologist. It was therefore with science founded on such researches that the traditional doctrine had to be brought into contact.

However, his knowledge of scientific matters seemed to him insufficient. But this was not to prove a drawback. At that time Charcot's theories on mental disease were all the rage, and we find among the pupils of the famous Paris physician, assiduously following his courses and his clinics, a certain Dr. Mercier, who is none other than our Canon of Malines. Later at Louvain he followed courses in physiology, chemistry, and mathematics. In the laboratory of Van Gehuchten he attended the experiments and witnessed the discoveries of that great neurologist; he became the disciple of the celebrated chemist Louis Henry. He requested Paul Mansion to unveil to him the profound meaning of mathematics, and Msgr. de Harlez to initiate him into the secrets of linguistics. He passionately followed the admirable researches of Van Beneden and Carnoy. No scientific domain remained unfamiliar to him; his mind was nourished with the same abundance of facts, he accustomed himself to follow the same methods as the practitioners of observation and the experimenters of the laboratory. And he had an advantage over them in that he could point out in what way their verifications were insufficient, their theories inadequate, and along their own beaten paths he led them on to the problems and the solutions presented by philosophy.

Immediately after his inauguration in October, 1882, Mercier began his exposition of Thomism. The students of the various faculties who out of curiosity attended his first lectures, were surprised, for each one heard the language of the science he was studying: comparative grammar, cellular biology, the physiology of the nervous system, etc. Is this, then, the doctrine of the Middle Ages which was expected to be all a-bristle with antiquated and bizarre notions? Yes, it is the same; for the moment the findings collected by the sciences group themselves and harmonize as general ideas, there at once appear the scholastic formulas of St. Thomas, and it so happens that their old Latin, paraphrased by the professor, says nothing else than what the statement of the problem led one to expect and foresee. This Thomism was very modern; it was living, actual, interesting. And jurists, philologists, physicians were all seized with zeal for a thorough study and discussion of Scholasticism.

Such was the success of Canon Mercier's lectures, as complete as it had been unlikely. Ere long it gave rise to larger projects. In a few years the higher course in philosophy had covered all the philosophical branches; it had compared the ideas of St. Thomas with those of Taine, Spencer, Kant, Ribot, Bain, John Stuart Mill, and a score of others; it had shown these ideas to be in harmony with the data of science. But the horizon of researches widens in proportion to their progress; one glimpses directions which cannot be followed up; one draws outlines the framework of which he alone cannot fill out. However great may be his power for work, the task is too vast for one man. Besides, each discipline calls for an appropriate mentality, to be acquired only by prolonged specialization. To achieve a philosophy of all the sciences it would be necessary to have sifted all the sciences to the bottom; for this each one of them would require a lifetime. How was the difficulty to be solved? By bringing together the representatives of the various disciplines and setting them to collaborate in a common work. There must be created a milieu where contact is established between the researches, where the savants can follow the projects of the philosophers and the philosophers receive and ponder the suggestions of the savants.

This idea led to the founding of the *Institut Supérieur de Philosophie or École Saint Thomas d'Aquin,*—obviously, a grand and imposing idea, inspired not alone by Catholic interests, but by those of human thought in its widest sense. Leo XIII enthusiastically approved the project. As

early as July 15, 1888, he requested the University
to actualize it, he insistently repeated the request,
himself contributed towards defraying the expenses
of the undertaking, conferred a Roman prelacy on
Canon Mercier, added the whole weight of his authority to clear the way for the new work and to
set it up solidly in the very heart of the University.

According to the mind of the Pope and that of
its founder, the *École Saint Thomas* was to have a
twofold aspect. This was not to be an institution
in the ordinary sense of a school, intent upon dogmatically dealing out a finished and definitive doctrine to its hearers. It would of course teach, so
as to spread its influence and recruit and train
workers. But first and foremost it would be a
center of study and research where work would
be done on "science in the making." Whence
would a higher institution of learning draw the
notions which it spreads around itself if it did not
at the same time endeavor to elaborate them? It
would have to get them elsewhere, and immediately drop to a tributary and inferior rank, while
at the same time creating above itself another institution which would work out the doctrine, and
alone and truly be the higher one. Science is a
living thing; it is constantly made and re-made;
only those possess it truly who labor to advance it.
Now this advancement is not realized except by a
vast collaboration which, above all national fron-
tiers and across the very strife of adverse opinions, unites all the researchers of humanity. This

was one of the master-ambitions of Msgr. Mercier:
to see his *Institut* take a place of first rank in the
international movement of thought. It manifests
itself in all his writings, in all the discourses contemporaneous with the foundation.

In 1894 Msgr. Mercier founded the *Revue Néo-
Scholastique*.[1] It was to be for the world the
mouth-piece of the new school, and its name alone
meant a programme. Alongside of it, the *Biblio-
thèque de l'Institut Supérieur de Philosophie* was to
bring together the more copious works; in the first
place, it published the successive volumes of the
*Cours de Philosophie: Psychologie, Logique, Cri-
tériologie, Ontologie*. This professorial work is
marked by a spirited manner of treatment. Despite the didactic form which, for practical reasons,
it has taken, it shows none of the stiff and impersonal manner of a text-book. However, it is
likely that the learned author is most himself when,
released from the unavoidable trammels of a manual, he unfolds his thought with complete ease,
as he does in his numerous articles in reviews
and books like the *Origines de la Psychologie Con-
temporaine,* and *Définition Philosophique de la
Vie*.[2]

[1] It continues to appear as a quarterly at Louvain, under the
direction of M. De Wulf, one of the first collaborators of Msgr.
Mercier.

[2] All these works, as well as those of the collaborators and
pupils of Msgr. Mercier which we shall cite in the following
pages, are published at the *Institut Supérieur de Philosophie,*
Louvain.

To-day one can appraise the rôle played by this work in the Thomistic revival.

To be sure, this work must not be considered apart from the living teaching from which it issued, nor from the labors which the teacher prompted and organized around him. Undoubtedly, too, in reading these writings we should note the date they bear and keep in mind the growing distance which separates us from the end of the nineteenth century. And it is precisely by resetting them in their framework,—before the reactions they called forth and before the numerous works they directly inspired,—that we grasp the full significance of the new revelation which they bring; at the same time we understand how the directions they give are still actual and fit into the new conditions of the development of ideas.

To seek in present-day discussions the points of insertion where the old Thomistic teaching could gradually enter, prove itself fruitful, form alliances, grow young again by the intus-susception of fresh sap—is not such the formula, to-day as yesterday, according to which Scholastic philosophy must advance? No doubt the atmosphere has changed, the sciences are being subjected to a stringent criticism, Positivism is dead, Kantianism has gone back to the objective idealism of its founder, a new spiritualism is being born of psychology and the needs of action. But in the face of these new doctrines the same tactics must be taken up again.

To-day other thinkers—in France, Belgium, England—are following this method of *rapprochement*. But how many of them were found to do this before the example was set by Msgr. Mercier? The minds congenially inclined to modern philosophy lost sight of orthodoxy; those loyal to tradition did but wrap themselves in a shy and sullen isolation, or "refute" their opponents from the heights of an unchangeable doctrine, without, moreover, taking the pains to gain an exact knowledge of their thought.

How much more sensible, skilful, and—to say everything—Christian, was the attitude of Msgr. Mercier! With him the spirit of the Gospel bore its rarest fruit: that intellectual charity which the zeal of orthodoxy frequently stifles. To insure a welcome for itself, his Thomism began by extending a welcome to others; before discussing an opponent it made an honest effort to understand him; in this manner it in turn obtained a hearing and an understanding.

Let us enter for a moment into the more technical details. It would be difficult to exaggerate the importance of the revolution brought into Scholastic philosophy by the *Critériologie*. Before its appearance there had been no frank grappling with the problem except by those who solved it against us. The apparent silence of St. Thomas and the Scholastics concerning a problem unknown to their age had been taken as a solution by their over-timid followers. These latter deemed it necessary to deny the existence of such a problem, to refuse to discuss it, and, before any examination, to assert the capacity of the mind for knowing truth. "Certitude," they exclaimed triumphantly, "has forestalled doubt on the threshold of philosophy." But this *parti pris,* instead of engendering, could only shake confidence. Here Msgr. Mercier boldly substituted the tactics of radical sincerity. There was to be no longer an arbitrary affirmation, imposed on reflection and withdrawn from its investigation; no longer a criterion of salvage, embarking the menaced certitudes on incontrollable guarantees. For the mind's disquietude there is no other remedy but that of full clearness. To achieve it we must resolutely raise all possible questions without stopping, except at the point where there is no other question to put, where no distance longer separates the mind from its object, and where this object itself is disengaged from every admixture and every complexity. Before an object that is simple and immediately present, the mind can no longer put a question nor can it yield to further doubt. There is but one method for reaching this point where one holds the solution of every question: fearlessly to try the experiment of universal doubt.

Msgr. Mercier showed how St. Thomas and Aristotle had recommended this method; following St. Thomas, he brought the mind back upon itself and, instead of gratuitously asserting its aptitude for truth, made it touch that truth immediately in its judgments. Thus armed, he could follow Kant on his own terrain, and for the first time one could see the famous *Critique of Pure Reason* at close quarters with a Thomist in serried discussion. At the call of the master, the old stones of the traditional doctrine ranged themselves in a new order, where their solid and perennial qualities could repulse the assaults of scepticism. Thus one could *rethink* Thomism in function of contemporary problems and present-day needs.

To rethink Thomism: this formula has been stereotyped and is repeated throughout the world; now that the practical application of it has led to the formation of a vast movement whose victorious progress is daily asserting itself, account is no longer taken of the novelty and the daring for which it once stood. Msgr. Mercier was one of the first to conceive it and to give a concrete and practical example of its realization. Had he done nothing else, this alone would be worthy of immortal glory. In the history of thought achievements come slowly; they are the fruits of unremitting effort and loyal collaboration; they are within the reach of any one who, equipped with good sense and patience, will persevere in the endeavors prescribed by method. But to give to these endeavors new and precise direction, to divine and open up new ways, this is properly speaking the work of a genius,—work reserved for men of great initiative, and which for a long time guides the progress of learning.

But the *Critériologie* contained decidedly more than the indication of a way to follow: it was unquestionably an imposing construction. There one found the objectivity of necessary and universal judgments established, and the legitimacy of metaphysics firmly grounded against Positivism; there one found a very exhaustive discussion of all the doctrines which in the course of the nineteenth century had essayed to found certitude on subjective bases,—on faith, sentiment, or ethics. So, too, in various works the foundations of realism were examined and solidly established. The theory of substance was firmly fixed and given a happy and clear-cut explanation. Modern phenomenalism falls foul of an imaginative notion of substance; it substitutes the immediate, unavoidable, but as yet insufficiently disembroiled notion which our mind has of a substantial reality grasped in the very bosom of sensation. From this basis as a starting-point all metaphysics unfolded itself; it preserved a tight linkage with experience to the very end, up to the very proof of the first cause.[3]

In logic the value of the syllogism was clearly set free from the confusions of Positivism, while

[3] A young American philosopher, Fulton J. Sheen, a pupil of the *Institut* of Louvain, has published a notable work on the notion and proofs of God, entitled *God and Intelligence in Modern Philosophy*, London and New York, 1925.

the problem of induction found itself brought back to the metaphysical horizons which alone could give it its true import. In ethics, the foundation of duty, so often connected arbitrarily with the will of the Creator, was shown to consist in the exigencies of rational nature. The notion of freedom was very happily disengaged from the idea of a preference or a choice which gives rise to many difficulties. Finally, Aristotelian vitalism was brought into agreement with the advances of biological science, and here the ideas of Msgr. Mercier forestalled the orientation which has more and more taken shape with all who study the phenomena of life as a whole.

However, above all these theses it was necessary to point out a more general idea and one that would perhaps best mark the manner of the *ensemble* of Neo-Thomism and its relation to the diverse movements of contemporary philosophy. At different times Msgr. Mercier made it a point to denounce the mischievous effects of Cartesian dualism. To isolate "thought" and "extension" meant not only to break up the unity of man, but at the same time to multiply the insoluble problems which breed materialism, mechanism, idealism, and subjectivism. To isolate "science" and "ethics" in another domain was once more to spread the ferment of disorder and anarchy, the deplorable fruits of which we see multiplying around us. To separate "positive science" from "metaphysics" was to take away from the former the logical control and the sure groundwork of which it stands in need at every step, and to reduce the latter to a vague discipline and inconsistent poetry the manner of which each one would modify to please his own fancy. And in the end, do not all these unwholesome abstractions emanate from one primal source,—the divorce which, after the period of Humanism, gradually established itself between reason and faith, nature and grace?

In numerous pages of Msgr. Mercier's works one meets this general view of the history of modern thought. And there the dominant idea of his doctrine gives a masterly answer. The work of philosophy is a synthesis: it should unite all the powers of the soul, all the information furnished by science, all the points of view revealed by partial analyses, and all the divergent reflections which some over-narrow meditations have suggested to thinkers. Unity is at once the last word of the doctrine and the goal where the strifes of ideas can draw to an end in a beneficent collaboration. With good reason Msgr. Mercier sees there the fundamental trait of Scholastic philosophy and the profound cause of the successes to which it can still look forward.

In later years the growing burdens of his episcopal office stopped all personal publications by Msgr. Mercier. But the center of studies which he founded at Louvain has continued to show great vitality and ample development. The *Institut Supérieur de Philosophie* has at present eleven professors with about two hundred students. Among the latter some are specialists who devote themselves exclusively to philosophy and give their time to researches and private work. Others, pursuing various studies at the University of Louvain, come to philosophy for light on their work in science, law, or literature. All together they form the *élite* of the 3,500 students who pursue higher studies at the University. (In Belgium the studies corresponding to those of an American college are not made at the university.) There is another course in philosophy, less thorough, designed for the mass of the students.

In accordance with a method proper to it, the *Institut* of Louvain continues to bring renovated Scholasticism into close relations with the experimental sciences. It has a laboratory and a seminar of experimental psychology which is continually growing. Professor A. Michotte, director of the laboratory and an erstwhile pupil of Külpe at Würzburg, has for twenty years been organizing numerous researches in all the domains of experimental psychology; the results of these researches form the collection *Études de Psychologie,* published under the direction of A. Michotte, and well-known in the world of psychologists for the technical perfection of its experimental processes and the critical rigor of its methods. Many of these labors have attempted to attain a very precise experimental knowledge of the higher processes of attention, thought, and volition. To be sure, it is not a matter of solving philosophical problems along these lines alone; it is rather a question of seeing more clearly where these problems place themselves and to throw light on their solution by accumulating the data of experience upon which reflection will be able to construct its syntheses. This work of synthesis has not yet been reached. The laboratory methods of Louvain do not admit of hasty conclusions. Before passing on to ideas of the whole, it is indispensable to have pushed the programme of researches and experiments to the most complete fulfilment. But the experimental results obtained are of the first importance and have met with the greatest favor in the world of international science. To-day pupils of M. Michotte occupy chairs of psychology at the Universities of London, Utrecht, Milan, Toronto,[4] Ghent, and the labors of the laboratory are cited among the fundamental authorities in all works on psychology. When the conclusions on the *ensemble* appear, they will be founded on a solid basis.

Another collaborator of Msgr. Mercier, Professor Nys, has devoted himself to the philosophy of the sciences of matter. To him we are indebted for a monumental work, many times republished and revised. Under the title of *Cosmologie* he studies in four volumes the philosophic problems of the constitution of bodies, of time and space. This study is carried on at once from the viewpoint of

---

[4] We cite the recent work of G. B. Phelan, of the University of Toronto: *Feeling Experience and its Modalities,* Louvain, Institut de Philosophie.

the history of philosophical systems and from the viewpoint of theories and scientific facts. It shows how, of all the systems, the Aristotelian-Thomistic is that which best accords with the data of scientific experiment as well as every-day experience. Since the first edition of the work, the sciences have undoubtedly witnessed a profound change in all their conceptions; but M. Nys took special pains to remain *au courant* with these modifications, which leave his fundamental position unaltered. To-day, after thirty years of teaching, he is completely recasting his work in agreement with the latest scientific theories. On these, and particularly on the theory of Einstein, a young collaborator of M. Nys, M. Renoirte, has recently contributed a remarkable study to the *Revue Néo-Scolastique.*[5]

Among the main results achieved by the *Institut* of Louvain is the elaboration of a synthetic history of Scholastic thought. It is the work of Professor De Wulf. His *Histoire de la Philosophie Médiévale,* which just now appears in a new edition of two volumes,[6] is the outcome of more than thirty years of teaching. For a long time M. De Wulf has directed a seminar of medieval philosophy, out of which have issued numerous works of detail, publications of sources, and the resurrection of personalities hitherto unknown and of works hith-

[5] *"La theorie physique"* (November, 1923); *"La critique einsteinienne"* (August, 1924).

[6] The first volume of the English translation by E. C. Messenger has appeared. (Z.)

erto ignored. For the most part they have appeared in the collection *Les Philosophes Belges*, published with the aid of the Belgian government in the prosperous period before the war. But De Wulf's chief merit consists in having condensed the vast material contained in works which, during half a century and in all scientific centers of the world, have brought to light the life and the writings of the doctors of the Middle Ages. He is the only one, up to the present, who has disengaged from this immense mass the lines of a general history of ideas in connection with medieval life and civilization. The central thesis which he has constantly defended is that there existed in the Middle Ages a current of dominant thought joining the principal doctors into one school, of which St. Thomas is the apogee, and which rallies around a common philosophic system. I say, a system, and not an *ensemble* of coincident ideas, determined by external factors such as the authority of Aristotle and of the Fathers, the pressure of social environment, or the belief in Catholic dogma. A system, hence a whole, consisting of coherent ideas, united by an organic bond and engendered, it would seem, by one method. This system no doubt encounters opposition, but none the less it dominates the Middle Ages and its dominance is in proportion to the intensity and the value of the philosophic movement. Thomism is one and perhaps the most perfect form of it; but it is not the only one. In this way this system is truly the philosophy of the School; it gives to the latter its unity. Here, then, the term "Scholastic"—which since the Renaissance designates the philosophy prevalent in the preceding age —finds its natural meaning. It is the name of a doctrine.

And so we reach this conclusion: a doctrine is in its objectivity detachable from the environment in which it lives, from the contingent factors which contribute to its success, from the errors of detail attaching to it, and from the consequences that may be drawn from it. *Scholasticism* can be transported to our epoch; it must be *rethought* in function of the sciences of to-day and of contemporary philosophy: this will be the *New Scholasticism*.

Another collaborator of Msgr. Mercier, Msgr. S. Deploige, has devoted himself to the study of the social philosophy of St. Thomas. An important work, *Le Conflit de la Morale et de la Sociologie,* has placed him on a parallel with the works of the sociological school directed not long ago by M. Durkheim in Paris.

Have we still an ethics? Or has it dissolved into an experimental science of manners and customs?

The conflict between ethics and sociology is the outcome of old ideas. Step by step Deploige has followed the development of these ideas in all their ramifications since the eighteenth century; but of this vast and reliable erudition only the conclusions appear, in well-balanced and vigorous strokes. The reaction against natural law affects only the modern natural law, abstract, deductive, and verbal. In this reaction positivist sociology is the heir of criticisms repeated during the entire nineteenth century by various Catholic schools. The Thomistic method can take up on its own account whatever there is of the positive in modern sociology. This is in keeping with the spirit of that method which is founded on observation. But what practical conclusions are to be drawn from the laws deduced from observation? Here sociology comes to a standstill; it lacks a criterion and a theory of ends. The Thomistic method supplies both. Alongside of this basic demonstration, Deploige took occasion to pull down the sociological theses of Durkheim by disclosing their sources and unveiling their weaknesses. *Le Conflit de la Morale et de la Sociologie* aroused considerable comment and had a wide success.

In this manner the plan of studies outlined by Msgr. Mercier is being carried out in all directions by the painstaking efforts of his collaborators and followers. They also widened this plan, and by going beyond Scholasticism endeavored to regain immediate contact with the thought of Aristotle, as it is found not only in St. Thomas, but in the original Greek text; this they aimed to study with all the resources of philology, and at the same time with that philosophical understanding which is frequently absent in philologists and which an environment nourished by Scholastic thought can best reach. Under the direction of Professor A. Mansion, the collection *Aristote, Traductions et Études*, seeks to attain this end. It is to include a French translation, with commentary, of the works of Aristotle together with studies on the essential points of his teaching. This will also afford the opportunity of making a thorough study of the meaning of Scholastic notions by comparing them with their source.

However, since the time when Msgr. Mercier wrote, the movement of present-day philosophy, as stated above, has called forth forms of thought quite different from those which were contemporaneous with the beginnings of the new Scholasticism. On the other hand, the advances made in the historical studies on Thomism enable us to view it to-day in a manner which, while not fundamentally different, presents certain delicate nuances not descried at the outset. Moreover, it is not enough to stick to the letter and the surface of Thomistic thought; a deeper reflection should seek to grasp beneath this thought the foundations which it implies, but does not express.

While the philosophy of to-day is coming back to metaphysical problems, traditional metaphysics on its part can and should progress. For several years the Neo-Scholastic movement has been making very significant advances in this order. They are not yet completed, and it would be difficult to characterize with precision the work that is still going on. It can be foreseen, however, that in a few years Neo-Scholastic philosophy will be much more precise and detailed than it is now.

At the *Institut* of Louvain certain works were delayed by the war. Professor Noël has published *Notes d'Epistémologie Thomiste,* in which he seeks to give an exact exposition of the Thomistic theory of knowledge, and in particular to determine its starting-point by comparison with the ideas of M. Bergson and M. Blondel in France, and of the New Realism in England and America.[7] To him this starting-point seemed to be the reflexive verification of an immediate grasping of the real. On the other hand he shows how indirect realism is an untenable position. He points this out particularly in the instance of Kant, whose historical development he studies, disclosing his relations with decadent Scholasticism and with Thomism. Obviously, all this is but the point of departure of a complete theory and of a critique of knowledge which this work contains only in germ.

Professor Balthasar endeavors to make clear, from a critical viewpoint, the fundamental notions of Thomistic metaphysics. The articles he has thus far published are chiefly concerned with the "analogical" character of metaphysical notions, and in particular of the notion of "being." [8]

[7] A collaborator of Prof. Noël, R. Kremer, has recently published a work entitled, *Le Néo-Réalisme Américain,* which has been highly appreciated.

[8] *L'Etre et les Principes Métaphysiques";* also, *"L'Abstraction et Analogie de l'Etre.*

The *Collège Philosophique et Théologique* of the Society of Jesus, likewise established at Louvain, has for some time been a center of very remarkable Neo-Scholastic efforts. We will cite only the great work (not yet completed) of P. Maréchal entitled, *Le Point de Départ de la Métaphysique*.[9] With marvelous erudition the author traces the history of the critical problem from the Greeks on to contemporary philosophy, in order to show how the Aristotelian-Thomistic tradition contains the solution of that problem. Of this tradition he seems to offer an original interpretation, all the more interesting as it brings that tradition much nearer to certain modern doctrines, especially to the philosophy of Kant. This *rapprochement* does not suppress the existing differences; on the contrary, it tends to show more exactly where these differences lie by translating Thomistic ideas into Kantian terms and inversely Kantian ideas into Thomistic terms.

It would take too long to enumerate all the centers of study outside of Louvain, where Scholasticism is cultivated along scientific and modern lines. First of all, there are the numerous institutions of ecclesiastical studies where philosophy is studied in its connection with theology, and for the most part in Latin. The Neo-Scholastic movement has found its way into these institutions; while their chief aim is the study of the old Scholastics, to-day they are familiar also with the problems of

[9] Published by Beyaert (Bruges).

modern thought and science. It is with eyes fixed on these problems that the old masters are studied; and so these quarters, where a deep knowledge of the Scholastic tradition prevails, are able to bring much valuable light to the advancement of the movement.

Several periodical publications issue from the various religious Orders. The *Revue Thomiste* of Toulouse, and the *Revue des Sciences Philosophiques et Théologiques* of Kain (Belgium), are both published by the French Dominicans. Especial attention should be called to the excellent and complete *Bibliographie Thomiste* published by the former, and to the bulletins which the latter devotes to all branches of philosophy and which are quite the most complete and important to be found in the French language. The *Archives de Philosophie,* [10] published by the French Jesuits, also contain some very notable works. Then there are the *Études Franciscaines,* which make important contributions to philosophical questions.

From these same quarters have come works of capital importance for a knowledge of the history of Scholasticism and for the understanding of medieval thought. Here we can mention only the works whose chief aim is to bring Scholasticism in touch with modern thought. Very important are the works of P. Garrigou-Lagrange: *Le Sens Commun et la Philosophie de l'Être,* and *Dieu.*[11]

[10] Paris (Beauchesne).
[11] Paris (Beauchesne).

The author explains Thomism according to the loyally preserved tradition of the Dominican Order,
but the questions he essays to answer are those put
by present-day thinkers as to the foundations of a
demonstration of the existence of God. Another
work of the first importance is that of the lamented
P. Rousselot, *L'Intellectualisme de St. Thomas.*[12]
A genial thinker, unfortunately carried off by the
war,—he was killed in the battle of *Les Eparges*
while at the head of a battalion,—he could not
offer a finished conception in this work, which was
presented to the Sorbonne as a thesis for the doctorate in letters. Such as it is, however, it opens
up new horizons and reveals profound originality.
It seems that P. Rousselot sought to achieve a certain *rapprochement* between the philosophy of St.
Thomas and the recent systems of Bergson and
Blondel. This is clear especially in the articles he
contributed to the *Revue Néo-Scolastique* under
the title *"Métaphysique Thomiste et Critique de la
Connaisance,"* [13] and to the *Revue de Philosophie*
under the title *"Amour Intellectuel et Synthèse
Apperceptive."* [14] Some critics regarded this interpretation as a deformation of Thomism. Had he
lived, P. Rousselot undoubtedly would have attenuated certain paradoxical ideas; perhaps he wished
to insist on some disregarded aspects of a philosophy which is more delicately shaded than shallow

[12] Paris (Alcan); the new edition is published by Beauchesne.
[13] 1910.
[14] 1910.

commentators had led us to believe. At any rate he has pointed out the hidden bond that links some Thomistic theses, in appearance rather distant from one another, and he has well established the difference,—not always sufficiently stressed,—between the Thomistic theory of knowledge and a narrow intellectualism which could be coupled with Positivism.

Among the university centers connected with the movement of the Scholastic revival we must note the University of Fribourg (Switzerland). The teaching there is half in French and half in German. In philosophy, it is directed by the Dominicans and therefore permeated by the Thomistic tradition. Some very fine historical works as well as works on the relations of Scholasticism to the sciences have issued from this University. We may mention especially P. de Munnynck, whose articles on various questions of psychology and of the philosophy of nature reveal an extensive scientific knowledge.

In France the freedom of teaching is but imperfectly realized. The privileged position of State universities renders the progress of free institutions extremely difficult. On the other hand, the persistent disfavor with which the French State for a long time opposed religious ideas, has made it difficult for the Scholastic movement to penetrate into the schools under governmental direction. The free Faculties of Paris, Lyons, Lille, Angers, and Toulouse are valiantly and perseveringly contending with great obstacles. They are all centers of the Scholastic revival. At Paris, especially, in the favorable environment of a great city, the movement has taken on a remarkable significance. The Faculty of Philosophy has there been reorganized in accordance with a programme inspired by that of the *Institut de Philosophie* of Louvain. It publishes the *Revue de Philosophie*.[15] P. Peillaube, the director of this review and dean of the Faculty, is to-day amply rewarded for the enduring efforts he has devoted to the creation of a Neo-Scholastic movement in Paris.

From the viewpoint of teaching we should note one interesting result obtained at Paris. The free Faculty confers academic degrees on its students. But the French law recognizes only such degrees as are regulated according to a programme fixed by itself and obtained through examinations passed at the State universities. The students of the free Faculties are admitted to these examinations; but up to the present time, it was thought necessary to prepare them by closely following the programmes fixed by law and by the teaching of the official universities. Now, for some years the experiment has been made at Paris to present for the legal examinations students prepared in accordance with the Scholastic programme. The experiment has yielded most gratifying results, not alone for the licentiate degree, but also for that of bachelor, which, in France, is a degree marking the transition from

[15] Paris (Rivière).

intermediate to higher education, and is open to very young students. Of course the students trained in the Scholastic discipline are not directly and servilely prepared according to the directions of the legal programme; they know a certain number of things which this programme ignores, especially in metaphysics; but they likewise know modern philosophy and the philosophy of the sciences; what is more, they know things with a greater personal penetration because of the deeper principles they are taught.

The French free Faculties have made important contributions to the Neo-Scholastic movement. In the first place should be cited the work of P. Sertillanges, *Saint Thomas d'Aquin*.[16] It is the only synthetic exposition of Thomistic doctrine thus far achieved. There is no doubt that it faithfully expounds the teaching of St. Thomas in its historic form with constant reference to contemporary problems and presents a complete system of philosophy which can be placed on a parallel with modern systems.

At Lille, M. Dehove strives to put Scholasticism in touch with the data of present-day psychology. P. Peillaube is doing the same in Paris; to him we owe among others a notable work entitled *L'Image*.[17] In Paris, too, M. Voisine is very competently studying questions of the philosophy of nature, M. Simeterre is devoting himself with distinc-

[16] Paris (Alcan).
[17] Paris (Rivière).

tion to the history of ancient philosophy, P. Blanche expounds metaphysical doctrines with penetration, while M. Rolland-Gosselin studies problems of ethics and social philosophy. At Lyons, P. Valensin is making a thorough study of metaphysics in a spirit greatly resembling that of P. Rousselot, and we are indebted to him for various articles of great value.

We owe a special mention to M. Jacques Maritain. As a pupil of Bergson, and an *agrégé* of the official instruction, he discovered Thomism when his philosophic training was already finished, and that under the influence of ideas quite contrary to the Thomistic philosophy. He has a thorough mastery of modern philosophy, combined with a full knowledge of the natural sciences, especially biology. Scholasticism appeared to him as a novelty to which he forthwith became attached with the enthusiasm of a neophyte. And it is for this reason, and because of a reaction easily understood in a convert, that he manifests towards modern philosophy, and occasionally towards scientific method, a severity which at times approaches scorn. This cannot be regarded as the result of ignorance. Quite the contrary. If any one has the right to pass judgment on modern philosophy it is surely one who has received all the training it could offer, above all if at the same time he has a mind of a higher stamp; and this is certainly true of M. Maritain. One should rather ask whether he is not dazzled by the splendors discovered in Thomistic philosophy and whether he does not shut his eyes too much to the shadows which, like every human work, it contains, and which minds always nourished by this doctrine have become more accustomed to see there. But be that as it may, the work of M. Maritain belongs to those that will count in the history of French thought. It is not certain whether he would accept the title of a Neo-Scholastic; perhaps he would rather call himself a Scholastic, or better still, simply a Thomist. But he is playing an important part in the advancement of the Scholastic renaissance. Moreover, with his vigorous thought and perfect knowledge of modern problems he is, in spite of himself, a Neo-Scholastic in fact. When he combats the Neo-Scholastics' solicitude—in his opinion excessive—to study the moderns and to become familiar with the sciences, he perhaps forgets that for himself this work was already done when he arrived at Thomism, and that it is for this very reason that he understands its meaning better than others.

M. Maritain enjoys very great success due not only to the vigor of his philosophic thought, but also to the artistic charm of his style. Enthusiastic young students gather in large numbers around his chair at the free Faculty of Paris.

A collection of articles entitled *Antimoderne* [18] says enough by its title; perhaps it exaggerates the author's bent, inasmuch as M. Maritain is hostile only to modern errors and is far from living apart

[18] Paris (*Revue des Jeunes*).

from his times; rather, he believes that these very errors are of yesterday and already out of date. The dialogues called *Theonas* [19] contain, in a literary form that is pleasing as well as purposely archaic, very interesting discussions of actual problems. In *Réflexions sur l'Intelligence* [20] M. Maritain studies with great penetration the foundations of intellectual life. *Trois Réformateurs* [21] traces the decadence of the modern mind from Luther to Descartes and Rousseau. Finally, M. Maritain is working on a hand-book of philosophy which will unquestionably be a production of great importance. The *Logique,* the only part so far published together with the *Introduction,* thoroughly explains Aristotelian logic, such as it has been handed down and perfected by tradition; some intentionally summary remarks bear witness to a full mastery of contemporaneous works on logic.

Since the time when Msgr. Mercier wrote, the Neo-Scholastic movement has succeeded in compelling the attention of the most hostile quarters. As early as 1901 the German philosopher Rudolf Eucken noted the growing progress of Thomism in his resounding article: *"Thomas von Aquino und Kant. Ein Kampf zweier Welten,"* and pointed to Louvain as "the scientific center of present-day Thomism." Many others recognized the value and actuality of the movement. At Paris, M. Picavet,

[19] Paris (Nouvelle Librairie Nationale).
[20] *Ibid.*
[21] Paris (Plon).

who gave a course on medieval thought at the Sorbonne, in his chronicles in the *Revue Philosophique* regularly followed the progress of Neo-Scholasticism and noted its modern and scientific character.

To-day matters have taken on another aspect. The representatives of modern philosophy have begun to treat St. Thomas and the other Scholastics no longer as writers who may arouse interest but are out of date; rather, they look upon them as teachers from whom modern thought has much to learn. M. Étienne Gilson, who occupies the chair of M. Picavet at the Sorbonne, is perhaps not a Thomist, but he certainly is an admirer of St. Thomas, whom he regards as the father of modern thought, and shows Descartes' dependence on Scholastic thought in many points. M. Blondel, once an adversary of Thomism, is approaching it by ingenious interpretations. On every side the Scholastics are being studied with an interest which is growing sympathetic. This is perhaps the finest result of the long and patient efforts of the Neo-Scholastics to have their philosophy accepted by the modern world.

But while representatives of scientific thought are thus making a new place for Scholasticism in their preoccupations, others seem to be outlining an opposite movement. Violently hostile to modern thought, they are turning to Scholasticism to seek therein the formula, so to speak, of this hostility. To tell the truth, many of them know very little about the nature of Scholasticism. Such is probably the case with certain journalists of the group of *L'Action Française,* about whom one may well ask whether they ever read or understood one line of St. Thomas.   But better informed minds are also found in these quarters; such is M. Gonzague Truc, whose treatise, *Retour à la Scolastique* [22] reveals a very interesting state of mind.

M. Truc is not a Catholic; this is true of many of the leaders of the *Action Française.*   To-day no more than yesterday does it admit our fundamental theses, such as the existence of God.   But it feels itself attracted by the intellectual character of Scholastic thought, and contrasts it with what it regards as the far inferior qualities of modern thought.   Surely, this is a new attitude; it is not the fruit of a *parti pris,* but rather of serious study and, to use the words of the author, "the crowning of a long philosophical career."

This fact shows that Scholasticism has ceased to be a dead thought, and has again become a living thought, fully justified in looking forward to an auspicious future.

[22] Paris (Renaissance du Livre).

CHAPTER VII

THE NEO-SCHOLASTIC MOVEMENT IN GERMANY

By Dr. Bernhard Jansen, S.J.[1]

As Petersen has shown in his recent work on *Aristoteles im protestantischen Deutschland*,[2] in the seventeenth century even the system of Melanchthon was dislodged by Scholasticism, owing especially to the influence of Suarez. Conversely, during the period of *Enlightenment,* Christian Scholasticism to a large extent gave way to the specifically modern philosophy of Kant and Wolf. What is more, Catholic prelates were wont to send their most talented students to Königsberg, there to be initiated into philosophy by Kant.

During the era of *Romanticism,* of speculative Idealism, some highly gifted minds like Friedrich Schlegel and Joseph von Görres turned their attention to Catholic thought. However, quite in keeping with the genius of the times, they became im-

[1] Dr. Jansen was professor of philosophy for many years. He is now engaged in writing and editing philosophical works (some of which are cited in Part III), and is on the staff of that admirable monthly, *Stimmen der Zeit.*

[2] *Geschichte der aristotelischen Philosophic im protestantischen Deutschland,* Leipzig, 1921.

pregnated less with the more conceptual and deductive temper of St. Thomas than with the intuitive bent of the Fathers. The works of the Bohemian priest Bernhard Bolzano were destined to remain a barren and unknown capital for the time being. The attempts of Anton Günther to blend Christian-Scholastic with modern conceptions proved abortive. Also the speculations of Martin Deutinger on epistemological, religious, and esthetic problems met with little response owing to the frame of mind of Catholic Germany at that time, and to some of his peculiar conceptions.

Meanwhile the ground was being gradually loosened for the reception of Scholastic doctrines. This was in no small measure due to the bankruptcy of German Idealism, which followed close upon Hegel's death, and especially to the rapid development of the physical sciences. The positive factors working in this direction were the growing religious vigor of Christian life, and above all the rehabilitation of Plato and Aristotle. To be sure, this historico-philological and philosophical occupation was as yet mainly in the hands of non-Scholastic scholars like Schleiermacher, Zeller, Bonitz, and Schwegler. It was especially Adolf Trendelenburg who, by his substantial historical works and much more by his ingenious systematic theories, developed principles which are thoroughly congenial to Scholasticism. We need only call attention to his propositions on logic, teleology, and natural law. Trendelenburg exercised great influence on thinkers like

Franz Brentano, Otto Willmann, Georg von Hertling, and Friedrich Ueberweg.

As a real movement, however, Scholasticism gathered strength only in the second half, or more exactly, in the last quarter of the nineteenth century. It was encouraged to some extent by the then dawning Neo-Scholastic revival in Italy, in which men like Liberatore, Taparelli, and Sanseverino became prominent. Even before this, the Spanish philosopher James Balmes had done notable work in achieving a fruitful synthesis of the old and the new. His timely books, written in a lively style, received much attention in Germany. German scholars also drew nourishment from the works of French investigators of medieval philosophy like Jourdain, Victor Cousin, Rémusat, Hauréau.

A pioneer in the new movement was the *Philosophie der Vorzeit* by Joseph Kleutgen, S.J., published in 1860–1863. In a classic method of exposition, together with the constant analysis and appraisal of modern philosophy and its way of stating problems, Kleutgen produced a vigorous and lucid elaboration of the fundamentals of the Scholastic theory of knowledge and ontology; moreover, he set forth the medieval principles on nature, man, and God. At the same time Franz Clemens, Paul Haffner, Alois Schmid, Georg von Hertling, and especially Albert Stöckl grappled with the actual problems of the day from the Scholastic standpoint. In addition to this, Stöckl and Karl Werner dealt in a fruitful manner with the history of Scholasticism. Thus the intellectual treasures of the Middle Ages and of the sixteenth century, which had almost completely vanished from Christian consciousness, were gradually and vividly called to mind again. Modern philosophy scarcely took notice of this—with the exception, perhaps, of the historical treatises of Erdmann and Ueberweg. Prantl's *Geschichte der Logik im Abendlande* did indeed bring out sundry valuable details, but its author showed no understanding of the spirit of Scholasticism.

These favorable beginnings,—which of course had little to hope for from the philosophical tendencies then prevalent in Germany, with its all-dominating materialism, mechanism, evolutionism, and specialism,—witnessed the event which was to unite and increase the small forces hitherto working separately, and to make them fully conscious of their aim. On August 4, 1879, appeared the epochal encyclical *Aeterni Patris* of Leo XIII, whose genius for leadership, far-sightedness, conciliatory spirit, theoretical, political, and practical endowments held the whole cultured world in reverential admiration for a quarter of a century. He called upon Catholic scholars,—in the face of the disruption, scepticism, subjectivism, and materialism of the time, —to return to the objectivism, universalism, and idealism, the realistic theory of knowledge, metaphysics, the teleological and theistic world-view, natural law and theonomous ethics, of Scholasticism, particularly of St. Thomas Aquinas. On the other hand, with admirable broad-mindedness and far-sightedness for the progress of the individual sciences and modern criticism, he emphasized the duty of discussing and evaluating their methods and results, of working them into the assured heritage of thought, and, where necessary, of abandoning or modifying medieval theories for scientifically established truth.

As in other countries, so in Germany there now began a fertile era of philosophical investigation, which was constantly intensified and is being continued with unremitting energy; in the twentieth century it grew to such strength and eminence that to-day Scholasticism has attained a respectable standing in circles which formerly declined to give it any consideration or were positively hostile towards it. To-day not only is its relative, that is, historical value recognized, but it is even believed that in view of the triumphant breach made by metaphysics and the victory over historicism and idealism as a theory of knowledge, something may be learned from its content and method.

In point of time and psychologically, this rehabilitation was most effectively achieved by researches into the history of medieval philosophy, founded on a broad basis and carried on with the aid of modern ways and means. The high standing of the historical method and the empirical, positive mode of working on the one hand, and the deep-going antagonisms as to world-views between the Scholastic doctrine of being and modern Criticism on the

other, for a long time made this to be the most
effectual way of calling attention to the significance
of Scholasticism.

Even though the more recent editions of a Bonaventure, Thomas, and other Schoolmen were printed
abroad and but partly procured by German scholars,
nevertheless, owing to the philological, historical
and critical attitude of their editors, they met with
due consideration in Germany. The exact and
richly productive researches of two world-famous
scholars, the Dominican Heinrich Denifle and the
Jesuit Cardinal Franz Ehrle, proved truly epoch-
making. Since the nineties there have been appearing the *Beiträge zur Geschichte der mittelalterlichen
Philosophie,* by Clemens Baeumker, who has been
deservedly placed on a footing of equality with Zeller and Windelband. The twenty-five imposing
volumes of this series contain a great many new
texts and surprising new conceptions. The Franciscan and Dominican schools worked in the same
direction. The Scholastics of the Jesuit Order,
above all the great independent and critical metaphysician Suarez, were seen in a new light. Of
contemporary researchers may be mentioned,—besides Mathias Baumgartner, editor of the second
volume of Ueberweg, and Franz Pelster,—the in-
defatigable and prolific Martin Grabmann. He is
esteemed as an eminent Thomistic scholar and is
probably the best connoisseur of the manuscripts of
medieval Scholasticism.

The upshot of these labors, which science had to

recognize willy-nilly, is briefly this: the Middle Ages have a genuine philosophy, independent of theology and faith, that is, a science founded on reason alone, and with its own peculiar sources of knowledge, means of demonstration, and working methods. Scholasticism is not the monotonous, amorphous structure it was thought to be. The medieval period appears as an age instinct with life and vigor, marked by powerful tensions, various tendencies, diverse schools, violent contrasts. A significant and organic progress must be recognized in medieval thinking. Side by side with due respect for tradition and authority there is proof of a strong personal force and much critical discussion and appraisal of problems and opponents. Despite the predominance of the deductive method and the preponderance of the strictly conceptual way of thinking, there is evidence of a strong sense of reality, of experience as the point of departure, of respect for the material supplied by facts. Alongside of Aristotelianism there flows a powerful current of Platonism and Augustinianism. It is true that the critical investigation of knowledge, empirical psychology, and the history of philosophy are still far in the background; the methodical cultivation of the natural sciences is as yet unknown. All the more admirable, therefore, are the clarity and keenness of concepts and definitions, the momentum of syllogistic reasoning, the span, uniformity, and architectonic of systematization, and the wealth, depth, and clearness of the problems of reality there

treated. This holds true alike of theoretical philosophy,—with its exposition of rational psychology,
teleology, cosmology, theology, general ontology,
categories like quantity, time, space, relation, cause
and effect, substance, person,—and of practical philosophy, ethics, jurisprudence, and political science.

In the second place, the systematic works of its
representatives are naturally of great importance
for the standing of Neo-Scholasticism. To evaluate them objectively it is to be noted that their position is incomparably more difficult than that of the
representatives of specifically modern philosophy,
even than that of the adherents of distinct schools,
say, of Kantians, Hegelians, Spinozists. A thinker
who has his footing in Scholasticism and who acknowledges the truth of Christian revelation, when
critically discussing antiquated viewpoints of the
past, assimilating the assured results of modern philosophy and the positive sciences, and blending them
logically and systematically with the old, and hence,
even under the most favorable conditions, will never
appear as original, creative, personal in the eyes
of our times as, for example, the representatives
of the Baden school, Windelband and Rickert, or
even those of the Marburg school. Those at a
distance only too readily get the impression that
the old is being reproduced without deep intrinsic
analysis and appraisal, without the problems gripping the thinker in a living, personal way. Psychologically, though not logically, there is even the
danger of interior dependence and constraint.

That all these difficulties can be overcome is shown by men like Fröbes, Geyser, von Hertling, and Wasmann. That the Scholastic philosopher is theologically shackled, that the solution of problems is settled for him *a priori* by faith, and that therefore his work is but a verification or conceptual grasping of truths already established,—such are well-known objections against Scholasticism. It is, of course, granted that in case of an eventual contradiction between the outcome of his thinking and the dogmas of the Church,—not, be it well noted, mere opinions of theologians,—the Christian philosopher must revise the former. It would take us too far from the present subject to show how this is logically well founded and psychologically necessary. One point, however, should be emphasized in this connection: modern philosophy is not at all entitled to vaunt its freedom from presuppositions and its independence of authority; whoever has devoted a little study to the history and mental attitude of the moderns knows what is to be thought of these current fictions. For the rest, in many questions it is quite immaterial for dogma and theology whether this or that solution of philosophical problems is reached, as is evident from the differences and discussions between Thomists, Scotists, and Suaresians. Finally, faith as such never gives an intrinsic insight into the truths accepted; its motive and formal object is wholly the testimony of God. From all this it is clear that there can be no question of an aprioristic fixity and uncritical repetition of another's thoughts. One of the fundamental theses of St. Thomas is that the same truth cannot at the same time be known and believed.

After these preliminary remarks I shall give a brief survey of the main achievements of Neo-Scholasticism in Germany.

To begin with, there is a series of German and Latin text-books which treat either more conservatively or more freely all branches of Scholastic philosophy, with constant regard for the actual problems of to-day, and the inclusion of recent results. Their nature, number, and high editions indicate the quickened pulsation of intellectual life in Germany and the great progress made over the thirteenth and the sixteenth centuries. Such treatises on logic, theory of knowledge, cosmology, psychology, theodicy, and ethics are provided by Stöckl, Hagemann, Willems, Reinstadler, Steuer, Donat, Lehmen, Schulemann, the *Cursus Philosophicus* (6 volumes), the *Philosophia Lacensis* (8 volumes). Among the modern exponents of the theory of knowledge Joseph Geyser is prominent by virtue of his critical acumen, metaphysical vision, productive energy, and many-sided knowledge. In an eminently happy fashion he assimilates and blends the new and the old. As Geyser's way of viewing things manifests the decidedly Aristotelian type, so Switalski, in his works on the theory of knowledge and on psychology, shows an avowedly intuitive and

Platonic-Augustinian bent, directed more to the great metaphysical correlations. In the domain of natural philosophy may be mentioned *Die grossen Welträtsel,* by Tilmann Pesch. Though the work is no longer abreast of more recent research, it was none the less an achievement commanding respect at the time of its publication (1883), when mechanism prevailed. We can only refer to Stölzl, Pfeifer, Dressel, Schneid. Quite recently Schwertschlager (*Philosophie der Natur*) gives evidence of a significant fixedness of principles as well as familiarity with the auxiliary sciences, together with critical independence. It is well-known that Father Wasmann, the world-famous animal psychologist, combines speculation with experience and experiment, conservatism with progress in an equally felicitous manner. The works of Ettlinger tend in the same direction; moreover, he has applied himself successfully to the history of modern philosophy.

Psychology, especially on its rational side, as well as cosmology and theodicy, were cultivated by the versatile, erudite, mathematically well trained Gutberlet, editor of the Neo-Scholastic organ, *Philosophisches Jahrbuch.* Experimental psychology was furthered in model fashion by Fröbes and Lindworsky. The former, in his *Lehrbuch der experimentellen Psychologie,* professionally recognized as the best in this field, has brought together all the results of this young science in a manner that is clear and renders the material easy to survey.

Lindworsky, like his teacher Külpe, is engaged in investigating the higher intellectual and affective life of the soul. Marked success has crowned the thorough, lucid, and comprehensive way in which V. Cathrein treated ethical problems on an Aristotelian basis, after the mind of St. Thomas and Suarez. His detailed discussion of Socialism was highly esteemed by Socialists themselves. In his three volumes on *Die Einheit des sittlichen Bewusstseins* he shows, on the basis of extensive observation, the universal moral disposition of man. Here he comes in very close touch with the famous ethnologist Wilhelm Schmidt, the editor of *Anthropos*. The border domain of natural and Christian morals is ably treated by Mausbach. Beside Cathrein and Mausbach—and even prior to them—Georg von Hertling, familiar with the ways of the world and experienced in political life, energetically championed natural law as against Positivism, a task for which he was qualified alike by his studies in the history of philosophy and by his metaphysic, which took its bearings from Lotze. In a manner meeting with high and general esteem, Heinrich Pesch, brother of the above mentioned Tilmann, made a fruitful application of the principles of Scholastic philosophy to the social and economic order in his large *Lehrbuch der Nationalökonomie* (5 volumes). Otto Willmann, trained in the Herbartian school, is prominent in pedagogics and didactics. A rare speculative power and mental fertility characterize Hermann Schell in his constructive work on God and religion; he goes his own way, occasionally deviating from Scholasticism. In our own day the attempts to analyze and appraise the work of Scheler, who meanwhile has turned from Catholicism, have focussed investigations on the problem of God, and led to lively discussions on Augustine and Thomas, on the intuitive and abstractive knowledge of God; here Przywara and Geyser are prominent.

Besides these works, the *Philosophisches Jahrbuch,* the *Divus Thomas,* and other periodicals, we have the *Staatslexikon* of the Goerres Society and the *Lexikon der Pädagogik.* Recently a special institute for scientific pedagogy,—for research and teaching, and with a quarterly publication of its own,—was founded at Münster (Westphalia). The *Albertus Magnus Akademie für Neuscholastik* has been opened in Cologne; owing to economic handicaps, its beginnings are modest. In Salzburg, a short time ago, a faculty of philosophy was established at the Catholic University, which is gradually to receive further additions. In a three years' course the Jesuits of Innsbruck are giving lectures on Scholastic philosophy and its positive auxiliary sciences to students of the various faculties; the same is done by the Dominicans in Fribourg (Switzerland). In the many educational institutions for students of theology,—there are about ten such institutions,—conducted alongside the universities, philosophy is likewise eagerly cultivated. Many of the writers mentioned above spent a lifetime there in silent activity. In addition, there are the colleges of the various religious orders—the Benedictines at Beuron with Mager, the psychologist of religion, the Franciscans with the Scotistic scholar Minges, the Jesuits with their *Ignatiuskolleg,* where, besides Cathrein and Fröbes, the Assyriologist Kugler and the physicist Wulf are teaching. Furthermore, it is to be borne in mind that every German university with a Catholic faculty of theology is required by the State to have a Catholic professor in the department of philosophy to teach Neo-Scholasticism. In conclusion, attention should be called to the *Philosophische Handbibliothek,* [3] planned to consist of about sixteen volumes,—ten have already appeared,—which is apt to give the best insight into Neo-Scholastic endeavors and tendencies in content and method alike.

To these two main factors of historical and systematic productivity there was added a third, which considerably enhanced the standing of Scholasticism in non-Scholastic circles. In the first instance it is connected with the names of Husserl and Brentano, and harks back to Bolzano and Leibniz. The logical investigations of Husserl created a sensation by their energetic combating of psychologism, by their championing of the absolute character of truth and the proper position of logic. The *Phenomenology* founded by Husserl was for a time the most important tendency in Germany;

[3] Published by Josef Kösel and Friedrich Pustet K.-G., München. (Z.)

its method found many adherents and fructified the cultivation of various philosophical branches. At the same time the influence of Brentano, who, far removed from the world of academic activity, had hitherto affected a small circle of select thinkers, began to make itself felt in a wider field. The so-called Austrian school, with Meinong as its leader and scholars like Ehrenfels, Höfler, Martinek, and Witasek as members, had its origins in Brentano. Now Brentano, despite his breach with the Church, remained a lifelong and enthusiastic adherent and champion of the Aristotelian way of thinking, both as to form and content, and thereby indirectly paved the way for Scholasticism. What is more, Husserl himself was most strongly influenced by Bolzano. The latter's Scholastic conception of propositions in themselves, ideas in themselves, truth in itself, is to be found again in Husserl, even though only in a modified form.

Thus the ground for a certain *rapprochement* and understanding was prepared long ago. Occasionally these had appeared even earlier. Lotze's theory of knowledge, his metaphysics and idea of God lead through Leibniz to Suarez and St. Thomas. Grabmann has fully discussed Külpe's points of contact with Scholasticism. In their important investigations Driesch, O. Hertwig, Hartmann, Troeltsch show many traits that have a kinship with Scholastic thought. Reinke has struggled up entirely from his empirical, biological standpoint to an almost unqualified Scholasticism:

realism, an intellectually apprehensible world of being, life, teleology, soul, theism, ethics.

What since the beginning of the twentieth century was working consciously or unconsciously, intellectually or voluntaristically in philosophy and the individual sciences, in professional theories, in collective consciousness and the spiritual attitude of the educated, has burst forth with elemental force in the post-war period: a sobering down as to one-sided specialism and as to historicism, a passionate yearning for a deeper world-view and more adequate religious and ethical conceptions, a retreat from Mechanism, Idealism, and Criticism, a movement toward Realism, metaphysics, contemplation of the totality of things. In the year of his jubilee, 1924—the second centenary of his birth —Kant, hitherto a living force, was honorably entombed as a historical figure during the commemorative exercises at Königsberg, by Harnack, Vaihinger, and Driesch. And as early as the meeting of the *Kantgesellschaft* at Halle, in 1925, Heimsoeth, Hartmann, and other philosophers passed from the general programme over to the fruitful and detailed work of completing the structure of metaphysics. This also betokens a change of attitude towards Scholasticism,—a change which is clearly evident in the reviews of Neo-Scholastic works, say, in the *Kantstudien*. To mention a personal experience, small in itself but quite characteristic: before the *Philosophische Monatshefte der Kantstudien* appeared, the editor amiably ap-

proached the present writer with a request for a
dissertation on "The Significance of Scholasticism
for Metaphysics," because, it was explained, the
standing of Scholasticism made it desirable to insert
one or the other Catholic contribution in an early
number.

Having outlined the process of formation and
set the framework of Neo-Scholasticism, we must
now sound and appraise its spirit. What is its
programme? What its attitude towards medieval
thought, say, towards St. Thomas, or the later
Suarez? what towards modern philosophy, say
Kant? what towards the results of the individual
positive sciences? Does it recognize freedom of
thought, does it mean an advance over the Christian
past, does it exercise creative power?

It is self-evident that such a judgment in the
aggregate will remain one-sided and will naturally
shift with the shifting of the idea and ideal of philosopher and philosophy. He who lays the main
stress on the critical and the personal element in the
discussion of problems will apply a different standard than he who sees the task of the thinker in an
impersonal surrender to objective reality. The
strength of Leibniz lies in his universalism, his
breath of view, his adjustment of the old and the
new, his wealth of ideas; his weakness is the lack of
clear-cut concepts, of critical analysis. The reverse
holds true of Kant: his genius shines forth in his
way of stating problems, in critically following out

some few central questions; but the content shows gaps everywhere. Plato's greatness is conditioned by his metaphysical intuitions; despite all his errors of detail he remains one of the few great thinkers of all times. His pupil Aristotle has consigned to posterity an immeasurably greater number of lasting truths, and yet he stands far beneath Plato in philosophical depth and creative power. St. Thomas is the greatest systematizer and the foremost classifier of knowledge in all history, his works are conspicuous at once for their clearness and consistency; but for all that, our admiration is still more aroused by St. Augustine.

In the second place, one must bear in mind the intellectual attitude of our time if one is to pass a fair judgment on Scholasticism. The individual philosophical branches have received an intelligent and devoted cultivation. Critical self-examination and analysis have reached an almost incredible degree. The empirical substructure for the search after a world-view seems to be secured for ever more. Intuition, the abundance of ideas, the variations of the new and the personally elaborated excite a well nigh sensational and fashionable interest. In inverse ratio to the undeniable advantages stand the obscurity of ideas, the dialectic helplessness, the lack of organic, historical continuity and development based on the achievement of previous thinkers, the absence of understanding for the given world of reality, the want of detachment from the isolated self and of objective devotedness to metaphysics; finally, and above all, there is lacking the synthesis that fashions the results of individual researches into a uniform, harmonious world-view.

I can now attempt to submit my unbiassed opinion on the spirit and value, the excellences and defects of Neo-Scholasticism in Germany.

Measured by the achievements of the Scholasticism of the thirteenth and sixteenth centuries, the Neo-Scholasticism of to-day presents a much lowlier appearance both as regards power of thought and richness of speculation.   But instead, by far greater than at that time is the abundance of the material supplied by the positive sciences and to be philosophically assimilated, the wealth of the problems raised by the history of philosophy, the demand made on critical thought because of the progress of culture.   Moreover, the general philosophical *milieu* was but little favorable to Scholastic thought; indeed, it was rather a hindrance to it.   About the middle of the last century the Scholastic traditions had wholly died out; in fact, until 1900 the understanding for metaphysics, spiritualism, teleology, and theism was almost totally extinct; until recently there was the one-sided dominance of Criticism, Mechanism, exaggerated Specialism in psychology, theory of knowledge, and natural science.   For the most part Scholasticism met with disregard, derision, disdain because it was not known and, as is now candidly confessed, is not yet known to-day.

Finally, in order to form a just estimate it should

be remembered that our time has but few notable philosophical achievements to its credit. Measured by the Rationalism of the seventeenth century and the German Idealism of the beginning of the nineteenth,—not to speak of Greek philosophy and Kant,—the performances of even the more prominent thinkers of to-day, of a Brentano, Külpe, Husserl, Cassirer, Driesch, make but a modest showing. With philosophy it is much the same as with other cultural domains, say, the representative arts and poetry: it would seem that many generations must prepare the ground so that during a brief and fertile period of flowering one creative genius, or several, may gather up the fruits and bequeath them to posterity. If various signs are not misleading, hopeful times are preparing during these years for a significant rise of a teleological and spiritual metaphysics. Psychologism, Empiricism, Positivism, Mechanism were overcome years ago; to-day Kantianism, Idealism, Historicism, and Relativism are meeting with the same fate.

Taking all these conditions into due consideration, it must be granted that Neo-Scholasticism represents an important development, which is of great worth not only to its adherents, but to philosophy in general. To begin with, in the bosom of Neo-Scholasticism the imperishable fundamental views of Platonic, Aristotelian, and medieval philosophy have again become a mental heritage that is being worked out in a living manner.

To enumerate only a few of the fundamental propositions. One of them is the doctrine that our thinking reaches out beyond what is subjective and can know not only what is material, but also what is spiritual,—nay, can even lay hold of the Infinite, though only inadequately and analogically. Another is the conviction that at the bottom of all the changing phenomena there is a permanent substratum; this holds true not only of the world of physical phenomena or bodies, but also of the psychical occurrences or the personal Ego that determines itself freely and works itself out ethically. Another is the thesis that the world has a meaning, is purposefully arranged, is developed in accordance with law; that there exists an essential difference between lifeless and living substances, between the animal which acts by instinct, not by reason, and man, who has intuitive, conceptual, reflective, and spiritual knowledge, and who, on the higher side of his being, could not possibly have evolved from the beast. Another is the vindication of an order of morality and law which is independent of all positive, changeable, historically conditioned data, views, fashions, customs, arbitrary measures; the doctrine, moreover, that the family exists prior to the State, and hence the latter cannot be the final source of right and morality for the individual, but that, on the other hand, the State is a requirement founded on the immutable nature of man and thence has its proper rights and duties. The ultimate point of unity and support in this metaphysic,

the focus to which all its rays convergently bend,
is the necessary, uncaused, unchangeable, personal,
infinite Being whom we call God. He is the
fountain-head, not only of the existing order, but
also of the world of ideal possibilities and truths,
not only the Creator of the universe, but also its
supreme, absolute, and ultimate end.

The demonstration of these paramount truths,
—which like so many suns throw a flood of light
on all the groping, unfinished, sceptical, dismem-
bered, and dim phases of many modern systems,—is
brought about quite independently of Revelation,
the Bible, the faith of the Church, and theology.
It betrays ignorance and misconstruction of the
rational and scientific character of Scholastic philosophy to believe that its thought processes are
merely a verification of doctrines pre-established
by faith. Aside from the fact that the methods
and proofs are fundamentally different in Scholastic philosophy and theology, the impossibility of
the alleged position becomes unmistakably clear
when it is realized that many of the philosophical
theses are in no way vouched for by faith, and are
of no consequence whatever for the content of
dogma; hence the Church broadmindedly allows
opinions the most diverse, often quite divergent, or
standing in polemical opposition to one another.
Moreover, there is a further, highly important
point that proves convincingly the marked advance
of present-day Scholasticism over the past. Even
though the above mentioned fundamental truths

were the common property of early Scholasticism, the ways leading up to them are in many respects quite new. Confronted with the problems raised by the consciousness of the times, by the history of modern philosophy, by the gigantic progress of the individual sciences, in a word, by the objections and methods of to-day, Neo-Scholasticism in many instances had to furnish new proofs and open up new ways of approach. Compare, for example, the proofs for the existence of God as formulated by Aristotle or St. Thomas with those of a Gutberlet, Hontheim, Schell; or the earlier manner of establishing the foundations of religion with that followed, say, by Wunderle, Schmidt, Geyser, and Przywara. How scanty do the earlier expositions of substance, causality, consciousness appear beside the deep-laid, critically temperate, psychologically grounded investigations of a Geyser or Switalski. What rich historical, ethnological, and philosophical material from modern times has been analyzed in the researches of a Cathrein, Hertling, and Mausbach on the State, on law and moral philosophy: their monographs have essentially outgrown the works of the great moral philosophers of the sixteenth century. Another instance is Schwertschlager's *Philosophie der Natur*. His footing is on Aristotelian-Scholastic ground, yet he maintains a large measure of freedom, deviates from it in essential points, and certainly one-half of the problems treated by him had not even been raised before. Similarly Pesch, Stölzle, and Wasmann combine the old and the new. When von Hertling, Geyser, Gutberlet, Willems, —to name at random some of the Neo-Scholastic representatives of epistemology and metaphysics,— systematically analyze and discuss Idealism, Kantianism, Phenomenalism, and Relativism, they are handling problems which the Middle Ages did not even know.

This finally brings us to the much debated question as to freedom, flexibility, and the personal element in Scholasticism. Here we come forthwith to the parting of the ways. One who, like many moderns, sees the proper task of philosophy in the raising of problems, in living through the experience of doubt, in the individual aspect under which things are viewed,—generally, in what is new, and, on the other hand, regards the truth of the content as something subordinate, has, of course, almost unlimited freedom experientially or psychologically; personally and emotionally he will be strongly gripped by the awe, anxiety, incentives that go with the search for truth, and by the gratification of finding it. For the most part, therefore, his thinking will also be keenly alive to what is peculiar to the content and method of the present, and hence attractive for the moment and but little abstract. That these qualities are characteristic of the specifically modern philosophy far more than of Scholasticism is an *a priori* truth the confirmation of which is met with time and again in oral lectures and literary productions.

Scholasticism believes in a truth that is valid independently of the thinking subject; it believes in its organic and gradual disclosure and development; for that reason, like all other sciences, it builds on the assured results of the past. But, on the other hand, it also knows how infinite is the ocean of being and truth, how narrow and small the spirit of man, how, therefore, there are human ways of grasping wisdom and forms of presenting it that widely differ from one another. They are all different, and yet not false. Each one of them, from its own standpoint, sees the whole. This in turn conditions agreement in the final result, despite every difference of detail. A splendid and thoroughgoing proof of this is the synthesis of Platonism and Aristotelianism which was achieved in the golden age of Scholasticism. In Germany recently, side by side with the predominant Thomism, there has been a successful and fruitful revival of Augustinianism. The important but unfortunately too much neglected Franciscan school, with its Bonaventure, Roger Bacon, Aquasparta, Olivi, Scotus, is again receiving marked attention. I know full well that within Neo-Scholasticism there are also narrow, intolerant tendencies which on the whole would like to base our times on the thirteenth century. But this spirit,—prevalent, perhaps, in the Latin countries,—could not thrive in Germany. Precisely the most distinguished representatives of German Neo-Scholasticism, like Baeumker, Ehrle, Gutberlet, Geyser, von Hertling, Switalski, have always advocated a large measure of freedom.

In my books, *Wege der Weltweisheit* (Freiburg i. Br., 1924), and *Der Kriticismus Kants* (München, 1925), I repeatedly compare Scholastic with so-called modern philosophy, and seek to present the advantages and defects of each in an objective manner. I may, therefore, conclude these reflections with the wish that the representatives of both tendencies earnestly strive for a better mutual understanding, so as to complement and further their efforts. The goal of philosophy is truth,— and there is but one truth, objectively given. Its possession is an ideal to which we must ever aspire, but which we can never fully realize. It confronts every age with new and stimulating problems and for that reason holds the ever restless spirit of man in a tension replete with vitality. If on occasions the Neo-Scholastics have too faint-heartedly kept aloof from the advantages and achievements of the present, their opponents should be slow to censure them, for they themselves have been far more timid in avoiding contact with Scholastic philosophy. Only recently it is dawning upon them how many metaphysical treasures are stored in the depths and heights of Scholasticism.

CHAPTER VIII

ITALIAN NEO-SCHOLASTICISM AND ITS RELATIONS TO OTHER PHILOSOPHICAL CURRENTS

By Professor Msgr. Fr. Olgiati, of the Catholic University of the Sacred Heart, Milan, Italy [1]

I

THE Italian Neo-Scholastic movement, whose full and vigorous development centers round the *Rivista di Filosfia Neo-Scolastica* and the Catholic University of the Sacred Heart, at Milan, deserves special attention in its relation to other philosophical currents.

Until a few years ago, the attitude of our adversaries, who belong to various schools and champion the most diverse systems of philosophy, was one of Olympian disdain, of scornful silence,—broken occasionally by some ironic sally,—of utter indifference to Christian philosophy. Positivists, Kantians, Idealists, or, if names be preferred, Robert Ardigò, Cesare Lombroso, Carlo Cantoni, Francesco Fiorentino, Bertrando Spaventa, though hope-

[1] In a recent letter to me Professor A. E. Taylor of Edinburgh University wrote: "Professors Olgiati, Chiocchetti, and Gemelli seem to me the outstanding men of the Neo-Thomist movement in Italy at the moment." (Z.)

lessly divided among themselves, were at one in their
opposition to, and compassion for, the protagonists
of Thomistic thought, whom they regarded as poor
Egyptian mummies, disinterred by a papal encyclical
and exhibited in diocesan seminaries and monasteries for the admiration of obdurate obscurantists.

To-day the atmosphere is changed. It is true,
opposition between Neo-Scholasticism and the other
philosophical tendencies actually flourishing in Italy
continues, and from time to time finds expression in
lively debates. But Positivists and Idealists alike
respect our doctrines, devote essays and critical reviews to our publications, and, what is more, fully
realize that the Neo-Scholastic movement is en-
joying a fresh and promising spring, that it has only
just begun its task, and that it has a future. It no
longer causes surprise when the leading representative of Italian Neo-Scholasticism,—Dr. Agostino
Gemelli, who has shown such great wisdom and
marvelous energy in initiating this new cultural life,
so full of youthful vigor,—takes part together with
his colleagues in international congresses of philosophy, as spokesman for the doctrines of his school.
We all remember the splendid success achieved last
year (1924) during the International Congress held
at Naples, by the commemoration of the centenary
of St. Thomas, which the directors of the public sit-
tings intrusted to the illustrious Franciscan of
Milan.[2]

[2] The Very Rev. Dr. Gemelli is a member of the Order of Friars
Minor. (Z.)

The legal recognition which the Italian government has granted to the Catholic University of the Sacred Heart is another proof of this changed state of mind.   Whoever desires further evidence on this point has but to read the reviews that oppose us. I shall limit myself to quoting one of them, the *Giornale Critico della Filosofia Italiana,* directed by Giovanni Gentile, who, together with Benedetto Croce, is the foremost exponent of Italian Idealism. In 1923 this periodical devoted a long article[3] to *"The Most Recent Neo-Scholastic Activity in Italy."* Its author, Vincenzo La Via, a disciple of Gentile, praises the Italian Neo-Scholastics for "a characteristic attitude of theirs, growing ever more decided and conscious, of a sincere and lively preoccupation with the gravity of the problems put forward by modern thought, and with the difficulty and seriousness of the work to be accomplished if there is to be a true balancing of accounts with that thought."   He continues: "For this reason, as well as for the rigorous methods of study which make our Italian Neo-Scholastics so far superior to the few remaining Positivists, and above all for the spirit of honest and thoughtful search for truth which animates the better representatives of our movement, they deserve the honorable post of opposition to idealistic spiritualism,—an opposition neither insignificant nor sterile, but undoubtedly serving to clarify con-

[3] *Giornale Critico della Filosofia Italiana,* September, 1923, pp. 237–271.

sciences, inasmuch as it is not ingenuous nor extrinsic, but aware of the inherent difficulties of its task."

In like manner Vincenzo La Via expressed himself about the *Rivista di Filosofia Neo-Scolastica*: "The unceasing interest in the general movement of contemporary culture, which had previously been proved by the large space which the *Rivista* devoted to accurate information and bibliographical analyses, to numerous notices on cultural life and calm discussions of doctrine, not only did not abate in the years following 1914,—not even during the Great War during which the Neo-Scholastics gave a noble example of that serene and disciplined activity which distinguishes true scholars under such circumstances, —but rather continued to grow more intense; certain less disputable achievements of modern thought began to be regarded with an ever increasing sympathy, or at least with greater spiritual liberty and, what is of more importance, the critical and speculative efforts of Neo-Scholastics were concentrated more resolutely and visibly on the problems of contemporary idealism, which is the point of confluence of modern speculation."

I could add many similar quotations from Italian philosophical reviews which represent the various present-day tendencies and which, while combating our Thomism, are full of deference for our researches. But I prefer to seek for the innermost reason of such a consoling change of attitude, that is to say, for the motive which has changed disdain into esteem and silence to fruitful and elevated discussion.

II

We may synthesize the reasons for the progress achieved by saying that deeds are of greater force and value than words. On the one hand, the positivistic school of thought charged Neo-Scholasticism with not being abreast of the scientific conquests of to-day; on the other, the idealists looked with a pitying eye on a philosophy which was a system of the thirteenth century and which failed to place itself in contact with modern and contemporary philosophical conceptions.

To those who denied the existence of motion, the Italian Neo-Scholastics replied by setting themselves in motion. . . . In the first period, owing especially to the initiative of A. Gemelli, they devoted themselves to the cultivation of the sciences (such as biology and experimental psychology), which, because of their very nature, brought to the fore purely philosophical problems. The laboratory of psychology, for example, which to-day is under the direction of Father Gemelli, is the best among the laboratories of all the Italian universities, so much so that an adversary like Giuseppe Prezzolini, in a recent work on *La Coltura Italiana,* acknowledges that "the Catholicism of Gemelli and of those who work with him shows that it can hold its own beside everything: the microscope and the telescope, the card catalogue and the quotation of texts, studies in psychology and philosophy." It is true that the objection and the reproach is made against us of not having achieved "an intimate fusion" of our culture and our faith, and of resting satisfied with a merely external approach; but, prescinding from the fact that our adversaries know but very little about our religion and its assimilative power, no one to-day may venture to despise Neo-Scholasticism because of a lack of scientific culture. Besides, it is not the machines and instruments of laboratories which can raise a difficulty against our system; on the other hand, in the philosophical principles of old the follower of the metaphysics of St. Thomas finds many a precious treasure and a perennial soul of truth which can vivify all modern discoveries. To-day the very progress of the sciences goes to confirm such a position. While the mechanistic conception is losing ground, we see vitalism gradually asserting itself in biology, nor does it fear to appeal with Driesch even to the Aristotelian entelechy; and in psychology the introspective method is making rapid strides towards victory; in its final affirmation this method bids farewell to psychic atomism and to the conception of psychology as structural analysis, the while it turns to the study of psychology from a functional point of view.

In its second period, with a view to meeting the facts, the preoccupations, and the prejudices of Idealism, Italian Neo-Scholasticism plunged into the sea of modern philosophy. The works of Professors Emilio Chiocchetti, Amato Masnovo, Giuseppe Zamboni, Paolo Rotta, Dr. Antonio Padovani, and some of my works on modern thinkers, indicate the orientation of our researches. Anglo-American pragmatism, the idealism of Josiah Royce, the intuitionism of Henri Bergson, the philosophy of Kant, the systems of Benedetto Croce and Giovanni Gentile, the epoch of Humanism and the Renaissance, were all examined by us, amply and faithfully expounded, and honestly criticized. In the near future new and exhaustive works on other philosophers will make their appearance; and in the course of about ten years we hope with our united efforts, —now grouped around the Catholic University of the Sacred Heart in Milan,—to be able to devote a critical work to each of the great systems which have arisen since the Middle Ages. The fervor of research coupled with a strong and enthusiastic will vivifies the movement. In view of our publications it would be ridiculous for any adversary to charge Neo-Scholasticism with ignoring modern thought. They may of course aver that we have not overcome it, that our reasoning does not convince them, that they cannot accept our fundamental point of view, which is Thomistic: and as to all this we can well continue our discussion; but it would be pitiable for any one to insinuate that we are in the dark as to the results of modern and contemporary speculation.

For these reasons Neo-Scholasticism, in Italy at least, is no longer reproached with having little of scientific and philosophic modernity; the legend that we do not discuss actual problems or that our system is exclusively deductive is no longer repeated; even that other preposterous charge, formerly so generally made, has gone out of fashion, namely, that Neo-Scholasticism is not a true philosophy, but rather "a philosophy by decree," whose conclusions are imposed in advance by the Church, instead of issuing from the free exercise of human reason.

To be sure, we Italians have had certain conditions that were favorable to the dissipation of this last charge. Above all, Agostino Gemelli, the organizer of our movement, did not defend Neo-Scholasticism *a priori*. In former days he was a militant member of the positivist camp; but having become convinced of the truth of Christianity, he renounced everything and donned the habit of St. Francis. Together with divine grace, it was *conviction*, patiently and painfully acquired, and *not a decree*, that brought him to our ranks. A similar scene was repeated last year (1924). A young disciple of Giovanni Gentile, Professor Mario Casotti, —the author of several works on idealistic pedagogy, associate director of idealistic reviews, associate professor of philosophy,—abandoned his system, came to us, took the chair of pedagogy at the Catholic University, and made known his conversion in his book, *Lettere su la Religione*, based not on dogmatism, but on sound reasoning. Moreover, no one among the Italian Neo-Scholastics has any personal interests to defend, each has made and gladly makes heavy sacrifices for the Catholic University, and it is wrong to suppose that we are so lacking in good sense as to act in this manner in consequence of a decree, and not from a properly motivated conviction.

For the rest, when have we ever addressed our opponents in a dogmatic tone? At times it would rather seem that some one of their number is dogmatizing. In philosophy we follow the example of St. Thomas, who *reasoned,* and who was loyal to the principle that *locus ab auctoritate infirmissimus.* And there is yet another point to be noted: the attitude of the Italian Neo-Scholastics is in part quite new; hence it would be absurd to regard it as determined *a priori.* It will be to our purpose to say something more on this last point, so as to indicate what, in my opinion, is the *essence, the scope, and the method of Neo-Scholasticism* as it is being slowly elaborated in Italy. But as the movement is still in a stage of formation, one cannot exact full precision on this point nor look for unanimous agreement. I shall trace along broad lines the opinion which I prefer.

III

The greatness of St. Thomas undoubtedly consists in the immortal synthesis he has given us of the entire culture of his time and of antiquity. He represents the systematization of all the thought that went on maturing from the pre-Socratic thinkers through Socrates, Plato, Aristotle, St. Augustine, and all the living currents of his own time.[4]   Leo XIII and his successors have designated him as the Master of the Catholic schools, not because to single out St. Thomas means to exclude the other great Christian thinkers, but to point out his marvelous effort at synthesizing in one organism the living parts of truth found everywhere.

Does this mean that there was no progress in human knowledge after St. Thomas, or that he is the goal rather than a beacon-light?   No one who believes in the action of Providence in history can for a moment suppose that God has abandoned the modern and contemporary world to the devil.   God employs the errors and evils of the past and the present to compass the triumph of truth and goodness.   As I see it, then, it is imperative to conceive St. Thomas not only as he is,—that is to say, in relation to the whole of ancient culture,—but also in relation to all the achievements of the centuries that followed.   Hence it is necessary for the Neo-Scholasticism of the twentieth century to take into account the progress that has been made from the Middle Ages on, in every field, but above all in that of science and philosophy.

I know that our Idealists will object: "Ancient philosophy, as well as Thomism, is a *philosophy of being* which thought mirrors, thus originating the

---

[4] Dr. Olgiati has shown this lucidly in his work *L'Anima di S. Tommaso,* which I have translated: *The Key to the Study of St. Thomas* (B. Herder Book Co., St. Louis, 1925).   (Z.)

dualism of object and subject, and of an object that *transcends* thought. Instead, modern philosophy, —from Descartes on, and especially through the work of Immanuel Kant and those who came after him,—is a *philosophy of the subject,* and of a subject that *creates the object,* and as a consequence implies absolute *immanence* and monism." I also know that the Positivists interpret the modern epoch as a gradual elimination of the Transcendent whose place is taken by Nature. But it is precisely upon these points that we take issue with our opponents. To our mind the modern and contemporary era has neither done away with God nor eliminated being, and for that reason it has not destroyed the validity of the Thomistic synthesis. In my judgment the value and significance of modern speculation and history is quite different. While antiquity and St. Thomas studied reality chiefly by means of the *abstractive process,* modern thought and culture studied it by the *method of concreteness*. But as there are but few who have clear and distinct ideas about "abstract" and "concrete," it will be well to begin by giving a precise definition of these concepts. This will also serve to obviate misunderstandings and solve many objections.

1. What is *abstraction?*—A thousand preconceptions conspire to becloud the true meaning of abstraction as it was understood in pre-modern philosophy.

I look at a plant and, prescinding from the rest

of the plant, concentrate my attention on one of its leaves. I have an image, a representation, and I regard only one side of it. I view a battlefield and consider only one wounded soldier, without concerning myself about the others. When I do this, when in the consideration of a concrete object I analyze it into its *concrete* elements, study one of them and prescind from the rest, have I performed a true act of abstraction? Many modern scholars maintain that I have; of course, if they wish to call such a process "abstraction," they are free to do so, but it is not true philosophical abstraction.

According to the older thinkers, true abstraction does not take in one of the elements as distinguished from the rest, but it reaches the *nature* of a being and tells us what a thing is—*quid sit res*. When the mind considers a determinate circle, for example, the metaphysical abstraction does not consist in regarding the material with which it was drawn, and prescinding from the rest, or in fixing attention on this or that particular note of a given circle, but in grasping in *this* circle the *nature* of circle, in laying hold of that which makes it to be a circle and not a square.

When I perform such a mental operation, that is, when I prescind from the individualizing notes, from particulars, from the individuality of a being or an image, so as to confine myself to their nature, then I have the true *abstract idea,* which I call *universal,* inasmuch as it may be repeated in an indefinite number of things.

Now then, in my opinion the process of abstraction,—the fruit of centuries of philosophical speculation,—gives us the true character and temper of all pre-modern philosophy, in so far as this philosophy was, in a particular manner, the study of being, of reality, by means of abstraction.   The pre-Socratic thinkers prepared the way for the discovery, and it was only by means of the *concept*, of the abstract, that Socrates could overcome the Sophists.   Plato enlarged the field of the Socratic concept, limited by his great predecessor to "human affairs," to the interior life, to the subject; and the Platonic *ideas*, —whether we consider the system from the point of view of knowledge or of metaphysics,—are nothing else but the abstract regarded as eternal, immobile, perfect.

The discovery of Aristotle is the *form*, that is to say, the Platonic idea, no longer wrenched from things and existing separately, but immanent in them as the innermost dominating force that pervades the elements, coordinates them, synthesizes them, as the intrinsic principle of the nature and the specific activity of every being.   And what else is abstraction but the concept which gives us the *form* of things?   For the Stagirite our conceptual knowledge is a knowledge of forms and through forms; and St. Augustine, too,—despite his profound sense of interiorness and his programme of *"in te ipsum redi, in interiore homine habitat veritas,"*—remains within the orientation peculiar to the abstractive process.

The fundamental intuition, the germ and explanation of all Augustinian philosophy is *veritas,* truth, which in the depths of his soul the great thinker of Hippo contemplated as eternal, immutable, perfect, and which was not explained to him by the becoming of the world nor by our Ego, but only by God. And this *veritas* (which, as was well observed by the Thomists later, is nothing else, but the result of abstraction) is really the abstract; it is that which gives us the *ratio rei,* the nature of a being.

It is scarcely necessary to insist that St. Thomas remains unintelligible to those who fail to study him from this point of view. If we were to take away *abstraction* from his philosophical doctrine, everything else in it would crumble—from the theory of knowledge to the metaphysics of *being,* from psychology (where abstraction forms the convincing and conclusive proof for the spirituality and immortality of the human soul) down to theodicy.

And were not all the discussions about *universals* carried on with the origin and validity of the abstract as the central point of debate? *Nominalism* reduced the abstract to a name; *Conceptualism* resolved it into a pure concept of the mind; *Exaggerated Realism* gave it an existence in things, even in so far as it was abstract; *Thomistic Realism* closed the question by adopting moderate realism.

To conclude: in pre-modern times there were, of course, philosophical currents with an orientation toward concreteness. And it was natural that there should be, inasmuch as abstraction is not sufficient for *life;* and as at that time, despite the vigorously flourishing speculation, life also had its rights to assert, it is not surprising that from time to time a strong craving for the concrete made itself felt in the scientific, religious, and moral domains. Mysticism, Stoicism, Epicureanism,—to mention only a few examples,—yield to it; and the significance of a Roger Bacon, and still more so of the Nominalism of Ockham, clearly manifest the same urgent demand.

But if we view the broad stream of pre-modern philosophy,—not secondary and lateral rivulets,— if we fathom the soul of that philosophy, we cannot but recognize its outstanding characteristic to be *the study of reality by means of the abstractive process,* provided the word "abstraction" be taken in its true metaphysical sense.

2. But does this abstractive process comprise all knowledge and exhaust the domain of reality? By no means. If I know only the essence of a being, if, for example, I know that Paul, with whom I do business, is a man, I know very little about him. If I knew of an action *only* that it was performed freely, I should know nothing about its particulars, its individuality, or, as the Scholastics put it, the *individualizing notes* of this action. After the study of the universal there evidently had to come an epoch in which the eye would turn to the *individual;*

after the era of *abstraction* bourgeoned the era of concreteness.

The attempts to satisfy the pressing needs of concreteness by the abstract were made in vain. The makeshift was worse than the lack of any remedy whatsoever. For it stands to reason that when one tries to apply to particular elements, to individual notes, to the manifold, to the concrete, what belongs only to the universal, to the abstract, to the principle of unity, one no longer remains in the field of abstraction, but passes into that of *"abstractism."* If, for example, in the study of astronomy one should attempt to follow the motion of the stars not by means of observation or the telescope of Galileo, but by the principles of metaphysics and the criteria of Cremonini, one would fall into an abyss of errors, —and that not through the fault of abstraction, but because of an abstractistic, illegitimate procedure.

As the pre-modern era had devoted itself *especially* to the philosophic examination of the *nature* of reality, so modern times had to dedicate themselves *especially* to the research of the *concrete*. And by this term I mean, in general, everything that is real, but does not belong to the essence of beings. Thus we have concreteness when psychological investigation does not stop short at the nature of the Ego, but proceeds to scrutinize the Ego in its development, in the origin of its ideas, in the association of its images or percepts, in the variety of its utilitarian tendencies, in the pulsation of its moral life, in its uninterrupted duration caught in its full richness, in its activity taken in the widest extent, in the whole of is phenomenology, or also in its subjective unity which has the function of a presence unifying the psychic facts, and, finally, in its own little history as organically linked with the great history. We have concreteness when we investigate the phenomena of the universe, no longer regarded in their essence, but in their particularity. The same holds true of the mechanistic method, and the efforts of the scientists to utilize (not to comprehend) the natural forces; of the researches about the evolution of the worlds and of living organisms; in a word, of all modern science in its various branches and manifold applications. We have concreteness when human acts are viewed as they issue from the root of freedom, in their full and precise individuality and their relations to all other facts. We have concreteness, therefore, when we place a fact within the texture or framework of history, or when we see the individual in the whole, search out the organic linkage of affairs, in short, when we consider reality historically. And it goes without saying that there are *varying degrees of concreteness.* No one, for example, would liken the sense of concreteness in *l'action* of Blondel to that of Anglo-American pragmatism; no one can confuse Baconian concreteness with that of Giambattista Vico.

Now, beginning with Humanism and the Renaissance, there was this change of direction in philosophy. During that period investigation overlooks the nature, the essence of beings, the abstract, the universal; with eagerness and confidence it turns to the particular, the individual, the concrete.   In art and literature, in politics and pedagogy, in religion and jurisprudence, but above all in philosophy and science, we can verify this new orientation, as I have shown in my work on *L'Anima dell' Umanesimo e del Rinascimento.*

The psychological study of man in his rich complexity; art, which is not the abstract universal but the individual, the concrete beauty and harmony; the ancient codices, ancient culture, ancient history; effectual truth in politics; interiorness in religion; the particular in the universal, or the individual in the whole, in philosophy; nature explored, subdued, dominated; nature, the object of aspiration in the discoveries of Columbus, in the attempts of magic, in the researches of astrology, and, finally, in the new scientific methods of Leonardo and Galileo,— in a word, every manifestation of thought and life in this period presents this physiognomy and vibrates with this soul of concreteness.   The true conception of abstraction disappears, it is forgotten, it is confused with "abstractism," it is scorned because it does not seem to answer to the new exigencies.

In Nicholas of Cusa the *universal,*—as was to happen later in all modern philosophy,—takes on a new meaning: it is no longer referred to the abstract, but to the whole concrete.   Being, reality, is not considered with a view to grasping its essence or nature, but with the aim of seeing the organic nexus of the singular with the whole of reality. Nicholas has a most vivid sense of concreteness; perhaps no one more than he was permeated and inspired by the soul of the epoch: every theory, every work, every line of his says it in a thousand ways. The same holds true of the other philosophers of the Renaissance, especially Giordano Bruno. The Sceptics, too, of this period, from Ramus to Sanchez and Montaigne, questioned only the validity of ancient science, that is to say, of the abstractive method and its results, but they were eager for things, for experience, for the concrete individual.

Leonardo and Galileo were bent on the inculcation of this programme: we are not to waste our energies in the conceptual elaboration of reality, but should turn them to the consideration of nature, to observation, to experiment, to the connection existing between phenomena, in a word, to the realm of the concrete. They wished to be well rid of the encumbrance of a "pseudo-philosophy" (which was no longer abstraction, but "abstractism"), and to put scientific concreteness in the place of the philosophic concept.

The difference, therefore, between Aristotle and Galileo is a difference of attitude in the face of reality. Aristotle, too, was a great observer, keensighted and patient, athirst for facts, eager for experience, filled with an insatiable curiosity that reached out to every domain, from botany and biology to the constitution of States; he truly set out on the "hunt of Pan" many centuries before Bacon came to advocate it. But at what did Aristotle aim in his search and examination of facts? At the *form*, that is to say, the essence of beings, the *knowledge* of things in their profound reasons and nature. All this has no interest for Galileo. He starts from experience with the purpose of dominating things. And to achieve this dominion he has no need of the *essence*, the abstract, but of the concrete, which he studies by means of the mechanistic method and the application of mathematics to physics. Aristotle scrutinized reality from the viewpoint of abstraction, Galileo from that of concreteness.

In like manner Socrates and Montaigne analyze the *subject;* but what a difference between the two! To Socrates the Ego reveals the *concept,* the abstract; to Montaigne, on the contrary, the Ego appears in its concrete richness and gives him, not abstraction, but our living personality with its tendencies, its innermost character, its particular coloring. Not only Humanism and the Renaissance, then, but the whole of modern philosophy is stamped with the same characteristics.

I do not deny that at least some of its great representatives devoted special attention to the *subject;* neither do I deny that (not all, but) some systems contain theories which, taken in themselves, are opposed to the ancient doctrines (just as in these, too, the various thinkers defend theses that clash with each other) ; I only maintain that the historical significance of modern thought and life does not consist in the affirmation of nature as the center of all things, nor in the immanentistic and monistic tendencies, but in the various achievements of concreteness.

What is important from the historical point of view are not so much the intentions, the illusions, and the expressions of this or that person, but the real influence which such illusions, intentions, expressions exercised in the development of thought. And, besides, to appraise a system, one should not stop at one or the other of its parts, but should reconnect every point with the whole system and then interpret it according to the fundamental intuition that animates the single theories. But it is only too true that in our days there is not much exactness on either requisite. The point of departure is an initial preconception: "Modern philosophy must be monistic, immanentistic"; and instead of a faithful reconstruction of the whole thought of a philosopher, we distort it by clever manipulation; here and there a selection is made of those passages which seem to favor one's own aprioristic principle and, either gently or violently, a thinker is laid on the Procrustean bed of one's own system. Small wonder, then, if the entire history of modern philosophy takes on the meaning which one has aimed to impose upon it *a priori*.

One should begin, instead, to rethink the doctrines of one philosopher after the other without any preconceptions. Then it will become clear, for example, that in Bacon of Verulam there is no affirmation of the *subject,* but that the true key to his thought is furnished by that special kind of concreteness which means the utilization of nature through the method of scientific induction. It will become evident that Giambattista Vico was never an immanentist, no more than Descartes, Malebranche, Pascal, Berkeley, Leibniz. It will be seen that even the immanentism of Spinoza should not make us forget the thesis of his *Ethics,* according to which the intellect and the will of God are to our intellect and will as the *"canis, signum caeleste"* is to the *"canis, animal latrans";* and that,—to refer to another thinker,—the affirmations of transcendence in Fichte are such as to lead many immanentists to suspect that there are two philosophers in him. In short, just as the method of the Positivists,—who in the various periods of the history of philosophy see nothing but a preparation for the scientific period,— is shown to be wrong inasmuch as science is not the *soul* of modern philosophy, even though in many philosophers it furnishes a *material* by no means to be despised, so in the case of Kantianism and Idealism we must protest against the deformations,— now in vogue and blindly accepted,—which, for example, place the *soul* of all modern systems in absolute immanence, in the gradual elimination of being and the affirmation of the *subject* as the creator of reality.

The single systematic constructions, taken in the spirit that animates them, are not an expression of such theses, but represent partial conquests of reality, no longer studied in its nature, but in its concrete determinations, From Bacon,—who in an epoch of scientific discoveries extols the utilization of nature and seeks to find the key to its domination through *induction,*—to Vico and Hegel, who teach us the meaning of history; from the psychogenetic conceptions of Locke to the keen analyses of the sentiments and affections made by the English sentimentalists, and to Bergson's study of the real duration of consciousness; from the glorification of the Ego during the whole romantic period to the *action* of Blondel and the "historicism" of Croce: always and everywhere there is heard but one voice—the voice of concreteness.

3. Does Neo-Scholasticism, then, accept modern philosophy? The answer can now be readily given, inasmuch as it flows from the premises just stated.

If modern philosophy had the meaning attributed to it by the Positivists, the Kantians, and the Idealists; if, for example, it consisted in the reduction of the object to the subject, of being to thought, Neo-Scholasticism evidently could not give adherence to the philosophic speculation developed from Descartes,—and, also, from the Renaissance,—down to our own time. Moreover, if the acceptance of modern philosophy implied the favorable reception of all the theories upheld by the various thinkers, then not only the Neo-Scholastics, but all would be constrained to reject it. How, for example, could a Hegelian idealist like Giovanni Gentile accept the theory of Pascal about God, of Leibniz on the monads, of Kant on the *noumenon?*   And how could we Neo-Scholastics subscribe to the materialism of Büchner, to the pantheism of Hegel, to Gentile's conception of the spirit as a pure act of thought?

The only plausible meaning of the question is this: given that several centuries of thought and life cannot be considered as representing only purposeless errors; given, therefore, that modern philosophy must have a meaning and a value; given that such meaning and such value consist in the fact that, in opposition to pre-modern philosophy, whose orientation was towards reality as grasped by an abstractive process, the new epoch tends to lay hold of reality in its concreteness,—given all this, we may reasonably ask whether Neo-Scholasticism can and must accept modern philosophy?

For us the answer is beyond doubt affirmative, because it seems to us that although *abstraction* and *concreteness* stand for different ways, they are nevertheless not opposed, but must be used to complement each other.   We are, in fine, *Neo-Scholastics* because we recognize as eternally true certain results attained in the domain of philosophy by our pre-modern thinkers, especially St. Thomas, through the abstractive method: we believe, moreover, that in metaphysics, taken in its Thomistic meaning, no new discovery has been made since the Middle Ages, and that no one has explored reality from the viewpoint of its nature and essential notes with greater perfection than the great Greek and medieval thinkers.   But we are *Neo-Scholastics of the twentieth century,* who propose to synthesize into one organic whole the immortal truths of pre-modern thinkers with the contributions made by modern times in the scientific and philosophical investigations of concreteness. Such is our programme, our method, our system. Such too, perhaps, is the battlefield on which will take place the philosophical engagements of the future. Such, at any rate, is my Thomism and such the reason of our opponents' attitude toward Italian Neo-Scholasticism.

CHAPTER IX

SCHOLASTICISM AND AMERICAN POLITICAL PHILOSOPHY

By M. F. X. Millar, S.J., Professor of Constitutional Law, Fordham University

THE problem most congenial to the American mind would seem to be that of organized social life. But as the problem has come to present itself, especially since the war, there is an urgent need for an intelligible account of life, and especially of the part that affects social relations and political institutions. But the American mind has thus far concentrated its attention on the practical problem and disdained speculative considerations.

There is a grave necessity for a sound intellectual accounting for the realities of life if the practical problem is to be properly approached. The recent tendency has been to trust to mere organization [1] and manipulation. The present demand is for standards wherewith to evaluate the present and past organized conditions of society, and to judge of

[1] Bertrand Russell in *Icarus, or The Future of Science*, p. 28, has well said: "To a rational mind the question is not, do we want organization or do we not? The question is, how much organization do we want, and where, and when, and of what kind?"

what should be done in the future. The consciousness that our former exuberant energy can no longer
indulge in the hit and miss policy, and finds itself
confronted with complex problems for which intellectually it is all too little prepared, is at present
engendering something of a dangerous scepticism
that leads so easily to a spirit of indifference and
surrender. Nothing short of an intellectual sifting
of our institutions and social traditions, whereby
the nation as a whole will be brought to share [2] in a
common understanding of what is sound, and will be
in a position to criticize fairly and intelligently what
needs amending, can keep us on the path of normal
development. There must be enlightenment in the
sense of education taken in the etymological meaning
of the word if there is to be any proper deepening
and enlargement of character.

This implies that we are faced with a twofold
problem, that of convincing the American mind that
there are such things as abiding standards involving
immutable and universally applicable principles, and
that, morally speaking, all persons, by reason of the
natural disposition of their minds, can be brought
to recognize these and appreciate their value. The
problem is clearly not one for the politician, the ora-
tor, the social engineer, or the political scientist, but

[2] "A law is in a person not only as in one that rules, but also
by participation as in one that is ruled. In the latter way each
one is a law to himself, in so far as he shares the direction
that he receives from one who rules him." (*Summa Theol.*, I^a II^ae,
qu. XC, art. 3, ad 1.) The quotations from St. Thomas are taken
from the Dominican translation, except when otherwise noted.

for the philosopher, who should courageously take his stand on the higher ground of intellectual speculation, and give the law to the former, especially to the political scientists, regardless of their supercilious attitude, their grand "scientific" assumptions, their tendency to monopolize the whole field to the exclusion of philosophy, all of which is attributable to minds improperly trained and ignorant of their own proper powers.   As one recent author has put it, "Intellectual restoration is the condition of political and economic restoration." [3]   This is precisely the phase which the political and social scientists insist on overlooking in their determination to confine themselves to purely inductive methods.   In the words of one writer (whom we quote merely by reason of his statements being typical of what we have in mind), "The statement of the social objective in progress is an evolution of the substitution of new and ever more highly objectified and inclusive, as well as constantly more rigorously tested generalizations regarding the ultimate consequences of human adjustments, for the older and narrower, more subjective and less inclusive and less accurately tested generalizations regarding the ultimate results of human social adjustments."

With such an aim, looked at from the strictly scientific viewpoint, we would not quarrel even on the ground of its pretentiousness.   But when the same writer solemnly informs us that "only gradually have we come to see that there are no fixed entities

[3] F. J. Sheen, *God and Intelligence*, p. 8.

or absolutes back of our generalized viewpoints, and that the cosmos, nature, even our own narrower social world, are only ways of looking at things in orderly fashion from a human—though objectified—viewpoint," [4] we easily recognize the *parti pris* of the scientific dogmatist, who insists on pulling the wool over his own eyes and paying himself in words whenever he touches on things outside the sphere of his own special knowledge. This tendency, so marked in the case of those who inherit a Protestant culture, to thrust out of all consideration whatever appears to conflict with one's own point of view, reveals in modern form a mental disposition that derives traditionally from that *fiducia* [5] or self-

[4] L. L. Bernard, *The Concept of Progress,* Social Forces, Sept., 1925. Walter Lippmann, in a work otherwise deserving of real consideration, in this respect starts off on the wrong foot with a statement that, "to judge the whole universe, you must, like a god, be outside of it, a point of view which no mortal mind can adopt," turns to "the realm of man's interests and purposes and desires" and concludes: "There is no human point of view here, but only points of view of men. None is valid for all human beings, none for all human history, none for all corners of the globe. An opinion of the right and the wrong, the good and the bad, the pleasant and the unpleasant, is dated, is localized, is relative. It applies only to some men at some time, in some place, under some circumstances." (*The Phantom Public,* p. 97.)

[5] An instance of what we mean is furnished by Richard Hooker. "No man," says he, "can love things which in his own opinion are not. And if they think those things to be which they show that they love when they desire to believe them, then must it needs be that by desiring to believe they prove themselves true believers. For without faith no man thinketh that things believed are. Which argument all the subtlety of the infernal powers will never be able to dissolve." (*On the Certainty and*

assurance and wilful trust which Luther evoked to replace the intellectual assent of Catholic faith, and suggests the fundamental defect in the American ventures into the realm of philosophy.   In their desire to solve the practical problems, Americans have been misled into confining themselves to the purely empirical aspect of each problem as it arose, and owing to the present stress laid on physical sciences, due to the overweening position such sciences have gained in consequence of the temporary enlargement of material interests, the philosopher has subordinated his own proper function to that of the scientists.   But action presupposes knowledge, and courageous, vigorous, normal and sane action presupposes clear and certain knowledge that derives from a definite intellectual grasp of the realities of life. But this, history itself would testify, requires a return to the traditional metaphysics.

Our first question, then, is, what is metaphysics and what connection has it with the problem of standards in practical matters?   Except in the case of those who, owing largely to extrinsic and unworldly reasons, have managed to keep their hold on this Ariadne thread that stretches through the

Perpetuity of Faith in the Elect; Works, 1839 ed. p. 579.)   We find something the same in the view entertained by Newman in the days of his Protestantism. "This, indeed, is its [faith's] trial and its praise, so to hang upon the thought of Him [God] and desire Him as not to wait till it knows for certain from infallible informants whether or no He has spoken, but to act in the way which seems on the whole most likely to please Him." (*Via Media,* Vol. I, p. 86.)

labyrinth of the past, these questions admittedly are now puzzling the best minds. A striking instance of the complete departure from what has been traditionally meant by metaphysics is furnished by Alfred N. Whitehead in his recent book, *Science and the Modern World*. Speaking of the difficulties that surround the problem of induction, he says,

"We must observe the immediate occasion and use reason to elicit a general description of its nature. Induction presupposes metaphysics. In other words, it rests upon an antecedent rationalism. You cannot have a rational justification of your appeal to history till your metaphysics has assured you that there is a history to appeal to; and likewise your conjectures as to the future presuppose some basis of knowledge that there is a future already subjected to some determinations. The difficulty is to make sense of either of these ideas. But until you have done so, you have made nonsense of induction" (p. 62).

What the author, however, means by metaphysics is revealed in another passage, where he states that the "reasonable harmony of being which is required by the unity of a complex occasion, together with the completeness of the realization (of that occasion) of all that is involved in its logical harmony is the primary article of metaphysical doctrine. It means that for things to be together involves that they are reasonably together. This means that thought can penetrate into every occasion of fact, so that by comprehending its key conditions the whole

complex of its pattern of conditions lies open before it" (p. 39). Whatever may be said for this
concept of metaphysics with "reasonable harmony"
as its primary doctrine, it is certainly not the traditional view. Nor is this departure insignificant nor
unimportant, as is made clear by what the author has
to say about the "notion of periodicity":

"The general recurrences of things are very obvious in our ordinary experience. Days recur, lunar
phases recur, rotating bodies recur to their old positions, beats of the heart recur, breathing recurs. On
every side we are met by recurrence. Apart from
recurrence, knowledge would be impossible. Nothing could be referred to our past experience. Also,
apart from some regularity of recurrence, measurement would be impossible. In our experience, as we
gain the idea of exactness recurrence is fundamental." [6]

In this one should note again the fallacy of re-
stricting all knowledge to a particular kind of knowledge. The statement in itself is characteristic of
the common one-sidedness of the mind of the specialists.[7] Yet even they, in their moments of lapsing
into common sense, act on the certainty of their
knowledge in respect to many things that do not
recur. But the point we wish to call attention to is
that the scientist here confines himself to the acknowledgment of recurrence as a mere fact and as

[6] *Loc. cit.,* p. 45.

[7] Strangely enough, W. himself is most emphatic in pointing
out the dangers of professionalizing knowledge. (*Ibid.,* p. 275.)

the subject-matter for scientific measurement, without attempting in any way to account for the recurrence itself. Like the dog in the manger, he would stand over this and refuse to allow the human intellect to satisfy its innate desire to seek the reason for the recurrence. The author himself, in the beginning of the book, has put the problem off with the statement that "there can be no living science unless there is a widespread instinctive conviction in the existence of an *Order of Things* and, in particular of an *Order of Nature*." [8]

The science that answers to this particular desire to find the sufficient reason of things is precisely what is properly meant by metaphysics in the traditional sense, and it is this principle of sufficient reason, functioning in terms of being,[9] and not reasonable harmony required by unity, together with complete realization of what is involved in logical harmony, that constitutes the primary article of metaphysical doctrine.

Thus the intellectual grasp of the realities of life we stand so much in need of as a nation presupposes a solid basis in sound metaphysics, and involves, therefore, something more than a mere rational harmony or consistent view of things, based on "experi-

[8] *Ibid.,* p. 5.
[9] For the fundamental significance of this for genuine metaphysics see the brief but eminently adequate presentation given in *The Key to the Study of St. Thomas,* by Olgiati-Zybura. Maritain, in his *Reflexions sur l'Intelligence,* ch. 7, *De la Métaphysique des Physiciens,* analyzes very clearly the relation of scientific relativity to the absolute of the metaphysician.

ence," which is the point from which American philosophies, in their subservience to science, insist on taking their start.[10]   The fundamental bias in this respect may undoubtedly be traced historically to the earlier Protestant insistence upon "justification by faith alone," "personal inspiration," and "private judgment," which, whether believed in or not, remain part of the traditional mental posture with which the American mind is predisposed psychologically to face all problems of thought.[11]

It is this, perhaps, more than anything else that has severed American thought from any proper appreciation of that *philosophia perennis* which, however obscurely or confusedly apprehended, lies at the foundation of the whole civilization of western Christendom.   It is more than mere ignorance; it is an inability, artificially induced and contrary to the spontaneous tendencies of the normal mind, to appreciate and properly evaluate such principles of this philosophy as tradition has preserved in the common-sense views of life.

The fact that there is one true way of thinking has become utterly obscured by the quest for new ways of thinking.   In their concern to ascertain how we do think they are constantly misled into con-

---

[10] An interesting criticism of the effects on Western civilization's present lack of a sound metaphysics may be found in René Guenon's *Orient et Occident*. We do not agree, however, with the author, that there is any need of our turning to the Hindus for enlightenment in this matter.

[11] James B. Pratt stresses this apriorism of the pragmatist in *Essays in Critical Realism*, p. 100.

siderations of the way of thinking, which again become confused in their minds with the quite other question of the why and how of thought or cognition. This accounts for their persistence in confining themselves to psychological data in their attempt to analyze the problem. But "first principles are not of psychological origin, nor the fruit of a subjective interpretation of mental data, nor the urge of the will. Their sole explanation is in the intellect as a faculty, which belongs to man in virtue of his human nature. Experience gives the matter. Abstraction is the necessary condition, and the objective and immediate evidence the formal reason of the consent." [12]

Though this is a scholastic philosopher's way of accounting for the foundations of knowledge and the true and normal method of thought, we find something of a welcome return to what traditional scholasticism has thus perennially stood for in the statement of one of our critical realists.

"It is impossible," he says, "to identify either the datum or the images which introspective analysis discovers with the independent and common object which common sense as well as all realistic philosophy believes in. The fact that this is not realized in perception is of much less significance than the wider considerations which necessitate the conclusion; and it is hard to see any good reason why the thinker should shut his eyes to these unavoidable facts and confine himself to a description of the

[12] Sheen, p. 149 sq.

way one feels before one has begun to think at all." [13]

Now it should be noted that the two statements just quoted, when combined, give us findings substantially the same as those which Aristotle ascertained to be the constitutive elements of prudence.

"The intuitive reason," he says, "deals with ultimate truths at both ends of the mental process; for both the first and last terms, i. e., both first principles and particular facts, are intuitively and not logically apprehended, and while on the one hand in demonstrative reasonings it apprehends the immutable first terms, on the other, in matters of conduct, it apprehends the ultimate or contingent term which forms the premise of the syllogism; for it is truths of the latter sort which are the first principles or original sources of the idea of the end or object of human life. As the universal law, then, is derived from particular facts, these facts must be apprehended by perception, or in other words by intuitive reason." [14]

But where the critical realist confines himself to pointing out the fact that we do know the particular facts in themselves from which Aristotle would have us derive the universal laws or standards of action, and would hand the question of the inner and ultimate nature of facts over to the scientists and metaphysicians is precisely where the scholastic, with

[13] James B. Pratt, *loc. cit.*, p. 96.
[14] *Ethics*, VI, 12. (Welldon's Translation). Cf. *Summa Theol.*, I^a II^{ae}, qu. XCIV, art. 2.

his traditional metaphysics, would insist that in the case of the facts as well as of the first principles it is a question of their intelligibility as apprehended by the intelligence and not by way of any process of ratiocination, as the scientists with their eighteenth century rationalism have assumed to their own present confusion. The Scholastic way of accounting for both intelligibility and intelligence is that "we receive our knowledge from natural things, of which things God by His knowledge is Cause. In each thing, therefore, there is the *ratio,* the principle of its intelligibility. But this principle of intelligibility is there only in potency. Coming from the Mind of God into matter it has lost its character of universality, necessity and transcendence, which makes it the direct and immediate object of the intelligence. It has fallen into extent, number, movement and contingency. In order that 'it may revive in the mind in its proper characteristics it is necessary that the reality coming into our mind by sense perception in some way make a return to its source, disincarnate itself from matter, and go in the opposite way from that which individuation in matter imposed on it. The individuation realized by the generation of a being is an attraction of the idea in matter.' In order to know, there must be a contrary action, an extraction or abstraction." [15]

Extraordinary as this way of accounting for knowledge must seem to the modern, it is nothing

[15] Sheen, p. 138. The incorporated quotation is from A. D. Sertillanges, *St. Thomas,* Vol. II, p. 165.

more than the Scholastic's ultimate analysis of the traditional idea of *ratio*.   And here it might be well to note that by philosophical tradition we mean a formulated body of truths based upon a number of simple yet universal principles, immanently wrought from the findings of many minds, tested by the accurate thought of eminent thinkers and sifted in the light of experience.[16]   To take the word *ratio* as used above in connection with the intelligibility of things and our intelligence of them, we find the term *rita* among the early Hindus used to express that which is at once the organized principle of the universe and the divine ordering of earthly life.[17] Among the Greeks the word φύσις indicates the order or constitution of nature developing from the spontaneous energy inhering in material objects without the intervention of human artificial agencies.[18]   It was on this basis that Aristotle made his momentous distinction between that which is natural in the sense of deriving from nature and that which is natural in the sense of being demanded by nature in view of the final end.   Among the Romans, *rita* becomes

[16] Cf. Sheen, p. 65. "The growth of modern philosophy is not organic. It grows not from within like a living organism, but from without like a crystal. It grows on contradictions. Swinging always between the two extremes, it passes precipitately from one extreme to the other. Traditional thought, on the contrary, which is a philosophy of a school and not of individuals, grows and expands by the development of first principles. It remains in the mean, and would fall into error only if it moved toward the extremes."

[17] Berolzheimer, *The World's Legal Philosophies*, p. 37.

[18] *Ibid.*, p. 47.

the *naturalis ratio,* which signifies the objective and external order of nature. This was further analyzed by St. Augustine and transmuted into the doctrine of *pax,* which became an essential part of mediæval philosophy. But this, it should be observed, is not peace, but that which brings peace, a blissful sacred order.[19] Following St. Augustine, St. Thomas completed the analysis in his doctrine on the *lex aeterna,* where, supplementing St. Augustine's statement with regard to the *lex veritatis,* viz., "that we see a law above our mind called truth," [20] he points out that the intellect is measured by things.[21] In his further analysis, the *lex naturalis*

[19] *Ibid.,* p. 96.

[20] The importance of this doctrine of St. Augustine in its historical connection with the early formulation of the mediæval principle of the supremacy of law, which later became embodied in the common law, and now finds its fullest development in our own Constitution, has been too little noticed. Its influence on the theory that underlies Magna Charta may be clearly detected in the "Song of Lewes," the authorship of which is probably to be attributed to a Franciscan friar, and where, among much else to the point, are to be found such statements as these: "The affairs of the commonalty are best managed if the realm is directed by the way of truth," and, "Let liberty be limited by the bounds of right, and when those limits are despised let it be deemed error," and again, "It is commonly said, 'As the king wills, the law goes.' Truth wills otherwise, for the law stands, the king falls." (C. L. Kingsford, *The Song of Lewes,* p. 51, 52.) For an early application of this doctrine of St. Augustine see the letter of Charles the Bald to Pope Adrian II (Migne, *P. L.,* Vol. 124, col. 892).

[21] *Summa Theol.,* Iᵃ IIᵃᵉ, qu. XCIII, art. 1, ad 3. For a proper understanding of the term "measured" see Maritain, *Réflexions sur l'Intelligence,* ch. 2, "La Vie Propre de l'Intelligence," and ch. 9, "Le Réalisme Thomiste."

is seen to be a participation of the *lex aeterna,* the manner in which the participation is affected being described in the quotation given above.

As to the natural law itself, it is of first importance to observe that the Scholastic way of accounting for it is in no way to be identified with the mathematically expressed laws of nature with which it is generally confused in the minds of our contemporaries.[22] Nor is it the same as the natural law of the Stoics, who identified reason with the force behind nature,[23] a notion which falls very far short of the Scholastic analysis, but which was revived by

[22] A striking instance of this confusion will be found in Carl Becker's treatment of the philosophy of the Declaration of Independence, in *The Declaration of Independence,* ch. 2 and 6.

[23] Cicero, in his *Pro Milone,* speaks of the *"lex nata non scripta."* That this was to be understood in an exclusively subjective sense is clear from the various passages in his works which deal with the natural law. Seneca, in his Epist. 76, gives the fundamental Stoic notion in the statement that a man "is good if reason is properly developed and properly constituted (*recta*) and in conformity with the will of his nature." This view, as revived, was apparently held by Jefferson. Writing to Adams he says: "I believe that it [justice] is instinct and innate, that the moral sense is as much a part of our constitution as that of feeling, seeing, or hearing, as a wise Creator must have seen to be necessary in an animal destined to live in society." (*Correspondence of John Adams and Thomas Jefferson,* by Paul Wilstach, p. 145.) Commenting again on the same topic in a letter to Francis W. Gillmer, he says: "Assuming the fact that the earth has been created in time and consequently the dogma of final causes, we yield, of course, to this short syllogism, Man was created for social intercourse. But social intercourse cannot be maintained without a sense of justice. Then man must have been created with a sense of justice." (*Jefferson et les Idéologues,* by Gilbert Chinard, p. 245.)

the Renaissance naturalists and embodied in the Calvinist tradition, and now survives as the main assumption of that present mental muddle known as Modernism, which in essence is nothing more than radical Protestantism shorn of all the positive elements of Christian doctrine which the earlier forms of Protestantism managed to retain for a time in arbitrary and unfounded condition after the initial break with Christian tradition of revealed doctrine. As St. Thomas says, "Every act of reason and will in us is based on that which is according to nature, for every act of reason is based on principles that are known naturally. Every act of appetite in respect to the means is derived from the natural appetite in respect of the last end. Accordingly, the first direction of our acts to their end must needs be in virtue of the natural law." [24]

The same writer makes a very significant distinction between natural law in the sense of the laws or tendencies of nature, and natural law in the stricter sense.

"Even irrational animals," he says, "partake in their own way of eternal reason, but because the rational creature partakes thereof in an intellectual and rational manner, therefore the participation of the eternal law in the rational creature is properly called a law, since a law is something pertaining to reason. Irrational creatures, however, do not par-

[24] *Summa Theol.*, I^a II^ae, qu. XCI, art. 2, ad. 2.

take thereof in a rational manner, therefore there is no participation of the eternal law in them except by way of similitude." [25]

The singularity of the manner in which man participates in the eternal law stands out more clearly in another passage in the body of the article from which the above is taken.

"The rational creature is subject to Divine Providence in a most excellent way, so far as it partakes of a share of Providence by being provident both for itself and for others. Wherefore it has a share of the eternal reason whereby it has a natural inclination to its proper act and end, and this participation of the eternal law in the rational creature is called natural law."

Thus far the natural law has been considered in its psychological aspect. Man, it will be seen, is psychologically necessitated [26] to seek both the good and the true, and equally necessitated or determined to assent to the evidence of first principles such as the principle of contradiction and the principle that good is to be done. It is in this way that St. Thomas meets the demand so strenuously made by the social and political scientist that man be included in nature, a demand which never would have had to be made

[25] *Summa Theol.,* I[a] II[ae], qu. XCI, art. 3, ad 3.

[26] Rev. Michael Cronin, "On the Moral, Social, and Political Philosophy of St. Thomas," in *St. Thomas Aquinas,* ed. by Rev. C. Lattey, S.J., p. 153.

except in view of the Manichæan element of Protestantism, and the corresponding implications in
the idealism of Descartes.[27]   It is this, for instance,
that Professor Barnes should have meant when he
said that "no human characteristic has yet been discovered which clearly violates the natural laws discovered and expounded by scientists." For he is
clearly not talking as a scientist when he adds, "The
combined implications of cosmic and biological evolution have destroyed completely the foundations
for the hypothesis of human uniqueness or primacy." [28]   But for us there is the further question
with which we are chiefly concerned, viz., the metaphysical necessity of the law of nature thus taken in
its stricter sense.

"Human reason," says St. Thomas, "is not of itself the rule of things.   But the principles impressed
on it by nature are general rules and measures of all
things relating to human conduct, whereof the natural reason is the rule and measure, although it is

[27] Referring to Descartes' refusal to start with things and with
sense experience in the attempt to see truth immediately in God
Himself, Jacques Maritain says: "In reality, such a presumption
did not merely destroy the hierarchy of our intellectual virtues,
metaphysics becoming, to speak truly, no longer the crown of our
knowledge, but the introduction to the science of phenomena
and to the practical domination of nature." (*Réflexions sur l'Intelligence*, p. 29.)   Professor Whitehead points out the connection
in this respect. "Luther," he says, "asked, 'How am I justified?'
Modern philosophers have asked, 'How do I have knowledge?'
The emphasis lies upon the subject of experience." *Loc. cit.*,
p. 195.)

[28] H. E. Barnes, *History and Prospect of the Social Sciences*,
p. XIV.

not the measure of things that are from nature." [29]
The meaning of this, the metaphysical significance
of the phrase, "principles impressed by nature," will
be better understood in the light of the following:

"Contingent things can be considered in two ways:
either as contingent or as containing some element
of necessity. Since every contingent thing has in it
something necessary, *e. g.*, that Socrates runs is in
itself contingent. The relation of running to motion is necessary, for it is necessary that Socrates
should move if he runs. Now contingency arises
from matter, for contingency is that which may
either be or not be. But potentiality belongs to
matter, whereas necessity results from the nature of
form, because whatever flows from form belongs of
necessity to the informed subject. But matter is
the individualizing principle, whereas the universal
comes from the abstraction of the form from the
particular matter. Moreover it was laid down
(Art. 1) that the intellect of itself and directly has
the universal for its object, while the object of the
sense is singular, which in a certain way is the indirect object of the intellect, as we have seen above.
Therefore the contingent considered as such is known
directly by the sense and indirectly by the intellect,
while the universal and necessary principles of contingent things are known only by the intellect.
Hence, if we consider the objects of science in their
universal principles, then all science is of necessary
things. But if we consider the things themselves,

[29] *Summa Theol.*, Iᵃ IIᵃᵉ, qu. XCI, art. 3, ad 2.

some sciences are of necessary things, some of contingent things." [30]

From this it may be gathered what the basis is for maintaining the reality of those fixed entities or absolutes back of our sound generalized viewpoints, and the manner in which the cosmos, nature, and even our own narrower social world are ascertained to be something more than mere ways of looking at things in orderly fashion from a human viewpoint. To sum up, the natural law may be said to be the objective content of the intellect representing by its natural tendency the proper interrelation between the elements of the universe and that due order to which the will ought to conform in consequence of the contingency of the whole.[31]

The chief obstacle in the way of anything like a sympathetic consideration of this Scholastic doctrine is of course the peculiar prejudice in the American mind in favor of what is called "experience," that is to say, a peculiar distrust of anything in the order of knowledge that has not or cannot be put to a personal, practical test, and a tendency to relegate all else in knowledge to a mere matter of information.

[30] *Summa Theol.,* I[a], qu. LXXXVI, art. 3, translation by Sheen, *loc. cit.,* p. 159.

[31] For a fuller explanation of this definition see *The State and the Church,* by J. A. Ryan and M. F. X. Millar, S.J., p. 143. "Moral evil, sin, is a breach of the order established by the Creator; it consists in not acknowledging in practice and trampling upon the value of beings and their coördination in reference to the Supreme Being. Goodness and virtue, on the contrary, consist in the observance of the order flowing from the nature of being." (Olgiati-Zybura, *loc. cit.,* p. 104, 105.)

The Scholastic answer to this is the distinction it makes between confused and distinct knowledge.[32] Much that Scholasticism thus lays down already forms an inalienable acquisition of the least trained mind, though known without analysis or discernment in reflex processes of its parts or of its predicates. The same, when subjected in other minds to processes of rigid analysis, only assume a more explicit form and easily commend themselves when thus presented by reason of the objective identity of the principles in either case. It was of this distinction that Burke was thinking in a noted passage in his *Reflections on the French Revolution*.

"We are afraid," he says, "to put men to live and trade each on his own private stock of reason; because we suspect that the stock in each man is small, and that the individuals would do better to avail themselves of the general bank and capital of nations and of ages. Many of our men of speculation, instead of exploding general prejudices, employ their sagacity to discover the latent wisdom that prevails in them. If they find what they seek, and they seldom fail, they think it more wise to continue the prejudice with the reason involved than to cast away the coat of prejudice and to leave nothing but the naked reason, because prejudice with its reason has a motive to give action to that reason, an affection which can give it permanence. Prejudice is of ready application in the emergency, and previously engages the mind in a steady course of wisdom and

[32] Cf. Sheen, *loc. cit.*, p. 182.

virtue, and does not leave the man hesitating in the moment of decision, sceptical, puzzled, and unresolved. Prejudice renders a man's virtue his habit, and not a series of unconnected acts. Through just prejudice his duty becomes a part of his nature."

The name of Burke suggests the importance not only of the distinction between confused and distinct knowledge, but also of the Scholastic traditional metaphysics [33] as a whole in their relation to our own American political tradition. Americans, in their tendency to simplicism, which is a natural consequence of the exclusive stressing of personal experience, fail to recognize what a complex yet intelligible thing our Constitution is when properly viewed in the light of genuine tradition, thought and law, which historically lies behind it. Its provisions have been interpreted in the popular mind in the light of the use to which they have been put by the politician or demagogue, rather than in the light of the interpretation which the courts have gradually settled upon with regard to them. By way of reaction, the political scientists, misled by the prevalent impression that the Constitution was framed as well as ratified by the people, and who inclined to look to "public opinion" rather than to the nature of things for the basis of their theories, would have us

[33] Students of Burke would find considerable light thrown upon certain misinterpreted aspects of his political philosophy in what M. Gilson has to say of St. Thomas' doctrine with regard to law, custom, and changes in the law, in his *St. Thomas d'Aquin,* p. 246–250.

reject all such ideas as inalienable rights, equality, government by consent, and divided sovereignty.[34]

Yet these ideas have gone into our formation as a nation not as "forces" merely, expressive of emotional tendencies or reactions, but as fundamentals, expressive of realities variously apprehended by statesmen and people, yet ever molding in their effect and in such fashion as to argue, when duly considered in the light of results, a basic consonance with human nature. Referring to the second paragraph of the Declaration of Independence, Arthur T. Hadley, the former President of Yale, declares: "Few of us at the present day would be ready to subscribe to quite so broad a statement as this. We know that the right to liberty is not inalienable, but may be forfeited by misconduct. We know that the supposed equality of all mankind is something that has never been actually realized in human history. In fact, the signers of the Declaration of Independence themselves can hardly have meant what they said to be taken literally. Most of them were aristocrats, many of them were slave-holders; some of them defended human slavery on principle. They

[34] As Harold J. Laski, in his review of Professor McIlwain's book, *The Political Idea of James I,* has pointed out, "Nothing to-day is more greatly needed than clarity upon ancient notions. Sovereignty, liberty, authority, personality,—these are the words of which alike we want the history and the definition; or rather, we want the history because its substance is in fact the definition. No period has so illuminated these questions as the Counter-Reformation. It is in some sort the birthplace of the modern state." (*Political Science Quarterly,* June, 1919, p. 304.)

were simply stating the theory of democratic government as it was understood in their time, and as it has been expounded by the great prophet of modern democracy, Rousseau." [35]

Again, Walter J. Shepard says:

"The Declaration of Independence is still cited as approved authority on occasion, though its doctrine of equality, (if the term be given in a political signification), inalienable rights, government by consent, are decisively belied by the evidence of current events. One of the tasks of the political scientist is to rid men's minds of outworn theories. He is often looked upon as a closet philosopher, who spends his time in spinning useless abstract doctrines, but it is the man on the street and the public official who really are devotees of ancient dogmas. More vigorous efforts towards the eradication of such ideas as those just mentioned—strenuous educational campaign towards the clarification of the pop-

[35] A. T. Hadley, *The Conflict between Liberty and Equality,* pp. 1 and 2. The author makes the common mistake of confusing physical liberty with moral liberty; moreover, what is forfeited is not taken, in the sense that it ceases to be inalienable. To argue from the inconsistent actions of some of the signers to the falsity of the theory of the Declaration is to forget that it is possible, in the words of Marshall in Marbury vs. Madison, "to overthrow in fact what was established in theory." Claude G. Bowers, the latest biographer of Jefferson, in his book entitled *Jefferson and Hamilton,* says: "There is no sillier assertion in history than that his [Jefferson's] democracy was born of association with the men of the French Revolution." While Charles E. Hughes, in *American Citizenship,* ed. by Josiah Marvel, p. 72, says, "The Declaration spoke with the tongue of Magna Charta, Petition of Right, and the Bill of Rights."

ular mind—is one of the urgent duties of political science." [36]

Both of these passages are typical of many recent statements in the same strain. All are based on the superficial and therefore unscientific assumption that there can be but one possible meaning to the terms to which they thus unanimously object. As a matter of historical fact, there are two very definite traditions respecting the meaning which these words are supposed to convey. The one that traces back to the medieval and Scholastic tradition stresses intellectual apprehension of the proper relation of things as the basis, and reason as the fundamental norm of human conduct. The other derives from the debased form of Scholastic thought in the later Middle Ages, beginning with Ockam [37] and Mar-

[36] *History and Prospect of the Social Sciences*, p. 431.—As Browning says in *Old Pictures in Florence*, " 'Tis looking downward that makes one dizzy."

[37] With reference to Ockam, Imbert de la Tour in *Les Origines de la Réforme*, Vol. III., p. 14, has this to say: "Let us make sure that there were no greater intellectual revolutions even before the Reformation. In destroying the correct idea of law, criticism of Ockam thrust aside the whole synthetic and realistic movement of the Scholastic thinkers. On the one hand, it divorced philosophy from theology, severed and even set up in mutual denial the two spheres of thought—where, in the one, reason penetrates into the world of phenomena, and in the other, is raised by faith to the supernatural,—and thus proclaims the existence of two so-called 'truths,' which at times could be irreconcilable and even, it might be, contradictory. On the other hand, once reason was dethroned, the world no longer appeared except as a system of unrelated individual activities. The will became the one predominant faculty, and, not being able to conceive of itself otherwise than as endowed with absolute autonomy,

siglio of Padua,[38] and finds ultimate synthetic expression in Rousseau, the dominant characteristic throughout being the exaltation of will at the expense of intellect or any objective normative basis.

the entire sacredness of our being was concentrated in the one sovereign power of self-determination and free choice or liberty." For a valuable contribution on the "theories of the will," see Irving Babbitt's *Democracy and Leadership,* Appendix A.

[38] J. W. Allen, in *The Social and Political Ideas of Some Great Mediæval Thinkers,* pp. 177 and 178, says of Marsiglio of Padua after summing up the latter's theories expounded in the *Defensor Pacis:* "Government is concerned first of all with the repression of the perverse will in man. Its primary business is to force men to act in their own interests. . . . The writer is thinking in terms of mere need and necessity. The recognition of need involves will, but he is thinking of will only as something produced by need. He is not thinking in terms of 'right' at all." Law, again, in Marsiglio's view, is essentially "a judgment as to what is just and advantageous to the community. It is an imperative expression of the common need, formulated by reason, promulgated by recognized authority, sanctioned by force. Just because it is this, the legislator must needs be either the whole community or its *valentior pars.*" It goes without saying that these views of Ockam and of Marsiglio of Padua run counter to the whole of the earlier mediæval theory of law and government. There is, we think, a whole chapter in history to be written showing the influence of the revival of Roman law on this unfortunate trend in Scholastic thought. In the Civil Law, liberty is defined thus: "Freedom, from which is derived the term free as applied to men is the natural power of doing what we each please unless prevented either by force or by law." Here we see will and force confronted, with no objective ground for delimitation except the positive determination of the law as this proceeded from the *imperium,* which was only will in another form. The influence of this may be detected in the case of Scotus, who held society to be a purely artificial fact; while he exaggerated the freedom of the will, he went counter to St. Thomas inasmuch as he depreciated the individual and overemphasized the power of the sov-

In the older and sounder of the two traditions, which the historians and political scientists persistently ignore or evade,[39] equality was understood to mean that no man of himself had any right to impose

ereign. (See *Duns Scot,* by Bernard Landry, p. 231 sq.) Coke quotes the civil law definition of liberty with approval. (*Institutes,* Part I, Book II, ch. II, of Villanage, sect. 172.) Bacon adapted it to his purposes in the case of the Postnati. "Our law is grounded upon the law of nature, and these three things [life, liberty, and dower] do flow from the law of nature. Preservation of life natural, liberty, which every beast or bird seeketh and effecteth naturally, etc." (2 Howell's Trials, 594.) This view of liberty, it may be noted, was uppermost in the minds of the Puritans during the Puritan Rebellion. The contrast which this presents to the theory of liberty as implicit in our common law has been lucidly set forth by Roscoe Pound in his *Interpretations of Legal History,* p. 56 and 57, although he himself, if we are to judge from some of his views as to law, does not seem to have grasped the full implications of his observation. "If we must find," he says, "a fundamental idea in the common law, it is relation, not will. If the Romanist sees all the problems in terms of the will of an actor, and of the logical implications of what he has willed and done, the common law lawyer sees almost all problems—all those, indeed, in which he was not led to adopt the Romanist point of view in the last century—in terms of a relation and of the incidents in the way of reciprocal rights and duties involved in or required to give effect to that relation. Magna Charta, the foundation of our public law, is not the expression of the idea of individual freedom, but a formulation of the rights and duties incident to the relation of the king and his tenants in chief."

[39] Two striking instances of this may be noted in two recent works. Charles E. Vaughan in his *Studies in the History of Political Philosophy,* Vol. II, p. 53, dealing with Burke's statement in the *Reflections on the French Revolution* on the social compact, assumes that because Burke evidently did not have the theory of Hobbes or of Locke in mind, he therefore attached little meaning to the term, whereas had he but read what Bellarmine

either his will or his ideas upon another.[40]   Government based upon the consent of the governed followed as a necessary consequence in the sense that
no man or body of men could legitimately claim the

has to say in his *De Laicis,* ch. V and VI, he would have realized
that what Burke had in mind is not only significant but vital.
Holdsworth, on the other hand, in his *History of English Law,*
Vol. VI., p. 280, dismisses Bellarmine as an advocate of revolutionary doctrine identical in character with that of Calvin and
the Puritans, when as a matter of simple historical fact Bellarmine emphatically takes up in the *De Laicis,* where his alleged
views are to be found, the same position against Calvin and
the Reformers which Burke adopted later in his opposition to the
French Revolutionists.

[40] The Stoics, it is true, maintained the equality of men, and
their view found embodiment in the civil law. In the words of
Ulpian, "As far as the natural law is concerned, all men are
equal." But the Stoic doctrine is something quite different from
the mediæval concept. To the Stoics, all men are equal because
they all have the same origin in nature, but this furnishes no
basis for any such thing as inalienable rights. In the mediæval
concept, all men are equal, having both the same origin and
the same destiny, and hence the inalienable right to the necessary means to the attainment of their final end, which is ultimate happiness. For Madison's criticism of this term as used
in the Declaration of Independence, see *The State and the
Church,* p. 175. The distinction is not unimportant, as may be
seen from Edwin DeWitt Dickinson's observations on the evil
results that followed from the influence of the naturalists on
international law, who revived the pagan notion in this matter
and applied it to the equality of states. (*The Equality of States
in International Law,* p. 42 sq.) The misleading effects of in-
sisting on holding this pagan Roman law view of equality for
the only traditional one is illustrated in the confusion displayed
by William A. Dunning in his posthumous article, "Liberty and
Equality in International Relations," in the *American Political
Science Review,* Feb., 1923, p. 1 sqq. The American constitutional doctrine as to the equality of the states under the Constitution stands out strikingly in Kansas vs. Colorado, 206 U. S. 46.

right to rule *de iure* where the claim was not based
on the agreement, at least tacit, of the people.   Sovereignty again, on this same basis, resolves itself into
the ultimate power or right to decide in any particular matter, with the correlative obligation on the
part of the subject or citizen to conform in consequence of his social nature.[41]   Taken in the above

[41] Since Bodin revived and popularized the pagan civil law notion of sovereignty as a most high, absolute, and perpetual power
over the citizens subject in a commonwealth not subject to law
(*Six Books of a Commonwealth,* Book I, ch. 8), the idea that
sovereignty must be identified with force has been kept alive
by Hobbes and John Austin, and is now generally accepted by
the American political scientists. Even Irving Babbitt seems
unaware of the fact that this was not the earlier mediæval view.
He is guilty of a grave misconception when he states in *Democracy and Leadership,* p. 332, that "The genuinely mediæval conception of sovereignty is very different from the conception I have
been associating with the *lex regia* and Roman law. For the
Christian, sovereignty does not derive from the people as in
Roman law, but from God, who is conceived primarily not as
Reason but as Will." The following gives us the early 13th
century theology on this point: "We believe that God . . . desires the truth. One alone is called and is king in truth through
whom the world is ruled by pure majesty, who needs not as-
sistance whereby He may be able to reign, nay, nor counsel, who
cannot err." (*The Song of Lewes, loc. cit.,* p. 47), St. Thomas
gives the Christian philosophical emendation of the *lex regia.*
"Reason," he says, "has its power of moving from the will: for
it is due to the fact that one wills the end that the reason issues
its commands as regards things ordained to the end. But in order that the volition of what is commanded may have the nature
of law, it needs to be in accord with some rule of reason. And
in this sense is to be understood the saying that the will of the
sovereign has the force of law; otherwise the sovereign's will
would savor of lawlessness rather than of law (1ᵃ 2ᵃᵉ, qu.
XC, 1, ad 3). Bracton on the other hand gives the legal theory
in emendation of the same. "Although," he says, "the king is the

sense, equality is logically the necessary presupposition to the common law and American constitutional
principle of the supremacy of law. Historically,
on the other hand, the doctrine of consent developed
into the bilateral contract of the coronation oath and
the feudal oath of mediaeval times, and now stands
at the basis of our own Constitution, but with lim-
iting effect in consequence of the fact that the people
have conferred none but enumerated powers upon
our national government. Sovereignty, moreover,
as defined in accordance with this tradition, is clearly
divisible,[42] although the question of the nature and

minister of God he possesses no other power on earth save only
that which he has by law, nor is that a hindrance which states
that what is pleasing to the ruler has the force of law, since there
follows at the end of the law: 'since by the *lex regia* passed concerning his authority,' that is, not everything is presumed to be
from the will of the king but from his intention of making laws,
and that which, by the advice of his magistrates, the king mani-
festing his authority after reflection and consideration of the
matter, shall have been rightly defined." (Bracton, *De Legibus
et Consuetudinibus Angliae,* Vol. II, p. 305.) Professor Charles
H. McIlwain, in *The High Court of Parliament,* p. 142 sqq., points
out the difference between the common law use of the word *absolute* and that which we have just seen to constitute the meaning
of Bodin and his followers. It may be interesting to note that
as late as the reign of Henry VII an act of Parliament was held
void by the king's judges because in conflict with the canon law.
(*Ibid.,* p. 277). The American definition of sovereignty is best
gathered from the opinion of Justice James Wilson in Chisholm
vs. Georgia (2 Dallas 419).

[42] Madison has recorded the intent of the Federal Convention in
this matter. "It has hitherto been understood," he says, "that the
supreme power, that is, the sovereignty of the people of the
states was in its nature divisible, and was in fact divided, according to the Constitution of the United States, between the states in

manner of the division again depends upon the initial fact of consent or agreement. To illustrate, St. Thomas held, "To order anything to the common good belongs either to the whole people or to some one who is vicegerent of the whole people, and therefore the making of a law belongs either to the whole people or to a public personage who has care of the whole people, since in all other matters the direct-

their united and the states in their individual capacities, and so viewed by the Convention in transmitting the Constitution to the Congress of the Confederation; so viewed and so called in official, in controversial, and in popular language. Of late another doctrine has occurred, which supposes that sovereignty is in its nature indivisible. . . . This discord of opinions arises from a propensity in many to prefer the use of theoretical guides, technical language, to the division and depositories of power as laid down in the constitutional charter. . . . If sovereignty be in its nature divisible, the true question to be decided is whether the allotment has been made by the complete authority; and this question is answered by the fact that it was an act of the *majority* of the people in each state in their highest sovereign capacity, equivalent to a *unanimous* act of the people composing the states in that capacity." (James Madison: *Sovereignty Selections: Private Correspondence of James Madison from 1813 to 1836*, published by J. E. McGuire, Washington, 1853, pp. 370, 372.) And yet Professor Westel W. Willoughby has been misled by his Kantianism and German authorities on law to the extent of declaring in his *Fundamental Concepts of Public Law*, p. 250, that "It is plain that the constituent states have no sovereignty of their own, and that such autonomous powers as they now possess are had and exercised by the express will or by the constitutional forbearance of the national sovereignty." President emeritus H. P. Judson of the University of Chicago is, we think, likewise in error when he states in *Our Federal Republic,* that "each one of the states is subject to the authority of the United States and hence no one of the states is itself sovereign."

ing of anything to the end concerns him to whom the end belongs." [43]

Later, Bellarmine summed up the mediaeval theory in this respect in these words:

"[Secular] power resides as in its subject immediately in the whole state, for this power is by Divine law. But Divine law gives this power to no particular man, therefore Divine law gives this power to the collected body. For there is no good reason why, in a multitude of equals, one rather than another should dominate. . . . By the same natural right, this power is delegated by the multitude to one or several, for the state cannot of itself exercise this power, therefore it is bound to delegate it to one or to several, and this authority of rulers considered in general is both by natural law and by Divine law. Nor can the human race, even were all men to agree together, decree the opposite, namely, that forsooth there are to be no rulers or leaders. . . . Individual forms of government in specific cases are from the law of nations, not from the natural law, for, as is evident, it depends on the consent of the people to decide whether kings or consuls or other rulers are to be placed over it. And if there be a legitimate cause, the people can change a kingdom into an aristocracy or an aristocracy into a democracy, and vice versa." [44]

Commenting on this, Suarez adds, "If a people transfer power to a king, yet retain it in themselves

[43] *Summa Theol.*, I[a] II[ae], qu. XC, art. 3.
[44] *De Laicis*, ch. VI.

for certain affairs or for things of greater moment, it is allowable for them to use it and to maintain their right. Such a right, however, ought to be sufficiently ascertained either from ancient and authentic documents or from immemorial custom." [45]

When, in the famous decision in Marbury vs. Madison, Marshall approached the question as to whether an act repugnant to the Constitution can become the law of the land, we find him laying down this identical doctrine as basic to our whole structure of government.

"That the people," he says, "have an original right to establish for their future government such principles as in their opinion shall most conduce to their own happiness is the basis on which the whole American fabric has been erected. The exercise of this original right is a very great exertion, nor can it nor ought it to be frequently repeated. The principles, therefore, so established, are deemed fundamental, and as the authority from which they proceed is supreme, and can seldom act, they are designed to be permanent.

"This original and supreme will organizes the government, and assigns to different departments their respective powers. It may either stop here or establish certain limits not to be transcended by those departments. The government of the United States is of the latter description. The powers of the legislature are defined and limited, and that those limits may not be mistaken or forgotten the Consti-

[45] *Defensio Fidei Catholicae*, III, 3, 3.

tution is written. . . . The distinction between a government with limited and unlimited powers is abolished if those limits do not confine the persons on whom they are imposed, and if acts prohibited and acts allowed are of equal obligation. It is a proposition too plain to be contested that the Constitution controls any legislative act repugnant to it, or that the legislature may alter the Constitution by an ordinary act." [46]

When, in the case of McCulloch vs. Maryland, Marshall stressed the peculiar character of our national government as one of enumerated powers, he said, speaking of the Constitution itself: "Its nature, therefore, requires that only its great outlines should be marked, its important objects designated, and the minor ingredients which compose those objects be deduced from the nature of the objects themselves." [47]

Later, in the case of Cooley vs. the Board of Wardens of the Port of Philadelphia, Justice Curtis, dealing with the question as to whether Congress' power under the Commerce Clause to regulate the qualification of pilots is exclusive of state action, reiterates the same doctrine, saying:

"In construing an instrument designed for the formation of a government, and in determining the extent of one of its important grounds of power to legislate, we can make no such distinction between the nature of the power and the nature of the sub-

[46] 1 Cranch 137.
[47] 4 Wheaton 310.

ject on which that power was intended practically to operate, nor consider the grant more extensive by affirming of the power what is not true of its subject now in question." [48]

These broad legal rules of construction, it should be noted, bring our Constitutional law into strict conformity with the Scholastic doctrine of the natural law viewed as a norm.   If we turn now to the question of divisibility of sovereignty, we find Bellarmine maintaining, in keeping with St. Thomas,[49] the mixed form of government to be the best, but adding, "This mixed form evidently requires that there should be in the commonwealth one supreme ruler, who, while issuing commands to all, should himself be subject to none.   Those, on the other hand, who preside over the provinces and cities, should not be vicegerents of the king or mere annual judges, but let them be real rulers subject in obedience to the supreme ruler, yet in such a manner as at all times to hold the regulation of their respective provinces or cities to be a matter of concern to themselves and not the concern of another.   Thus the commonwealth will enjoy the benefits of a monarchy under a king and of an aristocracy under a select body of rulers.

[48] 12 Howard 299.

[49] One striking instance, among many, of St. Thomas' influence in this respect upon English constitutional theory in the days previous to the Revolution, is furnished by Sir Roger Twysden in his *Considerations upon the Government of England* (Camden Society), p. 90, where he says: "It seems to me Aquinas as hee determines that for the best government comes neerest to what wee see establisht here."

If in addition to this it were provided that neither the supreme ruler nor those who ruled under him should attain to such positions of dignity by hereditary succession, but that those best fitted should be selected from the body of the people and elevated to them, the commonwealth would then possess some of the attributes of a democracy." [50]

In another place Bellarmine explains the basis upon which such a division of sovereignty becomes feasible. In his controversy with Barclay, who held the Gallican theory in regard to the question of the relation of the state to the Church, he says:

"Barclay states that one power cannot be subordinate and subject to another unless the dignity and function which pertains to the subordinate exist also in the one to whom it is subordinate. For all Catholics teach that the political power is subject and subordinate to the Church. But we do not admit what Barclay concludes from this. For this subordination may be understood in two ways: the one, whereby the power which resides in the subordinate derives from the one to whom he is subordinate, as in the case of a vicar, who derives his power from him whose vicar he is, and of a legate, who derives it from the prince who delegated it, and of a judge or presiding officer, who derives it from a king. In such cases undoubtedly the power of him to whom they are subordinate comprehends their power as subordinates. The other, whereby one power is not derived from the other, but is subject and subor-

[50] *Opera Omnia*, I, p. 467.

dinate to the other for this reason only, that the end
for which one exists is subordinate to the end for
which the other exists, as is the case with that form
of subordination and subjection whereby the various
arts are subordinate to what may be called the regal
art of ruling people." [51]

In close conformity to this theory we find Marshall describing the nature of state government under our Constitution, and the relation of states to
the national government.   Speaking of the manner
in which the Constitution was proposed to the people for ratification in state conventions, Marshall
says:

"This mode of proceeding was adopted by the
Convention, by Congress, and by the state legisla-
tures the instrument was submitted to the people.
They acted upon it in the only manner in which they
can act safely, effectively, and wisely on such a subject, by assembling in convention.   It is true they assembled in their several states, and where else
should they have assembled?   No political dreamer
was ever wild enough to think of breaking down the
lines which separate the states, and of compounding
the American people into one common mass.   In
consequence, when they act they act in their states,
but the measures they adopt do not on that account
cease to be the measures of the people themselves,
or become the measures of the state governments."
Further on, "If any one proposition could command
the universal assent of mankind, we might expect

[51] *De Potestate Summi Pontificis,* c. 2.

that it would be this, that the government of the Union, though limited in its powers, is supreme within its sphere of action. This would seem to result necessarily from its nature. It is the government of all, its powers are delegated by all, it represents all, and acts for all. Though any one state may be willing to control its operations, no state is willing to allow others to control them. The nation, on those subjects on which it can act, must necessarily bind its component parts."

In another passage in McCulloch vs. Maryland he describes the manner in which the division of sovereignty was effected, and incidentally provided, as it were by anticipation, a refutation of Calhoun's main contention, which Webster on his part later failed to meet in the great controversy over state rights.

"It has been said that the people had already surrendered all their powers to the state sovereignties, and had nothing more to give. But surely the question whether they may resume and modify the powers granted to government does not remain to be settled in this country. Much more might the legitimacy of the general government be doubted had it been created by the states. The powers delegated to the state sovereignties were to be exercised by themselves, not by a distinct and independent sovereignty created by themselves. To the formation of a league such as was the Confederation, the state sovereignties were certainly competent. But when 'in order to form a more perfect union' it was deemed necessary to change this alliance into an effective government possessing great and sovereign powers and acting directly on the people, the necessity of referring it to the people and of deriving its powers directly from them was felt and acknowledged by all.   The government of the Union, then, (whatever may be the inference of this fact on the case), is emphatically and truly a government of the people.   In form and in substance it emanates from them; its powers are granted by them, and are to be exercised directly on them and for their benefit."

And yet, as he added later in Gibbons vs. Ogden: [52]

"Although many of the powers formerly exercised by the states are transferred to the government of the Union, yet the state governments remain, and constitute a most important part of our system."

While Justice Field in the Tarble's case says: [53]

"There are within the territorial limits of each state two governments, restricted in their spheres of action, but independent of each other and supreme within their respective spheres.   Each has its separate departments, each has its distinct laws, and each has its own tribunals for their enforcement. Neither government can intrude within the jurisdiction or authorize any interference therein by its judicial officers, of the action of the other.   The two governments in each state stand in their respective

[52] 9 Wheaton 1.
[53] 3 Wallace 397.

spheres of action in the same independent relation to each other, except in one particular, that they would if their authority embraced distinct territories. That particular consists in the supremacy of the power of the United States when any conflict arises between the two governments."

That all this reasoning is based logically upon the doctrine enunciated in the Declaration of Independence that "all men are created equal and that they are endowed by their Creator with certain inalienable rights, that among these are life, liberty, and the pursuit of happiness, that to secure these rights governments are instituted among men, deriving their just powers from the consent of the governed," should be sufficiently clear once the meaning of equality in its sound traditional sense is placed in its true light. Some have sneered at the introductory statement that "we hold these truths to be self-evident," and while it is true that the evidence in question would undoubtedly not appear to a Hindu [54] or a Chinaman or to anyone not sharing in that tradition, there is a sense in which the statement may be held to be emphatically correct. As St. Thomas says:

"The precepts of the natural law are to the practical reason what the first principles of demonstration are to the speculative reason, because both are self-evident principles. Now a thing is said to be self-

[54] For an interesting discussion of the absence of any such idea in the Hindu mind, see the English periodical, *The Month*, November, 1925, p. 433.

evident in two ways, first, in itself, secondly, in relation to us. Any proposition is said to be self-evident in itself if its predicate is contained in the notion of the subject, although to one who knows not the definition of the subject it happens that such a proposition is not self-evident. . . . But some propositions are self-evident only to the wise who understand the meaning of the terms of such propositions." [55]

In conclusion, and by way of modern commentary, may there not be a saving wisdom in Carlyle's remark, where, referring to the confusion and futilities of the modern world, which he attributes to its having departed so radically from that tradition which was meat and drink to Abbot Sampson in the twelfth century, he says: "We have taken up the fact of this universe as it is not. We have quietly closed our eyes to the eternal substance of things and opened them only to the shows and shams of things. We quietly believe this universe to be intrinsically a great unintelligible. Perhaps; extrinsically, clear enough, it is a great, most extensive Cattlefold and workhouse, with most extensive kitchen-ranges, dining tables—whereat he is wise who can find a place. All the truth of this universe is uncertain; only the profit and loss of it, the pudding and praise of it, are and remain very visible to the practical man." [56]

[55] *Summa Theol.*, I^a II^{ae}, qu. XCIV, art. 2.
[56] Book III, ch. 1.

CHAPTER X

THE NEW SCHOLASTICISM AND ITS CONTRIBUTIONS
TO MODERN THOUGHT

By Professor James H. Ryan, of the Catholic University of America

"THE Scholastic tradition reigned undisputed for nearly three centuries, and it did not die with the Middle Ages. Not only did it survive in England as we have seen. . . . In the system of Hegel, and even, though in a less degree, in that of Kant, Aquinas's influence is apparent. Hegel indeed had first studied from Thomistic manuals, and he owed more to them than he owed to Heracleitus. In our own times we have seen a more obvious revival of Thomism. After considering the systems of Gioberti and Rosmini, the Vatican gradually decided to make Thomism its official philosophy. The result has been far-reaching. In Italy, where, as ever, Dante is studied, Scholasticism accompanies the neo-Hegelianism of Croce and Gentile. Cardinal Mercier was the leader of the revival in Northern Europe. He founded the school of Louvain, and he re-wrote his lectures in a considerable volume. Scholasticism regains its hold on Germany, and we gather from the fourth and fifth books in our list that it is beginning to arouse respect also in Great Britain."

Thus writes the editor of the *Times Literary Supplement* (London, November 5, 1925) apropos of a lengthy review of a series of new books on Scholastics and Scholasticism written by such well-known scholars as Étienne Gilson, Francesco Olgiati, Jacques Maritain, and Henri Ghéon. The revival of interest in England in the thought of the Scholastics is being paralleled in the United States by a similarly awakened interest in things mediaeval, and especially in mediaeval philosophy. The creation of the Mediaeval Academy of America, and the announcement of a new review, *Speculum, A Journal of Mediaeval Studies,* are signs which point in only one direction.

The realistic trend of American philosophy owes more than it suspects to the classical thought of the thirteenth century. While it would be an exaggeration to maintain that the New Realists arrived at their theory of knowledge because of an appreciation of the principles of Dualistic Realism, since few, if any, of them betray even a nodding acquaintance with the philosophy of Saint Thomas, nevertheless it can be contended honestly that they have been affected to no small extent by Thomistic thinking, from whatever source originally they gained a knowledge of it. Nor is this renewed interest in Thomistic thinking to be looked upon as momentary, superficial, and likely to be overthrown at the appearance of some new fad in philosophy. If the interest were purely archæological, it might be

waved away as one of the passing fashions of the
day, and we could hope from it nothing more conse-
quential than an increase of appreciation of the truly
stupendous literary and artistic creations of the Middle Ages.   But Scholasticism, in its twentieth century dress, that is, as the New Scholasticism, is not
presenting itself to modern thought as something
very old, decked out in up-to-date clothes; a corpse
brought to life by a magic process of artificial intellectual respiration.   Quite the contrary.   The New
Scholasticism maintains that it is a vital current of
present-day thinking, that it has a message for the
modern philosophical world, that in the practical affairs of life it can point a way out of the various difficulties which seem to have swamped many thinkers
and left them helpless before the tide of scepticism
and unbelief threatening the future and even the
present.

In the dark night of the intellectual anarchy which
has followed upon the war, the Neo-Scholastic holds
out for acceptance a systematic thought which, like
a great light, penetrates the obscurities of the dungeon in which much of our thinking seems to be confined, and indicates the road to safety, sanity, and
salvation.   We know that the light which will penetrate this darkness is not an illusion.   The eager
search for it proves that mankind, too, realizes both
its existence and its need.   That men shall see and
accept and be guided by its blessed rays depends on
the energy we manifest and the skill we use in making known our belief to an age whose eyes have be-

come unaccustomed to the strong white light of
truth.

We have alluded to the vitality of Scholastic
thought. Its reappearance as a contender in the
arena of warring systems of philosophy cannot but
appear to many observers as little short of a resurrection from the dead. For Scholasticism had been
interred, and without the honors of war, by such
renowned thinkers as Descartes, Locke, Hume, and
Kant. So accustomed had philosophy become to the
idea that nothing was to be expected from the
thought of the Middle Ages that it passed over in
amused silence the strenuous efforts which were being made to rekindle the spark of life in its supposedly dry bones.

The renaissance of Scholastic thought began in
Italy as early as 1850. Its rebirth, like the birth of
any great man or movement, passed unnoticed. Its
early appearance to the modern world, in the form
of commentaries and compendia written in Latin,
served to confirm the widespread belief that as a
philosophy it was hopeless. The first real impetus
given to Scholastic philosophy came from the Encyclical *"Aeterni Patris"* of that great Pope, Leo
XIII. The world, well aware of the modernity and
soundness of Pope Leo's thinking on other subjects,
could not but give ear to his fervent plea for a revival of philosophical studies. It saw, too, that the
Pope was in earnest when he stated his conviction of
the need of a sound philosophy, and from that day
forward Scholasticism became an element in think-

ing that had to be reckoned with. The influence of Cardinal Mercier and the University of Louvain in spreading the ideals of Leo was determining. The twentieth century opened with the army of the New Scholasticism drawn up in fighting array, prepared to battle for the great principles that had shown such vitality in Ancient Greece and Imperial Rome, and had helped to mould the Middle Ages from a barbarous incoherency into a logical and highly efficient culture.

The New Scholasticism has a long and difficult road to travel before it can hope for anything approaching the recognition given in intellectual circles to certain modern systems of philosophy. No one is more acutely aware of this fact than the Neo-Scholastics themselves. The difficulties involved are of many kinds, not the least being the patronizing attitude generally assumed towards a system of thought which is so deeply rooted in the past. Again, modern thought has become strangely and, we feel, unreasonably suspicious of any intellectual position which seems to imply the acceptance of defined dogmas of religion. The whole trend of our thinking has been in the direction of secularism, of the divorcing of science and philosophy from the tenets of religious faith, be it Christian or non-Christian. It is true that religion has come to be accepted by many people as a dignified and useful sort of sentimental experience. But its intellectual influence is either denied outright or passed over in mild contempt. The result of such an attitude has been to discount beforehand every system of thought tinctured by or associated with religious dogma. In modern times, the *odium theologicum* has thus acquired a new and startling meaning.

The aforementioned difficulties must sooner or later yield to a sound and clear presentation of the Scholastic position, if we are prepared to make it known in a way and under circumstances which will appeal to thinkers. What I mean is that, considering the actual situation, the medium of presentation is often of as much importance as the arguments advanced to sustain one's position. Interest in a philosophical or scientific movement soon wanes if its leaders are not anxious to make themselves understood in a language which the modern man can comprehend. The mode of presentation, therefore, as well as the language used, are tremendously important elements to be considered when one is committed to the difficult task of making his thought known and acceptable to others. It is quite generally conceded that any failure of the New Scholasticism to attain the commanding position in modern thought which it deserves because of the clarity and sanity of its thought constructions, is due primarily to the weakness it has exhibited in the methods used to bring such principles before the public. On occasions when this thought has been well and logically expressed, it has been received with an appreciation and even enthusiasm that is as surprising as it is gratifying. All of which suggests the idea that it is not Scholasticism *in se* which is repellent to modern

thinkers.   Prejudiced as many are, and indifferent
as many more are, to our system of philosophy, the
great majority of its opponents will be found among
those who are almost entirely ignorant of Scholastic
principles.   This may be due either to an unwillingness or an incapability of approaching this thought
in the severe dress in which it is often presented.   A
good example of this latter handicap is seen in the
late Professor James.   Few philosophers exhibited
a more genial broadmindedness than the great
leader of American Pragmatism.   In many of his
best ideas James was closer to the philosophy of the
Schools than he ever suspected.   In spite of all this,
he betrayed again and again an obscurantist attitude
toward Scholastic philosophy which is in startling
contrast to his ordinarily impartial treatment of
points of view opposite to his own.   The only plausible explanation of this strange treatment of Scholasticism on the part of James seems to be that he
did not know what the Scholastics taught, but formed
his ideas of their teachings from the tradition current in idealistic circles, or that he did not feel himself quite equal to consulting the sources from which
alone a fair and scientific view of that position can
be obtained.

By all this I do not mean to assert that opposition
to Scholasticism is due solely either to ignorance of
its teachings or to our own ineffective methods of
presentation.   Many modern thinkers, and the number is on the increase, understand only too well what
these fundamental positions are.   However, be-

cause of their acceptance of a radically opposite starting-point which, generally speaking, is monistic, they confess themselves incapable of harmonizing Scholastic conclusions with their own accepted premises. Their position, of course, is quite logical, conceding the truth of the monistic philosophy. These thinkers, therefore, oppose the New Scholasticism, conscious of the fact that as a system it is definitely and uncompromisingly pluralistic just as mediaeval Scholasticism was. I can see no way of bringing such thinkers to an appreciation of the strength of Scholastic philosophy until we have fought out the differences which divide the monist from the pluralist, that is, until the dualist position has become so fortified against attack that every species of Monism will willingly capitulate to the convincing force of its logic. Until recently it was the conventional thing to regard Monism as the only sound approach to the problems of the universe. Professor Ladd expressed that attitude when he wrote "that Dualism arises—at least in modern times—almost altogether as a protest against some form of Monism which is deemed extreme or dangerous."

The confidence of present-day philosophers in monistic thought is scarcely that of Professor Ladd. This confidence has been shattered in the last two decades. Many thinkers, it is true, are not as yet prepared to throw Monism overboard and to proceed in their quest, guided by an out-and-out Pluralism. On the other hand, despite lingering attachments to Monism, a fairer and juster estimate is quite universally made of the claim of Dualism that it represents a legitimate explanation of the nature of reality, and that only in a pluralistic universe can thought and experience ever come into harmonious and satisfying relations.

There is a general feeling that Scholastic thought is so bound up with mediaeval ideas of science that anything like a *rapprochement* between it and modern philosophy is unthinkable. The philosophy of Saint Thomas was developed in a period and in a *milieu* which were wholly unscientific. The physics, chemistry, and biology of the thirteenth century strike us as only a bit less childish than the animism of certain Australian semi-savage tribes of the present day. Not only did the Middle Ages lack scientific knowledge; its atmosphere was positively anti-scientific because of over-emphasis of the deductive process which it regarded as the sole means of acquiring truth. It is for some such reasons as these that many feel that a philosophy developed under such unfavorable circumstances has little or nothing substantial to offer modern thinking.

The objection involves a theory of the fundamental relations of science to philosophy, which must be analyzed before we can accept it; it exhibits, too, a picture of the scientific condition of Europe in the thirteenth century which does not harmonize with recent historical investigations. To take the latter point first. That the condition of the sciences in the Middle Ages was not at all like the portrait traditionally drawn, anyone can discover for himself who will take the trouble to read the writings of Haskins, Thorndike, and Duhem on the history of mediaeval Science. The genuine scientific spirit never died, even in the darkest days. The story of its accomplishments in the thirteenth and fourteenth centuries is as moving and dramatic as anything which modern science presents for our admiration. Particularly at Oxford was the pure spirit of investigation held in great honor. Such an attitude resulted in a series of achievements which are not only noteworthy but clearly opened the way to the more brilliant and better known discoveries of the seventeenth and eighteenth centuries.

The student of the history of mediaeval philosophy, too, is well aware of the analysis of the inductive method made by Ockham and the disciples of his school. Without such preparatory studies the advance of science would certainly have been delayed for a long period. Moreover, the great Scholastics were well acquainted with the methods and progress of the sciences of their day. That this progress in no way approaches what has been done in the nineteenth century, that the methods of science then in vogue were crude as compared with our own, do not seem to justify us in sweeping away at one stroke the solid and lasting accomplishments of those stirring days of the re-awakening of the human mind. To praise our own times, it is not necessary to condemn the past.

The New Scholasticism, as far as science goes, is not mediaeval but modern. As a matter of fact, that is one of the reasons why it is a *new* Scholasticism. We are quite conscious of the scientific handicaps under which Bonaventure, Albert, and Thomas labored. We would consider it nothing short of suicidal to fail to make use of every item of information laboriously achieved by modern research and investigation. The New Scholasticism cannot accept the physics, the chemistry, or the biology of the Middle Ages, nor does it make any pretense to justify the scientific views of that period. In this attitude we but follow along the lines pointed out by Pope Leo when he wrote: "We hold that every word of wisdom, every useful thing by whomsoever discovered or planned, ought to be received with a willing and grateful mind. . . . If anything is taken up with too great subtlety by the Scholastic doctors, or too carelessly stated—if there be anything that ill agrees with the discoveries of a later age, or, in a word, improbable in whatever way, it does not enter Our mind to propose that for imitation to Our age." Certainly, no one can quarrel with such sound and prudent advice. This being so, it becomes a laborious task to explain the view of those who assert that the advance of science has rendered useless the Scholastic synthesis but has left unscathed other philosophies, practically all of which antedate the great scientific accomplishments of our own day.

Perhaps the best indication of the willingness of the New Scholasticism to accept the proved results of modern science is the scientific work which believers in this philosophy have done.   In every field of investigation we have made substantial and important contributions to present-day knowledge. We have accepted, too, the results of other investigators and have attempted to interpret them in terms of our general philosophy of nature.   Where these results have contradicted theory, we have not wavered in sacrificing theory to facts.   That we have not bowed before the "idol of scientific method" nor gone over unreservedly to a mechanistic view of the universe will hardly be laid to our discredit. Present-day philosophy is not at all convinced of the wisdom of the wholehearted surrender which nineteenth century philosophy made to mechanistic science.   In fact, it has again and again repudiated this surrender and is working its way in a direction almost the very contrary to that pointed out by the science of the last century as the safe road to pursue.   Again, it is only a reactionary view of science which condemns a philosophy because it refuses to succumb to the mechanical view of nature.

The New Scholasticism is not mechanist, neither is it materialist.   If to be scientific it is necessary to become one or both, then Scholasticism will never become "scientific."   But what philosopher will accept the pretensions to intellectual autocracy made so often by materialistic science?   To do so, would be to confess our impotency before the problems of our own special field of knowledge.   Philosophy cannot be expected to sign its death warrant even at the demand of modern science.

Few things are more necessary to-day than a clear delimitation of the respective fields of science and philosophy. Science has been slowly but surely encroaching on the realm of philosophy until it has actually usurped command of all the approaches to knowledge, and claims for itself nothing less than the divine right to rule as dictator over all the provinces of human thought. It was certain that a reaction would come against such unjustifiable and absurd claims. The only surprising thing is that it was so long in coming. We are now in the full tide of that reaction. The scientists have finally awakened to the fact that modern philosophy is prepared to throw off the old yoke of servitude.

A new note, that of intellectual self-sufficiency, has been struck by philosophy, a veritable declaration of independence from the rule of science has been announced to the whole world. Philosophy is ready now to write its own charter of rights and in terms which it can understand, accept, and live under. The opinion of thinkers like Dewey and Russell, who favor the experimental method as the sole adequate philosophical method, is fast yielding to the viewpoint which refuses to submerge philosophy in the all-encompassing sea of laboratory science. As Hoernlé has so well remarked, "a philosophical theory is rarely such that it can be proved or disproved by some action devised *ad hoc*." If philosophy could be proved in the laboratory, it would cease to be philosophy, and would become science. Reality is so wide and so deep that no experiment can ever hope to fathom all its intricacies or all its profundities. The relationships of things, too, are so manifold that it is hopeless to attempt to bring them all under the head of a single carefully prepared test. One may play with the idea that, say, Utilitarianism or Absolutism may some day yield up their secrets to an experimental search. But the absurdity of the whole thing will strike us when it is realized that there are philosophers who actually work on the assumption that a particular experiment can be devised to test out the truth or falsehood of an inclusive view of the universe, a view which of its very nature involves both intangibles and imponderables.

The New Scholasticism cannot accept either the extreme of Experimentalism or the extreme of Deductionism. Taken as an exclusive method of approach to the problems of philosophy, both views are inadequate and false. Each, however, has a great deal to contribute to an ultimately achievable synoptic view of the universe. Thus, philosophy must be "scientific" in the sense that it cannot but accept the proved results of science. These results are both a starting-point and the crucial test of the validity of its speculations. But philosophy, because of the innate limitations of pure science, must ever soar above the formulations which are presented to it by science. It must also return to these same formulations in order to check up the truth of its own thought constructions. In both ways, therefore, science aids and even controls philosophy, for first of all, it starts philosophy on the right road to truth, and then it calls her back to this road whenever, because of the hardihood of her speculations, she strays into the by-paths of error or falsehood, or, what is worse, into blind alleys which lead nowhere.

Deductionism, too, has a part to play in the building up of a sound attitude towards reality. The manifest exaggerations which have resulted from an exclusive use of deduction in philosophy should not close our eyes to the validity of the process itself. The human mind, given axioms and postulates, is quite capable of arriving at the truths contained in them. That philosophers have abused the deductive method and brought it into disrepute is an unfortunate fact, but not a deciding argument against the method. Deduction, which does not involve *a priori* assumptions and is willing to be controlled by direct observation and scientific experiment, can be of untold value to philosophical progress. It is some such combination of the experimental and deductive methods that the New Scholasticism champions. The thought must strike every one that this *via media* presents itself as both rational and useful. To combine analysis and synthesis into a working method is a sure way of conserving the best that science has to offer, while discarding the worst that uncontrolled speculation is likely to afflict us with.

The widespread acceptance of the Darwinian theory is regarded in many quarters as having given the death-blow to every philosophy which admits the existence of God and of the spiritual, or which takes a teleological view of nature. Evolution is supposed to have made untenable any theory about nature which is not rigorously deterministic on the one hand, and essentially materialistic on the other. Evolutionism has been particularly devastating as far as Scholasticism is concerned, since it displaces man from his position as the central figure in the universe, regarding him merely as the end result of a progressive natural development which has taken millions of years to achieve. Copernicus, Kepler, and Galileo in physics and mathematics, and Darwin in biology, are supposed to have thrust all purposiveness out of the universe, including human purposiveness, and in its place to have erected "forces, motions, and laws, changes of mass in space and time, and the like" into guiding principles for modern mathematics and modern philosophy. In such a universe man plays a very minor rôle. Mind, conscience, and values are admittedly non-existent.

It is very much of a question, even granting the truth of the Darwinian theory of evolution (which, of course, we do not, as no one to-day does) whether such awful consequences for philosophy flow from an acceptance either of the evolutionary hypothesis or of the Copernican revolution. I am not at all concerned here with the evolutionary movement in its biological aspects. Whether it be true or false biologically is a question which only biologists can determine. Even if it is true, there are few aspects of it which cannot be harmonized with the Scholastic view both of life and of man. But evolutionism as philosophy is quite a different thing, and it is to evolutionism as philosophy that we object. This translation of a working theory from the realms of biology to the wider reaches of philosophy has been accompanied by assumptions which startle us because of their naïveté as well as by leaps in logic whose perilous, even disastrous, consequences ought to be and would be recognized by any thinker not prepossessed in favor of his own pet ideas. How the truth of biological evolution gives one the right to postulate that *ab initio* everything was a primordial undifferentiated mass of atoms, or that thought and matter are at bottom one and the same, or that noumenal and phenomenal are but aspects of a common reality, or that human ethics is either a matter of conventions or the result of economic determinations, or that God is but the construction of our own fear impulses—all of this has as much to do with the results of biology as the fantastic elephant which supported the fantastic tortoise which supported the world of Indian mytho-philosophy has to do with modern physical science. And while we are on the question of mythology, what a grandiose myth the evolutionary philosophy constructs to explain the origin of this world of ours! Is it any wonder that philosophers have begun to rebel against the irrational pretensions of a theoretical biology of this type? Philosophy has no serious quarrel with scientific biology. As a matter of fact, it is greatly indebted to biological investigations. It welcomes, too, into its camp speculations founded on sound

biological data.   But philosophy can scarcely remain true to its own better nature should it longer
permit the biologists to run wild in the field of philosophy.   To do so would be to allow the tail to wag
the dog.

Philosophers to-day are in revolt against biology;
perhaps it would be more exact to say, against biologists.   They are in revolt, too, against many of
the other tyrannies of the nineteenth century.   So
oppressive in fact was the overlordship which science
for a hundred years had been exercising, that it is a
matter of constant wonder that philosophy did not
rebel sooner.   In particular it has rebelled, or rather
it is rebelling, against many of the unacceptable assumptions of the biological philosophers.   Professor Urban, in his presidential address to the American Philosophical Association in December, 1925,
pointed this fact out as one of the most significant accomplishments of philosophy in the past twenty-five
years.   "The last 25 years," he said, "have marked
the gradual drawing of the limits of the concept of
universal evolution.   I should say that we are at
the end of the biological philosophies of the last
quarter-century.   The brute fact is that the pan-
orama of evolution, that comprehensive plan of the
sequence of natural events as it seems to unroll itself before our intellectual eyes, is far from being
the obvious, intelligible thing that many simple
minds take it to be.   It seems to make our life and
the cosmos in which that life is lived intelligible to
ourselves, but it itself is far from intelligible.

"In his poem, 'The Passing Strange,' John Masefield expressed in unforgettable words how passing strange the whole things is:

> Out of the earth to rest and range
> Perpetual in perpetual change,
> The unknown passing through the strange.

"That is what a merely naturalistic evolution inevitably is—the unknown passing through the strange. Strange—eternally and radically strange—all the varied phenomena of change, unless they possess that intrinsic meaning which attaches itself solely to a will oriented toward purpose and value."

The New Scholasticism will never become acceptable if it comes to us merely as a defensive position designed to protect its adherents from the exaggerations of naturalistic philosophy. Modern thought asks of the diverse philosophies which are called before its judgment seat more than that they be strong defensive positions. It asks them, first of all, to present their credentials in the name of philosophy itself, and this Scholasticism is prepared to do. The New Scholasticism is not a protest. It is a positive doctrine and, as such, exhibits a set of principles which must be evaluated on their own merits as on their general availability for the purposes of modern science and life. We feel, too, that this philosophy has a peculiar contribution to make towards the advance of human knowledge. It is on the basis of such contributions also that both its timeliness and truth are to be judged.

The body-mind problem and the problem of knowledge are the chief questions which divide philosophers to-day. A moment's thought will cause us to realize why these questions have assumed such large proportions in present-day philosophical speculation, so as almost to exclude the consideration of all other problems. The solution, for example, given to the epistemological question colors one's psychology inasfar as it is explanatory and not merely descriptive, one's metaphysics, and one's ethics. On the other hand, to profess parallelism or behaviorism or some sort of materialistic monism involves the acceptance of a group of psychological and metaphysical assumptions which cannot be squared with the postulates of the Interaction theory. In both cases the solutions offered are of immense significance for philosophy by reason of the consequences involved, as by reason of the attitude towards reality and experience which each theory necessarily implies. That the Neo-Scholastic theory of knowledge and of the psycho-physical relation is daily gaining ground and becoming more and more the accepted viewpoint of both science and philosophy, is an indication of the construction possibilities for thought contained in that position.

Let us first look at the Neo-Scholastic solution of the problem of knowledge. The New Scholasticism, as far as knowledge goes, is realistic. It accepts the reality of thought; it also accepts the reality of the object known by thought. Such a position involves a dualistic reading of nature. It is by a process of mental correspondence that the real object is brought within the knowing range of the mind. Given such a correspondence, truth results from the relationship; in the absence of correspondence, we have doubt or error.

Dualistic Realism is fully aware of the immense difficulties which flow from an acceptance of its philosophy of the knowledge relation. There are many points in the theory, particularly in the field of sense perception, which require a fresh and minute examination. While its analysis of error is the most profound and consistent that has ever been presented, there remains a great deal to be done in clearing up the obscurities of conception and judgment, to say nothing of that as yet unexplored field of knowledge, intuition. The foundations of the theory, however, are sound. Every advance in epistemological science abundantly proves this contention. Moreover, the consequences of Realism for all branches of science and knowledge are so important and decisive that one cannot think of giving it up unless he is prepared at the same time to overthrow practically all the certainties upon which life and knowledge depend for their meaning and value.

As a knowledge theory the New Scholasticism is profoundly intellectualist. It therefore approaches more closely idealistic theories than the voluntarism of Pragmatism. Yet, it sympathizes deeply with pragmatic strictures on the "inhumanity" of the cold, narrow intellectualism which has always characterized idealists, both subjective and objective.

What is more, the utility theory of truth can be accepted by us, but not in the sense in which Pragmatism propounds it.   If a thing is useful, undoubtedly it is true; it is not utility however which makes truth, for utility presupposes truth already made.   We acknowledge, too, the value of the coherence theory, but cannot come to regard it as the final test of truth.   Over and above the simple fact that the Real Whole, with which individual truths must cohere in order to gain truth, is for human knowledge a pure metaphysical abstraction, or, if not, then it is an unattainable acquisition, coherence presupposes a more ultimate criterion by which we are to judge the truth or falsehood of a particular proposition presented to the mind before it is capable of being brought into relation with the whole of truth.   If we are not mistaken, Realism can be presented as a higher synthesis of both Idealism and Pragmatism, for by a series of distinctions the differences between Scholasticism and these theories can be resolved into a higher and more acceptable philosophy.

Again, the New Scholasticism endeavors to steer a safe course through the exaggerations of radical empiricism, mysticism, and intuitionism.   Whatever place must be accorded experience, pure, mystical, or intuitive in life and knowledge, we are convinced that these experiences in no sense exhaust the possibilities of knowledge.   They do not even touch the heart of real human knowledge, which is the product of intellect alone.   Nor can we accept the substitution of the will-to-believe for the intellect-which-knows.

The philosophy of the place of the will in knowledge must be presented in sound and defensible terms if we are not to enmesh ourselves in a host of difficulties which will obscure rather than clarify the question at issue. The distinction between intellect and will must be maintained at any cost. It is a distinction which we present to modern philosophy, and which we consider one of the greatest contributions that the New Scholasticism has to offer to the solution of the epistemological problem.

The realistic trend of modern epistemology is something more than a reaction against Idealism. Some historians have seen it only as a protest against the ineptitudes of Idealism. This appears a superficial view of a movement which arose out of convictions and not out of animosities. Both in its new and in its critical forms, Realism has gone on the offensive and has presented a constructive programme of metaphysical thinking which is not to be despised. However much we may deplore the monistic, and in some cases the materialistic tendencies of the New Realism, we are forced to acknowledge that philosophy, after three centuries of hopeless wandering in the bogs of speculative thought, has at last put its feet firmly on the ground. And if one's feet are on the ground, the chances of an advance movement are not to be despised.

The New Scholasticism feels itself in friendly company when it associates with modern Realism. So many of our fundamental positions are the same, as our starting-points are identical. We feel, too, that we possess a something in the shape of clarity and precision of thought which is of incalculable value to the realist cause. Moreover, the arguments upon which Dualistic Realism is founded are of such a character that they are easily adaptable to the New Realism, and could serve the useful purpose of convincing thinkers, in whom there still linger strong attachments to Idealism, that there exists a convincing basis for the realist solution.

Towards a solution of the psycho-physical problem, the New Scholasticism offers a series of ideas of vast importance, not only for this particular question, but for psychology as well. Its specific contribution to the problem at hand is the Interaction Theory. Parallelism is admittedly inadequate, and involves difficulties which are well nigh insurmountable. There has followed upon the breakdown of philosophical mechanism a decided reaction against every phase of Psychical Monism. Professor McDougall, who has done so much to make Parallelism untenable, contends that the body-mind problem can only be solved in one way, that is, by some form or other of animism. Crude animism is, of course, out of question. However, it is animism, but a philosophical and scientific one,—what we call the Mind-Substance Theory,—that the New Scholasticism presents to the consideration of philosophy. We are quite conscious of the fact that of all the ideas which we defend, the idea of substance, and in particular mind-substance will probably be the very last that modern thought will accept. Since the days of

Hume, the functional viewpoint has held undisputed sway and has acquired the prestige of being regarded almost everywhere as axiomatic. The functional idea, however, must be blasted out of the modern treatment of mind problems. In its place we must substitute a dualistic and dynamic philosophy of act and potency, substance and accident. These categories are of as vital importance for metaphysical thinking to-day as they were in the days of Saint Thomas and Aristotle. That the conceptions current of these categories are scarcely better than cartoons is due perhaps as much to our lethargy as to the inadequate presentations which we have made of such necessary and far-reaching principles of thought.

The New Scholasticism also has its own contributions to make to the philosophy of nature. Space does not permit a detailed discussion of these offerings, attractive as the question undoubtedly is. To give only one example, we may say that it possesses a theory of the fundamental principles which all science, descriptive and explanatory, assumes to be true, but makes no effort to justify. In the explanatory field, especially, metaphysic is of supreme importance, since upon a sound analysis of the categories of causality, actuality, and potency, the truth or falsehood of the laws of science rests.

No aspect of philosophy has been so manhandled by modern writers as the ethical. The introduction of the historical method into the treatment of ethics by Herbert Spencer has very often served to obscure its real problems. By this I do not mean that the history of ethical ideas has nothing of value to say to ethics *qua* ethics. It has a great deal to say, but it should say it in an illustrative and confirmatory, and not in an argumentative manner. The historical method has carried along the false and harmful assumption that all ethics is in constant flux, that no sound principles of thought underlie its construction; in a word, that morals are mere conventions. The result of such confusion has been that philosophers continue to discuss the idea of Hobbes, Bentham, and Mill as if these systems had any present-day import. The fact is that Hedonism, either in its ancient form or in its modern dress— Utilitarianism, is an exploded theory. We have given up completely the sensationalism of Locke. How can we continue to hold on to Hedonism, which is nothing less than the Lockian materialism translated into ethical terms?

I do not think it too strong an assertion to contend that the New Scholasticism has more to offer philosophy in the field of ethics than in any other field. The theoretical basis of its formulations is essentially sound. The practical application of these principles to present-day conditions of industry, politics, social life, education, and religious belief is easy to make. A large and respected wing of Neo-Scholastic thought is hard at work in Europe and America making such applications, following the lead of Pope Leo XIII, who, probably more than any other man, succeeded in calling universal atten-

THE NEW SCHOLASTICISM

tion to the significance of these principles and their
applicability especially to modern industrial conditions. All of which suggests the thought that it is
through the gate of ethics that the New Scholasticism should enter in its onward movement towards
a better understanding and appreciation on the part
of modern philosophy.

PART III

SCHOLASTICISM
AND THE PERIOD OF TRANSITION

AND

STATUS AND VIEWPOINT OF THE NEW
SCHOLASTICISM

By J. S. Zybura, Ph.D.

PART III

SCHOLASTICISM
AND THE PERIOD OF TRANSITION

AND

STATUS AND VIEWPOINT OF THE NEW
SCHOLASTICISM

By J. S. Zybura, Ph.D.

CHAPTER I

SCHOLASTICISM AND THE PERIOD OF TRANSITION—
THE NON-SCHOLASTIC VIEW

"WITH the exception of the period which witnessed the transition of the pagan into the Christian world, the history of mankind hardly offers one more striking than that of the transition from the Middle Ages to modern times." [1] For well nigh a century and a half there had been a growing restiveness and discontent with things as they were, a passionate desire for the new, the nature of which, however, did not as yet appear in clear and definite outlines. These pent-up feelings burst forth with an elemental violence in the political, social, economic, scientific, religious upheavals of Humanism, the Renaissance, and the Reformation. Here we are concerned with this springtime of the modern epoch and heyday of the modern spirit only in so far as it affected the fortunes of Scholasticism.

I

A thorough study of the transition period is likely to call up wistful visions of "what might have been"

[1] Ludwig Pastor, *The History of the Popes* (St. Louis, 1902), Vol. I, p. 1—G. Voigt expresses the same view in his *Wiederbelebung des Klassischen Altertums.*

the course of Western thought and culture if at this juncture the genuine conquests of the new era had been fitted into the substantial framework of the tried and abiding values of the old, if a harmonious assimilative union had been accomplished instead of the disastrous division and attempted break of continuity, with all the sinister brood that have been the bane of our civilization for the last four centuries. As it was, the leaders of the new movements and tendencies were for the most part carried away by the first flush of their fiery but purblind enthusiasm. Recklessly they spurned the philosophic thought of the immediate past and eagerly turned to the exclusive study of antiquity, of man, of nature,—and sowed the seeds whose germination, flowering, and fruitage resulted in the world-views and life-views of to-day. On the other hand Scholasticism, which but a short time before was at its zenith and celebrated its greatest triumphs in Aquinas, began to decline at an early stage of the period of transition. It continued on its downward course in proportion as the new movements were reaching their meridian. After a brief revival in Spain and Portugal, it ceased to be a living influence in subsequent movements of thought and life.

Such are the facts. What is their true explanation? Was this rapid decline owing to some fatal flaw in the system itself, rendering impossible the assimilation of the *nova* by the *vetera,* or was it caused by extraneous factors, for which the system *as such* is not to be held accountable? Were the Scholastics of the period animated by the spirit of the old masters and did they, in harmony therewith, make an earnest effort to bring the old into a sympathetic and fruitful contact with whatever was true in the new science and philosophy? In other words: was it the authentic Scholasticism of its golden age, or only a degenerate semblance of the system, that was put to the test, found wanting, and superseded? Evidently, the true answer to this pertinent formulation of the problem is of vital moment to the New Scholasticism. For it is mainly to what is regarded as perennial in the thought of the thirteenth century, and can therefore serve as the foundation and guidance for further development, that the Neo-Scholastics look for light and inspiration in order to the solution of present-day problems through a fruitful synthesis of the lasting values of the old and the new: *vetera novis augere*. If, as many still hold, the tocsin of revolt in other domains eventually proved to be also the knell of Scholasticism *as such* in the realm of philosophy, then, of course, the Neo-Scholastics are championing a lost cause. Then they are indeed like weeping willows around a magnificent medieval mausoleum containing the remains of a system dead and buried several centuries ago. Then the only correct attitude towards Scholasticism would be what some of our non-Scholastic friends [2] take to be the common one to-day: "the historical retrospective attitude, as to a system that has had its day" (Professor Perry). For "the sense is still

[2] See Part I, Chap. I.

strong among those educated in different traditions that the starting-points of Scholasticism were superseded in the period of the Renaissance" (Professor Hocking). "Most academic philosophers regard Scholasticism as a dead issue, of historical interest only, representing a stage in the history of philosophy" (Professor Hudson). It is clear that such an attitude challenges the very right to life of the New Scholasticism. It must then be squarely met and fairly answered. In this chapter the non-Scholastic view of the fortunes of Scholasticism during the period of transition is considered. In the following, the Scholastic interpretation will be given.

The passing of Scholasticism *as such* was inevitable, it is averred, because the innermost spirit, the essential viewpoint, the dominant tendency of the new life and thought were in direct and radical antithesis to the very spirit and the fundamental content of medieval speculation. The old was tested in the crucible of the new and it disintegrated. The outworn system, like many another stronghold of tradition, had to encounter the formidable onslaughts of "the storming Titans" and was forced to surrender its scepter in the realm of philosophy. But the question at once arises, what was the nature of this ruling spirit that is said to have enlivened all the tendencies and movements of this period, and to have dealt the death-blow to Scholasticism? On this point there is vacillation and difference of opinion. Nor is this surprising. The age was an age of transition, and therefore one of fluctuation.

With unparalleled and almost savage effort, with unexampled dash and energy, it sought to create its own directives in every domain of thought and action. Everywhere there was such a luxuriant flowering of deeds, theories, events, that the many glittering colors of the fascinating spectacle dazzle one and render difficult the discovery of the one vital principle, the one vivifying breath of a springtime so exuberant in every field.

The difficulty is much the same when we limit ourselves to the evaluation of the transition-philosophy. Owing to its variegated and fluid character, its striking contrasts and frequent contradictions, it can hardly be brought under one formula without doing violence to history. How, for example, can we reduce to a common denominator the various phases of Nicholas of Cusa's teaching on knowledge and on God,[3] the metaphysics of Giordano Bruno, the life-views of the Platonists, Stoics, Sceptics of that time, the political theories of a Machiavelli, Bodin, Althusius, the fantastic cosmologies of a Paracelsus, Agrippa of Nettesheim, Cardanus?[4] And this is not all. The numerous currents of this philosophy were, like the literary and artistic movements of the Renaissance, revivals of the ancient systems.[5] Almost all the Greco-Roman theories, from the old

[3] Cfr. F. Olgiati, *L'Anima dell' Umanesimo e del Rinascimento*, Milan, 1924, p. 429 sqq.

[4] B. Jansen, S.J., *Wege der Weltweisheit*, Freiburg i. Br., 1924, p. 151.

[5] F. Klimke, S.J., *Historia Philosophiae*, Freiburg i. Br., 1923, Vol. 1, p. 288.

Ionians down to the Neoplatonists, were brought to life again; but their developments took divergent and often opposite directions.[6]   To be sure, the representatives of these developments were at one in their more or less emphatic and disdainful repudiation of all that savored of the speculation of the centuries immediately preceding.   But this entirely negative characteristic does not go to the core of the aspirations of that epoch, nor does it suffice to explain the elemental and creative forces which were then set free in such variety and profusion.   Besides, what really matters is not what, under varying degrees of self-delusion, these men wished to assail, but what they actually antagonized.   From this objective standpoint it is much nearer the truth to say that the deeper and broader characteristic of the time-spirit was the aim thoroughly to emancipate the natural from the supernatural, from the revealed and the hierarchical on the one hand, and the consequent individualistic and autonomous, anthropocentric and naturalistic bent on the other.

And so modern thinkers fix upon a principle of unity in the various philosophical tendencies of that time, which are then regarded as the branches of one tree: though stretching out in diverse directions, they none the less belong to a single organism, destined to grow on to our own day.   The Idealists find the principle of this unity, the soul of this organism, in the glorification of *man,* the Positivists in

[6] W. Windelband, *A History of Philosophy,* New York, 1905, pp. 353, 357.

that of *nature*. Thus, they say, it is not merely the *negative* factor of war on Scholasticism and Christian Aristotelianism that unifies the various systems: there is likewise a positive element of unity, namely, the immanentistic and naturalistic tendencies that stamp the speculation of this period. And it was the combination of these two elements which, in their opinion, compassed the downfall of Scholasticism. The first period of the transition philosophy,—the "process of purification," as Kuno Fischer designates it in his *Einleitung in die Philosophie*—seeks to strip Greek philosophy of the Christian vesture by which the Schoolmen had disguised it. The second attempts to lay the foundations of a new philosophy in keeping with the new vision of the universe. The first, wholly anti-Scholastic, finds its fulfilment in the Academy of Florence and the schools of Padua and Bologna. The Academy believes itself to be returning to the genuine Plato; the others think they are going back to the real Aristotle. Ficino and Pomponazzi [7] are the leading representatives of the efforts to purify, that is, to de-Christianize Plato and Aristotle. Bernardino Telesio [8] opens the second period, which, through Bruno and Campanella, [9]

[7] A. Douglas, *The Philosophy and Psychology of Pietro Pomponazzi*, Cambridge, 1910; Olgiati, *op. cit.*, pp. 531 sqq., and 584 sqq.

[8] V. Troilo, *Bernardino Telesio*, Modena, 1911; Olgiati, *op. cit.*, p. 702 sqq.

[9] Blanchet, *Campanella*, Paris, 1920; Olgiati, *op. cit.*, pp. 731 and 616 sqq. Also, H. O. Taylor, *Thought and Expression in the Sixteenth Century*, New York, 1922; the collection of Dyroff, *Renaissance und Philosophie*, Bonn, 1906 sqq.

reaches the very threshold of modern philosophy. In both periods, as has been said, the Idealists see the exaltation of man; the Positivists, that of nature.

II

According to the Idealists,[10] the humanistic as well as the natural science stage of the Renaissance are inspired by one and the same ideal, the emancipation and glorification of man. As Humanism is the exaltation of man in himself,—of his greatness, power, rights, achievements, aspirations, hopes, and in particular of his history,—so the Renaissance philosophy of nature takes the position of man in his relation to the world as the point of departure in all its problems.[11] This second view-point is essen-

[10] We here give the substance of Dr. Olgiati's excellent *Introduzione* to his thorough study (*L'Anima Dell' Umanesimo e Del Rinascimento*) of the spirit and historical significance of Humanism and the Renaissance, as manifested in their literature, art, political science, jurisprudence, religion, philosophy, and natural science. Without overlooking the sins and errors of that period, Dr. Olgiati seeks to discover the lasting contributions it has made. He finds that the outstanding characteristic of its various phases was *concreteness*. This quality is not contrary, but complementary to the *abstractive process* of medieval thought, and marks a true advance in the several domains of human culture and activity. In the *Rivista di Filosofia Neo-Scolastica* (Milano, 1926), Anno XVIII, Fasc. I, pp. 56–62, Dr. Olgiati answers the criticisms of this attitude towards the history of modern philosophy. Also, cfr. A. N. Whitehead, *Science and the Modern World* (New York, 1926), pp. 12, 14, 26, 57, 62.

[11] Cfr. W. Dilthey, *Auffassung und Analyse des Menschen im 15. und 16. Jahrhundert* (*Archiv für Geschichte der Philosophie*, IV, 604–652, V, 337–441; *Das natüliche System der Geistes-*

tially the same as the first, but widened so as to embrace nature within its scope. It is precisely in its gradual development from the Humanist revival of Greek learning to the ego-centric and naturalistic view of the world that the Idealists see and stress the radical antithesis of this epoch to the medieval conception of reality, to the metaphysics of being. That conception championed the absolute primacy of Being, of God: from Him all beings proceed, on Him they all depend; He is the source and center of all reality. Instead, the new era glorifies the dignity and inherent worth of man. This achievement alone, thinks Burckhardt,[12] is enough to make us forever grateful to this period. Numerous were the hymns in praise of man, now becoming aware of his rights and dignity: Giannozzo Manetti's *De Dignitate et Excellentia Hominis,* Marsilio Ficino's *Theologia Platonica,* Pico della Mirandola's *De Hominis Dignitate,* Leonardo da Vinci's *Trattato della Pittura,* Giordano Bruno's *Spaccio della Bestia Trionfante,* Galileo's *Dialogo dei Massimi Sistemi,*—these and a thousand similar panegyrics were synthesized in one of Campanella's poems on the might of man,

wissenschaften im 17. Jahrhundert (Ibid., V, 480–503, VI, 60–128, 225–301, 347–380, 509–545); *Die Autonomie des Denkens (Ibid.,* VII, 28–147). *Die Funktion der Anthropologie im 16. und 17. Jahrhundert (Sitzungsberichte der Königlich Preussischen Akademie der Wissenschaften,* Jahrgang 1904, 2–33). Also, H. Heimsoeth, *Die sechs grossen Themen der abendländischen Metaphysik und der Ausgang des Mittelalters,* Berlin, 1922.

[12] Jakob Burckhardt, *Die Kultur der Renaissance in Italien,* Leipzig, 1886; translated as *The Civilization of the Renaissance,* by S. G. C. Middlemore, London, 1890.

"the king, the sun, the harmony, the end of all things."

To be sure, the exaltation of human excellence was also the favorite theme in former times,—from the sublime chant of the Royal Psalmist to Dante's *Convivio,* from Ovid and Cicero to the Stoics and the Neoplatonists. But the likeness is only on the surface, the Idealists insist; for now there is a new spirit, born of man's awakening to the sense of his autonomy and central position in the universe. Formerly, despite occasional eulogies, man was as nothing in his own eyes, because unaware of his inherent worth and dignity. He was entirely at the mercy of Church and Empire,—both securely entrenched as the representatives of God. Such a man lacked self-consciousness, and therefore individuality. For him truth and law alike came from on high.

With Humanism and the Renaissance the scene changes. It is true that the identity of the human mind with the divine is not as yet asserted; but there is the dawning insight into the creative and autonomous initiative of man, together with that conception of the mind which looks upon reality as the mind's creation. "Hitherto," says Monnier in his work on *Le Quattrocento,* "man knew no other nobility but that of his origin, no other mission but that of preparing for the future by fasting and penance. Now, in the intense realization of present joy and beauty, man is everything: no longer a slave, but master; no longer a member, but the head; no longer a scholar, doctor, baron, draper, Guelph, Ghibelline, Christian,—he is himself, man.   He has made himself: 'I have made myself,' said Pontano.   He is his own end: 'man made for himself,' said Latini." In every phase and moment of this era Gentile [13] and other Idealists discern this new standpoint—a denial of the old one, a perfect antithesis to the metaphysics of being, and the cradle of the new metaphysics of the subject.   In every domain,—religious, philosophical, literary, political, social, scientific,—they see the medieval sun setting, and "a great forward step of the utmost importance being taken."

How, in their opinion, was this radical revolution brought about?   To free man's suppressed individuality from the yoke of that reality which was represented as transcendent by philosophy and theology alike, Humanism launches man into the free world of art, where he will never have to come face to face with that reality.   A frontal attack on the medieval world with its traditional science and its God was out of the question.   Hence antiquity is disinterred, not so much for its own sake,—for its mere restoration would have meant a retrogression instead of progress,—as with the aim of offering a new world, a fresh terrain on which autonomous thought can triumph.   Philosophy itself is now studied in the original texts.   Scholars are no longer constrained

[13] In the chapter on *"Carattere dell' Umanesimo e del Rinascimento"* of his work, *Giordano Bruno e il Pensiero del Rinascimento*, Firenze, 1920, pp. 241-269.

to test ancient teaching in the crucible of Christian dogmas, or to study that stifling theology in which the learning and science of the last century had become enmeshed. The Humanist lives and moves and has his being in a world wholly different from that of his contemporaries: their religion, ethics, politics concern him not at all. He treats them with the indifference and aloofness proper to the esthetic spirit. For reasons of practical exigency he may conform to the life around him, but it has lost all meaning and value in his eyes. In his new world he can roam without let or hindrance. Freed from the somber and oppressive shadows of the Transcendent, he serenely gives himself over to recollection and concentration. He raises aloft the standard of the liberty of the spirit to rouse men's minds and nerve them for an *immanentistic* conception of reality. At last he has grasped the greatness of man as the center of a world that calls for a radical reconstruction. Thus the new philosophy was being born, characterized by its outright antagonism to the Greek and Scholastic conception of truth as the knowledge of a reality already existing, and existing independently of the human mind. The first mewlings of the future metaphysics, *the metaphysics of the subject,* were becoming audible. Humanism and the Renaissance were the dawn,—as yet not quite clear,—of a radical transformation of philosophic thought. They were the first yearnings for an ideal intuitively glimpsed rather than fully understood,—the first steps toward a goal whose outlines

were but dimly seen.   Hence the shortcomings and
uncertainties of the period, and the faltering character of its initial movements.   But, says Windelband, the period of maturity, fermentation, and clarification is not far distant.   Then it will be seen that
the thought and history of to-day began in this sap-
ling of the transition period, which is destined for a
vigorous growth, while the cankered tree of Scholasticism is undergoing the inexorable process of dissolution.

Having steeped himself in the ideal world of
Greece and mastered the richness of its interior life,
man passes on from the abstract world of interiority,
as Windelband puts it, to the study of nature.
However, in the idealistic interpretation, this process *ad extra* is not opposed to that of inwardness,
but results from it as its consequence and development.   "The immanentism of the Renaissance,"
says Gentile,[14] "culminating in the new Platonism
of Ficino and Pico, in the naturalism of Pomponazzi,
Telesio, Bruno, Vanini, Campanella (a naturalism
so different from the naturalism of the pre-Socratic
period because of the historical moment that gave it
birth), is a continuation of the Humanist movement
itself.   It does not look to a return to the nature
over which had been spread that transcendent,
Platonic-Aristotelian world, revived and perpetu-
ated in medieval philosophy; rather, it goes back to
a nature rejuvenated and transfigured, because in-

[14] *Sistema di Logica come Teoria del Conoscere,* Bari, 1922 and
1923, 2 Vols.

timately pervaded by that ideal world in which,—as was taken for granted from Socrates on,—all truth was to be sought. *This nature of the Renaissance culminates in man,* who feels his own dignity, power, divinity,—in a word, who partakes of the sense of the divinity and absolute reality of spirit. . . . But this man attaches himself to nature and loves to identify himself with it, because for over fifteen centuries a common lot bound man and nature close together,—from the time when Plato, by opposing the reality that becomes to eternal reality, had limited all being and all value to the latter. *And it became necessary to vindicate all life, of man and nature alike, against the blighting oppression of supramundane reality."*

The naturalism of the Renaissance, then, means precisely this: man in his relations to nature, man and nature independent of God. According to Windelband,[15] it passed through three stages. First of all, philosophy began to detach itself from theology and took the study of nature for its task. Formerly all reality, man and nature alike, had to be studied in relation to God, because regarded as dependent on Him. Metaphysics had of necessity to be theology, as Aristotle wished and as St. Thomas realized in his *Summa.* "By Scotism and Terminism the faith-metaphysics of the Middle Ages had become disintegrated and split in twain; everything supersensuous had been given to dogma, and as the object of philosophy there remained the

[15] *Op. cit.,* pp. 354 and 366 sqq.

world of experience. But before thought had as yet had time to become clear as to the methods and special problems of this secular knowledge, Humanism and with it above all, the Platonic *Weltanschauung* burst in. . . . The supersensuous itself, and all therein that was connected with man's religious life, might be cheerfully left to theology; philosophy could dedicate itself to the task of being natural science, with a conscience all the calmer in proportion as it followed the Neo-Platonic precedent of apprehending nature as the product of spirit, and thus believed that in the conception of the deity it retained a point of unity for the diverging branches of science, the spiritual and the secular. Did theology teach how God reveals himself in *Scripture,* it was now the business of philosophy to apprehend with admiration his revelation in *Nature.* On this account the beginnings of modern natural science were *theosophic* and thoroughly Neo-Platonic." [16]

Thus in the second stage there arose the *philosophy of nature.* "The characteristic fact, however, is that in this revival of Neo-Platonism, the last dualistic motives which had belonged to the same were also completely set aside. . . . The fundamental tendency in the natural philosophy of the Renaissance was therefore the fanciful or imaginative conception of the *divine unity of the living All,* the admiration of the *macrocosm:* the fundamental thought of Plotinus of *the beauty of the universe* has been taken up by no other time so sympathetically as by

[16] Windelband, *op. cit.,* pp. 366–367.

this; and this beauty was now also regarded as a manifestation of the divine Idea. . . . With Bruno the symbol of the all-informing and all-animating primitive light is still dominant; with Böhme, on the contrary, we find that of the organism; the world is a tree which from root to flower and fruit is permeated by one life-giving sap, and which is formed and ordered from within outward by its own germinal activity." [17] The tendency toward an outright monism and pantheism is evident. The divine is humanized, nature is divinized. The *macrocosm* is not in opposition to the *microcosm,* nature is not in opposition to man, the Renaissance is not at war with Humanism. Quite the contrary. For from the metaphysical principle of Nicholas of Cusa and Giordano Bruno, that nature must be conceived organically and that she is contained in her entire indivisible essence in every one of her finite manifestations, flowed the theory of knowledge of that period: that man is the whole universe and therefore, by knowing himself, knows all. The knowledge of nature has its roots in self-knowledge (Weigel, Böhme, Campanella); the subject is not only not in opposition to nature, but it is only through the former that we can reach the latter; and, on the other hand, a fuller knowledge of nature resolves itself, in the last analysis, into a broader and deeper knowledge of man.

The third stage, that of *natural science,* was reached when the age of science and discoveries

[17] *Ibid.,* p. 367.

brought with it the rich development of the mechanical arts and the triumphs of Galileo. From a subjective, fantastic, speculative knowledge of nature man is urged on to the penetration of her secrets. He seeks to know the forces of nature so as to control them, to subdue them by knowledge and will. The then flourishing magic, superstition, astrology, reading of dreams and signs, necromancy, the medical doctrines of Paracelus, alchemy, the dream of the "philosopher's stone,"—what else were these but so many attempts to surprise nature which was as yet a closed book, to wrest her secrets from her and force them into the service of man? The discovery of America and the consequent widening of horizons, the increase of navigation, the new cosmographic knowledge, all added fuel to human hope and daring. Revived antiquity seemed to give man the dominion over history, Gutenberg over thought, Columbus over the earth. The concept of man is the soul that inspires all the discoveries, and inventions of the period, the scientific researches of a Leonardo and a Galileo. For Bacon, too, the *"interpretatio naturae* is but a means for *subjecting nature to the human spirit,* and his great work for the 'Renovation of Science'—*Instauratio Magna,* '*Temporis Partus Maximus,*'—bears also the title *De Regno Hominis.*" [18]

The essential and profound difference between the Middle Ages and the Humanism-Renaissance period is the difference between transcendence and imma-

[18] *Ibid.,* p. 386.

nence.   Such is the conclusion the Idealists reach from their interpretation of the centuries of transition.   During this epoch, as they see it, partly the tendency, partly the downright effort to eliminate transcendence dominates everything: the psychological discovery of man, the radical revaluation of the supreme values of life,—of theoretical truth, moral perfection, religious insight,—the assertion of the autonomy and value of nature, all draw their inspiration from this one ideal.   Therein Rudolf Eucken [19] sees the deepest reason of the success of this era in creating a new world of thought and life. His portrayal of this process hits off admirably the dawning of the "modern" time-spirit; it is therefore summarized here.

The Christianity of old, he says, had issued in an ascetic negation of this world for the sake of a remote beyond.   In its youthful ardor the new spirit feels itself ever more irresistibly drawn to this world and ends by placing therein the center of its true life: the idea of a beyond pales and gradually vanishes.   Religion is neither attacked nor rejected, but it is despoiled of that rigid and hieratic solemnity with which it ruled medieval humanity.   It is brought nearer to the immediate world of intuition and sensation.   Its forms take on a more human aspect and come down benignly into the midst of our every-day life.   This humanization of the divine is at once a sublimation of the human: the abyss between the two worlds gradually disappears.

[19] *Lebensanschauungen grosser Denker*, Leipzig, 1922, p. 298 sqq.

Our existence, instead of being in opposition to the divine, becomes its expression and reflection. It is especially art that brightens the world with this new light and transfigures it into a home of the spirit. Such a gladsome sense of life links the two worlds that the inherent contradiction is as yet not noticed. The transformation is living and profound. Nature and spirit,—these forces for so long hostile to each other,—are drawn together once more. An exalted feeling of joy reigns everywhere and finds expression in the beauty of form and the splendors of culture. Modern man exults as one recovering from a long and serious illness. Freed from the incubus of ultramundane restrictions, he enters upon that vigorous development of subjectivity which forms the outstanding characteristic of the Renaissance. Relying on his own powers, he becomes the true center of life, is quite untrammeled in his movements, and stamps his activities with the seal of his own individuality. Thus are fashioned personalities with a more intense vitality and clear-cut outlines than were ever found amid the thousand interdependencies and the drab uniformity of the Middle Ages. This renovating energy of the modern man, this triumphal process of his emancipation, penetrates and embraces the whole civilized world. The "interiorization of life" now becomes the germinal principle of a glorious future with boundless horizons and countless problems. Henceforth everything must be tested by the law and standard of man; it must become subject to his criticism and compulsion, and serve his will and pleasure. Sentiment, too, with its aspirations for happiness, becomes profoundly different from the medieval spirit. Its consolation is no longer the faith and hope in a beyond: it demands immediate satisfaction, and with burning passion looks for perfect happiness here below. The flourishing new life purifies things from the mists of traditional prejudices so as to grasp their real nature; and while making external reality its own, the spirit endows it with life and contemplates it esthetically. The union of power and beauty,—or better, the flowering beauty of life,—becomes the supreme and dominant ideal. Thus an esthetic conception of the world, of life and conduct asserts itself. The life of the individual becomes more self-conscious, more vigorous, more the work of man himself. Social life is stamped with refinement and culture, joy and laughter. The State is conceived as a work of art. The sentiment of glory is intensified. The spirit of autonomy, the independence of the individual, prevails in every domain. It is the seed which will flower into the modern States and modern nationalities, in complete separation from the Church. It holds in embryo the new economic world, no longer dominated by the Christian principle, as were the medieval corporations. From it, in a word, will issue all the actualities of modern life.—Such is Eucken's picture of this period.

An immanentistic orientation as against transcendence,—this is the clear-cut and violent antithesis between the new and the old. The Scholastic edifice had been reared on the foundation of transcendence, with the supreme and supramundane, infinite and personal Being as its corner stone. Into this medieval basilica Humanism and the Renaissance hurl a firebrand which eventually flames into a devastating conflagration. On the ruins of the temple of God is built the temple of man. The altars of the Transcendent are being replaced by a new altar dedicated to the dawn of a radical immanence whose noonday splendor is assured. Henceforth man and nature are regarded as independent of God. With deeper feeling and self-assurance man extols his own infinity and divinity. A new viewpoint has been gained,—*the viewpoint of the subject,*—from which Humanism and Naturalism must be studied if they are to be understood. This dominant idea of the period, says Gentile, will be taken up again and find disciples elsewhere and in greater numbers than in Italy. The metaphysics of being, of the object, is inexorably doomed to crumble. Beside its ruins the metaphysics of the subject will gradually rise—and it will rise by virtue of this period because "it is the Italian Renaissance-philosophy that will enable the modern philosophy of Europe to get under way."

III

Not a new vision of man, but a new vision of nature, say the Positivists, is the central idea, the vivifying principle, and the source of inspiration of the transition era.   The new viewpoint is not man and the absorption of nature in man, but nature and the comprehension of man in nature. Humanism and the Renaissance are the birth of the modern scientific conception of reality, and the consequent death of abstract speculation, metaphysics, and theology. Against the mystic dreams and ascetic aberrations of the Middle Ages they vindicate the indefeasible rights of nature, the value of facts, the purely natural character of *all* phenomena, the genuine idea of science as knowledge based on direct evidence for its truths. In this new conception man, too, with his mind and thought, is a fact among facts. He must be explained in conjunction with other phenomena and with the whole of nature.[20] He must be analyzed by the same direct and positive criteria.

The new movement, beginning with the Italian Renaissance, spread very rapidly. In Germany it developed into the Reformation, which was a re-awakening of the sense of individuality and personal freedom as against the inconsiderate and unnatural pretensions of an all-absorbing authority. In France it issued in the Revolution, with its promulgation of the new table of the rights of man. The present epoch is the fruition of the three preceding: the rational principles of the Renaissance evolved into the positive sciences of to-day; the sense of individuality of the Reformation gave us our effective civil and religious liberty; the rights of man asserted by the Revolution became the present laws of soci-

[20] Cfr. G. Fonsegrive, *L'Évolution des Idées dans la France,* Chap. III, Paris, 1921.

ety. Speculatively, nothing has value to-day unless
based on observation and experiment; practically,
the morality of labor is held in highest esteem.   But
all these characteristics are the very antithesis of
medieval mysticism and asceticism, and by that token the fulfilment of what the Renaissance initiated.
—Such is the Positivist's interpretation of the origin,
development, and ideal value of the period of transition.

In matter of fact, they say,[21] its new standpoint
originated in a return to the pristine ideal of philosophy, which, at its dawn, was the philosophy of
the object, of *nature*.   In the change that followed,
philosophy first turned from nature to man, then attempted to rise from man to something outside and
above man and nature, to God.   Thus were created
the fatal dualisms of spirit and matter, soul and
body, heaven and earth: another world—that of
ghosts and divinities—was superimposed on the
world of nature.   In the stagnancy resulting from
this other-worldliness, the finite was stifled for the
sake of the infinite, man for God, beings for Being.
The theoretical *credo quia absurdum* and the practical *fuga saeculi* gave rise to the grotesque aberrations of the Patristic and Scholastic period.   However, the dualism of *understanding* and *believing*
had one saving feature: it admitted of an initial development of the positive side of the mind.   This

[21] Their position is well stated by Erminio Troilo in his works
on *Idee ed Ideali del Positivismo*, Roma, 1909, and on *Il Positivismo ed i Diritti dello Spirito*, Torino, 1912.

was unconsciously elaborated by the Nominalists and Conceptualists, by Duns Scotus, Ockham, and the "Franciscan Positivist," Roger Bacon. The dark shores of the Middle Ages are receding. Philosophy is about to burst the cerements of medievalism and to hail the flash of a new light coming from the great Leonardo da Vinci. The freed and purified spirit of man is about to triumph in Positivism. With Leonardo everything undergoes a positivistic renovation: *method* becomes inductive, *science* is proclaimed to be *nature herself transformed into discourse,* nature is regarded as superbly *autonomous.*

And in this luminous renewal the mind moves and rises—but always within the confines of this world, —by means of aims and processes that constitute the new and natural, no longer the old and mystical, *itinerarium mentis.* The thought of Leonardo foreshadows the Renaissance asserting itself by its feverish activity and Dionysiac enthusiasm, reviving the soul of paganism and enlivening that Greek Positivism which the Middle Ages had smothered. These latter, however, are not laid low at one blow: their shadow still lingers and stirs in the theosophy, mysticism, magic, astrology,—a dark, bizzare mass, suggestive of doctrines that are like the gray zone between the old thought and the new. Small wonder that even some of the most virile thinkers of the period of transition are still subject to their influence. But these psychological *aurae* are quite negligible in view of the modes of thought now triumphing with Pomponazzi and Telesio, Patrizzi and Bruno,

Vanini and Campanella. To be sure, this triumph provokes opposition and persecution. On the one side stands the Platonic-Aristotelian tradition, a congealed conglomerate of idealism, metaphysics, mysticism,—become Christian dogma and Catholic authority, and protected by the secular arm. On the other is the materially weaponless thought that is renewing itself in the fresh flowering of the positivistic ideas and ideals of the pre-Socratic physicists, of the Atomists and the Stoics, of Epicurus and Lucretius. The final battle against spiritual and material tyranny is fought in the face of Inquisition and dungeon, torture and the stake,—and Positivism appears not only as the supreme philosophy, but also as a teacher of direct revolutionary action in the cause of human dignity and human liberty: the way to modern thought and life was marked by thought sublime and noblest blood. Thus *the era of new values* was ushered in: the violent negation of nature yields to a solemn affirmation of it; the conception that execrated and shunned nature as man's foremost enemy gives way to a philosophy that is a frank and virginal intuition and glorification of it, similar to that of the earliest Greek thought.

The clash of the two philosophic conceptions was a clash of two civilizations,—the Christian and the modern. The revolution was far-reaching and profound. After a long and troubled dream man bestirs himself and shakes off the nightmare of the Transcendent. He retakes possession of living reality, contemplates it with a well nigh mystic ardor, and penetrates it in a thousand ways. By discovering new lands and new things he widens the boundaries of the world. He extends the limits of the mind and of practical activity by painstaking research, epochal inventions, the fortunate disinterment of books, documents, and works of art,—tokens of the wisdom and glory and beauty of the past. Manifold and daring enterprises enable him to reconstruct the form and transfigure the spirit of art and literature. He withdraws the history of political and social vicissitudes from the control of Providence. He renews the methods and instruments for the attainment of knowledge and thereby transforms, directly or indirectly, the standards of value and conduct. The very excesses of the period, countenanced in the courts of princes and prelates, point to a radical revaluation of values. Medievalism is dead indeed. Desperate reactionary efforts of men like Savonarola are doomed to utter failure. The new principles and the new values triumph, and with them the new and true philosophy.

While this appraisal is shared by other thinkers and many men of letters, it is typical of the positivistic mentality and common to all representatives of this philosophy. It is found in Taine's *Philosophie de l'Art* and Comte's *Cours de Philosophie Positive*. And though Comte has words of praise and recognition for the Middle Ages (in the sixth volume of his work), nevertheless these centuries are for him the theological age of his three stages of development. They had "the great intellectual function, evidently transient, of preparing under the theological régime the elements for the reign of Positivism." Despite its many excellent aspects, he thinks this stage bore within itself the germs of dissolution, and its hostile attitude to science hastened the process. The period of struggles within the Church, marked by the clash of the spiritual and the temporal power, by the flowering of heresies and disputes, together with the period of open and systematic rebellion culminating in Protestantism and Deism, represent for him the critical and metaphysical era,—the transition, that is, from the theological stage to that of Positivism. Beginning with the fourteenth century there is noticeable everywhere a positivistic reconstruction in the domains of industry, esthetics, science, and philosophy. And the phase from Copernicus to Galileo and Bacon marks "the first direct founders of positive philosophy."

This substantially unanimous agreement of Positivists as to the origin and development of Humanism and the Renaissance, likewise stamps their estimate of the *essential character and value* of this new movement of ideas and of life. It was not a process toward inwardness, they insist, not a reduction of nature to man. On the contrary, it was a decided orientation toward the external, a reduction of man to nature, a tendency to study everything, psychology included, by naturalistic methods and criteria. Humanism and the Renaissance appropriated the fairest heritage of Epicurus,[22] with his mechanical conception of the world, his liberation from the religious yoke, his serene view of life. The Epicurean teaching, deadened for so many centuries by the mysticism reborn of Platonic ideas, and by the ascetic transcendence of the Middle Ages, is revivified during the Renaissance and brings in a breath of fresh and powerful life that purifies the atmosphere of the modern world. The thousand sinister powers nestling for ages in the dark and unknown depths of nature are ruthlessly driven out of every quarter. The mysterious threats of some dismal Nemesis from an impossible heaven can no longer terrorize the stupid credulity of the masses. Metaphysics and religion had turned aside the scientific evolution of humanity, and had ensnared and beclouded the spirit of man. At last the medieval night is over and the world is flooded with the benign rays of the sun of nature and the serene and sacred fatality of her laws. The Platonic elements of the Renaissance only served to arrest the advance of science by keeping alive those transcendent velleities which, even after three centuries of scientific progress, are not as yet eradicated. So, too, the feudal and ascetic phases grafted on that period are but lingering vestiges of an age whose sun had set never to rise again.

A strange survival of medievalism would be the attempt to force nature into second place and adjudge the primacy to man and the problems of his

---

[22] G. Trezza, *Epicuro e l'Epicureismo,* Firenze, 1877.

mind.   In the eyes of science "man is but a mechanical joke perpetrated by omnipotent nature."   Certain problems would never be broached if nature's
mechanical laws and their eternal necessity were better understood.   What means the universe with its
measureless motions, and whither is it bound with its
nebulous constellations in the immensity of space?
What part do we mortals play in the scheme of
things?   Why this torment of ideals?   Why this
tragic conflict in which reason and folly prevail by
turns?   Why the unquenchable thirst for truth, and
why the boredom that ever dogs its discovery?
Why beguile the heart with the hope of a distant
immortality, only to be plunged again into the ruth-
less whirl of eternal atoms?   What would this
proud sphinx that plants itself in our way, plies us
with riddles, and then destroys us with a scornful
grin on the dolorous way of truth?   Whence do we
come?   Why are we here?   Whither do we go?
Foolish questions all, children of the pride that
would fain make us the center of the universe, as if
the whole of nature with all her laws gravitated
around the atom called man, and had to give the
slightest heed to his questions and aspirations.

Nature, then, not man, is the epochal discovery
of Humanism and the Renaissance; nature, independent of the fantastic Transcendent of the old
metaphysics and of the God of religion; nature,
evolving itself by eternal and fatalistic laws in a perennial process of development, of which man is a

necessary product. Whatever at first blush seems to fall foul of this thesis is but a residue of the past, —the noxious incidentals which the life of history ever drags in its train, the scars of medieval folly showing even after centuries of scientific sanity. But this nature is not limited to material phenomena. It is much more comprehensive: it includes man, that is to say, all the phenomena bound up with his thinking and willing, both in the individual as studied by anthropology, and in the inclusive life of humanity, as studied by the philosophy of history and by sociology. These phenomena, too, are governed by fixed laws resulting from the very nature of the forces which produce them and from the conditions in which they operate. Besides forming a special class, these phenomena, too, are integral parts of the grand totality of the universe.—For the confirmation of their thesis the Positivists appeal not only to Leonardo, Galileo, Bacon, but also to the philosophers of this period. If, for example, we examine the work of Pomponazzi, what outstanding doctrines do we find? The independence of reason in science, the positive method in philosophy, the psycho-physical conception of the soul,—nature everywhere, in the world of matter and of spirit. Precisely the same is true of Bruno, whose marvelous insight enabled him to anticipate the concepts and supreme criteria of modern science and civilization. He divined the identity of force and matter, the infinity of worlds forming the sidereal universe, the principle that the concept of the unity of things originates in the logical process whereby the mind synthesizes the many and dissimilar data of sense observation. It may be truly said that Bruno anticipated the physics, the cosmology, and the positivistic psychology of to-day.

CHAPTER II

SCHOLASTICISM AND THE PERIOD OF TRANSITION: THE NEO-SCHOLASTIC VIEW

THE two phases of the non-Scholastic interpretation differ sharply as to the initial viewpoint; but they are at one in regarding Humanism and the Renaissance as a formidable and triumphant assault upon the very core of the medieval philosophic conception. In that conception God is the true center from which all reality and history must be regarded if it is to be understood and explained. The new center fixed by the period of transition in the interpretation of the Idealists is *man,* in that of the Positivists, *nature.* In the one, it is man who is emancipated from all divine transcendence; he substitutes the free consciousness of his own powers for submission to an ultramundane will, and lets the vivid sense of earthly reality and his own invincible energy take the place of God. In the other, it is nature that "creates" man and, mechanistically conceived, has no need of a God to explain it. The one turns from the metaphysics of the object to that of the subject. The other repudiates metaphysics root and branch. Both strike at the very heart of the old metaphysical conception, in which the Absolute, the Transcendent, was the ultimate explanation of man and nature. During the transition period the foundations of modern philosophy were being laid, with outright immanence as the cornerstone of the new edifice: man and nature are self-explanatory and self-sufficient. Formerly the standpoint was theocentric and other-worldly; now it becomes anthropocentric and this-worldly.

No antithesis more clear-cut and radical than this could well be conceived. And it is all-inclusive: there is no longer a question of this or that thesis, of this particular method or that individual theory. The point at issue concerns the very soul that inspires all thought, all life, all history. Is God, or are man and nature, the Alpha and Omega of reality? The alternative chosen will decisively affect the very source and center of man's individual and social thinking and living. It will determine his world-view and his life: it will definitely fix his standpoint on all problems,—philosophical, religious, political, economic, social, literary, artistic.

According to the non-Scholastic interpretation the choice was made by Humanism and the Renaissance. They overturned the Scholastic position and shifted the center of reality from God to man and nature. Thus was planted the root-cause of all those abysmal differences and glaring contrasts that mark off the modern and contemporary from the medieval thought and time-spirit. Will this interpretation stand the test of historical criticism, or is it merely a half-truth, an undue stressing of one phase of the period, a typical instance of the clever manipulation of facts and doctrines to make them fit the Procrustean bed of preconceived theories?

The answer of Neo-Scholastics, and of Catholic scholars generally, may be summarized as follows: [1]

I. *In point of principle,* the Scholastic metaphysics of being, with its conception of God as the creator, conserver, and ruler of all reality, in no way militates against the rights of man or nature.

II. *In point of fact,* the Renaissance cannot be reduced to one formula, to a single inspiring principle. On the contrary, within the movement itself there were two distinct currents, the pagan and the Christian. Whatever was sound in the various phases of the new science, thought, and life could have been readily assimilated by Scholasticism.

III. The failure of Scholasticism in this respect was not owing to a fatal flaw in the system itself, but to factors extrinsic and utterly alien to its true spirit: the causes of this temporary decline in no way invalidated its essential doctrines.

It is the aim of the following pages to substantiate these important points, as a true conception of the fortunes of Scholasticism during the transition period is indispensable for a correct attitude towards the Scholasticism of to-day.

I

It is a striking fact that the motives by which one current of the Humanism-Renaissance movement

[1] F. Olgiati, *op, cit.,* p. 58 sqq.

sought to justify its offensive against Scholastic metaphysics were identical with those advanced by paganism, many centuries earlier, for its hostility to nas-
cent Christianity: both conceptions were attacked
as implying a religion, a philosophy, and a life an-
tagonistic to the rights of man and nature, to worldly
joys and the free development of individual and social activities. Tacitus branded the Christians as
haters of the human race. Celsus denounced their
religion as antihuman. The early apologists,[2] repeatedly called upon to repel these and similar
charges, spared no effort to make it clear that it was
not the condemnation of human activities, of the interests of the Empire, of natural joy and beauty, of
literature, art, and culture that the Christians had at
heart, but the proper subordination of them all to
the sovereign will of God, and the rendering unto
Caesar the things that are Caesar's and unto God
the things that are God's.[3]   And the earliest Christian actualities confuted these charges more elo-
quently than could be done by any apologist. A new
civilization was burgeoning.[4] The worth of the individual was recognized even in the slave. The sacredness and importance of family life was upheld.

[2] Cfr. J. Tixeront, *History of Dogmas,* Vol. I, p. 203 sqq., St.
Louis, 1921.
[3] Cfr. *The Great Encyclical Letters of Leo XIII,* New York,
1903, p. 107: *On the Christian Constitution of States* (Encyclical
Immortale Dei), and p. 180: *On the Chief Duties of Christians
as Citizens* (Encyclical *Sapientiae Christianae*).
[4] T. W. Allies, *The Formation of Christendom,* London and
New York, 1906.

The dignity and duty of labor were emphasized.[5] Human activities were sanctified. Nature spoke a new language, to which an Augustine hearkened with enthusiastic emotion. A new joy was spread abroad,—not the bestial merriment of pagan orgies, but the serene gladness welling up from a soul divinely blithesome.

Man was not belittled nor was nature despised by the early Christian and medieval conception. The Renaissance was not the age of the "discovery of man." It was not the Humanists nor the Italian despots, but Christianity that imbued a vast portion of mankind with the proper sense of its inherent worth. For the Gospel and the medieval *Summae* [6] man is of a high dignity because he is created in the image and likeness of God, endowed with a spiritual soul, destined for immortality, an adopted son of God. The least of human beings is a person, and may not be treated as a mere thing.[7] Indeed, the only genuine and all-inclusive Humanism is that championed by the Church and Christian philosophy, and practically developed to a high degree especially in the twelfth and thirteenth centuries. "Human

[5] Cfr. C. S. Devas, *The Key to the World's Progress*, New York, 1923, Part II, Chapters I–V.

[6] Cfr. St. Thomas, *Summa Theologica*, I[a], qu. XXX, art. 3, ad 2; *Contra Gentiles*, II, qu. 59, c. 7 and 8.

[7] Cfr. De Wulf, *Philosophy and Civilization in the Middle Ages*, Princeton, 1922, pp. 55 and 277. Also, the Encyclical of Leo XIII *"Rerum Novarum"* (*On the Condition of the Working Classes*), loc. cit., p. 208.

nature and the problems to which it gives rise had
been studied by St. Augustine, St. Thomas, and many
others with a precision and minuteness by no means
less than those which were brought to bear upon
them by the writers of the Renaissance." [8] Some
of the latter neglected Aristotle the *metaphysician*
for Stoic philosophy, and therefore failed to revive the genuine Greek humanism, of which the outstanding characteristic was its metaphysics, setting
off Western civilization from Orientalism with its
subjective bent. The great achievement of St.
Thomas was Christian Humanism, the harmonious
fusion of Greek Humanism and Christianity, of
Greek naturalism and Christian supernaturalism.
This synthesis "guarantees the perfect development
of the natural man and of reason in the name of the
supernatural and of Revelation. The Renaissance
was to be but the consequence,—the achievement at
certain points, at others a mere falling short,—of
this Christian Humanism set up in the mid-thirteenth
century. Even to-day it still represents, as the heir
of Athens no less than of Bethlehem and of Rome,
Western thought in its most complete form, determined to sacrifice nothing of whatever may give man
more truth, more beauty, more love and order.
This is the reason why Thomistic philosophy, accepting and gathering up the whole of human tradition,
legitimizing and arranging it in order, deserves still

[8] A. Baudrillart, *The Catholic Church, the Renaissance and the
Reformation,* London, 1908, p. 14.

to-day that we should turn to it for counsel; for it bears the very semblance of our highest ideal." [9]

Throughout, St. Thomas and the Scholastics display the deepest reverence for nature and human nature.[10] Hence they regard the great truths founded on universal consent as the gifts of nature, look upon common sense as the natural regulative principle of philosophy, and on natural law,—the unwritten law of the ancients,—as an imprint of the eternal law, of divine wisdom, on the human soul. Hence, also, in determining the fundamental principles of ethics, they consult and take as guides the essential tendencies of human nature. The animate and inanimate nature outside of man likewise comes from God, and is a revelation of His power, wisdom, and beauty. Nothing whatever debars us from studying, interpreting, and subjecting it with a view to availing ourselves of whatever in it conduces to our advancement in harmony with the will of God.[11] Dante, the loyal disciple of St. Thomas, asserts that "by despising nature and her goodness" we commit an offence against God Himself. Before

[9] Étienne Gilson, *The Philosophy of St. Thomas Aquinas,* St. Louis, 1924, p. X.—Christian Humanism was the subject of Professor Gilson's address on *"L'Humanisme de St. Thomas d'Aquin,"* at the International Philosophical Congress (Naples, May 4–9, 1924); cfr. *Rivista di Filosofia Neo-Scolastica,* Milan, 1924, Anno XVI, pp. 287, 288.—Cfr. R. A. Cram, *The Substance of Gothic,* Boston, 1917, pp. 132, 140.

[10] Jacques Maritain, *Réflexions sur L'Intelligence,* Paris, 1924, p. 307 sq.

[11] From the first, man was bidden by God to subdue the resources of the earth. Cfr. Devas, *op. cit.,* p. 80 sqq.

him the Poverello of Assisi sang rapturously of the
nature that had been purged of its pagan elements
by centuries of Christian expiation and asceticism.[12]
"No one to-day would commit himself to the prejudice, also not so old, that before Rousseau nature
was not understood and that the thirteenth century
was ignorant of its beauty.   All of those who are
familiar with the sculpture of the cathedrals and
with illuminated manuscripts, or who have read the
Divina Commedia of Dante and the poems of St.
Francis, know how unjust that reproach is; and they
never compare the thirteenth-century interpretation
of nature with that of our modern writers." [13]

As to civilization and culture,[14] St. Thomas con-

[12] Cfr. G. K. Chesterton, *St. Francis of Assisi,* New York,
1924, p. 36 sq. Also: Siegfried Behn, *Die Wahrheit im Wandel
der Weltanschauung,* Berlin, 1924, p. 156. "The early Church
was ascetic, but she proved that she was not pessimistic, simply
by condemning the pessimists. The creed declared that man was
sinful, but it did not declare that life was evil, and it proved it
by damning those who did. The condemnation of the early
heretics is itself condemned as something crabbed and narrow;
but it was in truth the very proof that the Church meant to be
brotherly and broad. It proved that the primitive Catholics were
especially eager to explain that they did *not* think man utterly
vile; that they did *not* think life incurably miserable; that they
did *not* think marriage a sin or procreation a tragedy. They
were ascetic because asceticism was the only possible purge of the
sins of the world; but in the very thunder of their anathemas
they affirmed for ever that their asceticism was not to be antihuman or anti-natural; that they did wish to purge the world
and not to destroy it." (G. K. Chesterton, *The Everlasting Man,*
New York, 1925, p. 277.).

[13] De Wulf, *op. cit.,* p. 9; also *ibid.,* p. 137.

[14] Maritain, *loc. cit.*—Cfr. M. Grabmann, *Die Kulturphilosophie
des hl. Thomas von Aquin,* Augsburg, 1925.

stantly insists that these go astray and grow corrupt
when they cease to carry on the work of nature and
isolate themselves from it or do it violence. And
so positive laws are not just laws if they run counter
to the natural law. Education, like the art of heal-
ing, must be an art co-operating with nature by as-
sisting the active principle and developing the natural aptitudes of the pupil who is the chief agent
in the acquisition of knowledge. Science derives its
validity from the natural intuition of first principles.
Art is an imitation of nature; hence the Thomist
Dante calls it the grandchild of God, who is the
Author of nature.[15]

Evidently, this reverence for nature is far removed both from the "following of nature" advocated by the paganizing Humanists,[16] and from
the dictum of Rousseau that "all our primal pro-
pensities are lawful." And this for two reasons.
In the first place, it insists that man is *by nature* a
rational being: the use of intelligence, of right reason
is indispensable for maintaining the proper poise
and holding steadfastly to the golden mean and
right co-ordination of all human faculties, inclina-
tions, activities, individual and social alike, if they

[15] Cfr. the works of Ralph Adams Cram on medieval art, and
Joseph Kühnel, *Von der Enkelin Gottes,* Freiburg i. B., 1926.
[16] How they interpreted the Stoic axiom, *"Sequere naturam,"*
is sufficiently evident from their writings (Valla, Beccadelli,
et al.), and their lives; for them it meant the complete "emancipation of the flesh," the unbridled satisfaction of every instinct,
even the most ignoble.—Cfr. Baudrillart, *op. cit.,* p. 17; Pastor,
op. cit., Vol. I, pp. 16, 23; R. A. Cram, *op. cit.,* p. 177 sq.

are not to be tyrannized by the blindness of sentiment and the infatuation of desire. "Every really
human action is saturated with intellectuality. We
are truly men when we strive to act in conformity
with our rational nature, by subduing our animal in-
stincts and impregnating being and action with
thought. This victory over the body by means of
the mind, this penetration of the idea into the field
of practical activity, sums up the entire moral teaching of St. Thomas: man's goodness consists in living according to reason." [17]   Secondly, this respect
for human nature was judiciously tempered by a full
recognition of the truth that it is a fallen nature, en-
feebled in its faculties and tainted by sin: it stands
in need of supernatural light for the intellect and of
supernatural strength for the will in order to reach
its full fruition. This conception steers a clear
course between the Scylla of humanistic and naturalistic optimism, and the Charybdis of Lutheran pes-
simism. Human nature is not wholly good or self-
sufficient, but neither is it totally corrupt or utterly
helpless. Though considerably impaired, man's
higher faculties remain capable of a marked degree
of efficiency in the domain of sensible reality. He
can also reach supersensible truth, goodness, and
beauty. On the rungs of this ladder of nature he
can mount to a true knowledge of the existence, and
of some of the attributes, of the Author of all, by
the principles of causality and analogy. He can

[17] Olgiati-Zybura, *The Key to the Study of St. Thomas,* St.
Louis, 1925, p. 109.

know that God has not only spoken through nature, but that he has revealed Himself directly: he is able to substantiate the fact of a supernatural revelation. The true, the good, and the beautiful of this supernatural order can never frustrate the same properties in the natural order; the former can in no way be a negation of the latter, but its sublimation and elevation only. For He who *is* infinite Truth, Goodness, and Beauty is the Author of both orders. Hence He can raise the lower to the higher, but He cannot make the one to annul the other, to contradict the other,—for He cannot contradict Himself. The higher is *super*-natural and *super*-rational, not *anti*-natural or *anti*-rational: it is above, not contrary to, nature and reason. It is the superstructure and complement of both. No real conflict is possible between the *truths* of reason and revelation, of philosophy and theology,[18] of science and religion.[19] A seeming conflict ensues when

[18] Cfr. Olgiati-Zybura, *op. cit.*, p. 140 sq.

[19] Cfr. Sir B. Windle, *The Church and Science,* London, 1924. J. Donat, S.J., *The Freedom of Science,* New York, 1914.—In dedicating the radio station of the Paulist Fathers in New York (Sept. 24, 1925), Cardinal Hayes said that religion gladly pays tribute to science and "rejoices that in God's providence another page of the book of nature has been unrolled, revealing to mankind the wonders of the radio. . . . Religion and science reverence profoundly the truth that revelation after revelation of God's wonderful handiwork in creation will continue until the crack of doom." He paid the Church's tribute to scientists in these words: "Patiently, unselfishly, perseveringly, in the laboratory and the machine shop, on earth and sea and in the air, they have toiled at their self-imposed tasks that all mankind might enter into the fruits of their labor and share the secrets of

one or the other side advances opinions as truths,
theories and hypotheses as facts. "If, then, Scholastic philosophy effected the most perfect conciliation of reason with faith, we must not take it for
granted that the conciliation was brought about at
the cost of the independence of philosophy. The
Schoolmen were as far removed from fideism as
they were from rationalism. They attached independent value to philosophy as well as to theology,
while they contended that philosophy and theology
can never contradict each other. In this way,—
and herein lies the philosophical significance of
Scholastic philosophy,—the Schoolmen established
between the natural and the supernatural the relation which the Greeks had established between matter and spirit, the relation of distinction without opposition. This doctrine of the continuity and independence of the natural with respect to the supernatural order of truth is the core of Scholasticism." [20]

Finally, the Christian and Scholastic recognition

their new, amazing knowledge. . . . There is a further acknowl-
edgement we must make. Science, real, not false science, discloses to its followers a lofty ideal worthy of the reverence of
every man. This ideal is truth, always, everywhere, at any cost.
Without selfishness or passion or prejudice, at the sacrifice of
health and wealth, of fame and friendship and life itself, the
real scientist worships at truth's altar, realizing, as the Church
teaches, that there can be no vital conflict or contradiction between the truth revealed to man by God in the natural order
and that made manifest by Him in the supernatural."

[20] W. Turner, *History of Philosophy* (Boston, 1903), pp. 419, 420.
Cfr. Gilson, *op. cit.*, p. 17 sqq.

and vindication of the dignity of man and the rights of nature differ abysmally from the *deification of physical and human nature* revived by neo-paganism. Christianity and Scholastic metaphysics acknowledge God alone as the Absolute. Monotheism, not monism, is the true interpretation of reality, the true world-view. God alone *is* Being. From Him all creatures *have* being. He alone is necessary and self-subsistent. They are contingent and dependent. Man and nature do not make the laws of their being and activity, but must observe them,—man freely, nature of necessity.[21] This implies no opposition whatever to man's energies or to the full development of his faculties in every field of endeavor. Rather, it is favorable to them. For when man violates the law of God he does not further life, but destroys the beauty, value, and effectiveness of human activity. Far from being a hindrance to man's progress and self-fulfilment, the infinitely perfect Being not only grants him the power and grace to rise ever higher, but imposes on him the moral obligation of unremitting effort to "be perfect as the heavenly Father is perfect." Surely, this is not a belittling of human values. That activity alone is condemned which rebels against the order, harmony, and law flowing from the very nature and relations of beings. The transcendent God has never hurled an anathema against man's true self. On the contrary, He has endowed him

[21] Cfr. F. J. Sheen, *God and Intelligence,* London and New York, 1925, p. 273 sq.

with the consciousness of his own dignity. He has
made him capable of being perfected by the marvelous efficacy of the interior life, which achieves true
life by way of mortification, true redemption by the
way of the Cross, true resurrection by the way
of sacrifice. What is more, He has divinized man
by grace and elevated him to the supernatural state,
thus making him "a sharer of the divine nature." [22]

In the preceding chapter we have seen how
strongly the non-Scholastic interpretation stresses
what it regards as the irreducible opposition between
transcendence and immanence. Now such an irreconcilable antithesis is utterly alien to the Scholastic conception of reality.[23] For Scholastic metaphysics strikes the golden mean in a synthesis of immanence and transcendence, expressed by the formula: God in all *and* above all. This theistic conception neither cuts reality ruthlessly in twain and
separates it by an unbridgeable chasm, nor does it
violently mass, fuse, and identify all being in one
impossible whole. Its idea of transcendence is not
such as to make God a stranger to His world, after
the manner of the Deists for whom He is more remote than the farthest star.[24] Nor does its concept of immanence confuse God with the world and
man, as do the Pantheists. From these extremes it
is saved by its basic principles of causality and of the

[22] Olgiati, *op. cit.,* p. 60.

[23] Cfr. F. J. Sheen, *op. cit., passim.*

[24] The whole universe is intimately related to God, who is the
exemplary, efficient, and final cause of all things. Cfr. Sheen, op.
cit., pp. 246 sqq.

analogy of being,[25] on both of which it founds its doctrine of immanent transcendence and transcendent immanence. While infinitely transcending all creatures and ever remaining essentially distinct from them, God is most intimately present to each,— intellectually by His knowledge, dynamically by His power, substantially by His essence,—and permeates the efficiency of all created causes by His *concursus*.

A brief exposition of this fundamental teaching will show the radical difference between the theistic immanence of Scholasticism and the pantheistic immanence of Monism. It will also make clear what is to be thought of the charge that Scholasticism "created the fatal dualism" of God and the world. The things of direct experience have a causal influence on one another. Now, "a closer examination will convince us that a finite thing can never be the adequate cause of any effect, but is always, metaphysically considered, only a part cause, ever needing to be completed by another cause. Every effect is,—at least under one aspct, at least as an effect,—something new, something that was not there before. Even were the effect contained,

---

[25] For the explanation and application of these principles, see P. Coffey, *Ontology,* New York, 1918, pp. 381 sqq., 36 sqq.; G. H. Joyce, S.J., *Principles of Natural Theology,* London and New York, 1923, pp. 18 sqq., 244, 289; Sheen, *op. cit.,* p. 168 sqq.; M. Debaisieux, *Analogie et Symbolisme,* Paris, 1921, especially Part I and II; B. Franzelin, S.J., *Die neueste Lehre Geyser's über das Kausalitätsprinzip,* Innsbruck, 1924; J. Maréchal, S.J., *Le Point de Départ de la Métaphysique,* Paris and Bruges, 1923, *Cahier* I, p. 77, *Cahier* V.

formally or virtually, in the cause, it is certainly not identical with this latter, for if it were, there would be no causality, nothing would 'happen.' In all causing and happening, something which was heretofore only possible, becomes real and actual. But things cannot determine themselves to influence others, or to receive the influence of others, since they are not dependent in their being on one another. Hence the necessary inference that all being, all happening, all change, requires the concurrence of an Absolute Principle of being.   When two things act on each other the Absolute Being must work in and with them,—the same Absolute Being in both,—to relate them to each other, and supplement their natural insufficiency."

"Such is the profound teaching about the divine *concursus* with every creature.   Such, too, is the grain of truth contained in the monistic doctrine of causation.   It is utterly false when Monism represents the Theistic conception to mean that God, once having created things, lets them operate with full independence from His power, according to their immanent laws, and only occasionally interrupts this conformity to natural law by a personal intervention, that is, by a miracle.   God works in all and with all.   He permeates all reality, everywhere; there is no being beyond Him or independent of His conserving and concurring power.   Just as creatures are brought into being only through God's omnipotence, and have no independent reality of themselves, so they need the self-same ever-present, all-

sustaining power to continue in this being and develop it by their activity.   Every event in Nature is
a transitory, passing phenomenon, so bound up with
conditions and circumstances that it must disappear
to give place to some other.   How could a mode of
being so incomplete discharge its function in existence without the concurrence of the First Cause?" [26]

But is this not tantamount to harking back to the
monistic doctrine of the essential connection of all
things with one another and with the Absolute Principle of being?   God is in all things, He works in and
with them; there is nothing outside Him.   Is not
this Monism pure and simple?   No, for the likeness is only superficial.   "With all this similarity
one should by no means overlook the essential differences between the theistic and the monistic teaching on divine immanence.   In Theism things have
an existence of their own, really distinct from God;
in Monism they are essential constituents of the
Absolute,—their being is really identical with, not
distinct from, the absolute being.   Hence in Monism it is only in an improper sense that one can speak
of the dependence of things on the Absolute.   It
is always one and the same being, regarded from
another point of view; it is but a different manifestation or appearance of one and the same absolute
essence.   In Monism things have no activity of their
own, but all activity is that of the Absolute; in Theism, on the contrary, things themselves are really ac-

[26] F. Klimke, S.J., *Der Monismus und seine philosophischen
Grundlagen*, Freiburg i. Br., 1911, p. 185.

tive, even though they stand in need of the divine concurrence. In Monism there is but a purely immanent operation; in Theism there is co-operation with creatures. According to Theism God is indeed in all things, everywhere and always; but He does not annul their own individual reality. For this reason Theism is able to avoid the insufferable contradictions into which Monism necessarily falls when it identifies individual things with the divine substance. If these contradictions are not everywhere so glaring in the monistic systems, this is because the empirical individuality of things is safeguarded despite monistic presuppositions, and because allowances are made which are totally independent of the metaphysical foundations." [27]

In applying this conception of immanence-transcendence to man, Scholastic metaphysics makes its own the profound thought of St. Augustine: "Thou wast more interior to me than the innermost part of my soul, and superior to the highest part thereof." [28] This memorable phrase formulates that simultaneity of "God within us *and* above us"— *Deus interior et exterior*,[29]—which is of paramount importance as the formal principle of man's moral and religious life. That God is at once more intimate to us than our most intimate self and towers

[27] *Ibid.,* p. 186.

[28] *The Confessions of St. Augustine,* in the translation of Sir Tobie Mathew, Kt., Revised and Emended by Dom Roger Huddleston, New York, 1923, Book III, Chapter VI.

[29] E. Przywara, S.J., in *Stimmen der Zeit,* Freiburg i. Br., 1923, Vol. 105, p. 343.—*Id., Religionsbegründung, ibid.,* 1923, *passim.*

immeasurably above us as the infinite and incomprehensible Divine Majesty, that He makes himself known to us in imparadising mystic *nearness* as well as in cold, awe-inspiring *distance*,—the living realization of this immanence-transcendence engenders the true fundamental attitude of the spirit towards Him, the interior polarity of "fearing love and loving fear": a fear not like that of a slave, but inspired by the love which dreads to lose its Beloved; a love kept sacredly sober and tenderly reverent by a holy fear of the transcendent majesty of God. The "God in us" corresponds to the element of love; the "God above us" to that of fear. If both are intimately interwoven and properly balanced, the immanence of "God in us" will not lead to pseudo-mysticism or degrade God to the level of man; and the transcendence of "God above us" will not elevate man to equality with God. Thus, on the one hand, "man is raised out of himself beyond the narrow circling round his own personality; and he enters a realm of mysticism, aiming at intimate union with an indwelling God and at some participation in the divine nature"; on the other, he is "ever held in check by the divine law and the transcendent majesty of the Creator; so that the fountains of self-deceit are stopped up, and man cannot become a law to himself, his own master, nay his own God, self-centered, self-complete, reducing science to autosophy and action to autonomy." [30] But the disruption of this mutual interpenetration, the disturbance

[30] Devas, *op. cit.*, p. 74.

of this fine spiritual equipoise of immanence and transcendence, will inevitably result in eliminating the duality of God and man: in the case of immanence—if God is *only* "in us," He becomes either an objective constituent, or a subjective state and experience, of human nature; in the case of transcendence—if God is *only* "above us," then man ultimately becomes independent of God and, to all intents and purposes, becomes his own god. In either case the true idea of God is lost.

Thus the seemingly paradoxical position of Scholastic metaphysics,—grasping with its two hands the transcendent-immanent God,—is the *tutissima via media* between excessive objectivism, hostile to every thought of a "God in us," and extreme subjectivism, deaf to every mention of a "God above us"; between a rigid religious legalism, which demolishes the very groundwork of all religion,—God's kinship with the immortal soul issuing directly from His hand,— and an unbridled religious individualism, which debases God to the expression of an immanent evolution.   It may also be noted that with such a conception of reality as a natural basis, reason does not find it difficult to believe that God has deigned to answer the cry of the soul for a "word" from Him,[31] and through the God-Man has bridged the distance between creature and Creator in a manner ineffably more sublime than that of the natural order.[32]

[31] Plato, *Phaedrus,* 85, C.D.
[32] Cfr. E. Wasmann, S.J., *Christian Monism,* St. Louis, 1923, p. 41 sqq.

II

In the light of historical criticism, the reduction of all the thought and life of Humanism and the Renaissance to one dominant idea and one formula turns out to be inaccurate and incomplete. An unbiassed study of facts proves conclusively that neither "the glorification of man" nor "the mechanistic conception of nature as self-sufficient" can embrace all the main ideas and ideals of the transition period. *For within the very bosom of the new movement there was a violent clash of two diametrically opposed tendencies and programmes, the one radically pagan, the other essentially Christian.* But the non-Scholastic interpretation takes only the first into account, and by that token stands convicted of being a one-sided stressing of some aspects favorable to a preconceived theory, at the expense of others equally real and important.

"We must bear in mind," says Pastor, "that in this movement, which began in the realm of literature, there were from the first two conflicting currents." The contrasts discernible in its gifted founders, Petrarch and Boccaccio, became more and more marked as time went on. "On the one side the banner of pure heathenism was raised by the fanatics of the classical ideal. Its followers wished to bring about a radical return to paganism both in thought and manners. The other side strove to bring the new elements of culture into harmony with the Christian ideal, and the political and social civilization of the day. These two parties represented the false and the true, the heathen and the Christian Renaissance. The latter party, whose judgment was sufficiently free from fanatical bias to perceive that a reconciliation between existing tendencies would be more profitable than a breach with the approved principles of Christianity and the development of more than a thousand years, could alone produce real intellectual progress. To its adherents the world owes it, that the Renaissance was saved from bringing about its own destruction. Not a few Humanists wavered between the two streams. Some sought to find a happy mean, while others were in youth carried away by the one current and in mature age by the other." [33] For the detailed proof of this thesis of the *two* Renaissances we must refer our readers to the standard works cited below. With this correct appraisal of the period as the point of departure, we proceed to show that *whatever was true, good, and beautiful in the various tendencies of the new era, could have been readily assimilated by Scholasticism.*

From the very beginning Christian thinkers were

[33] Pastor, *op. cit.*, Vol. I, pp. 1 and 13 sqq. Also, Olgiati, *op. cit.*, p. 62 sqq.; H. Janitschek, *Die Gesellschaft der Renaissance und die Kunst,* Stuttgart, 1879; A. Wesselofsky, *Il Paradiso degli Alberti,* Introd., Bologna, 1867; J. M. Stone, *Reformation and Renaissance,* London, 1904; A. Baudrillart, *op. cit.; Catholic Encyclopedia,* articles "Humanism" and "Renaissance"; De Wulf, *History of Medieval Philosophy* (newly tr. by Messenger, Vol. II, London, 1926); P. Duhem, *Études sur Léonard da Vinci,* Paris, 1906–1913; Id. *Histoire des Doctrines Cosmologiques de Platon à Copernic,* Paris, 1914–1917.

imbued with that spirit of right universality embodied in the admonition of the great Apostle of the Gentiles: "Prove all things: hold fast to that which is good." [34] They were ever quick to appreciate and eager to appropriate the *spolia Ægyptiorum,*—the true, the good, and the beautiful of every culture with which they came in contact. They looked everywhere for the "seeds of the Logos" and for the rays of His Light. To them may be applied what Cardinal Newman says of their Church, which has ever been "sitting in the midst of the doctors, both hearing and asking them questions; claiming to herself what they said rightly, correcting their errors, supplying their defects, completing their beginnings, expanding their surmises, and thus gradually by means of them enlarging the range and refining the sense of her teaching." [35] Thus while combating pagan superstitions and immorality, they absorbed what was best in the intellectual culture of the Greeks and the Romans. They regarded the attempt of Julian the Apostate, to deprive the Christians of classical education, as more hostile and dangerous to Christendom than the bloody persecutions that had gone before. They realized the moral and religious dangers that lurked in classical literature and counselled the necessary precautions. But St. Gregory Nazianzen and the majority of the Fathers severely condemned those

[34] I Thess., 5, 21.—Cf. V. McNabb, *The Catholic Church and Philosophy,* New York, 1927, p. 11 sqq.

[35] *Development of Christian Doctrine,* p. 381, 16th Impression, New York, 1920.

unenlightened and often self-seeking zealots who espoused the cause of ignorance and frowned on classical studies, science, and culture.   Clement of Alexandria warned them that "the heathen philosophy is not deleterious to Christian life, and those who represent it as a school of error and immorality, calumniate it, for it is light, the image of truth, and a gift which God has bestowed upon the Greeks; far from harming the truth by empty delusions, it but gives us another bulwark for the Truth, and, as a sister science, helps to establish Faith.   Philosophy educated the Greeks, as the Law educated the Jews, in order that both might be led to Christ." [36]   St. Basil and St. Augustine, St. Gregory and St. Jerome keenly appreciated the beauties of ancient literature and the value of culture in general.   St. Augustine sought to assimilate what was best in Platonism and Neo-Platonism.   During the stormy and dark times that followed, the intellectual treasures of antiquity were carefully guarded in medieval monasteries and, even under the very difficult and unfavorable conditions of that period, were turned to account in the interest of Christendom.   Men like Alcuin, Anselm, and Peter Lombard were preparing the ground for the true springtime of the modern era, the thirteenth century,[37] which reached its full flowering in

[36] *Stromata*, I, 5.

[37] "In the reversal of so many verdicts upon history, which today we witness, nothing is more remarkable than the transference, increasingly felt as due, of the name *Renaissance* from the XVth to the XIIIth century.   The XIIIth was the true creative period; the XVth imitative largely."   C. C. Martindale, S.J., in *Intro-*

the immortal synthesis of all preceding thought,—
Christian and non-Christian,—achieved by St.
Thomas Aquinas. "Indeed from the time of St.
Augustine, the central figure in history, who was the
heir of all ancient wisdom, the starting point of all
new, the Church has handed down with unbroken
continuity a *philosophia perennis*,[38] ever growing
more comprehensive and gaining force from every
controversy, those yielding perhaps the greatest contribution who have been in appearance, from Por-
phyry to Kant, her greatest opponents." [39]

Manifestly, then, the genuine spirit and centuries-
old tradition of Patristic and Scholastic thought,
far from conflicting with the assimilation of the
sterling achievements of the new science and speculation, imposed upon the Scholastics of the transition period the sacred duty of eagerly appropriat-
ing the fresh intellectual conquests for the invigora-
tion and expansion of the old. What actually took
place we shall see presently.

As to classical antiquity, the champions of the
Christian Renaissance rightly felt that the beauty
of classic form could become the appropriate artistic raiment and fuller expression of Christian
thought; that the good and the true of the classic
content had always been duly appreciated by the en-

duction (p. 93) to *Catholic Thought and Thinkers*, New York,
1920.—Cf. McNabb, *op. cit.*, p. 86.

[38] This is the main thesis of Otto Willmann's *Geschichte des
Idealismus*, 3 Vols., Braunschweig, 1907.

[39] Devas, *op. cit.*, Part II, Chap. I.

lightened leaders of Christian civilization. This was the attitude of the more judicious and mature humanists. This was the spirit in which the Popes [40] and ecclesiastical dignitaries enthusiastically welcomed and encouraged Humanism and the Renaissance, and sought to guide these movements along the lines of right reason and Christian principles. "The position occupied by the representatives of the Christian Renaissance in relation to the ancient world was the only true one, and they have in some degree solved the problem how justly to appreciate antiquity. Their enthusiasm for the intellectual treasures of the past never went so far as to endanger their devotion to the Christian religion. Unlike the extreme Humanists, they held fast to the principle that the works of the heathen are to be judged by a Christian standard. They saw the danger of idolizing the moral and religious teaching of heathenism so as to make it appear that by its means alone the highest end of life could be attained, thus ignoring the necessity of Christian doctrines and morality, of remission of sin and grace from on high. In the light of Christianity alone can the ancient world be fully and justly estimated, for the pagan ideal of humanity, as exhibited in its heroes and divinities . . . is not a full and complete one. It is but a shadowy outline, wanting in the color and life which something higher must sup-

[40] Cfr. Jean Guiraud, *L'Église et les Origines de la Renaissance* (Paris, 1902).

ply,—a fragmentary form, which has yet to find its complement in a more perfect whole." [41]

From this standpoint of the Christian Renaissance it is clear that there were positively no true, good and beautiful tendencies in the new movements of thought and life that could not have been readily absorbed by the old metaphysics.

When the Idealists insist that the "glorification of man" demolished the medieval structure of reality by sapping the foundations of the theistic conception, they are laboring under a partial and partisan view of the facts of this period. It is true that for some Humanists the alleged "new discovery" and affirmation of man's excellence was tantamount to the negation of the Christian God and the exaltation of heathen heroes and divinities as humanity's ideals. These paganizers were marked by an overweening self-esteem, a grotesque self-consciousness, a fluent shallowness, and a naïve grandiloquence. The saner and deeper group did not suffer their enthusiasm for the treasures of antiquity, their admiration for man's endowments and conquests, their recognition of his unique place in the visible universe, to unbalance or bedim their sober vision of reality. Man, they knew, is the noblest of God's visible creatures,—but always a creature, subject to all that this involves. With them, therefore, the exaltation of human power and dignity was by no means an inversion of right order and an annulment of the metaphysics of the Transcendent; on the contrary, it was

[41] Pastor, *op. cit.,* Vol. I, pp. 47 and 48.

quite consistent with, and implied, the recognition of God and the glorification of Him as the Author of man's being and faculties. Giannozzo Manetti is a typical instance. His work *De Dignitate et Excellentia Hominis* is acclaimed by the Idealists as "one of the characteristic expressions of Humanism." Now this noble-minded and distinguished scholar, "the friend of Pope Eugenius IV and Pope Nicholas V, was most deeply convinced of the truth of the Christian religion. . . . Although a layman, he was well versed in theology and literature, and translated the New Testament and the Psalms. He had studied three books so indefatigably, that he may be almost said to have known them by heart; these were the *Epistles of St. Paul*, St. Augustine's *City of God*, and the *Ethics* of Aristotle. . . . This great scholar was a man of exemplary life." [42] Other leaders of the Christian Renaissance like Ambrogio Traversari, General of the Camaldolese Order, "the first to introduce Humanist influences into the ecclesiastical sphere," Lionardo Bruni, Gregorio Carraro, Francesco Barbaro, Maffeo Vegio, Vittorino da Feltre, and Tommaso Parentucelli, afterwards Pope Nicholas V, found no difficulty in reconciling whatever was of sterling worth in the new movement with their Christian convictions. Some scholars combined Scholastic culture with the Humanist sense for form. Attempts were made to harmonize the content of ancient philosophy with Christian thought. It is true that men like

[42] Pastor, *op. cit.*, Vol. I, p. 40.

the gifted Marsilio Ficino and his young friend Pico della Mirandola, the most brilliant member of the Platonic Academy in Florence, failed in their well-meant efforts in this direction, but they wished to remain loyal to the teachings of Christianity.

The Renaissance, says Eucken, strove to draw all accessible realities within its horizon, to link them with man's life and force them into his service. It was an age of voyages, discoveries, inventions. Very true. But all these, far from militating against the old metaphysics, led sound reason to a more sublime conception of the power and wisdom of the transcendent God. The truth of man's desire to dominate the world and control its forces for his well-being and advancement does not contradict the other truth of his subordination to God. The first act of Columbus on discovering the new world was to set up the Cross of Christ. One of the first inventions of this period, the printing-press, found enthusiastic patrons in Popes and Cardinals. The Benedictine monks of Subiaco welcomed the first German printers, and forthwith proceeded to publish such works as the Latin Grammar of Donatus, Cicero's *De Oratore,* the *Institutiones* of Lactantius, and St. Augustine's *De Civitate Dei.* Surely, it never occurred to these good monks that by such activities they were undermining the foundations of Scholastic metaphysics.

Finally, the Positivists' assertion that the study of nature and the consequent scientific progress necessarily proved the unmaking of the old standpoint is not true. The greatest scientists of the period were firmly convinced that in the voice of nature they heard the voice of God. The attitude of Catholic and Protestant theologians of the sixteenth century towards the discoveries of Galileo and Kepler [43] was unfortunate. As to Scholasticism, "there is no inherent contradiction between the broad principles of Aristotelian and Scholastic philosophy on the one hand and the new physics and astronomy on the other. Aristotle had advocated the investigation of nature, and the greatest of the Schoolmen had insisted on the importance of building a science of nature on the basis of empirical knowledge." [44] Albert the Great and Roger Bacon had strenuously sought to foster the scientific spirit. It will not do to confuse the *Metaphysics* of Aristotle with his *Physics,* and then make the sweeping assertion that "the whole elaborate structure of St. Thomas has fallen before the challenge of modern science." St. Thomas took the *Physics* of Aristotle at its contemporary face-value. "We are aware from well-known and oft-quoted texts that they [the princes of Scholasticism] never meant to give all the scientific theories of their time the value of established theses, but rather of more or less probable hypotheses,

[43] Cfr. Sir Bertram C. A. Windle, *The Church and Science,* p. 25 and *passim,* London, 1924. Also: J. J. Walsh, *The Popes and Science,* New York, 1911; Ernest R. Hull, *Galileo and his Condemnation,* Bombay, 1913; Devivier-Sasia, *Christian Apologetics,* New York, 1924, Vol. II, pp. 275 and 479.

[44] William Turner, *History of Philosophy,* p. 433, New York, 1903.—The recent deciphering of Roger Bacon's code shows the wide extent of his scientific knowledge and his intense interest in scientific method. Cf. *The Fortnightly Review* (St. Louis), Jan. 15, 1927, p. 33.

*whose disproof and rejection would in no wise com-
promise their metaphysics.*[45]   So, for example, St.
Thomas, when speaking of the movements of the
planets,[46] makes use of these significant words:
'*Licet enim talibus suppositionibus factis apparentia
salvarentur, non tamen oportet dicere has supposi-
tiones esse veras, quia forte secundum aliquem
alium modum, nondum ab hominibus comprehensum,
apparentia circa stellas salvantur.*'   And his disciple,
Giles of Lessines, gives frequent expression to the
same view." [47]   Thus St. Thomas admits the possible advent of a theory which would subvert the entire structure of Aristotelian astronomy.   But were
not the Scholastic principles of general metaphysics
and cosmology dependent on the traditional astro-
nomical, physical and chemical theories, and did
not the overthrow of the ancient science involve the
ruin of the ancient philosophy?   "Not necessarily;
and that for this reason: amid the débris of the demolished science there remained untouched quite
sufficient data to support the constitutional doctrines
of Scholasticism." [48]   Moreover, scholars like
Pierre Duhem have shown that the beginnings of
modern science go farther back than the Renais-

[45] Italics mine.

[46] In Lib. II *De Coelo et Mundo,* lect. 17.—See also *Summa
Theol.* I^a, qu. XXXII, art. 1, ad 2.

[47] De Wulf, *Scholasticism Old and New,* p. 150, Dublin and
New York, 1907. Cfr. also E. Gilson, *The Philosophy of St.
Thomas,* p. 13, London and St. Louis, 1924.

[48] De Wulf, *op. cit.,* p. 149; also pp. 83 and 200.—Cfr. also F. J.
Sheen, *op. cit.,* p. 75 sqq.

sance.[49]   Unfortunately, the growing experimental
sciences did encounter neglect and opposition from
incompetent Scholastics.[50]   But this utterly mistaken policy was not motivated by the fear that the
dominion over nature would diminish divine sovereignty by widening the sphere of human influence
and activity.   As will be seen presently, it was owing
to factors quite foreign to the true spirit and fundamentals of Scholasticism.

It was a solemn and epochal moment in the history of the race.   The now vivid knowledge of his
glorious past, coupled with his growing mastery over
nature, made man keenly conscious of his powers and
possibilities: he must needs progress; his freedom
implies new conquests and new creations.   Every
tradition and principle of Christian thought put an
attitude of hostility or indifference to these legitimate aspirations out of the question.   The only
feasible course was the marvelous programme outlined by Pope Nicholas V.   With him the *genuine, i. e.,* the *Christian,* Renaissance, ascended the
Throne of Peter, amid the rejoicing of the Humanists and general acclaim.   The papacy once again
gave proof of that magnanimous and all-embracing
comprehensiveness which is a portion of its inheritance.   "With admirable large-heartedness, with a
fearlessness which has in it something imposing," [51]

[49] See the following chapter.

[50] The Scholastics were not alone in this matter; Aristotelians
like Cremonini held fast to the *Physics* of the Stagirite.

[51] Burckhardt, *op. cit.,* 3rd ed., p. 265.

with a gesture worthy of the successor of the Greg-
ories and the Innocents, Nicholas set out to make
the Capital of Christendom the capital of classic
literature and the center of science and art. His
very enthusiasm may have led him to overlook or
underestimate the dangers lurking in the heathen
and revolutionary Renaissance. But it is to our
present purpose to emphasize that in this enlightened Christian Humanist we have a shining, practical, palpable proof of the thesis that it was possible "to reconcile the admiration for the intellectual treasures of the past with the claims of the
Christian religion, to honor both Cicero and St. Augustine, to appreciate the grandeur and beauty of
heathen antiquity without being thereby led to forget Christianity." [52]

From all this it is clear that there was also a
Christian Renaissance and that it could have prevailed. Not the new activities as such, but their
pagan spirit, militated against the old metaphysics.
Unfortunately, this spirit soon gained the upper
hand. From the time of Paul II the Christian Renaissance began to lose ground and the pagan Renaissance triumphed.

This triumph is admitted by Catholic scholars.
Historically, they concede, Humanism and the Renaissance led to a standpoint radically new. These
movements meant more than merely some sort of
higher activity in literature, art, and science. They
betokened a decidedly new direction of reflective

[52] Pastor, *op. cit.,* Vol. I, p. 55.

thought: *gradually to emancipate knowledge from the control of supernatural truths, and specifically from the dogmatic doctrines of Christianity.* It is this intrinsic quality that constitutes their distinguishing mark; and it depends at once on the supreme principle from which they start and on the goal to which they aspire. The principle is that human reason is the sole source of knowledge; the aim is to know the internal world of man and the external world of nature. This scientific direction finds its telling expression in the term *Humanism:* it is wholly and purely a cycle of cognitions that begin and are achieved in and for man; and it detaches itself from faith.[53] The beginnings of the modern era were marked by the abandonment of medieval metaphysics; by the laying of the foundations of the modern sciences; by the transition from deduction to induction, from speculation to exact observation; by the consequent cultivation of the realistic scientific sense; by the growing mastery over nature and her forces; by the resulting progress of material culture, that is, "the rationalization of nature" in general, or rather of our knowledge of nature; this was followed by the "rationalization" of man's external life, of his social, economic, industrial conditions. Thus man tended to become more and more engrossed by the empirical world and the present life, to the neglect of the other world and the life to come. Instead of other-worldly, as in the medieval period, his manner of viewing and order-

[53] F. Olgiati, *op. cit.,* p. 72 sq.

ing his life grew more and more this-worldly. One metaphysical persuasion after another was rejected in philosophy, ethics, religion, with downright positivism as the result.[54] Subjectivism, the cult of personality, individualism, anthropologism—these characteristic notes of the transition philosophy—may be synthesized in one formula: "the coming of age of philosophy." For the core of all the aspirations of this philosophy was to be autonomous,—to rely exclusively on its own rational powers, not to be shackled by any ecclesiastical or purely human institutions, ordinances, dogmas, traditions, and so to solve the riddles of existence, above all those of man's interior and of nature, quite independently of any external tutelage.[55] The Renaissance philosopher attained his majority, it is true, but he failed to reach the full maturity and productiveness of manhood.

III

We now approach the crucial question in our appraisal of the fortunes of Scholastic philosophy during the period of transition. It is not enough to say, as some do, that the decline of Scholasticism was owing to a radical change in the attitude of mind, to the new standpoint and center of modern thought. This is granted. The point at issue is: why was

[54] F. Klimke, S.J., *"Indoles Philosophiae Recentis,"* in *Gregorianum,* Rome, 1923, Vol. IV, pp. 47–49.

[55] B. Jansen, S.J., *op. cit.,* pp. 163, 164.

the new standpoint of immanence and naturalism taken, and how came it to supersede the Scholastic conception? Did the defeat result from an intrinsic doctrinal defect of Scholasticism itself, or was it brought about by factors alien to the spirit and essence of the system as such? This, as was noted in the first chapter, is a matter of vital import to the New Scholasticism.

It is a gross exaggeration to speak of "the end of Scholasticism" and of "the last Scholastics" as if the system as such had been "annihilated" in the course of the Humanism-Renaissance epoch. The decline of Scholasticism *"must not be regarded as the death-agony of a philosophical system* killed by modern discoveries, but rather as a very complex intellectual movement, laden with many injurious influences *quite other than the philosophical doctrine itself*. An impartial study of these factors would go to show that the sterility of the period in question is to be laid at the door of the philosophers rather than of the philosophy." [56] Prof. De Wulf concludes his *History of Mediæval Philosophy* with the terse assertion that Scholasticism fell for want of men, not for want of ideas. Another scholar says: "It was not a question of the times having outgrown the system, but of the system being too big for the times." [57] "They [the Hu-

---

[56] De Wulf, *Scholasticism Old and New*, p. 145, New York, 1907.
[57] B. Otten, S.J., *The History of Dogmas*, Vol. II, p. 22, St. Louis, 1918; cfr. A. Stöckl, *The History of Philosophy*, New York, 1911, Vol. I, p. 420; F. Klimke, *op. cit.*, Vol. I, pp. 242, 271; M.

manists] were not able to value rightly the kernel, so full of character, which lay within the rough shell of the scholastic terminology." [58]

In the thirteenth century Scholasticism had been confronted, though on a smaller scale, with a problem somewhat similar to that with which it was brought face to face in the Renaissance period. After the taking of Constantinople, in 1204, the Christian world came in contact with the philosophical works of the Greeks,[59] Jews, and Arabians. But these new intellectual treasures did not find the Schoolmen unprepared, nor did they burst in upon them like a devastating torrent or a violent downpour. By an extraordinary intellectual activity and vigorous development Scholastic philosophy had become sufficiently matured, so as not to be overwhelmed by the fresh and varied material. Theoretically and intrinsically it was ready to assimilate and elaborate it by ripe judgment and careful winnowing. And so the thirteenth-century Scholasticism solved the philosophic problem of its time quite satisfactorily, "without, however, becoming the last word in the evolution of philosophy,—a point not seldom overlooked by some of its over-zealous protagonists." [60]   Practical and extrinsic factors, too,

Grabmann, *Die Philosophie des Mittelalters*, p. 110, Berlin und Leipzig, 1921.

[58] Windelband, *op. cit.*, p. 360.

[59] Later, at the request of St. Thomas, William of Moerbeke, an able linguist, made a more accurate translation of the works of Aristotle from the original Greek.

[60] B. Jansen, S.J., *op. cit.*, p. 165.

were favorable to this happy outcome. Western
civilization was then at the height of a unified, compact, well-articulated polity in Church and State.
The faith was the dominant and all-pervading influence in every sphere of life and thought. The
unity of Scholastic philosophy and theology was for
the Christian peoples the symbol of the concord between the spiritual and the temporal power. The
University of Paris had become the center of Christian culture. And there were intellectual giants in
the land,—thinkers like Albert the Great, Bonaventure, and, above all, Thomas Aquinas, "the greatest
synthetic genius the world has ever seen." His
epochal achievement was the harmonious synthesis
of all preceding thought.[61]

Quite the contrary in all these respects was the
situation at the coming of this second springtime of
European culture and civilization. If the momentous moral and religious conflicts that are part and
parcel of the period of his development find a man
wanting in the requisite maturity of mind and will, if
at this critical turning-point in life he has not experienced, clear-sighted, loving counselors who know
how to give his freedom and unfolding the proper
play without fostering lawlessness and libertinism,
then there exists the imminent danger that his whole

[61] Cfr. Olgiati-Zybura, *The Key to the Study of St. Thomas,*
Chap. I, St. Louis, 1925. Also: E. Gilson, *The Philosophy of St.
Thomas,* pp. 268 sqq., Cambridge and St. Louis, 1924. On the
unity of the Christian world in the Middle Ages see A. Gemelli,
L'Unità del Mondo Cristiano nel Medio Evo, in *Rivista di Filosofia
Neo-Scolastica* (Milan, 1924), Anno XVI, Fasc. V–VI, pp. 345–355.

future may be warped or blighted. Such, precisely, was the tragedy of the unpreparedness of the dawning modern era for the new developments in life and thought which it encountered in such variety and profusion during the period of transition. As in other domains, so also in that of philosophy, the results were disastrous and far-reaching. The influences that made impossible a repetition of the brilliant achievements of Scholasticism's golden age were theoretical and intrinsic, as well as practical and extrinsic. We shall consider the latter first.

A brief review of the history of the fourteenth and fifteenth centuries will suffice to disclose the external reasons,—the political, ecclesiastical, social conditions,—for the unreadiness of the Christian leaders and thinkers successfully to solve the grave problems presented by Humanism and the Renaissance. On September 7, 1303, when Nogaret, Philip the Fair's minister of vengeance, rode into Anagni to take Boniface VIII captive, the medieval, the sacred order of things, which had lasted under conflict during five centuries, expired [62] in that crime which Dante [63] has likened to the Crucifixion. During the "Babylonian Captivity" of Avignon the Popes were forced to rely on the protection of France. Their supremacy over the states was at an end and the resistance of the nations commenced.

[62] W. Barry, *The Papacy and Modern Times*, pp. 30 sqq., New York and London, 1911.

[63] *Purgatorio*, XX, 86–90.

The unity of Christendom was being disrupted; nationalism and Neo-Cæsarism were setting out to take its place. Under the flag of Louis of Bavaria, in his long quarrel with the Pope (1322–1347), were collected many influences hitherto separate; the quarrel "may be described as a rehearsal of the Reformation on a minor scale." The crown lawyers were supported by Marsilius of Padua, then high in the Paris University, and more strangely still, by the Franciscan General, Michael of Cesena, and by Ockham, in whom Luther later recognized his master. The doctrines of the *Defensor Pacis* of Marsilius (1327) anticipated Luther by two centuries. They became the inspiration of Henry VIII and Elizabeth. While Avignon, "the false Rome," flourished in the sun, the real Rome fell desolate. For the Humanist the glories of ancient Rome were surely more inspiring than the sorry spectacle Rome presented in the mid-fourteenth century, when cattle fed near what were once the altars of St. Peter's. In 1348 the Black Death devastated Europe and swept off at least one-third of the population. The Great Western Schism was an attempt, premature but fertile in consequences, to break up medieval Europe ecclesiastically among the French, Italians, Spaniards, Germans, and English. The "nations" that voted at Constance were superseding and casting aside the Empire. They were also, in fact, debating whether each of the European chief divisions should not have its own church. Wyclif, Hus, and Jerome of Prague had their day. When

Martin V confirmed the rules of the Roman Chancery, his action put off all serious amendment of abuses until the Council of Trent.

Manifestly, philosophy and the sciences could hardly flourish amid such general restiveness, turbulence, precariousness, disintegration. Nor was this all. Though the truth of the fundamental doctrines of Scholastic *philosophy* did not, of course, depend on the old order of things, that philosophy was none the less intimately associated in men's minds with the various parts of the medieval organism. Accordingly, the leaders and followers of the movements hostile to the latter, invariably directed their attacks also against the former.

During those two centuries discords, ignorance, enervation of discipline, dissolution of morals grew apace. And thus it came about that the fresh cultural developments found the men and times quite unequal to the situation. The new era burst upon a "generation intellectually and physically overwrought, and in many ways unhealthy." [64] After the laudable efforts of Nicholas V to Christianize the new movements, and those of Pius II to crush their dangerous tendencies, the paganizing spirit triumphed. There was a deplorable lack of that clear and far-sighted policy and energy which would have known how to discriminate between the sound and the unwholesome, the Christian and the pagan elements of the new culture. The very men who

[64] Pastor, *op. cit.*, p. 12.

should have controlled the various phases of the modern spirit and led the several currents into the proper channel, were themselves bewitched by the sweetly alluring and dissembling influences of Humanism and the Renaissance. It was only after the "modern," secular, naturalistic idea had waxed strong and from its Italian home had spread to the north and west of Europe, only after millions had become separated from Mother Church, that reform and restoration were seriously attempted. Thus side by side with the *negative* factor of unpreparedness resulting from the conditions of the centuries immediately preceding, there was at the time itself of the new movements the *positive practical* factor of *disloyalty in conduct* to the Christian and Scholastic ideal on the part of its leading representatives. This factor militated strongly against the old metaphysics at this critical period, and therefore deserves some consideration.

In his preface to *Heretics*, Chesterton says that the most practical and important thing about a man is his view of the universe, that is, his philosophy. "The question is not whether the theory of the cosmos affects matters, but whether in the long run anything else affects them." "I think with Mr. Chesterton in this matter," said William James in his first lecture on Pragmatism. "I know that you, ladies and gentlemen, have a philosophy, each and all of you, and that the most interesting and important thing about you is the way in which it de-

termines the perspective in your several worlds." [65]
Every man is a metaphysician because every man is
a rational animal, or, as Professor Maritain puts
it, *"l'homme est un animal métaphysicien."* [66] *Every*
mode of life is an application of a view of the universe just as every world-view issues in a life-view
and a line of conduct. Hence the worth of a man's
philosophy is measured by his life: it is known by
the fruits it bears. A philosophy that is a mere aggregate of abstractions floating free without anchor-
age or suspended in the air, is rightly regarded as
worthless. It must be anchored in the pulsating
reality of life and history; in turn it must exercise
a living and formative influence on both. These
truths will enable us to realize what a telling blow
was dealt Scholasticism at this time by those dis-
loyal churchmen whose sacred duty it was to translate its principles and spirit into conduct, to body
them forth in their lives, to apply them to the solution of the grave problems and to the direction
of the developments that were affecting almost all
departments of human thought and life. "This reaction [towards antiquity] in the Renaissance took
a special coloring and shape from the circumstances
of the time in which it occurred. It was a melan-
choly period of almost universal corruption and
torpor in the life of the Church, which from the
beginning of the fourteenth century had been mani-

[65] *Pragmatism: Popular Lectures on Philosophy,* p. 3, New York,
1916.
[66] *Réflexions sur l'Intelligence,* p. 303, Paris, 1924.

festing itself in the weakening of the authority of the Pope, the worldliness of the clergy, the decline of the Scholastic philosophy and theology, and the terrible disorders in political and civil life." [67]

In Catholicism Scholastic philosophy had always found not only an ally, but something more: Catholic theology had availed itself of Scholastic metaphysics to establish the *preambles of faith*. Nor was this all. While a clear-cut distinction was upheld between revelation and reason, the supernatural and the natural, theology and philosophy, metaphysical notions were laid under contribution to illustrate, elaborate, and systematize the data of revelation. Thus the leaders of Catholicism were looked upon as the representatives of Scholasticism. Besides, Scholastic metaphysics clearly called for the practical recognition and application of the principle of the subordination of all beings to God. From ontology flowed theodicy and ethics. Every human activity, private and public, was to be developed with reference to the Supreme Being. Now the lives of many churchmen of this period,— Popes, prelates, and priests,—flew in the face of the very fundamentals of that philosophy which they, above all others, were solemnly pledged to champion by word *and* deed. To preach and teach transcendence and other-worldliness, and at the same time to live as if this world were "the be all and end all," could have but one result: to undermine and discredit a system of ideas that was so

[67] Pastor, *op. cit.*, p. 12.

flagrantly belied in practice by many of its foremost representatives; and such mere lip-service was especially disastrous at a time when the tendency away from these basic doctrines of Scholastic metaphysics was so powerful and widespread.

This, however, does not mean to say that during this period the sun of Christianity had set and yielded undisputed sway to the sun of Jove, Homer, Epicurus, Ovid, Seneca. Despite the degenerate lives of many ecclesiastics, there were thousands of souls, among the clergy and the laity alike, who loyally held aloft the blazing torch of Christian ideas and conduct. As medieval Europe was not one vast monastery, where all were given to unceasing prayer, fasting and scourging, so neither was the Italy of the Renaissance a pagan temple, where all burnt incense to Jupiter and Venus and Bacchus. In his history Pastor [68] gives documentary evidence of the profound religious and moral sentiment asserting itself in various forms and in many quarters. But the fact remains that in the Rome of the Popes and elsewhere, in episcopal sees, in chapter-houses, in convents and monasteries, there existed deplorable disorders. The dire enervation of ecclesiastical discipline; the worldly spirit of the clergy; the lives of unworthy Popes like Sixtus IV, Innocent VIII, and especially Alexander VI; [69] the

[68] *Op. cit.,* introduction to Vol. I and V (of the English translation).

[69] The recent work of Msgr. Peter de Roo, *Material for a History of Alexander VI, His Relatives and His Time* (Universal Knowledge Foundation, 1925), seems to have been unsuccessful

scandalous conduct of Cardinals like Ascanio Sforza, Riario, Orsini; the simoniacal elections and nepotism; the warlike and political activities of some Popes, who devoted their energies to everything except the sacred duties of their office; the spectacle of a Leo X wasting time and treasure on amusements, buffooneries, and the chase at the very time when a large section of Europe was on the verge of revolting against the Church,—this calamitous state of affairs [70] at such a critical period enables us to realize the *practical causes* of the decline of a philosophy whose basic doctrines were flatly contradicted by the lives, methods, spirit of the very individuals who were looked up to as its leading representatives, and were in duty bound to be its foremost protagonists in theory and practice. The flood of an elegant corruption submerged for a time the solid foundations of the magnificent structure reared by an Albert and an Aquinas.

Such was the disastrous disloyalty to the spirit and principles of Scholasticism in the *practical* domain. To evaluate correctly the *theoretical* shortcomings of Scholastic philosophy as we find it at this critical period, and its consequent failure to measure

in its attempt to reverse the judgment of Pastor concerning this Pope. Cfr. *The Month* (London, April, 1925) on *"Pope Alexander VI and his Latest Biographer";* also, *The Fortnightly Review* (St. Louis), Vol. XXXII, pp. 183, 243.

[70] For details see Pastor, *op. cit.;* also, Pietro Tacchi-Venturi, S.J., *La Vita Religiosa in Italia durante la Prima Età della Compagnia di Gesù,* Roma, 1923.

up to the problems arising from Humanism and the Renaissance, it is important to remember that this decadent condition of the system was the result of a gradually increasing deterioration during the centuries immediately preceding. Attention should likewise be called to what an eminent authority says about certain overstatements regarding these centuries: "The fourteenth and fifteenth centuries can be called the period of the decline of Scholasticism in more than one respect. But it is inaccurate to see in these centuries *only* the time of philosophic decadence, just as it would be an exaggeration to wish to perceive in them *distinctly* the dawning of modern philosophy." [71]   The time of great syntheses, of philosophical and theological *Summæ* was past, but some acute and at times original thinking was done on particular questions of logic, noëtics, and psychology.

In the course of the thirteenth century philosophic speculation had reached its zenith; that is to say, Scholastic thinkers had exhausted and philosophically elaborated all the material available from everyday experience and from such positive sciences as existed at the time. "The efforts of Roger Bacon and of Albert the Great to reform scientific method had failed: the sciences were not cultivated." [72]   Further speculation, in order to be fruitful, stood in need of new experiential data, of a broader and deeper empirical substructure.

[71] M. Grabmann, *op. cit.,* p. 110 (italics mine).
[72] W. Turner, *op. cit.,* p. 398.

But before new sources and means of positive knowledge and new methods of research were discovered,—as they began to be in the Renaissance period,—before fresh empirical food for speculative thought was supplied, there existed in the interim the imminent danger that intellectual evolution would come to a standstill: the mind would begin to feed on itself, or rather, on the material already assimilated and, in the absence of vigorous and original thinkers, lapse into sterile repetitions and futile subtleties. The Scholastics of the fourteenth and fifteenth centuries for the most part succumbed to this danger; and those of the sixteenth and seventeenth failed to accept and assimilate the new empirical data furnished by the scientific progress of that period. Such was the *general theoretical cause* of the decline of Scholasticism: the lack of men of genius, of great thinkers, gifted with the true philosophic and scientific temper. From this flowed *the particular causes:* the deterioration of content, method, language and, during the Humanism-Renaissance period, the neglect of contemporary thought and life and of the natural sciences. We shall consider each of these in detail.

The glorious heritage of the golden age of Scholasticism was the Thomistic synthesis achieved in function of the idea of being.[73] Even in the system of Duns Scotus and in the flights of the mys-

---

[73] Such is the thesis of *The Key to the Study of St. Thomas,* cited above.

tics this fundamental idea had been left intact.[74]
Had the true Scholastic spirit and tradition of the
13th century been kept alive down to, and during
the 16th, Scholasticism would have triumphed instead of being superseded. Unfortunately for itself and for the future of philosophy, the degeneration of its *content and method* set in some fifty
years after the death (1274) of St. Thomas.[75]
"Now that the great constructive thinkers have dis-
appeared, the intellectual knight-errantry of Abélard's day once more comes into vogue, the minds
incapable of constructive effort devote themselves
to analysis and controversy." [76] Scotistic formalism had issued in a multiplication of metaphysical
entities. This called forth a reaction in favor of
simplification, which, however, soon "substituted
dialectic for metaphysics, advocated nominalism,
and ended in something dangerously near to sensism
and scepticism." This tendency, which exerted a
decisive influence on the destinies of Scholasticism
at this time, was ushered in a few years after the

[74] F. Olgiati, *L'Anima dell' Umanesimo e del Rinascimento*, p.
83; the traditional appraisal of Duns Scotus has undergone a
marked modification. The reasons for this are given in the Note
on p. 532.

[75] As early as May 8, 1317, Pope John XXII sent a warning to
the faculty and students of the University of Paris: "Some are
abandoning the true notion of philosophy, . . . others are unfit
and unworthy to teach, some are accepted as teachers without
due examination, others, even theologians, are occupying themselves with useless questions and subtleties." Cfr. Denifle, *Chartularium Universitatis Parisiensis*, II, 200, Paris, 1889 sq.

[76] W. Turner, *op. cit.*, p. 392.

death of Scotus by Durandus and Peter Aureolus, who thus became the precursors of Ockham, the true author, the *venerabilis inceptor,* of the revival of Nominalism. *"Non est ponenda pluralitas sine necessitate,"* [77] was his *law of parcimony,* his "razor," with which he proceeded to curtail the "unnecessary multiplication of entities."

After the bitter conflicts of the eleventh and twelfth centuries, the problem of universals had been solved in favor of moderate realism: one of the outstanding achievements of the thirteenth century was the vindication of the powers of human reason. In the early years of the following century [78] one of the first causes of the deterioration of philosophic content was the unwarranted distrust of these powers, the narrowing of the sphere of valid knowledge, the abandonment of the virile intellectual standpoint, the lapse into partial scepticism [79] and, on Ockham's part at least, into extreme voluntarism. Durandus began by denying the knowability of the divine attributes, but not of the exist-

[77] *Quodlibeta,* V, 5.—This formula did not originate with Ockham; it was current in the thirteenth century. Cfr. Thorburn, *The Myth of Occam's Razor, Mind,* July, 1918.

[78] On the connection between Scotism, the precursors of Ockham, and Nominalism, cfr. J. Maréchal, *op. cit., Cahier* I, pp. 81, 82, 121, 122, and *Cahier* II, p. 22. On the intellectual movement of the fourteenth century, cfr. F. Ehrle, *Der Sentenzenkommentar Peters von Candia* etc., (Münster, 1925) ; also Werner, *Die Scholastik des späteren Mittelalters.*

[79] Cfr. C. Michalski, *Le Source du Criticisme et du Scepticisme dans la Philosophie du XIVe Siècle,* in *La Pologne au Congrès International de Bruxelles,* Cracow, 1924.

ence of God. Ockham went further by denying the knowability of God's existence, and of the spirituality and immortality of the soul: these truths were relegated to the domain of faith. Such views were the result of Ockham's theory of knowledge: he denied all extra-mental value to abstract concepts, to universals; they are mere "signs" or "terms" of a number of individual realities; the individual alone is real, and the knowledge of it is intuitive; propositions, not things, are the object of scientific knowledge. "The principles which Ockham formulated led to materialistic scepticism. . . . If we exclude the element of faith and take his philosophy as it stands, we must pronounce him to be the forerunner of the anti-Christian philosophers of the Renaissance." [80] Nominalism, or Terminism as it was now called, subverted the very foundations of the old metaphysics. It was the philosophic canker of the age. It infected especially the Universities of Paris and Oxford, and from there spread to other seats of learning. At Paris it initiated quarrels lasting for a century and a half. Ockhamism became the *via moderna,* Thomism and Scotism the *via antiqua.* To what extent scepticism had taken hold of some of the Parisian Doctors shortly after Ockham's time may be gathered from several preposterous propositions defended by one of their number, Nicholas of Autrecourt, sometimes called the Hume of the fourteenth century; in 1348 he

[80] W. Turner, *op. cit.,* p. 407; cfr. Windelband, *op. cit.,* p. 360 sq.; C. Michalski, *op. cit.*

was removed from the faculty of philosophy because of his "loquacity and temerity." [81]   Gabriel Biel (died 1495), inaccurately called "the last of the Scholastics," though a man of great talent, could offer his pupils nothing better that a *Collectorium ex Occamo*. It must be granted, however, that Nominalism, by focusing attention on the individual both in external and internal experience, led to observation and scientific research: the precursors of modern natural science were philosophers of the school of Ockham.

The thirteenth century had been an age of men rather than of schools.   In the following period the *multiplication of schools* and the *spirit of partisanship* worked great harm by dissipating the energy of Scholasticism and thus contributing to the deterioration of its *content*.   Scotus had "inaugurated an age of criticism and formulated a system of voluntarism which should have stimulated the later Scholastics to enlarge and strengthen the philosophical synthesis of Scholasticism in presence of the dangers which were soon to threaten it." [82]   Instead, Thomists, Scotists, Nominalists, Terminists, Albertists, Ægidians, Averroists,[83] were lustily

---

[81] Denifle, *Chartularium*, II, 576.—Cfr. I. Lappe, *Nicolaus von Autrecourt*, Münster, 1905; Hastings Rashdall, *Nicolas de Ultricuria. A Medieval Hume*, Proceedings of the Aristotelian Society, 1907.

[82] Turner, *op. cit.*, p. 397.

[83] There was a recrudescence of Averroism from the middle of the fourteenth to the seventeenth century, especially at Paris and Padua.

wrangling about trifles and subtleties to the neglect
of essential matters. What is worse, they were increasingly losing contact with the actualities of their
time, and seemed quite unable to realize that vital
problems and epochal clashes were looming in the
distance. No heed was given to the errors of the
day. There was little or no originality of thought
amongst them. An outward show of learning replaced true scholarship. "The further development
of philosophy was arrested. Questions which had
already been sufficiently discussed were argued in an
unchanging round. In the treatment of these questions acuteness degenerated into hair-splitting." [84]
For the most part the works of this period were
mere "commentaries on commentaries." [85] A most
deplorable result of the partisan spirit was the wor-
ship of authority, in outright opposition to the
Thomistic principle that in philosophy the argument
from authority is the weakest of all arguments,—
"*locus ab auctoritate infirmissimus.*" Each small
faction followed its own master,—*iurantes in verba
magistri*,—adhered rigidly to the doctrines of its
own school, and defended them against all others.
The doctors of the religious Orders became the

[84] A. Stöckl, *History of Philosophy*, Vol. I, p. 421, New York
and London, 1911.

[85] Notable exceptions were the Thomists John Capreolus
(1380–1444), St. Antoninus of Florence (1389–1459), Francis
Silvester Ferrariensis (1474–1528), with his excellent commentary
on the *Summa Contra Gentiles*, Thomas de Vio (Card. Cajetan,
1469–1534), with his commentary on the *Summa Theologica.*—
Of the Scholastic revival in Spain and Portugal a word will be
said later.

authority for the students of those Orders.   Controversy and servility replaced original and profound research.   This condition could only produce stagnation.

Another factor detrimental to the *content* of Scholasticism was *ignorance of the teaching of the great Scholastics,* of the real meaning and character of their system, or of parts thereof.   There are instances of such misconceptions early in the fourteenth century.   Durandus misunderstood the Scholastic doctrine of sensible and intelligible *species* and of the function of the "active intellect."   Such ignorance grew apace.   The representatives of Scholasticism in the seats of academic authority misconstrued the fundamental concepts of Scholasticism, such as matter and form, species, faculties. They stood by the Scholastic formulas, but they either gave them a merely verbal meaning or mistook their real meaning, betraying equally in both cases the sane and rational metaphysics of the thirteenth century which they thought they were defending.[86]   Moreover, there were other influences that tended to produce a relaxation of the spirit of serious study and the decline of science and philosophy.   Of the many universities founded in the fourteenth and fifteenth centuries, some received the power of conferring academic degrees, others simply usurped it.   To attract students in greater numbers they made graduation easier.   The chairs of philosophy were held by teachers who fol-

[86] De Wulf, *Scholasticism Old and New,* p. 148.

lowed the minor philosophers to the neglect of the
great masters. In the seventeenth and eighteenth
centuries the very professors of Aristotelian philosophy were ignorant of the fundamental Scholastic doctrines.[87]

The *degeneration of method* went hand in hand
with that of content. And the root-reason was the
same: the lack of forceful, fertile thinkers and of
new empirical material. The Scholastic method,[88]
modeled on that of Aristotle, had been rounded out
in the thirteenth century and used effectively. But
the later Scholastics carried it to an extravagant
excess, until it often defeated the very ends of
method. Instead of the limpid and easy manner
of Aquinas there now appeared an endless series
of "distinctions and subdistinctions and divisions
and classifications, until finally all thought became
mystified and muddled in an inextricable maze of
schemes, systems and departments!"[89] It is very
difficult to follow one of these long-winded *quaestiones* without losing the connecting thread. The
Scotist school especially delighted in the excessive
cultivation of formalism and subtle abstractions.
One of its leading representatives, Franciscus May-
ronis, was characteristically styled the *magister
acutus abstractionum*. It neglected both method
and language to such an extent that, together with

[87] Klimke, *Historia Philosophiae*, Vol. I, pp. 243, 271.
[88] Cfr. M. Grabmann, *Die Geschichte der scholastischen Methode,* Freiburg i. Br., 1909 sqq. (not yet complete).
[89] De Wulf, *op. cit.,* p. 147.

the Terministic school, it contributed greatly toward the decline of Scholasticism.[90]   Dialectic formalism poisoned all the philosophical writings of the
sixteenth century.   Such chop-logic and captious
quibbling were reason enough for the caustic sally
of Galileo about "the quintessence of syllogisms
most subtilely distilled."   The fantastic notions that
were but a caricature of Scholastic doctrine fully
deserved the scoffs and sarcasms of Malebranche,
Arnauld, and Molière.

With this barren and obsolete method was
coupled the *corruption of Latinity and an artificial
terminology*.[91]   Much of the philosophical language had become a jumble of outrageous barbarisms.   The clear, easy, and attractive style of the
earlier Middle Ages had given way to an uncouth
and unadorned mode of expression.   Often grammar, syntax, even orthography were ignored.   Futile questions, idle subtleties, obscure thoughts were
clothed in language still more repellent and obscure.
These insufferable faults of method and style were
laid at the door of Scholasticism itself.   We can
well imagine how the elegant but shallow Humanists,—and the general public of a like calibre,—re-
acted to this contempt of the elementary demands
of esthetics at a time when the classic literary forms
of Rome and Greece were becoming generally
known, especially after the invention of the printing-
press, when beauty of language and grace of style

[90] F. Klimke, *op. cit.*, p. 249; A. Stöckl, *op. cit.*, p. 412.
[91] Some instances are given in the *Chartularium*, III, p. XI.

were idolized; when glittering imitations and alluring errors, robed in a rich and colorful raiment, had far more appeal than the content of thought and the substance of truth, especially when presented in tatters. The minds of the Renaissance preferred "humanistic works,—such as those of Vives or of Agricola or of Nizolius or of others even more superficial,—to the dry subtleties of the contemporary 'terminists.' " [92] "With their essentially esthetic disposition they had no longer any feeling for the abstract nature of that science of abstract conceptions. Thus they opened the battle in all directions with the weapons of jest and of earnest; *instead of conceptions they demanded things;* instead of artificially constructed words, the language of the cultivated world; instead of subtle proofs and distinctions, a tasteful exposition that should speak to the imagination and heart of the living man." [93]

Now, *the virile and constructive thinkers of the thirteenth century, had they lived at this time, could and would have been capable of giving the Renaissance minds all this and more.* Those men, possessed of the true philosophic temper and outlook, would have given the young and adventurous modern spirit not only the new *things* it demanded, but the tried directives and formative *conceptions* it needed to guide and guard it against the pitfalls

[92] De Wulf, *Philosophy and Civilization in the Middle Ages,* p. 7, Princeton, 1922.
[93] W. Windelband, *op. cit.,* p. 360.

and perils lurking in the new things. Without sacrificing one jot or tittle of what was *perennial* in
their *conceptions,* they would have *re-thought* and
re-interpreted them in reference to what was of
lasting value in the new *things,*—the new movements, currents of thought, scientific discoveries,
problems. Instead of maintaining a surly and suspicious aloofness, they would have extended a warm
welcome to whatever was true and good in the new
things, and fitted it into the broad and solid framework of the old synthetic *conception.* Instead of
being alarmed about their metaphysics because of
the new scientific springtime, they would have freed
Scholastic metaphysics from Aristotelian physics.
Instead of stubbornly prolonging the repugnant
union of the discredited results of their infant
science with the eternal principles of an immortal
metaphysics, they would have proceeded to elaborate
a more perfect and more fruitful synthesis of the
old metaphysics and the new science.[94] Instead of
fatuously clinging to sophistic subtleties and excessive abstractions, they would have complemented
and fructified the medieval *abstractness of concepts*
with the *modern concreteness of things.* And all
this they would have sought to do in the "tasteful
exposition" called for by the new culture. In a
word, those intellectual giants of yore would have
been equal to the new demands, opportunities, and
responsibilities. On a grander scale they would

[94] The attitude of the princes of Scholasticism in this matter has
been pointed out *supra.*

have repeated their glorious triumphs of the thirteenth century. They would have stripped the robust old oak of the *philosophia perennis* of its withered branches and ingrafted instead the sound shoots of the new thought and science: a living continuity would have been achieved, Scholasticism would have been spared the humiliation of centuries, and the course of modern thought would have been quite different.

Unfortunately, their decadent successors did none of these things at the critical turning-point in the history of science and speculation. For it was a doting and a doddering group of Scholastics,—with a philosophic system attenuated to a mere shadow of its former vigorous self by the blunderings of well nigh two centuries,—that faced the onrush of the exuberant and lusty modern spirit.

And so *the most potent cause* of the decline of Scholastic philosophy, especially in the sixteenth and seventeenth centuries, was *the neglect of the natural sciences and of contemporary history.* *"Historiam et naturae et temporis maxima ex parte ignorantes,"*—thus Francis Bacon justly reproaches the Scholastics of this period with their disastrous and inexcusable default. But this obscurantism and inertia was at once a most flagrant betrayal of the very soul of Scholasticism to which we have just referred,—that alert and far-sighted, soundly progressive and constructively assimilative spirit displayed by the old masters, who would have hastened to invigorate their minds and their philosophy

with the varied richness of the fresh empirical
nourishment. Instead, the closeted and purblind
pedants of the Renaissance period continued to ru-
minate lean abstractions, to fritter away precious
time on vain discussions of highly technical questions
and meaningless subtleties,—the while the world
round about them was teeming with new realities
and problems. While the great discoveries were
everywhere revolutionizing physical and mechanical
astronomy, physics, chemistry and biology, and the
mathematical sciences as well, while the geocentric
system of Ptolemy was being replaced by the helio-
centric system of Copernicus, and Galileo's telescope was revealing the secrets of the heavens, while
man's scientific conception of the universe was being reconstructed on altogether new lines, while
many of the scientific theories which the medieval
mind had incorporated in its synthetic view of the
world were now finally and completely discredited, [95]
while profound and far-reaching political, social,
economic changes were in progress, the minds of
the Scholastics seemed to be hermetically sealed
against the momentous import of all this new science,
thought, life: they quixotically attempted to make
a dogma of every word of Aristotle,[96] they te-
naciously defended the outworn astronomy and

[95] De Wulf, *Scholasticism Old and New*, pp. 148, 149.

[96] But in this they were not alone. It is said that Melanchthon
and Cremonini refused to look at the heavens through a telescope.
Galileo speaks of the Aristotelians who "rather than alter Aristotle's heavens in any particular, obstinately deny the reality of
what is visible in the actual heavens."

physics of the thirteenth century, they fatuously refused to distinguish the essential and permanent from
the accessory and changeable, to discriminate between
two things so absolutely different as metaphysics and
scientific theories. Their opponents took them at
their word and threw their metaphysics into the discredit and oblivion deserved only by their physics.

In outright disloyalty to the soul of the system,
its incompetent representatives during the period
of transition utterly ignored the new day of ideas
and events. And the new day repaid them in
kind—and in full: they and their system alike were
left wholly to one side in the subsequent development
of philosophic thought.[97]   The new systems were
built upon Baconian empiricism or on Cartesian rationalism. It is true that when Cartesianism began
to gain ground, some Scholastics endeavored to appraise and counter it. But by that time their influence had dwindled too far to produce any
appreciable impression. After the Council of Trent
had initiated reforms in the practical domain, there
was likewise a vigorous revival of Scholasticism, especially in Spain, from where it spread to Portugal, Italy, and partly also to Germany.[98]   These
first Neo-Scholastics returned to the great systems
of the thirteenth century, examined them critically,
developed and applied them to new problems, particularly those of a political and social nature.

[97] Such, at least, was the intention; the following chapter will
show that it was not entirely realized.

[98] Cfr. F. Klimke, op. cit., Vol. I, pp. 273–276.

Windelband admits [99] that "Suarez was an important writer, clear, acute, accurate, and with a great capacity for a luminous disposition of his thoughts; he surpasses also, to a considerable degree, most of the older Scholastics in the form of his expression." Owing to external causes and a certain narrowness of attitude, [100] this intellectual awakening was of short duration. But it was sufficient to serve as an eloquent proof of the vital power of the perennial principles of Scholasticism when applied by men gifted with the true philosophic spirit.

[99] *Op. cit.,* p. 363.

[100] F. Klimke, *op. cit.,* p. 363; Maréchal, *op. cit.,* Cahier II, p. 23.

CHAPTER III

THE facts established by the foregoing review of the practical and theoretical causes off the temporary decline of Scholasticism lead to several conclusions that are of vital moment to the New Scholasticism.

I

The first and most important conclusion we can validly draw from the premises substantiated in the preceding chapter furnishes the true answer to the paramount question formulated at the beginning of the first chapter of Part III: *The decline of Scholasticism was attributable, not to some flaw in the system itself, but to causes quite extraneous, in fact contrary, to its essence and spirit; it was not the genuine Scholasticism of the thirteenth century that was put to the test and superseded, but a decadent semblance thereof; throughout the entire period the causes of decay left intact and sound the vital parts, the great organic doctrines of Scholastic philosophy.* Let us briefly review the salient facts which justify this conclusion, and note the main exceptions taken to it.

464

In the course of the *fourteenth and fifteenth centuries* the sterling content of Scholastic philosophy was indeed obscured by the sad condition of the times, by the practical disloyalty of its representatives, and by the theoretical incompetence of its exponents. This incompetence led to abuses of method, defects of dialectic, and barbarisms of language. But such factors alone cannot invalidate the essential soundness of a philosophic system: the fund of its genuine speculative truth remains unshaken and undiminished. None the less there are still some who maintain that the vicissitudes of Scholasticism were of a more radical nature. In the first place, there are those who assert that Scholastic philosophy succumbed to the process of "self-dissolution" or "self-destruction," owing chiefly to the corrosive action of Nominalism as revived by Ockham. Reason was denied the power of attaining a sure knowledge of the existence of God and of the spirituality of the soul, and so the proper object of natural theology and of psychology was eliminated; moreover, all science was rendered impossible by the denial of the objective validity of universal concepts. It is, of course, not to be gainsaid that the nominalistic tendency, left to itself, would have led Scholastic philosophy into the morass of empiricism and scepticism. It is likewise true that many Scholastics of the decadence period championed Nominalism. But it is also a fact that the Nominalists of the period never pursued their system to its logical consequences, nor did

they ever attain a commanding position. Above all,
—and this is a decisive factor in the question at issue,—Nominalism flew full in the face of the true
Scholastic tradition, of Aristotle, St. Augustine, and
all the great Scholastics of the thirteenth century
with St. Thomas at their head. Then, too, at the
very time when Nominalism was rampant at the
University of Paris, Realism was strenuously defended in other universities, such as that of Cologne.
Later, the restorers of true Scholasticism like
Cajetan, Soto, Suarez, and the rest, unanimously
combated Nominalism,[1] and gave a brilliant proof
of the lasting vitality of the core of Scholastic
doctrine. All of which goes to show that this
tendency, far from being representative of genuine
Scholasticism, was rather an aberration from it, a
betrayal of its fundamental principles through the
errors and levity of misguided individuals, a dissipation of energy at a time when the days of trial and
conflict were not far distant.

Others assert that Scholastic philosophy was
destroyed by the so-called Reformation. The essential characteristic of this philosophy, they allege,
was its vital dependence on revelation as proposed
by the authority of the Catholic Church. But this
authority was rightfully denied and destroyed by
the "reformers." Hence Scholastic philosophy, de-
prived of its life-giving principle, also ceased to exist, and was replaced by modern philosophy. The
minor of this argument is an assumption disproved

[1] H. Schaaf, in *Gregorianum*, Rome, 1921, Vol. II, p. 110.

by history and apologetics. But even if it were true, the conclusion would not hold because the major premise erroneously takes for granted that Scholastic philosophy had no autonomous existence whatever, but was *intrinsically* and *formally* dependent on theology. The falsity of this widespread notion is sufficiently evident from the statements of Neo-Scholastics,[2] based on the history of medieval philosophy.[3] However vague, confused, and at times reactionary, may have been the previous opinions on this point, by the twelfth century philosophy had become clearly distinguished from theology and its independence recognized. In the following century St. Thomas definitively traced the precise line of demarcation between the domains of faith and reason.[4]

In the *sixteenth and seventeenth* centuries another cause of decline was added to those already at work. In their short-sightedness and pitiable incapacity the decadent *Scholastics* of this period stubbornly refused to abandon discredited theories and to assimilate the new empirical material. But this in no way lessened the intrinsic value of *Scholasticism:*

[2] In Part II of this book.

[3] Cfr. De Wulf, *Philosophy and Civilization in the Middle Ages,* p. 50 sqq.; also his *Scholasticism Old and New,* pp. 8, 53 sqq., 190.

[4] Cfr. Olgiati-Zybura, *op. cit.,* p. 149 sqq.; E. Gilson, *The Philosophy of St. Thomas Aquinas,* St. Louis and Cambridge, 1924, pp. 17 sq. and 28; P. H. Wicksteed, *The Reactions Between Dogma and Philosophy. Illustrated From the Works of St. Thomas Aquinas,* London, 1920, *passim.* Also, Th. Heitz, *Essai Historique sur les Rapports entre la Philosophie et la Foi de Bérenger de Tours à S. Thomas d'Aquin,* Paris, 1909, pp. 145–167.

it merely showed that its incompetent representatives proved unfaithful to its true spirit. In this connection it is of capital importance to keep in mind the historical fact that *during this whole period neither the Scholastics themselves, nor the Renaissance scientists and philosophers instituted a thorough comparison,—as they should have done, —between the results of the new scientific progress and thought on the one hand, and the vital, fundamental doctrines of Scholastic philosophy on the other, with a view to ascertaining the compatibility of the latter with the former. This question,* therefore, *remained an open one:* the essential Scholastic doctrines themselves were not put to the proof. The entire conflict between the various camps raged only around side-issues and non-essentials of Scholasticism, such as Aristotelian physics, medieval scientific theories, and the deteriorations noted in the preceding chapter. Unfortunately, the Scholastics blindly identified these physical theories with their metaphysics, and the scientists and philosophers indiscriminately made the perennial metaphysics suffer the fate of the discredited physics. It was this fatal confusion on both sides that lent some plausibility to such wild statements as that "the progress of modern science demolished the philosophic structure of Scholasticism," that "the reduction of man to stellar insignificance, and the discovery of the infinite abysses of space, exploded all the axioms and postulates of mediaeval thought," [5] that Galileo and Copernicus destroyed not only the old astronomy, but also, without knowing or wishing it, the personal God of the Scholastics.[6]

It is one of the many tragedies of history that during the most critical period in the development of Western thought and culture, there was found no one possessed of the authentic philosophic spirit,— the assimilative and synthetic genius, of Aquinas, to institute a searching comparison of the old and the new, with a view to fusing them to the full extent of their compatibility. As it was, the sun of medieval Scholasticism was overcast for a season by a cloud of corruption and ignorance, of narrowness and error. The system lapsed for want of men, not for want of ideas.[7] Though incrusted in a hard and bitter rind, its kernel remained sound.[8] *Its great organic doctrines were in no way impaired by the period of decadence. Therefore, there is nothing whatsoever to militate, or create a prejudice, against the Neo-Scholastic programme for their restoration.* The effects of the Leonine encyclical *Aeterni Patris,* and the subsequent achievements

[5] F. J. C. Hearnshaw, in *Mediaeval Contributions to Modern Civilisation* (London, 1921), p. 38.

[6] M. Deussen, *Jacob Böhme,* Kiel, 1897, p. 20; cfr. Edgar A. Singer, Jr., *Modern Thinkers and Present Problems,* New York, 1923, p. 21 sqq.

[7] De Wulf, *op. cit.,* p. 153.

[8] A. Stöckl, *op. cit.,* p. 421.

of the New Scholasticism as outlined in this volume by some of its leading representatives of today, *are a concrete confirmation of our thesis.* No papal document, no Neo-Scholastic enthusiasm could infuse soundness into a radically vitiated system, or call a dead one back to life. That the Neo-Scholastic movement is not a mere galvanization has been amply shown by the severe test which it has stood for half a century. Here is the testimony of two eminent scholars who are above the least suspicion of partiality,—one a professor at the Paris Sorbonne, the other at the University of London. "It is,—so it has been said,—a merely artificial return to an obsolete Scholasticism, a movement, political-religious rather than strictly philosophical; what has not been alleged and invented to explain a movement of ideas whose depth and vitality are sufficient to disprove so mean an origin!" [9] For "Scholasticism is still very far from extinct; in fact it appears about to enter upon a phase of great revival; and in any settlement of the meaning of intelligence, it possesses an indubitable claim to be heard before all others." [10] Now, the true course of philosophy,—above all of metaphysics,—depends on the true conception of the nature of intelligence; [11] for, as St. Thomas says, "intelligence is

[9] E. Gilson, *op. cit.,* p. VII.

[10] C. Spearman, *The Nature of Intelligence and the Principle of Cognition,* p. 22, New York and London, 1923.

[11] Cfr. J. Maritain, *Réflexions sur l'Intelligence et sur sa Vie Propre,* Paris, 1924. Also, F. J. Sheen, *God and Intelligence,*

life and the greatest thing there is in life." [12] Accordingly, already from this one, but highly important, point, Scholasticism has something decidedly essential to offer to present-day thinkers. And what Cardinal Mercier says of Scholastic psychology [13] is equally true of Scholastic metaphysics: "It alone possesses at once a systematized body of doctrine and a framework sufficiently capacious to embrace and synthesize the ever-increasing results of the observational sciences."

On closer study, its perennial doctrines will be found sufficiently broad and deep, universal and progressive to welcome and assimilate every true development and discovery in the domain of philosophy and science alike. They will be seen to be vital and vigorous enough to exert a penetrating and salutary influence on the thought and life of to-day, if only they be put to work in the very midst of that thought and life. They can throw a flood of light on the problems that vex the modern mind,— not only such as are strictly philosophical, but also those of a social, political, economic, and broadly cultural nature,—if only they be properly focused on those problems. All this they can do, and more,— *provided the authentic spirit of the masters of Scholasticism's golden age animates and guides all*

New York and London, 1925; J. Maréchal, *op. cit.*, Cahier I, Introd., and *passim*.

[12] *Contra Gentiles,* lib. IV, c. 11; *Metaph.*, lib. XII, lect. 8.

[13] *Psychologie*, Préface, Louvain, 1923.

these efforts.[14]   The Neo-Scholastics have set out
to do what the men of the Renaissance period failed
to do, and they must be ever on the alert against
a recurrence of the disastrous blunders which caused
that failure.

The true Neo-Scholastic will not, like the Scholastics of the Renaissance period, uncritically cling to
the past just because it is old, or timidly shut out the

[14] That the Neo-Scholastics of *Europe* are alive to present-day
problems, and strive to keep in living touch with the modern
mind is sufficiently evident from the nature of the subjects discussed at the First International Thomistic Congress held in
Rome, April 15–20, 1925. Papers were read (followed by dis-
cussions) by Boyer, S.J., of the Gregorian University, *De
Problematis Critici Positione et Solutione;* by Gény, S.J., of the
same University, *De Ratione Problematis Critici Solvendi;* by
Noël, of the University of Louvain, *Comment poser le
Problème de la Connaissance;* by Dehove, of the University of
Lille, *La Psychophysique et la Théorie Thomiste de la Connais-
sance;* by Cordovani, of the University of the Sacred Heart,
Milan, *Il Concetto della Verità secondo l'Idealismo Italiano;* by
Rabeau, of the University of Lublin, *Sur l'Activité Constructive
de l'Intelligence;* by Krzesinski, of the University of Warsaw,
*Il Problema dell' Oggettività nel Criticismo Kantiano e nella
Filosofia Neoscolastica.* Other eminent scholars treated other
timely topics like *De Valore Theoriarum Physicarum; Utrum
Hylemorphismus cum Placitis Physicorum Recentiorum Componi
Possit; De Discontinuitate Materiae* (by MacWilliams, S.J., of
St. Louis University); *L'Adaptation de la Géométrie au Monde
Sensible; De Theoria Relativitatis; De Habitudine Psychologiae
Rationalis ad Experimentalem.*—These papers and discussions were
published by the Roman Academy of St. Thomas Aquinas, in the
volume *Acta Primi Congressus Thomistici Internationalis,* Romae,
1925. Cfr. *Rivista di Filosofia Neo-Scolastica* (Milan, 1925), Anno
XVII, pp. 224–227; *Stimmen der Zeit* (Freiburg i. Br., 1925),
Vol. 109, pp. 234–236; *Revue Néo-Scolastique de Philosophie*
(Louvain, 1925), XXVIe Année, pp. 389–393.

present just because it is new. His proper appreciation of what is of lasting value in the traditional will not be allowed to degenerate into an obstructive and narrowing ultra-conservatism; he will not become an undiscriminating *laudator temporis acti,* but will always keep his mind hospitably open to the new that has been adequately tested; he will have sight and insight for the kernel of truth wherever found. His repudiation of the insidious and corrosive "modernistic" mentality will not include the rejection of the "modern" when it is truly progressive and constructive.

He will have none of that authoritarian and partisan bias which idolizes names and schools; none of that unenlightened zealotry and purblind pedantry which cabins and stifles the true philosophic spirit. He will not "follow" the great thinker of Hippo because he was an Augustinian, or St. Thomas Aquinas because he was a Dominican, or Duns Scotus because he was a Franciscan, or Suarez because he was a Jesuit. What he will look for in each of these, and in all other great thinkers old and new, is the lasting contribution each has made to the common fund of *living and growing truth,* to the *philosophia perennis,* which is bound to no particular time or place, person or school. With Grabmann,[15] Gemelli,[16] and other leading Neo-

[15] *Der Gegenwartswert der geschichtlichen Erforschung der mittelalterlichen Philosophie,* Freiburg i. Br., 1913, pp. 35–38, 41, 46 sq., 78.

[16] *Rivista di Filosofia Neo-Scolastica,* Milan, 1924, Anno XVI p. 81 sqq.

Scholastics, he will insist that the narrowing of Scholasticism only tends needlessly to widen the breach between Scholastic and modern philosophy.

In method and criticism alike he will keep philosophy and theology strictly apart. He knows full well that formally and intrinsically his philosophical speculations are as free as those of any other thinker: here the light of reason alone is his guide. *Logically,* therefore, he can be at once a true philosopher and a true believer in supernatural revelation. On the *psychological* side, however, there lurks the danger that his intense theological convictions may influence,—unconsciously, for the most part,—his processes of philosophic thinking. In the past as well as in the present some have succumbed to this subtle danger. It is this influence that leads some Scholastics to assume, as Prof. Dewey says, "that the truth is so finally and clearly stated in Scholasticism that most modern European philosophy is a kind of wilful and perverse aberration." [17] "If everything that is generally offered in text-books of Catholic philosophy is to be considered as certainly known and proved by reason alone, then it would be difficult to see why theologians deem a revelation relatively necessary for the clear, sure, and ready knowledge of religious and moral truths." [18]

[17] Part I, Chap. I, *supra.*

[18] M. Pribilla, S.J., in *Stimmen der Zeit,* Vol. CVII, p. 272.— In a recent communication to *America* (Vol. XXXIII, No. 22, p. 519), one of its readers says: "The lack of the spirit of scholarship seems to show itself . . . in a certain dogmatism, by which

His use of the great achievements of the past will not consist in mere mechanical repetition and slavish commentary, without due regard for subsequent advances and contemporary contributions. "If there be anything that the Scholastic doctors treated with excessive subtlety or with insufficient consideration, or that is at variance with well-founded teachings of later date, or is otherwise improbable, we by no means intend that it shall be proposed to our age for imitation. . . . We certainly do not blame those learned and energetic men who turn to the profit of philosophy their own assiduous labors and erudition as well as the results of modern investigation; for we are fully aware that all this goes to the advancement of knowledge. . . . We proclaim that every wise thought and every useful discovery ought to be gladly welcomed and gratefully received by us, whatever its origin may have been." [19]   For the true Neo-Scholastic the great thinkers of the past are a beacon, not a boundary.   He turns to the past in order to progress.   It is not a stopping-place but a starting-point from which he goes forward, enlightened and invigorated, on the quest for more

mere systems, theories and opinions are erected into the rock-walled and bastioned fabric of dogma." This is "an attitude of mind too common among Catholic ecclesiastics who are teachers, and it is certainly not in accord with the spirit of true scholarship." —Cfr. Switalski, *Probleme der Erkenntnis,* II, Münster, 1923, p. 148 sq., where it is cogently shown that *theoretically* the Catholic can be the best philosopher, and where the *practical* dangers to be guarded against are pointed out.

[19] Leo XIII, Encyclical *"Aeterni Patris" (The Great Encyclical Letters of Leo XIII,* New York, 1903, p. 34).

truth. He realizes that the intellectual treasures of past ages will remain practically valueless if they are merely hoarded and admired, without being put out at interest to enrich the cultural capital of the present and the future. They must not be left a dead mass, but be made to become a quickening leaven for the newly acquired mental material.

Hence the real Neo-Scholastic abhors self-complacent or timid aloofness. He does not remain behind closed doors, fearing the living actualities of the day with their manifold complexities. Urged by the creative spirit he will bravely face present problems, bring them into an intrinsic and vital contact with Scholastic principles, and strive to solve them not by the convenient alternatives of accommodation or rejection, but by the strenuous method of creative criticism and critical creation. He will eagerly seek to have more and more of that keen, broad, far vision that made possible the synthetic achievements of the thirteenth century, and so convince contemporary thinkers that Scholasticism has the spirit of perennial youth.

His manner of exposition will not be that of the dull and deadening compendia into which much of the Scholasticism of to-day has shriveled,—in no wise mirroring the fulness of life and the richness of problems that once held tense the leading spirits of the past, who showed an open-mindedness, large-heartedness, and versatility that makes them akin to what is best in modern thinkers. The armory of Scholasticism holds an imposing array of finely tempered weapons; but they need to be refurbished and refashioned if they are to be effective in modern tactics. A soldier clad cap-à-pie in the best medieval armor would cut a sorry figure on the modern battlefield; but the fine material of his armor would do him excellent service if recast into a machine-gun.[20]

In a word, the aim and ideal of the Neo-Scholastic is to penetrate ever deeper into the deep thought of the great Scholastics of the past, to rethink and reinterpret it, whenever necessary, in reference to the new conquests and new problems, with fine discernment to search out the true in the old and the true in the new, thoroughly to assimilate both, and then to labor earnestly to contribute his share toward the eventual elaboration of a richer and more fruitful synthesis than has yet been achieved.[21] With such a goal in view the Neo-Scholastic rightfully resents the charge of being unprogressive, unscholarly, unscientific; he feels fully justified in looking to his non-Scholastic colleagues

[20] Cfr. Maritain, *op. cit.,* Appendix I, *Sur le Langage Philosophique,* p. 337 sq.

[21] One of the leading Neo-Scholastics of Germany thinks that present indications warrant the prediction that the near future will witness "an organic and at the same time critically well-founded combination of subjectivism and objectivism, of critical noëtics and metaphysics, which, like antiquity and the Middle Ages, sees its foremost task in the grasping of things, but, like the modern times, finds the way to that goal ultimately in consciousness and its data, that is to say, in science generally and in the individual sciences in particular." (B. Jansen, S.J., *op. cit.,* p. 230.) Cfr. Peter Wust, *Auferstehung der Metaphysik,* Leipzig, 1920.

for a fair hearing, an honest appreciation, a sympathetic co-operation. The same passion should urge both, the same ideal should inspire both: the passion for truth wherever found, and the ideal of its attainment in an ever fuller measure. For that is the very soul of a true philosopher,—*unice veritatis amator.*

"If we are to be philosophers in earnest we cannot afford to have any path which may lead to the heart of life's mystery blocked for us by placards bearing the labels 'reactionary,' 'unmodern,' and their likes. That what is most modern must be best is a superstition which it is strange to find in a really educated man. A philosopher at any rate should be able to endure the charge of being 'unmodern' with fortitude. . . . Abélard and Saint Thomas very likely would have failed as advertising agents, company promoters, or editors of sensational daily papers. But it may well be that both are better fitted than Lord Northcliffe . . . to tell us whether God is or what God is. In short, if we mean to be philosophical, our main concern will be that our beliefs should be true; we shall care very little whether they happen to be popular with the intellectual 'proletarians' of the moment, and if we can get back to truth we shall not mind having to go back a long way after it." [22]

Professor Webb sees the prospects of an understanding "growing greater . . . with the decrease

[22] A. E. Taylor, *Recent Developments in European Thought,* pp. 47 and 48, Oxford University Press, 1921.

of sectarian animosity," [23] which makes some men averse to Scholasticism because of its connection with the Catholic Church. May that animosity vanish altogether. It is utterly out of place in the mind of a true philosopher. Scholastic *philosophy*, old and new, is a body of doctrines, and the honest thinker will appraise it solely by their intrinsic worth.

II

The second conclusion warranted by the facts of the transition period is this: It was during the Humanism-Renaissance era that the terms *Scholasticism, Scholastic,* and the things they signify, were made synonymous with "the unscholarly, the unscientific, the out-of-date, the naïve, the product of a backward civilization, satisfactory only to the monks and clergy of a credulous age." The Scholasticism the Humanists and the scientists attacked, and the only one with which most of them were at all familiar,[24] was the decadent one described in the preceding chapter. It was this *magni nominis umbra* that became the butt of their stinging gibe and biting jest. Surely, when Laurentius Valla denounced that "superstitious and senseless race of professors" who made their pupils swear never to contradict Aristotle,[25] he could not have meant to in-

[23] Part I, Chap. II, *supra*.
[24] Cfr. B. Jansen, *op. cit.,* p. 161, 162.
[25] *Dialecticae Disputationes,* p. 643 (*Opera,* Paris, 1540). On Luther and Scholasticism, cfr. H. Denifle, *Luther und Luthertum,* (Mayence, 1904–6).

clude the great Scholastics of the thirteenth century without standing convicted of gross ignorance. When Ludovicus Vives unsparingly hurled his shafts of scorn at the masters of the University of Paris, who "rave and invent absurdities, and a new sort of language that only they themselves can understand," [26] he could not have been aiming at an Albert or an Aquinas without having his disdainful missiles recoil on himself. So, too, the Renaissance scientists. They made Scholastic *philosophy* responsible for the errors of medieval *science* because the Scholastics of their time had obstinately held the discredited scientific theories to be part and parcel of that philosophy.[27] "When we remember that for very many Scholasticism meant merely the old systems of astronomy and physics, we can understand at least to some extent why they should treat it with such sarcasm. They were not long about discrediting a system that defended such mistaken views. The necessity of making a clean sweep of the past became more and more apparent. And some, not satisfied with condemning all Scholasticism *en bloc,* went even so far as to condemn *all* philosophy. . . . The more moderate among the scientists, while repudiating Scholasticism with

[26] *In Pseudodialecticos, Opera,* ed. 1782, Vol. III, page 38.

[27] For the preposterous attitude of the "Aristotelians" in their university controversies with the Cartesians, see Feret's article, *"L'Aristotélisme et le Cartésianisme dans l'Université de Paris au XVIIᵉ Siècle,"* in *Annales de Philosophie Chrétienne,* Paris, April, 1903.

scorn, gave their adherence to some system or other of modern philosophy; for the latter had always professed its respect from the very commencement for the sensational scientific discoveries of the seventeenth century." [28]

The caustic strictures levelled at the Scholastics of the fifteenth, sixteenth, and seventeenth centuries, though at times excessive, were on the whole deserved. Unfortunately, subsequent critics and historians did not stop here. Without taking the pains to gain at least some idea of the content, method, and spirit of the great classics of the thirteenth century, and of those of the short but brilliant revival of the sixteenth, they included *all* Scholastic philosophers in the condemnation justly applicable *only* to the decadents. Owing to such summary and uncritical procedure, everything Scholastic was henceforth superciliously regarded as beneath the notice of the scholar. Bacon makes the sweeping statement that Scholasticism "disintegrated into subtle, vain, unwholesome and, so to speak, vermiculated questions." [29] The Encyclopedists echoed the refrain by pitying all "who devoted themselves to those miserable Scholastic subtilities that consist more in words than in things." They ridiculed Duns Scotus, in whose works they could find but "vain subtilities and a metaphysic which every man of common sense rejects"; "a man who would know

[28] De Wulf, *op. cit.*, pp. 151, 152.
[29] *De Augmentis Scientiarum*, l. I. c. 9.

fully all he [Scotus] had written, would know nothing." [30] Then came Brucker with his *Historia Critica Philosophiae*. Whatever merits this work may possess in other respects, it is anything but critical in its appraisal of Scholasticism. For Brucker's estimate is based solely on the uncritical and sweeping condemnations just mentioned. Small wonder that he looks upon the introduction of the writings of Aristotle to the Western world as ushering in a "downright degeneration of the human intellect." Scholasticism, he says, was never inspired by the sincere desire for truth; it consists merely of philosophical skirmishings, endless logomachies, excessive and affected subtlety, barbarous diction coupled with barbarous thought.[31] Coming from this first and "critical" modern historian of philosophy, such invectives against a system he never understood, could not but confirm and continue the Humanism-Renaissance-Reformation tradition as to the utter worthlessness of *all* Scholastic thought. For Taine the golden age of Scholasticism was an age of "imbecility," which "did not add a single idea to man's intellectual inheritance." [32]

It was in such wise that an undiscriminating "disdain for the past begot ignorance, ignorance begot injustice, injustice begot prejudice," uncritically

[30] *Encyclopédie des Sciences, des Arts et Métiers,* article "Aristote," Vol. I, pp. 663, 664.

[31] *Historia Critica Philosophiae,* Leipzig, 1766, pp. 712, 870, 871.

[32] *History of English Literature,* Vol. I, pp. 223, 225.—It is not surprising that minds filled with such prejudices should hail Descartes as the "savior" of philosophy.

passed on from generation to generation down to our own day. Hence the programme of a *Scholastic* revival, of a *Thomism* that would be *scientific,* "appeared nothing short of ludicrous to the enlightened moderns in their blissful ignorance of what medieval philosophy was and what it contained! For, what was medieval philosophy to them? It was a vast fabric of errors,—multiplied and monumental,—of errors that were grotesque in their puerility, and of distortions of fact that were hoary with age; such was the idol that passed for medieval philosophy, for Scholasticism, in the minds of 'the moderns,' and that stood unassailed until recent critical researches into the history of that period demolished the idol by shedding forth a light before which it has crumbled into dust." [33] Ignorance and prejudice are gradually giving way to sympathetic interest and appreciation.

III

Our third conclusion concerns *the law of continuity* as well as the *unhistoric and unphilosophic attitude* of one section of the Renaissance and of the moderns towards the Middle Ages in general, and towards Scholastic philosophy in particular.

It is of course true that the proximate causes of the profound changes that came about during the Renaissance period are to be found in the various new movements of thought and life which signalized

[33] De Wulf, *op. cit.,* p. 277.

that epoch. All these factors, however, were but the means by which the deeper law of human development was asserting itself. Now the law of all true organic development in nature, history,[34] and thought implies the law of a living continuity. "The whole succession of men," says Pascal, "should be considered as one man who lives on and never ceases to learn." There exists a causal and ideal nexus between the various phases of civilization and culture, as well as between the successive attempts of the human mind to reach a philosophic interpretation of the universe.[35] Thought flows in a continuous stream from one generation to another.[36] "The systematic development of thought, like that of nature, *non facit saltus*. . . . All differentiation and division of the history of philosophy can have no other than a purely empiric and pragmatic value,—for the convenience of cataloguing and study,—against which it is absolutely necessary to react as soon as we pass from school manuals to the direct sources. . . . As history has no meaning when studied atomistically as a discontinuous succession of events linked only by a chronological continuity, so also philosophy, which is the history of human thought, is rightly regarded as an organic development of a single and most profound spiritual movement, of which the various

[34] Cfr. Alfred Feder, *Lehrbuch der geschichtlichen Methode*, pp. 3 sqq. Regensburg, 1924.—An English translation of this excellent work is being made.

[35] F. Klimke, *Historia Philosophiae*, Rome, 1923, Vol. I, p. 5.

[36] Turner, *op. cit.*, p. 434.

systems represent only the epiphenomenon. And as moral and social anarchism lies at the bottom of the atomistic conception of history, so the abyss of scepticism, anarchy of mind, and disillusion of thought are at the root of that inorganic conception which makes of philosophy one vast motley conflict of insoluble riddles." [37]

This universal and essential principle of organic continuity also links the beginnings and development of the modern era with the history and thought of the centuries that constitute the medieval period. "What really took place [in the Renaissance period] was not so much a revival of learning as a flowering out of the learning of the preceding centuries. It is a capital error to hold that this epoch marks an abrupt and sudden resurrection of intellectual life after long centuries of darkness. In history, as in nature, there can be no effect without a cause. From nothing comes nothing; all things are bound together by the law of cause and effect. The movement of the Renaissance was in keeping with the laws of accelerated motion: it was but the natural, progressive and uninterrupted development of the society of the Middle Ages from century to century down to the opening of the present age. Modern genius had for its parent the society of the Middle Ages and grew up with it during the laborious and fruitful cen-

[37] P. Bondioli, in *Vita e Pensiero,* Milan, 1925, Vol. XVI, pp. 167, 168, 170. Cfr. F. Olgiati, *L'Organicità del Reale,* in *Rivista di Filosofia Neo-Scolastica,* Anno VII, No. 3 (August, 1915).

turies of its infancy; finally, it reached the heyday of youth, when, like an opening flower, it disclosed suddenly all its rich and magnificent vitality. This view of the Renaissance is in keeping with all the laws of nature and all the teachings of history. . . . The luscious fruits which ripen on the tree of civilization are the last results of an innumerable series of patient and disinterested efforts." [38] Humanism itself "was connected with the Middle Ages by an unbroken series of links from Nicholas V to Petrarch, from Petrarch to Dante, and from Dante to Charlemagne, without a break in the literary tradition of the classics and without any lagging in the enthusiastic study of these literary masterpieces." The various movements of the transition period are "a glad budding forth of a robust plant, which before opening to the sunlight and displaying its wealth and excellence must first experience the wondrous rising of the sap and undergo the patient and hidden work of vegetation." [39]

This rich and variegated flowering of the seeds of medieval culture and speculation was prevented from reaching its full fruitage because of the cankerous influences that resulted from the *violent*

---

[38] G. Kurth, *The Church at the Turning Points of History,* translated by Msgr. V. Day, Helena, Montana, 1918, pp. 123, 124, 127.

[39] G. Kurth, *What are the Middle Ages?* (*Ibid.,* 1921) pp. 29, 30. Cfr. Gilson, *op. cit.,* pp. 7 sqq.; S. Behn, *Die Wahrheit im Wandel der Weltanschauung,* Berlin and Bonn, 1924, pp. 164, 165.

and flagrant breach of continuity committed by the leaders of one section of the Renaissance movements. The paganizing Humanists, savants, and representatives of "the philosophy just come of age," *made the new rationalistic and naturalistic standpoint possible only by spurning the accumulated wisdom of the immediate past,* by utterly ignoring a thousand years rich in thought and culture, by uprooting man from the cultural soil, environment, atmosphere of the living present and transplanting him into the soil of ancient paganism. That was the fatal blunder, the results of which are still with us to-day. The real reactionaries were not the Scholastics, but those paganizers who repudiated the precious heritage of the tradition with which they were linked by every conceivable tie, only to pay homage to a strange and more remote tradition.[40] Thus the early dawn of modern thought, with its first attacks on the medieval conception, presents a strange spectacle to our view: on the one side are the conservatives, remaining loyally within the domain and continuity of history; on the other, the radical revolutionaries, taking their position on a terrain violently separated from the living reality of history and thought by what may be termed a "pseudo-historical abstractism." [41] We have seen that the Scholastics betrayed their system at this critical moment by failing to give

[40] Cfr. S. Behn, *op. cit.,* p. 169.
[41] Olgiati, *op. cit.,* p. 74.

it the development and adaptation of which it was capable, and so did it a wrong which the Neo-Scholastics are endeavoring to right.

The eighteenth century view of history, as exemplified by Hume, was also the atomistic, as against the organic, conception of it. "It is no wonder that history presented itself as a mere undeciphered maze to the eighteenth century thinkers, of whom Hume was the most complete representative. . . . Having abandoned the old theological and metaphysical synthesis, he reduced the race to a mere chaos of unconnected individuals." [42] "So, too, in philosophy, Sir W. Hamilton's standpoint was largely that of the eighteenth century. To him, in Mr. Alexander's words, philosophy was 'a number of separate problems falling apart like atoms in the void.'" [43] This mistaken conception is well described by Dr. Olgiati: [44] "The historic sense certainly never had such ardent panegyrists as to-day. And yet, it does not abound in the concrete domain of practical applications. One needs but to open certain manuals of the history of philosophy to get a clear and painful impression of the downright lack of that indispensable insight which knows how to lay hold of unity in multiplicity,— a unity, that is, which is living, dynamic, synthesizing the various phases of an idea or a system within

[42] Sir Leslie Stephen, *English Thought in the Eighteenth Century*, II, pp. 184 and 370.

[43] Wilfrid Ward, *Problems and Persons*, p. 41, New York, 1903.

[44] Olgiati-Zybura, *op. cit., Introd.*, pp. V–VII.—On the historic sense, cfr. O. Willmann, *op. cit.*, Vol. III, Chap. XVII.

the continuity of a gradual development. As a result, the history of philosophy becomes a collection of medallions, a whirling dance of conceptions that follow and chase one another, and take their turns with changing fortune and capricious unreasonableness. It is true that the individual philosophers are portrayed with a wealth of biographical and bibliographical information, together with a list of the doctrines they champion in logic, metaphysics, ethics, and so on. But not even a question is put as to what link binds the parts of a system (or entire systems) together, as to the interpenetration that exists between the diverse theories. . . . It is the immanent logic of truth and error alike that causes philosophical systems to unfold themselves. Hence, to the eye that looks beneath the surface, they no longer appear as scattered bits of a casual explanation, but as gathered up within the progressive development of the original germs." From this it appears how unphilosophic is the attempt to confine the various systems, from the dawn of philosophy down to our day, in water-tight compartments, as though they were not phases of a single comprehensive development of the quest for ultimate truth, and as though there existed no interaction and interdependence between mind and mind in the successive stages of this development.

Not so long ago the attempt to ignore the organic continuity and intrinsic linkage in the evolution of human affairs was especially evident in the determination to "leap clean across the Middle Ages" (the Germans' *Sprung über das Mittelalter*), on the plea that the thought and culture of that period could be safely relegated to the scrap-heap, or at most be regarded as a historical curiosity. As far as Scholasticism is concerned, this opinion was based on the unjust and uncritical Humanism-Renaissance-Reformation tradition which, as we saw, judged the whole of medieval thought by the period of its decadence. The Middle Ages were looked upon as "an intermediary stage, parenthetical, with no value saving that of connection between antiquity and the modern times." [45] A historian of philosophy expressed the attitude prevalent some years ago: "If philosophy is, as we have defined it, a free search, we may say that from the edict of Justinian (529) to the Renaissance in the fifteenth century there is a sort of interval during which there is, properly speaking, no philosophy. For, during all that period, Western humanity was subject in the region of speculation, to the dogmas that constitute the Christian teaching, and, in the region of morals, to the ecclesiastical discipline founded on those dogmas. We should, therefore, in the history of philosophy, simply skip that interval of eight or nine centuries and pass directly to the researches that prepared the way for modern philosophy." [46] Adopting

[45] De Wulf, *Philosophy and Civilization in the Middle Ages*, p. 6.

[46] M. Penjon, *Précis d'Histoire de la Philosophie*, Paris, 1897, p. 165.

this counsel, non-Scholastic writers of the history of philosophy were wont to dismiss medieval Scholasticism with a few brief paragraphs.[47]

This uncritical position, both as to medieval culture in general and Scholastic philosophy in particular, has been abandoned by all reputable scholars. It is now generally recognized that the Middle Ages laid the foundations of modern civilization and that especially the twelfth and thirteenth centuries were marked by an intense and a fruitful intellectual activity, producing imperishable treasures of philosophic thought, as well worthy of attention as any of the systems of antiquity. "Far from being intermediary between the ancient and the modern civilizations, the 'Middle Ages' are the beginning of modern civilization. . . . All that we have,—our religion and our political ideas, our nationality and our language, our esthetics and our social economy,—all these connect us with the Middle Ages and separate us from antiquity. We are heirs of the Middle Ages; we continue their work, not the work of the Renaissance. If there be any epoch to which we may apply the term 'Middle Ages,' is it not the Renaissance itself, which opened in the history of modern nations a parenthesis now closed or soon to be closed? The

[47] J. Rehmke, in his *Grundriss der Geschichte der Philosophie* (Leipzig, 1921), gives ten pages to the whole of Patristic and Scholastic thought under the pretext that it was merely a decline of ancient thought, and had made no noteworthy contribution to the development of philosophy. He devotes seven pages to Hobbes, and twelve to Descartes.

idols of the Renaissance are now overthrown, and
we turn away from its ideal. We try to keep
clear of royal absolutism and of the centralization
which is its logical consequence. We utterly repudi-
ate the famous maxim of the sixteenth century,
Cuius regio ejus religio. . . . Over the head of the
Renaissance (without denying our indebtedness to
it) we clasp hands with our ancestors of the Middle
Ages; we again tread the paths from which we
had been led astray by the Renaissance." [48]

Professor Longwell, of Princeton University, is
of a like mind with us on this important point:
"We are essentially of the same blood as our
mediaeval ancestors, and therefore we understand
them far better than we understand any of the
ancient peoples: their thoughts *are* our thoughts
and their ways our own. The development out of

[48] G. Kurth, *op. cit.,* pp. 24, 27, 28.—Cfr. R. A. Cram, *The
Great Thousand Years,* Boston, 1918, p. 7 sqq.; IDEM, *The Sub-
stance of Gothic,* Boston, 1917, pp. 109, 110, 134; H. O. Taylor,
The Mediaeval Mind, New York, new ed., 1925; *Mediaeval Con-
tributions to Modern Civilization* (cited above); Henry Adams,
Mont-Saint-Michel and Chartres; James J. Walsh, *The Thir-
teenth, Greatest of Centuries;* T. J. Shahan, *The Middle Ages;*
P. L. Landsberg, *Die Welt des Mittelalters und Wir,* Bonn, 1923.
This book, coming from a disciple of Max Scheler, made quite
a stir in Germany. In our country, the growing interest in the
Middle Ages is evinced by the recent formation of *The Mediaeval
Academy of America.* Its purpose is "to conduct, encourage,
promote and support research, publication and instruction in
mediaeval records, literature, languages, arts, archaeology, history,
philosophy, science, life and all other aspects of mediaeval civilization by publications, by research and by such other means as
may be desirable." It publishes a quarterly called *Speculum*
(248 Boylston St., Room 312, Boston, Mass.).

that age into our own has been one integral whole
without break; certainly there is no such rupture
as is commonly conceived around 1600. The so-
called Renaissance is simply a period of accelerated
growth in the development of our modern (Teutonic) stock; and it differs from preceding transition eras—e. g., in the 9th century or the 12th
century,—chiefly in intensity and volume. The
'new' had appeared long before that time; and it
continued to appear thereafter,—in increasingly
perceptible form. If one would look for the distinctly 'new' as definitively 'arrivé en bon port,'
he must place it near the end of the 18th century
rather than at the beginning of the 17th century.
But such effort is illusory, I am sure, for the history of philosophy. In any event, the entire movement from mediaeval times into our own day constitutes, I am convinced, a continuous development.
And that is why it turns out that the modern is so
much more mediaeval than is willingly admitted,
and the mediaeval so much more modern than is
commonly thought." [49]

Concerning the philosophy of the Middle Ages,
this same authority further says: "It is being seen
more and more that this field deserves closer attention not only for itself, but as a connecting link
between ancient and modern. It has long been my
own conviction that the so-called philosophy of the
Middle Ages is in reality the early or beginning

---

[49] From a letter to me.—Cfr. E. Gilson, *Philosophie au Moyen
Age*, Paris, 1922, II, p. 155.

modern philosophy; and that neither the one nor
the other is intelligible when viewed in the customary manner,—namely, as a distinct period in
and for itself." [50]   And Professor Gilson [51] looks

---

[50] Professor Longwell's statement in Part I, Chap. I, *supra*.

[51] *Études de Philosophie Médiévale*, Paris, 1921, p. V.—Cfr.
J. Maritain, *Saint Thomas d'Aquin, Apôtre des Temps Modernes*,
Paris, 1923; M. Cordovani, *L'Attualità di S. Tommaso d'Aquino*,
Milan, 1923, cap. 3, *"Modernità di S. Tommaso"*; L. Noël,
L'Actualitè du Thomisme, p. 1, *Notes d'Epistemologie Thomiste*,
Louvain and Paris, 1925; J. Feldmann, *Thomas von Aquin und
die Philosophie der Gegenwart*, Paderborn, 1924; in *S. Tommaso
d'Aquino, Pubblicazione Commemorativa del Sesto Centenario
della Canonizzazione*, Milan, 1923, Agostino Gemelli, *"Il Sig-
nificato del Centenario di S. Tommaso,"* pp. 22–40, Francesco
Olgiati, *"Il Tramonto di S. Tommaso e la sua Resurrezione,"*
pp. 302–317; in *Acta Hebdomadae Thomisticae*, Romae, 1924,
Card. L. Billot, *"S. Thomas et sa Philosophie a l'Époque Actuelle,"*
pp. 9–28, J. Maritain, *"Le Thomisme et la Crise de l'Esprit Mo-
erne,"* pp. 55–79; A. E. Taylor, *"St. Thomas as a Philosopher,"*
in *St. Thomas Aquinas,* Papers read at the Celebration of the
Sixth Centenary of his Canonization, held at Manchester, 1924,
Oxford, 1925, p. 33; T. F. Tout, *"The Place of St. Thomas
in History,"* ibid., p. 1; F. Aveling, *"St. Thomas and Modern
Thought,"* in *St. Thomas Aquinas* ed. by C. Lattey, S.J., St. Louis,
1924, p. 94; *Proceedings of the Aristotelian Society*, New Series,
Vol. XXIV, London, 1924, p. 169, *"The Thomistic Outlook in
Philosophy,"* by F. Aveling.—P. Mandonnet et J. Destrez,
Bibliographie Thomiste, Kain, Belgique, 1921. Also, W. H. Shel-
don, *Strife of Systems and Productive Duality*, Harvard University
Press, 1918, Chap. X, *The Practical Synthesis—Thomism;* Josiah
Royce, *"Pope Leo's Philosophical Movement and its Relation to
Modern Thought,"* in *Fugitive Essays*, Harvard University Press,
1920, pp. 408–429. *Mélanges Thomistes*, Le Saulchoir, Kain,
Belgique; *Miscellania Tomìsta*, Barcelona, 1924; *Xenia Thomistica*,
3 Vols., Rome, 1925; *S. Tommaso d'Aquino: Miscellanea Storico-
Artistica*, Rome, 1924; *Scritti Vari Nel VI Centenario della Canon-
izzazione di S. Tommaso D'Aquino*, in *Scuola Cattolica*, Milan,
1924.

upon St. Thomas as the first of modern philosophers: "He is the first, not because he has created
the principles and invented the attitude in which
we live, nor because all the directions of thought
by which the thirteenth century prepared the modern epoch were concentrated in his works; but because he is the first occidental of whom the thought
is neither enslaved to dogma nor to a system."
From every viewpoint the study of Scholastic
philosophy "appears as a necessary stage in our
philosophical education. Thus, it seems contrary to all reason to ignore that age, as has hitherto been done all too often. We must really
'traverse the Scholastic philosophy of the Middle Ages,' if we are to criticize or to go beyond
it." [52]

With increasing clearness present-day thinkers
are realizing that the law and fact of organic continuity, for a long time so nonchalantly overlooked,
must be taken into account in order to arrive at
a true understanding of the development of human
thought. This is evident from the statements of
some of our non-Scholastic contributors.[53] Thus
Professor Taylor well says: "The modern has to
learn that there really is no such thing as a breach
of continuity in the history of philosophy. There
was no arrest of philosophic thought between
A. D. 600 and A. D. 1600, which will allow him to

[52] De Wulf, *Philosophy and Civilization in the Middle Ages*,
p. 300.
[53] See Part I, Chap. I and II, *supra*.

jump from the Greeks to Descartes, and he will never understand Descartes himself without some knowledge of the thought of the thirteenth century, so much of which remains embodied in the *Meditations*." Professor Webb speaks of "the growth of that historical sympathy, in which the seventeenth and eighteenth centuries were in comparison with our time so lacking." Professor Longwell says: "In any event, the entire movement from the medieval times into our own day constitutes, I am convinced, a continuous development." Professor Everett admits that in his course in the history of philosophy he has found the treatment of certain features of medieval philosophy "essential to an appreciation of the continuity of thought." Professor Singer thinks that "the insistence now being put upon the continuity of history is rapidly restoring a balance which the beginnings of modern criticism upset." Professor Brett affirms that it can be shown that "the process of restoring a true philosophical attitude has been continuous from 430 A. D. to the present time; that consequently the fundamental task of making philosophy adequate to a growing experience . . . will in time be viewed as a common problem to which each period has made its specific contribution." Such ideas tally with the incontestable principle of continuity, of organic relationship between the various interpretations of reality propounded in the course of the ages.

It will be well to call attention here to some *fundamentals that have a direct and important bearing on the Neo-Scholastic position.*

The programme of the New Scholasticism to retain the great, constitutive doctrines of the old Scholasticism and, after having rethought and tested them by comparison with the conclusions of present-day science and with the teachings of contemporary systems of philosophy, to leaven contemporary thought and promote the solution of present problems with the aid of these *lasting* doctrines,[54]—the permanent achievements of Greek and Scholastic thought,—is at once an affirmation of another basic truth, akin to that of continuity and development, namely, *that there are such lasting doctrines.* It asserts that the whole of philosophy is not a thing of perpetual flux, changing completely from age to age; that radical relativism [55] and extreme evolutionism when applied to philosophy are errors; that to conceive of philosophy as a product which is merely relative to the needs of peoples, the tendencies of the times, the temperaments of philosophers,—to regard it as the reflec-

[54] These doctrines are summarized in Dr. Jansen's article (Part II, Chap. VII); also by De Wulf in his article "Neo-Scholasticism" in the *Catholic Encyclopedia,* and in his book, *Scholasticism Old and New,* pp. 211 sqq.

[55] The true sense in which our knowledge is relative and in which it is absolute, is clearly set forth in L. J. Walker's *Theories of Knowledge,* New York and London, 1919, *passim.* Cfr. Sheen, *op. cit.,* p. 276 sq.

tion of transient social conditions or of certain
economic interests, is tantamount to declaring the
bankruptcy of philosophy; that through the various
phases of human thought down the centuries, with
its variegated changes and frequent fluctuations,
there run golden threads of lasting truth; "that
alongside the changing elements that are peculiar
to any given stage of development in the life of
humanity, there is at every stage and in every
system an abiding soul of truth,—a small fraction
of that full and immutable truth which hovers
around the mind in its highest and noblest flights." [56]
In a word, the Neo-Scholastic standpoint affirms
the existence of a *philosophia perennis*.[57] The
truth of seven or of twenty-three centuries ago is
still the truth of to-day. "The truth for which
Pythagoras, Plato and Aristotle sought, is the same
as that pursued by St. Augustine and St. Thomas.
. . . In so far as it is elaborated in the course of
history, truth is the child of time; but in so far as
it embodies a content that is independent of time
and history, it is the child of eternity." [58]   About
the *maestro di color che sanno*,[59] Cardinal Newman
has written these memorable words: "While the

---

[56] De Wulf, in *Revue Néo-Scolastique*, 1902, pp. 13 and 14.

[57] On the *Philosophia perennis* cfr. O. Willmann, *Geschichte des Idealismus*, Braunschweig, 1907; James H. Ryan, *An Introduction to Philosophy*, New York, 1924, p. 378; Commer, *Die immerwährende Philosophie*, Vienna, 1899; P. Rotta, *Platone e la Filosofia Perenne*, in *Rivista di Filosofia Neo-Scolastica*, Anno XVII, 1925, pp. 8–22.

[58] Willmann, *op. cit.*, Vol. II, p. 550.

[59] Dante, *Inferno*, IV, v. 131.

world lasts, will Aristotle's doctrine on these matters last, for he is the oracle of nature and of truth. While we are men, we cannot help, to a great extent, being Aristotelians, for the great master does but analyze the thoughts, feelings, views, and opinions of human kind. He has told us the meaning of our own words and ideas, before we were born. In many subject-matters, to think correctly, is to think like Aristotle, and we are his disciples whether we will or no, though we may not know it." [60]

It is with this soul of truth as found in the great body of Greek and Scholastic thought, restored, rethought, and restated for our own day, that the New Scholasticism aims to vivify, permeate, unify, and organize the various branches of contemporary philosophic thought.[61] For "if reason be aught but a deceptive aspiration after the absolutely inaccessible, surely whatever has been brought to light, whatever our ancestors have unearthed and acquired in their pioneer labors, cannot have proved entirely worthless to posterity. . . . Instead of eternally commencing over again the solution of the great enigma of nature and of consciousness, would it not be wiser to preserve our traditional inheritance, and go on perfecting it? Can it be better to let the intelligence live on its own personal and ever-incipient thought than on

[60] *Idea of a University,* London and New York, 1919, p. 109.

[61] Cfr. F. Ehrle, S.J., *Grundsätzliches zur Charakteristik der neueren und neuesten Scholastik,* Freiburg i. Br., 1918.

the accumulated wisdom of centuries? Should
we not be better employed in adding to that common fund of doctrine than in changing it every
day—in the hope of attaching our names to some
new system?" [62]

However, from all that has been said in the
preceding pages about the nature, ideals, and
achievements of the New Scholasticism, it is sufficiently clear that this insistence on certain immutable and fundamental doctrines, this repudiation
of "the philosophies of everlasting flux," this rejection of "absolute" relativism in philosophy, by
no means signifies a denial of true development, a
championing of absolute and rigid immobility, or
the claim to the possession of "a finished, completely final system." Such an unenlightened attitude would flatly contradict the very *raison d'être*
and aims of the New Scholasticism, which is,
"vetera *novis* augere." It would flagrantly belie
the spirit and position of the great masters of
thought who, with St. Thomas, asserted that *opus*

[62] Van Weddingen, *L'Encyclique de S. S. Léon XIII et la
Réstauration de la Philosophie Chrétienne,* 1880, pp. 90 and 91.—
"Tradition is not the enemy of progress; it is the best friend
progress has, and for progress to disown it would be disastrous.
Tradition is the thing that makes progress possible. Tradition
is the secure possession of all the true and good and useful
things which past ages have discovered and stored up for us.
If every age as it comes along were to deny the existence of these
things, and have to start all over again in the re-discovery of
them, we would never make any progress at all. . . . For progress
to deny tradition is to deny the parent that gave it birth."
(*America,* New York, 1926, Vol. XXXIV, p. 369.) Cfr. Coffey,
Ontology, p. 31.

philosophicum semper perfectibile,[63] and, as Dr. Jansen says, "believed in the organic and gradual development of truth." It would mean stagnation and sterility, decay and death. It would indicate a titanic pride of intellect. The infinite depth and breadth of reality and truth on the one hand, and the manifold limitations of the human mind on the other, preclude the possibility of reaching complete finality here below. But the Scholastic position does mean that the human intellect is capable of reaching objective truth, and that a truth once established, always remains such, independently of the time and place of its announcement and irrespective of the transient conditions of an epoch. These may serve to explain the *origin* which the knowledge of a truth has had, but truth remains truth in virtue of its intrinsic value, of its objective evidence. Again, this does not say that it remains rigid, incapable of further development; for it can be deepened and broadened, it can receive new aspects, applications, adaptations. But true development is not destruction of the thing developed, true evolution is not revolution. The subsequent unfoldment of a truth does not change one concept into another, but renders the old concept deeper, fuller, clearer, more orderly and more precise. For as in all living development, so also in the historical development of truth in the human mind as it advances in its comprehension of reality, the past endures immanently in the present without the

[63] Cfr. Maritain, *op. cit.,* p. 289.

severance of life's continuity. Hence Professor Hocking [64] well says that "permanence of truth and growth of truth are not incompatible, any more than the identity of an individual is incompatible with his growth. When this truth is well understood, many of the difficulties between modernism and traditionalism, both in philosophy and in doctrine,[65] will disappear." So, too, in the sense explained, the Neo-Scholastic agrees with Professor Everett's statement that "philosophy is a progressive unfolding of human thought in the process of civilization, and that complete finality never is or can be reached. . . . This progressive view of philosophy does not mean that no secure truth is won and no problems settled, but rather that one's world-view cannot be rounded off to the exclusion of new discoveries and fresh insights." [66] But these latter, if true, cannot invalidate, but rather confirm, deepen and broaden, one's world-view in so far as it is true. For one truth cannot contradict another.[67]

[64] See Part I, Chap. I, *supra*.

[65] Cfr. Cardinal Newman's *Development of Christian Doctrine*, New York and London, 1920; Devas, *op. cit.*, Part II, Chap. IX; Eugene O'Doherty, *Doctrinal Progress and its Laws*, Dublin, 1924.

[66] Part I, Chap. I, *supra*.

[67] Neo-Scholastics could not admit that the progress of the observational sciences would induce St. Thomas to make any essential changes in the *great fundamentals* of his metaphysics, *rational* psychology, and ethics—in those doctrines, that is, which Neo-Scholastics regard as perennial, and which are summarized in Dr. Jansen's article.—This question has a direct bearing on

Finally, the Neo-Scholastics need to be on their guard lest they too lay themselves open to the charge of "jumping clean across" several centuries as worthless in the history of human thought. They must not create the impression that they consider "the truth so finally and clearly stated in Scholasticism that most modern European philosophy is a kind of wilful and perverse aberration"; [68] or that they believe "mankind have simply been playing the fool since 1274, . . . and all the most eminent philosophers from Descartes on have merely been talking puerile nonsense." [69] It is true that upon the appearance of the encyclical "*Aeterni Patris*," a position dangerously near to this unhistorical and unphilosophical one was assumed by a few individuals gifted with more zeal than insight and more heat than light. No true Neo-Scholastic of to-day takes this extremely reactionary attitude, and that for two reasons. In the first place, such a sweeping repudiation of the modern era outrages the principles and the spirit alike of the philosophy he champions. For Scholastic metaphysics maintains that reality and history are rational and purposive; that there is a Providence;

---

the problem of the extent to which metaphysics depends on the special sciences. The question of an "inductive metaphysics" and an "eternal metaphysics" was discussed at the First International Thomistic Congress, held at Rome in 1925.—Cfr. *Stimmen der Zeit*, June, 1925, Vol. CIX, p. 235; Maritain, *Réflexions sur l'Intelligence*, Chap. VIII, "*De la Métaphysique des Physiciens*."

[68] Prof. Dewey's statement, in Part I, Chap. I.

[69] Prof. Taylor's statement, Part I, Chap. II.

that every error contains some truth,[70] and furthers its development by the way of contrast and conflict; that every system has a special function to perform and a definite end to achieve, despite the admixture of many erroneous ideas. All of which means that nothing in the world is absolutely useless or harmful; that modern life and modern philosophy must have a meaning; that it is for us to discover and appropriate the elements of truth they contain. We are in duty bound to make a deep and earnest study of modern history and speculation, so as to determine what progress they mark in the upward strivings of humanity. The success and the glory of medieval Scholasticism lay precisely in this that it knew how to evaluate, assimilate and synthesize the best thought of the past and the present. As we saw, its spirit and attitude was always broad, open-minded, truly progressive. In the second place, that mistaken,

---

[70] "A prickly hull easily misleads one to cast it aside together with the kernel. And yet, the only means whereby any error can be definitively overcome is that of wholly disengaging from it the hidden grain of truth. Indeed, it is quite contrary to the Scholastic method to bring out only what is opposed to truth. In every distinction our method of disputation makes a *concedo* precede the *nego*. In this *concedo* must first be acknowledged whatever is true and right in the opponent's assertion. Only then, by the rules of the Scholastic method of disputation, may one reject the admixture of error. What a pity that this simple rule of schoolroom discussion is so frequently disregarded in public controversies." (A. Inauen, S.J., *Kantische und scholastische Einschätzung der natürlichen Gotteserkenntnis*, Innsbruck, 1925, pp. 1 sq.)

ultra-conservative zealotry of some of the first Neo-Scholastics not only alienated many from the movement at the very outset, but it flew in the face of the letter and spirit of the encyclical, and belied the very purpose of the Scholastic revival. These did not call for a wholesale condemnation of several centuries of speculation as being only a period of intellectual aberrations, but for a critical appraisal, a synthetic utilization, and a harmonious fusion of whatever was of lasting value in the philosophy and science of that period, with the perennial elements of medieval thought. The Neo-Scholastics were not to have "their eyes fixed solely on the past"; they were not to become "mere commentators of an outworn philosophy"; they were not to constitute "a school of mere mechanical repeaters," who "treat as a negligible quantity several centuries rich in thought, vibrant with life, fervid with struggles, glorious by conquests"; they were not to be "obscurantists, venerable mummies, who would fossilize the spirit that means life ever new." No; the spirit of the old Scholasticism and the programme of the new, imperatively demanded qualities and activities the very opposite of all these. And the true Neo-Scholastics proved loyal to the momentous task entrusted to them and, as their several contributions show, are energetically striving to accomplish it in an ever fuller measure.—So much about the *law* of continuity; now as to the *fact.*

There is a striking disparity, ludicrous at times, between willing and doing, between desire and achievement, on the part of the "heaven-storming Titans" of the Renaissance. They were prepared to sacrifice well nigh everything for the sake of "originality" and "individuality." In this they were distinctly "modern." Their avowed purpose was to cast all tradition to the winds. But they succeeded only in exchanging a nearer tradition and authority for those more remote. They decided to break entirely with the thought and culture of the Middle Ages. But the law of continuity proved more potent than they: *in matter of fact, there was no complete breach of continuity with the immediate and the medieval past.* Quite the contrary. Few other periods in history so palpably verify the universal law of an organic and gradual evolvement of all mental life as the one in question. Here Windelband finds the typical instance of continuous historical development. "The *continuity* of the intellectual and spiritual development of European humanity manifests itself nowhere so remarkably as in the Renaissance. At no time perhaps was the want for something completely new, for a total and radical transformation, not only in the intellectual life, but also in the whole state of society, felt so vigorously and expressed so variously and passionately as then, and no time has experienced so many adventurous and ambitious attempts at innovation as did this. And yet, if we look closely, and do not allow ourselves to be deceived, either by the grotesque self-consciousness or by the naïve grandiloquence which are the order of the day in this literature, it becomes evident that the whole multiform process goes on within the bounds of ancient and medieval traditions." [71]   In another place the same author says: "For this reason the Renaissance shows how this historical continuity forms the all-powerful background of European history, and how the European peoples, dissemble as they will, are inherently and permanently encumbered with traditions." [72]

We give some examples of this continuity in so far as it concerns our present subject.

If anywhere, the revolt against existing conditions was justified in the field of *natural science and research*.   Here Scholastic teaching was to a great extent petrified and outworn, and here the men of the Renaissance period, despite a certain one-sidedness, made valuable and lasting contributions to knowledge.   Here, it would seem, there had to be a thorough-going break with the past.   And yet, the recent epochal results of the painstaking and comprehensive researches of the famous physicist, Pierre Duhem,[73] have completely revolutionized the

[71] *Op. cit.,* p. 352.

[72] *Allgemeine Geschichte der Philosophie,* in *Kultur der Gegenwart,* p. 433.

[73] *Études sur Léonard de Vinci,* 3 Vols., Paris, 1906–1913; *Les Origines de la Statique (Ibid.)* ; *Le Système du Monde. Histoire des Doctrines Cosmologiques, de Platon à Copernic,* 5 Vols., Paris, 1914–1917; and other works.—Before him, J. Baumann had pointed out some connections between the new and the old

notions heretofore entertained concerning the scientific views of Scholastics during the late Middle Ages, and concerning the beginnings of modern mechanics, astronomy, and mathematics. In his preface to *Les Origines de la Statique,* he asserts that mechanical and physical science, of which modern times are so justly proud, derives, by an uninterrupted and scarcely perceptible process of perfectioning, from the doctrines professed in the bosom of the medieval schools. His findings have also markedly dampened the fervid self-complacency of modern science.[74] No intelligent person will question the creative genius of Galileo; however, in manifold respects he borrowed from his Scholastic predecessors without, as was his wont, acknowledging his indebtedness. The modern concept of motion,[75] which replaced the Aristotelian-Thomistic

in his work on *Lehren von Raum, Zeit und Mathematik,* Berlin, 1869; Olgiati, *op. cit.,* pp. 807–826.

[74] Cfr. *Mediaeval Contributions to Modern Civilisation,* London, 1921, p. 106 sqq.

[75] Dr. B. Jansen, S.J., who prepared a critical edition of the works of Peter Olivi (published as Vols. IV, V and VI of the *Bibliotheca Franciscana Scholastica Medii Aevi,* Quaracchi, Italy, 1922, 1924 and 1926), has discovered that this interesting Scholastic (lived 1248–1298) admitted the impetus theory, and defended it against the teachings of other Scholastics, especially of Albert the Great and St. Thomas. Dr. Jansen explains his discovery in the article, *"Olivi, der älteste scholastische Vertreter des heutigen Bewegungsbegriffs,"* in the *Philosophisches Jahrbuch der Görres-Gesellschaft,* Fulda, 1920, Vol. 33, pp. 137–152.—In his work on *Die Erkenntnislehre Olivis* (Berlin, 1921), Dr. Jansen refers (p. 95 sq.) to Olivi's teaching on optics and sense-cognition. Joseph Fröbes, S.J., the distinguished experimental psychologist, is of opinion that this teaching can be interpreted

idea of it, the law of inertia, the revolutions of
the earth around the sun, analytic geometry,—all
these Galileo found ready to his hand.[76] Nomi-

in the sense of the psychology of to-day.—Olivi is a very interesting Scholastic for two reasons: in the first place, he is a striking
instance of the energetic and rich life of scientific research that
pulsated in some quarters during the medieval period, especially
during the thirteenth century; secondly, his writings refute the
hoary charge that Scholastics recognized no independent philosophy. All his elaborations on matter and form, time and
space, knowing and willing, the lower and the higher powers
of the soul, furthermore, the sources of his argumentation which,
taking no account of Scripture, Tradition, Councils, Canon Law,
reverts again and again to Aristotle and the Arabians,—all this
is a most eloquent answer to some of the old prejudices against
Scholastic philosophy.—Cfr. B. Jansen, *Wege der Weltweisheit*,
p. 125, sqq.

[76] Cfr. Pierre Duhem, *Les Précurseurs Parisiens de Galilée.*—The
following works and articles are of interest on the question of
medieval science: T. C. Allbutt, *Science and Mediaeval Thought*,
New York, 1901; ID., *Palissy, Bacon, and the Revival of Natural
Science*, Oxford, 1914; C. L. Barnes, *Science in Early England*,
Smithsonian, 1896; A. Bartholomaeus, *Mediaeval Lore*, Oxford,
1924; R. W. T. Gunther, *Early Science in Oxford*, Oxford, 1921,
p. 22; F. S. Marvin, *Science and Civilization*, Oxford, 1923; C. H.
Haskins, *Studies in the History of Mediaeval Science*, Harvard
University Press, Cambridge, 1924; J. A. Thomson, *Science Old
and New*, New York; Lynn Thorndike, *History of Magic and
Experimental Science*, New York and London, 1923; J. J. Walsh,
The Popes and Science, Fordham Univ. Press, N. Y., 1908; J. A.
Zahm, *Catholic Science and Catholic Scientists*, New York; L.
Thorndike, *Natural Science in the Middle Ages*, Popular Science,
87: 271-91, Sept., 1915; *Peter of Abano, a Mediaeval Scientist*
(Amer. Hist. Ass'n Report, 1919, V, I, 315-326) J. J. Walsh,
Renaissance Clergy and Science, Scientific American, 101: 351 Nov.
13, 1909; *Science at the Mediaeval Universities*, Popular Science,
78: 445-59, May, 1911, *Mediaeval Science*, Catholic World, 109:
85-92, 1919; *Modern Science in the 14th and 15th Centuries*,
Science, n. s. 61: sup. 12-14, Jan. 1923, 1925. C. Baeumker,

nalists of the University of Paris [77] like John Buridan (died 1358), Albert of Saxony (died 1390),
Nicolas Oresmus (died 1382), had prepared the
way by an intense scientific activity.   Buridan was
the first to point out that the physics of Aristotle
was false, and must be replaced by new theories.

It should also be noted that during the fifteenth
and sixteenth centuries, little real progress was
made in the physical sciences.   The men of the
period were caustic critics of existing conditions, but
for the time being they followed the beaten track
until far into the sixteenth century.[78]   With sound
scientific temper Telesius, Paracelsus, and especially Francis Bacon, demanded the application of
the inductive method in the study of nature.   In
matter of fact, however, they gave little or no attention to the painstaking and wearisome work on
details.[79]   Accordingly, their theories,—even Bacon's theory of induction,—bore no fruit for the
scientific interpretation of nature.   At bottom
there was as yet merely a change in notions and
names.   It was only when men like Kepler, Galileo,
and Newton began to advance exact working hy-

Witelo, ein Philosoph und Naturforscher des XIII. Jahrhunderts,
in *Beiträge zur Geschichte der Philosophie des Mittelalters,* Band
III, 2.

[77] Cfr. Klimke, *Historia Philosophiae,* Vol. I, p. 247, and the
works cited above.

[78] Jansen, *Wege der Weltweisheit,* p. 154.

[79] In the 18th century the *Codex* of Avicenna was still used
as a text-book in medicine.

potheses, and in their light to examine individual objects with careful probing and mathematical accuracy, that the way was assured for the discovery of laws and the verification of theories.

The same interlocking and continuity of modern with medieval thought is to be found in the domains of *political science and jurisprudence.* Problems concerning the origin of the State and particularly of political authority, investigations about the contract beween ruled and ruler, theories of popular supremacy and of the concept of sovereignty, controversies about tolerance and the relations between Church and State, discussions on the various forms of government, treatises on natural, positive, and international law,—these vital and fundamental questions occupied the various thinkers under pressure of the political and economic events of that period. They call up names like Machiavelli, Bodin, Althusius, Gentilis, Thomas More, Grotius, Hobbes, Campanella, Soto, Suarez, Bellarmine, Lugo. There are fantastic Utopias like Campanella's *Civitas Solis,* beside classics like those of Soto and Grotius. Machiavelli's mirror for princes, a one-sided exaltation of political power and on the further side of good and evil, finds a worthy complement in Bodin's boundless religious indifferentism. Althusius, with his harsh accentuation of the inalienable sovereignty of the people, is the precursor of Rousseau. In general, several of the theories of that time contain in germ the further development they received from Locke, Montesquieu, Pufendorf, Thomasius, and Kant.[80]

Before the investigations begun some decades ago, particularly before the results of the model researches of Otto von Gierke [81] were published, all these theories were regarded as something quite new, as the achievements of modern thought. Only an astounding ignorance of the Middle Ages, and especially of the political philosophy of Saint Thomas [82] can account for this, and explain the unconcern with which Hugo Grotius was hailed as the creator of natural law, when he himself constantly refers to Aristotle, St. Thomas, and other Scholastics. His Dutch good sense together with his classical, philosophical, theological, and juristic training enabled him to turn the principles of the old Schoolmen to good account, and apply them to the economic and political conditions of the time.

[80] Jansen, *op. cit.,* p. 155 sqq.; Olgiati, *op. cit.,* pp. 219–350.

[81] Otto von Gierke, *Johannes Althusius und die Entwicklung der naturrechtlichen Staatstheorien,* Breslau, 1880, 2 Auflage, 1902; *Deutsche Genossenschaften,* Berlin, 1881, Vol. III; *Political Theories of the Middle Ages.*

[82] Cfr. P. Tischleder, *Ursprung und Träger der Staatsgewalt nach der Lehre des hl. Thomas und seiner Schule* (M. Gladbach, 1923); *Die Staatslehre Leos XIII (Ibid.* 1925); G. B. Biavaschi, *La Moderna Concezione Filosofica dello Stato* (Milano, 1923); J. A. Ryan and M. F. X. Millar, S.J., *The State and the Church* (New York, 1923); Fr. Millar's contribution to the present volume; S. J. McNamara, *American Democracy and Catholic Doctrine* (Brooklyn, N. Y., 1924); R. W. and A. J. Carlyle, *A History of Mediaeval Political Theory;* J. Neville Figgis, *The Divine Right of Kings,* and *From Gerson to Grotius* (Cambridge, 1916).

His originality consisted in rendering these principles fruitful for the elaboration of international law. The political and social ideas of the others were likewise no new creations, but rather developments of germs of thought found in the works of Nicholas of Cusa, Ockham, Marsilius of Padua, and St. Thomas.[83]

When we come to *philosophy proper,* we also find the law of continuity at work. The researches of the last decades have clearly shown that the very pioneers of modern thought,—even those whose avowed purpose it was to destroy tradition,—are more deeply rooted in the views of the past and have received far more intellectual nourishment from the Middle Ages than they themselves were aware of, and than was heretofore believed. As Prof. De Wulf says, "it would be worth while, from a critical point of view, to re-edit a book published in 1766 by an eclectic disciple of the Hanoverian philosopher, L. Dutens, under the curious title: *Recherches sur l'Origine des Découvertes Attribuées aux Modernes, où l'on Démontre que nos plus Célèbres Philosophes ont puisé la plupart de leurs Connaissances dans les Ouvrages des Anciens.*" [84] The researches of Freudenthal, von Hertling, Baeumker, and others give convincing evidence that the chain of the Scholastic tradition was never sundered, that Scholastic views continued to

[83] Cfr. De Wulf, *Histoire de la Philosophie Médiévale* (5 ed., Paris, 1925), Vol. II, pp. 207–216.

[84] De Wulf, *Scholasticism Old and New,* p. 161.

be a living influence in the consciousness of the cultured and the scientific world, that really great minds and noble hearts like Leibniz recognized the high merits of Scholastic philosophy,[85] that Bacon, Descartes, Spinoza, Locke, Leibniz, and others are indebted for central parts of their systems,—seemingly new and of a unique mould,—to the teachings of the great Scholastics.[86]

The recent volume of Koyre [87] has deepened and

[85] Cfr. Willmann, *op. cit.*, Vol. II, p. 533.—"Gierke, in an arresting sentence which, once read, is caught and imbedded in the memory, speaks of the great Leibniz as one 'who in so many directions went deeper than his contemporaries, and who, perhaps for that reason, so often turned his eyes backward towards mediaeval ways of thought.'" E. Barker, in *Mediaeval Contributions to Modern Civilisation*, p. 5.

[86] The following works deal with the indebtedness of modern thinkers to Scholastic philosophy: E. Gilson, *La Liberté chez Descartes et la Théologie*, Paris, 1913; *La Philosophie au Moyen Age*, Paris, 1922; also the last chapters of his *Études de Philosophie Médiévale*, Paris, 1921; E. Krakowski, *Les Sources Médiévales de la Philosophie de Locke*, Paris, 1915; P. Ramsay, *Les Doctrines Médiévales chez Jean Donne, le Poète-Métaphysicien d'Angleterre*, Oxford, 1916; J. Freudenthal, *Spinoza und die Scholastik* (in *Philosophische Aufsätze, Eduard Zeller gewidmet*, Leipzig, 1887, pp. 83-138); v. Hertling, *Descartes' Beziehung zur Scholastik* (*Sitzungsberichte der Münchener Akademie der Wissenschaften*, 1897, II, Heft 2, pp. 339-381; 1899, Heft 1, S. 3-36); M. Meier, *Descartes' Stellung zu den Alten in seinem Traktat "Les Passions de l'Âme"* (*Abhandlungen Georg Frhn. v. Hertling gewidmet*, Freiburg, i. Br., 1913), pp. 183-209; Glossner, *Zur Frage nach dem Einfluss der Scholastik auf die neuere Philosophie* (*Jahrbuch für Philosophie und spekulative Theologie*, 1899); Nostitz-Rieneck, *Leibniz und die Scholastik* (*Philosophisches Jahrbuch*, 1894); Jasper, *Leibniz und die Scholastik*, Leipzig, 1898.

[87] A. Koyre, *Descartes und die Scholastik*, Bonn, 1923.

broadened the evidence heretofore adduced for Descartes' indebtedness to patristic and medieval thought in a manner that eliminates every possible doubt on the subject. The book is highly significant because of the authentic, fully documented proof it furnishes for the dependence of Descartes, and therefore of at least an important section of the whole development of modern philosophy, on the Augustine-Bonaventure-Thomas-Scotus-Suarez tradition.[88] In other words, it establishes the continuity of philosophic thought from Augustine on to the moderns, who trace their intellectual lineage to the author of the *Discours de la Méthode* and the *Meditationes.* The Descartes to whom Koyre introduces us differs *toto caelo* from the Descartes with whom we were made acquainted by the manuals and lectures on the history of philosophy. There he was characterized as the bold adventurer in thought, burning all Scholastic bridges behind him, shaking off every particle of the dust of tradition, and like a free lance setting out undauntedly on the quest for a radically new philosophy.[89]

[88] E. Przywara, S.J., in *Stimmen der Zeit,* Vol. CVII (1924), p. 398.

[89] Koyre admits that it is not so easy to determine the sources of Descartes' inspiration and to disengage the foreign elements he embodied in his doctrines; for Descartes did his utmost to obliterate and to mask every trace of them. He wished to become the Aristotle of the New Scholasticism, and seemed to be obsessed by a craving for originality and by the fear of appearing to be in the least indebted to any one. He was quite familiar with Scholasticism; he had the *Summa* of St. Thomas and the *Disputationes Metaphysicae* of Suarez, and took them along on

Citing chapter and verse, Koyre unveils to our mind's eye a man whose fervently believing soul loyally treasures the whole intellectual heritage of his forebears and of his Catholic home, a thinker who strives with an intense earnestness to pass on to the modern world the varied richness of their thoughts and problems in a form modified by his own profound meditation and many-sided experience, a deeply penetrating metaphysician [90] instead of the shallow sciolist some believed him to be. Whosoever takes the pains dispassionately to verify and examine Koyre's authorities,—though he is likely to take exception to some of his assertions and inferences,—will see that it is no longer possible to subscribe to the old dogma set up by both sides and acting as a useless barrier to a mutual understanding,—the dogma, that is, of an absolute breach of continuity between Scholasticism and all subsequent philosophy.

his travels; with marvelous skill he utilized the works and basic doctrines of his predecessors; and yet he sought to create the belief that he never knew them or at least found nothing of value in them. Thus he put into circulation and fostered his own legend of being a self-taught man and the sole source of all his speculations. He did not succeed in misleading his contemporaries, but for a long time he did mislead posterity. In his remarkable personality, simplicity and extreme naïveté went hand in hand with a boundless ambition which resorted to wiles and diplomatic artifices. And so his moral qualities were not of the same high order as his intellectual endowments. (Koyre, *op. cit.*, pp. 7, 8, 158.) "Neither logically, nor psychologically, nor historically, was the philosophy of Descartes an 'absolute beginning.'" (Maréchal, *op. cit., Cahier* II, p. 25.).

[90] Cfr. Maréchal, *op. cit., Cahier* II, p. 25.

Neo-Scholastics and non-Scholastics alike must yield to the force of the facts here briefly reviewed, and recognize their profound significance for the advancement of philosophic thought. Instead of continuing to dissipate their energies in sterile controversies and futile recriminations, they should unite and direct them toward the constructive and fruitful work of clearing up the misunderstandings that have beclouded the course of speculation during the modern period; they should earnestly strive to bring order into the present chaotic condition of thought, and agree on a common language instead of the present philosophical Babel. There are gratifying indications of an initial realization by both sides of the supreme necessity of such a course. Twenty-five years ago it was still believed that Scholastic philosophy, far from having anything to offer towards enriching and enlightening modern thought, was a positive menace to its true progress. Today, as the various statements in our symposium show, clear-headed and far-visioned thinkers keenly realize that Scholasticism is in a position to make most valuable contributions toward the solution of outstanding philosophic problems. In 1901, Rudolf Eucken wrote of "a clash of two worlds," [91] meaning the Thomistic and the Kantian worlds of thought. In 1924, when the distinguished Neo-Scholastic, Fr. Agostino Gemelli, Rector of the Catholic University of Milan, outlined the progres-

[91] *Thomas von Aquino und Kant. Ein Kampf zweier Welten,* in *Kantstudien* (Band VI, Jahrgang 1901), pp. 1-18.

sive programme of the New Scholasticism [92] before
the philosophers of various schools and diverse nations assembled for the International Philosophical
Congress held at Naples,[93] he was given a most sympathetic hearing, and rewarded by whole-hearted
applause; it meant more than a general approval,
inasmuch as it was especially emphatic at those
points of his discourse which asserted the value of
the Scholastic conception of the universe, because
this conception is based on the granitic foundation
of the centuries-old tradition of realism.[94]   During

[92] His discourse is published in the *Rivista di Filosofia Neo-
Scolastica* (Anno XVI, 1924), pp. 81–96.

[93] The Congress was held May 4–9 in the venerable basilica of
S. Domenico Maggiore, where St. Thomas had often preached
and lectured some 650 years ago.

[94] Cfr. *Rivista di Filosofia Neo-Scolastica* (Anno XVI, 1924),
p. 280 sq.—The nature of the impression produced may be
gathered from some comments made on the address by non-
Scholastics. In the *Berliner Tageblatt* (May 20, 1924), Dr.
Petrone, of the University of Berlin, after stating that the outstanding features of the Congress were the commemorative ad-
dresses on St. Thomas (by Fr. Gemelli) and on Kant (by Prof.
Liebert), added: "The acute rector of the Milan University
delivered a deeply-grounded discourse. . . . No intolerant zealot
spoke here, but a man thoroughly familiar with the spirit and
achievements of modern science." In the *Resto del Carlino* (May
9, 1924) G. Tarozzi wrote: "Fr. Gemelli pointed out that it was
not the intention to substitute Thomism *in toto* for all contemporary science and philosophy, but that it is to be a central philosophy which, far from being in opposition to the achievements
of the modern epoch, can well become the basis for a new
synthesis of philosophy and science. . . . He did well to make
clear the programme of his school. . . . Once the position of the
one and the other side is established, a better mutual understanding will be possible."—The importance of the discourse was

THE NEW SCHOLASTICISM   519

the following session Prof. A. Liebert, president
of the *Kantgesellschaft,* referred to Fr. Gemelli's
address as a proof that the Neo-Scholastic programme was not to restore Thomistic philosophy by
way of a mere parrot-like repetition, but as a philosophy that was capable of facing and solving the
problems put by modern thought.   He further asserted that the usual dilemma, "Kant or Thomas,"
—in which the first was regarded as the representative of criticism, the second of dogmatism, and the
two systems as absolutely exclusive of each other,
—had no longer any justification.   With Fr. Gemelli he recognized that Thomism is an indispensable complement to the critical philosophy.

In a like constructive spirit, one of the leading
Neo-Scholastics of Germany recently wrote: [95] "As
in the recent researches of Hartmann [96] and Heim-

also noted by Alliotta, the president of the Congress, in *Italia che
scrive* (June 6, 1924); by Dr. H. Finke, professor of the University
of Freiburg (in Breisgau), and delegate of the German government, who wrote (*Kölnische Volkszeitung,* May 19, 1924) that
the discourse was the fundamental point of the Congress; by Dr.
J. Feldmann, of the Paderborn Academy (in *Theologie und
Glaube,* June, 1924).

[95] Erich Przywara, S.J., in *Stimmen der Zeit* (Vol. CVII, 1924)
p. 398.—Cfr. the excellent exposition of the ideals of the New
Scholasticism in Dr. W. Switalski's address (delivered Jan 22,
1923, at the opening of the Albertus Magnus Academy, the
Catholic Institute of Philosophy at Cologne), in *Probleme der
Erkenntnis,* II (Münster, 1923), pp. 147–164.—Cfr. F. Olgiati,
La Storia della Filosofia Moderna e la Neo-Scolastica Italiana,
in *Rivista di Filosofia Neo-Scolastica* (Anno XVII, 1925), pp. 23–39.

[96] Cfr. Nicolai Hartmann's latest work, *Grundzüge einer Metaphysik der Erkenntnis,* Berlin and Leipzig, 1925.

soeth the Marburg school presses on through the
pre-critical Kant to the old metaphysics,[97] because it
finds therein the settings in which the problem was
finally put by the critical Kant, so the New Scholasticism will have to go back to the truly original
sources. Between the great masters a true, life-
giving, *inward* explanation and appraisal was always and everywhere possible. Only petrified
schools can exist side by side without coming into
vital contact with one another. Accordingly, *the
philosophic programme of the future should be
. . . an inner* (not merely a polemic) *explanation
and understanding between the real Thomas and
the real Kant,*[98] from which will issue a really *new*
life instead of a romancing about ruins." [99]   The
same applies with equal force to the New Scholasticism and modern systems of philosophy.

Philosophy's quest is for ultimate truth.   Now
"Scholasticism believes in a truth that is valid independently of the thinking subject; it believes in

[97] Cfr. *Kantstudien,* Band XXIX, Jahrgang 1924, Heft 1 and 2.
[98] The Thomas-Kant relation is stressed alike by Neo-
Scholastics and non-Scholastics for reasons deeply rooted in the
historical development of philosophic thought, and which are of
capital importance for the proper appraisal of Scholasticism and
the modern systems. The Thomistic synthesis is the focal center
in which all the rays of Greek, Patristic, and early Scholastic
thought converge and from which, like sheaves of new light,
they radiate to illumine all subsequent Scholastic speculation.
Kant's philosophy, influenced by the modern systems that went
before, and revolutionizing the world of thought, became so to
speak the water-shed from which most of the subsequent currents
issue either in agreement, or modification, or opposition.
[99] Cfr. Appendix.

the organic and gradual disclosure and development of truth; for that reason, like all other sciences, it builds on the assured results of the past. On the other hand, it also knows how infinite is the ocean of being and truth, how small and narrow the spirit of man, how, therefore, there are human ways of grasping wisdom and forms of presenting it that differ widely from one another. They are all different, and yet not false. From its own standpoint, each one of them sees the whole. This, in turn, conditions agreement in the final result, despite every difference of detail. A splendid and thorough-going proof of this is the synthesis of Platonism and Aristotelianism achieved during the golden age of Scholasticism." [100]

"By the very exigencies of cultural development, the Thomistic synthesis inevitably had to be followed by a new analysis, which, in its turn, aims at a more perfect synthesis; this latter will not run counter to the former synthesis, but will be that same one, amplified, enriched, and embellished." [101]

[100] Dr. Jansen, in Part II, Chap. VII of this volume.
[101] From Fr. Gemelli's address at the International Philosophical Congress, *loc. cit.*

APPENDIX

ATTITUDE OF THE NEW SCHOLASTICISM
TOWARDS MODERN PHILOSOPHY

THE truly irenic and constructive method of criticism
by means of which the New Scholasticism seeks to discover
in modern philosophy every kernel of truth and all possible
points of agreement with the *philosophia perennis,* without
any slurring or minimizing of essential differences, may be
further illustrated by some recent works of German, French,
and Italian Neo-Scholastics on certain fundamental phases
of Kantian thought.

Dr. Inauen [1] begins his "Kantian and Scholastic appraisal
of our natural knowledge of God" with the pertinent remark that one serious obstacle to a thorough and just evaluation of Kant was the fact that Scholastics were wont to
study him too much apart from his contemporaries and historical background. Hence on several points he was taken
for an opponent of Scholasticism, with which he was not
familiar, when he was levelling his attacks against the rationalism of the Leibniz-Wolff school, when he was in fact
turning away from that school and drawing near to Scho-

[1] Dr. Andreas Inauen, S.J., *Kantische und scholastische Einschätzung der natürlichen Gotteserkenntnis,* Innsbruck, 1925, pp. 1–4.
—Cfr. the two chapters on Kant (pp. 224 and 254) in Dr. Jansen's *Wege der Weltweisheit* (cited above); this thoughtful work
displays the fine philosophic sense of its author, and contains
excellent appraisals and comparisons of ancient, medieval and
modern philosophy.

lastic doctrines. An objective and historic attitude is indispensable for a true appraisal. Moreover, it should be remembered that no error is definitively overcome until the grain of truth it hides has been duly recognized and fully disengaged.

Kant is praised by many and feared by many for having "shattered the proofs for the existence of God." Has he really done so? Did he mean to do so?[2] The repute alone is not decisive. It is quite possible that some are eager to still conscience by the authority of the great German philosopher, while others are prone to imagine the worst about their opponent. It needs but a simple consideration of the conditions of his time to evoke the questions: Has Kant shattered all proofs for the existence of God or only those of the rationalistic school of thought? Are his attacks directed also against the Scholastic formulation and appraisal of these proofs? A glance at the *Paralogismen der reinen Vernunft* should suffice to check a hasty answer. Looked at more closely, they prove to be fallacies by which the Wolffian school attempted to establish *a priori* the substantiality, spirituality, and immortality of the soul. The proofs offered by Scholastic philosophy in this matter are not affected by Kant's critique. Is it then not very probable that the criticism of the proofs for the existence of God is likewise wholly or partly directed against the rationalistic assertions, which are not shared by Scholastic philosophy?

We should bear in mind the apodictic, necessary and aprioristic certitude claimed by rationalistic philosophy for its assertions. In this it widely differs from the Scholastic cast of thought. The rationalist of the Cartesian-Spinozistic tradition undertakes to furnish mathematically certain proofs

[2] Cfr. Sheen, *op. cit.,* p. 23.

for every proposition of his system. The modern rational-ist, before whose mind mathematics continues to hover as the ideal of philosophy, demands them—at least from his opponent. The Scholastic, on the contrary, or at least the Neo-Scholastic, holds that "free certitude" is also true certitude. The mathematical-rationalistic type of thinker logically repudiates any influencing of the will or feelings in his statement of the proofs for the existence of God, whereas the defender of "free certitude" regards the co-operation of the will—and hence the proper disposition of it, as a downright necessity.[3]

Kant, as we know, freed himself in principle from the ideal of a philosophy on the mathematical pattern without, however, getting entirely away from it. Could it not be that he also saw the impossibility of mathematically evident proofs for the existence of God without reaching full clear-ness as to its appraisal? In that case his objections would be directed chiefly against the exaggerated valuation and formulation of the proofs by the rationalists of that time; and at bottom they would amount to the contention that the proofs for the existence of God produce only a "free certitude," though Kant did not give them a definite formulation. Dr. Inauen uses this conjecture as a working hypothesis for his investigation, which, despite several gaps, yields some interesting and valuable results. Following is a summary of those that concern the proofs for the exist-ence of God.[4]

In the first place, Kant's concessions to the cosmological

[3] E. Przywara, S.J., has made an illuminating study of Cardinal Newman's mind on this and kindred subjects, in comparison with Scholastic philosophy, in his *Einführung in Newman's Wesen und Werk*, Freiburg i. Br., 1922; cfr. especially pp. 18 sqq., and 43 sqq.; also his *Religionsbegründung*, cited above.

[4] Inauen, *op. cit.*, p. 85.

and teleological proofs, as well as his teaching on "doctrinal" and "practical faith" betray a conception of the
demonstrative force of these proofs which largely coincides
with the view of many Neo-Scholastics that they do not
beget necessary, but only free certitude. Thereby Kant
abandons the contemporary rationalistic pretension of furnishing mathematically cogent proofs, and draws near to
the Scholastic appraisal. Moreover, it is made clear that
in most of his objections against the proofs, Kant is far
more the adversary of the Wolffian school and of its manner
of formulating them than of the proofs as such and of their
Scholastic setting. Accordingly, only a fraction of his considerations on these proofs is irreconcilably opposed to Scholastic views, namely, his one-sided emphasis of the function
of the will in "doctrinal" and "practical faith," and his
radically ruinous doubt as to the trustworthiness of human
reason (in the appraisal of the teleological proof in the
Kritik der Urteilskraft), and the restriction of the law of
causality to the world of phenomena. After showing that
Scholastic philosophy has nothing to fear from Kant's opposition on these points, Dr. Inauen proceeds to institute
a like comparison between the Kantian and the Scholastic
teaching on the idea of God. Here, too, he reaches some
enlightening conclusions.

Dr. Maréchal in his erudite work[5] appraises Kant's
theory of knowledge in the same spirit that animates
Inauen's work. The *Revue des Sciences Philosophiques
et Théologiques* regards his as the best Scholastic criticism
of Kant in the French language. And Dr. Inauen con-
cedes[6] that there exists no better one in the German
language, above all none that approaches Kant so sym-

[5] *Op. cit., Cahier* III, *La Critique de Kant.*
[6] *Op. cit.,* p. 2.

pathetically. Dr. Maréchal seeks everywhere to penetrate to the kernel of truth that underlies the Kantian processes of thought, and to disentangle it from the manifold misunderstandings in which an all too distrustful criticism has enveloped it. In this way he discloses a series of important points in which Kant parts company with the empiricism and rationalism of his day and draws near to Scholastic Aristotelianism. He regards the following as one of the most significant:[7] "The modern philosophers who preceded Kant and followed Duns Scotus and Ockham failed to recognize the *complementary rôle* of sensibility and understanding in the knowledge of the 'object.' As a result, they had to reduce the objective contribution of these two faculties to the greatest possible homogeneity: hence the fatal confusion of the one with the other. But as this confusion could ensue indifferently from choosing the sensible or the intelligible object as the standard of assimilation, there followed, on the basis of a common error, a sharp conflict between idealism and empiricism: the conflict between the 'object-idea' and the 'object-sensation.'" "In *Cahier* II we have shown that this conflict had its source in the abandonment of a viewpoint familiar to the Scholastics of the thirteenth century, and drawn from the philosophy of Aristotle. This viewpoint presupposed a 'transcendental reflection' on the proper object of human knowledge. This object was not ascribed exclusively to sensibility or to the understanding, but to the simultaneous and strictly complementary activity of these two faculties. Sensation without the concept did not attain the rank of a knowledge of the 'object'; the concept without sensation was equally not objectified in consciousness: to constitute objective knowledge, the knowledge of 'something,' there

[7] *La Critique de Kant*, pp. 147, 148.

had to be a union of sensation as *matter* and of the concept as *form*. Thus the *unity of the object and the distinction of the faculties* were alike safeguarded."

"Kant leads us back to this medieval position; he solves the first great alternative (sensibility *or* understanding), bequeathed by decadent Scholasticism to modern philosophy, as St. Thomas would have solved it. The following lines from the *Kritik der reinen Vernunft* [8] measure exactly the extent of the progress, which is at the same time an unconscious return to tradition: 'Leibniz *intellectualized* phenomena, just as Locke had *sensualized* the concepts of the understanding. Instead of seeking in sensation and understanding two wholly distinct sources of representations, but at the same time two sources whose union is absolutely necessary for forming objective judgments on things, each of these two great men clung only to one of them, to the one which, in his opinion, immediately referred to the objects themselves, while the other (faculty) only served to blend or set in order the representations of the first.' "

"The Kantian analytic, therefore, restores to idealism as well as to empiricism the portion of truth contained in their interpretation of objective experience; but with the same stroke Kant demolishes the most fundamental presupposition which engendered the antagonism between these two tendencies. He refutes by conciliating. And his principle of conciliation repeats, in scarcely different terms, the old Aristotelian and Scholastic principle of the 'synthetic (sensitive-rational) unity of the object of experience.' Nevertheless, it should be remembered that history,—also the history of thought,—like life, does not repeat itself

---

[8] Edition of K. Rosenkranz, p. 222; in notes the popular Reclam edition gives the pagination of Rosenkranz.

servilely. With Kant the Aristotelian principle reappeared, supported by a new critical justification [9] and enriched by the philosophical experience of several centuries, but, on the other hand, impoverished and attenuated through the timidities of an agnostic methodology." In the same way the other points of agreement and divergence between the Kantian and the Scholastic theory of knowledge are brought out.

In his introduction to the collection of articles by professors of the Catholic University of Milan in commemoration of the second centenary of Kant's birth,[10] Dr. Gemelli outlines the standpoint taken by the scholars of that alert center of Italian Neo-Scholasticism in their study of modern philosophers in general, and of the Sage of Königsberg in particular. Heretofore, he says, the uncritically accepted interpretation of Kantian thought was the one imposed by absolute idealism. Modern philosophy is said to begin with Descartes and to be differentiated from all preceding thought because it made the *subject* the center, the constitutive principle of reality, as well as the pivotal point of knowledge. This "subjectivation" of reality is said to have reached its apogee in Kant and his successors. It is likewise generally accepted that Kantian Criticism inevitably leads to idealism and to the absolute negation of the object and of all divine transcendence. Thus Willmann, in his *Geschichte des Idealismus,* sees an unmitigated opposition between Criticism and Thomism.[11] As

[9] Cfr. Jansen, *op. cit.,* p. 231.

[10] *Immanuel Kant (1724-1924). Volume commemorativo del secondo centenario della nascita,* edited by P. Agostino Gemelli, O.F.M., Milan, 1924.

[11] As was noted above, there was a strong reaction, on the part of Thomists and Kantians alike, against the "Thomas *or* Kant" dilemma at the International Congress of Naples.

genuine idealism reached its highest point in St. Thomas, so spurious idealism found its most authentic representative in Kant.

This strong contrast, thinks Dr. Gemelli, is born of a superficial examination of modern as compared with pre-modern philosophy. In his opinion it is one of those conventional modes of thinking, transmitted by teachers to pupils, enclosed in the shell of meaningless, parroted formulas, uncritically accepted and handed down as the quintessence of human wisdom. Was not the Socratic philosophy one of interiority ("Know thyself!"), aiming to solve the problem of reality by solving the problem of life? Stoicism, too, was at bottom an affirmation of the subject as the center of reality; it was a philosophy of life rather than a theory of things. The same holds true of Epicureanism. And St. Augustine anticipated Descartes in setting self-consciousness [12] at the base of all certitude by his famous *si cogito sum, si volo sum, si fallor sum.*

"On the other hand, does not Kant,—whom it is sought to set in opposition to pre-modern philosophy by making him the great champion of the *subject,*—lead man from the subject to the object, from self-consciousness to objective reality? [13] What is more, does he not build on the self-consciousness of the subject a metaphysical structure where God, the soul, and the cosmos with its finality are declared independent of self-consciousness, that is, objective? . . . Whoever studies, not one side of Kant, but the *whole Kant,* such as he results from *all* his works as well as from the recent researches concerning his thought, perceives at once

[12] Cfr. Jansen, *op. cit.,* p. 79 sqq.
[13] Cfr. A. Dyroff, *Kant und die Scholastik,* in *Philosophisches Jahrbuch der Görres-Gesellschaft,* Fulda, 1924, Band 37, Heft 2, p. 98 sqq.

that the much blazoned Kantian immanentism and alleged negation of transcendence exist not in the brain of the author of the three *Critiques,* but solely in that of his interpreters, who distort the true Kant of history for their own ends. . . . Paulsen, who made a most objective study of Kant, wrote that '. . . *the impulse toward transcendence is the very soul of his philosophy.* . . .' Of course, we cannot make our own the road mapped out by Kant toward transcendence; for us it is theoretical reason before the practical that guides man from the *mundus sensibilis* to the *mundus intelligibilis,* from the world of phenomena to that of the noumena; for us the ideas of reason,—already in the domain of pure reason,—are not only regulative but 'real,' in the sense that an objective reality corresponds to them. On closer observation it seems that Kant himself conceded to theoretical reason the power of penetrating in some way to the supersensible world, not only by an impulse towards it, but also by a veiled discovery of it."

The differentiation of pre-modern from modern philosophy has a purely empirical value, and one cannot definitely establish where the first ends and the second begins. Dr. Gemelli sought to make this clear in his address at the International Congress of Naples.[14] Philosophy is a continuous current without any hiatus or sharp turns. *Est quaedam philosophia perennis,* which assumes diverse attitudes, but asserts itself everywhere in its essential elements. In its modern phrase more stress was laid, from the viewpoint of the theory of knowledge and of metaphysics, on the subject than before; the activity of the mind in the constitution of reality was given a greater value; there were excesses in bringing out the subjective element as against the objective. But despite all the efforts and errors, the

[14] Cfr. Part III, Chap. III, *ad finem.*

objective element held its ground, either as a co-agent in the cognitive process, or as a presupposition and postulate of ethics, or as both. To be sure, there are modern systems, especially those after Kant, in which the mind's activity seemingly absorbs every activity of the object, just as in pre-modern philosophy the object seems to absorb the subject. But a closer study shows that pre-modern philosophy has a very good knowledge of the subject, if not as the creator, then surely as the re-creator, of reality; and the subject is ever the point of departure and the point of arrival in its philosophic processes.

As true Scholastics, continues Dr. Gemelli, we seek to correct the excesses of ancient and modern subjectivism by a due regard for a sane objectivism. But we are far from considering modern philosophy as an exclusive affirmation of the subject, because we find that it also contains the assertion of that objectivism which after Plato and Aristotle has not ceased to stamp itself on all philosophical currents. We are anti-Kantian, it is true; but loyal to historic objectivity, we verify also in Kant the affirmations of that *philosophia perennis* which, whether wanted or not, permeates the speculation of all times. We are convinced that St. Thomas, with his vigorous conception of life, continues to live even in those who regard themselves as his most pronounced opponents. For the synthesis of Aristotelianism and Platonism created by his genius represents the most rational achievement of human speculation. Like a vital fluid it courses through all systems. It is then our duty to enter upon the terrain of our opponents and there find proof of the perennial vitality of the fundamental principles of philosophy.

Note to p. 450—Recent researches have invalidated much of the usual criticism of Duns Scotus, by placing his doctrines in a more favorable light. This is especially true of the work, *La Philosophie du B. Duns Scot,* by Ephrem Longpré, O.F.M. (Paris, 1924), wherein the author shows that the two treatises, *De Rerum Principio* and *Theoremata,*—hitherto ascribed to Scotus and forming the chief source of the accusations against him,—are not genuine.— Cfr. the article, *Auf dem Wege zur Wahrheit,* by Dr. Bernhard Jansen, S.J., in *Stimmen der Zeit,* July, 1926, Band CXI, Heft 10, pp. 251–265; also, the fifth French edition of M. De Wulf's *Histoire de la Philosophie Médiévale* (Paris and Louvain, 1925), Vol. II, p. 66 sq., p. 72 sqq., p. 80, which show considerable modification of the unfavorable appraisal of the *Doctor Subtilis* contained in the fourth edition.

INDEX